A Design and Construction Handbook for
ENERGY-SAVING HOUSES

A Design and Construction Handbook for
ENERGY-SAVING HOUSES

by **Alex Wade**

with drawings by Bob Dakin and Frank Gilbert;
photographic assistance by Jeremy Blodgett,
Dennis Simonetti, and Woujie Dwyer;
and technical coordination by Felicia Knerr

Rodale Press, Emmaus, Pennsylvania

Printed in the United States of America on recycled paper, containing a high percentage of de-inked fiber.

Library of Congress Cataloging in Publication Data
Wade, Alex.
    A design and construction handbook for energy-saving houses.
    Bibliography: p.
    Includes index.
    1. House construction—Handbooks, manuals, etc.
2. Dwellings—Energy conservation—Handbooks, manuals, etc. I. Title.
TH4813.W3   728.3   79-20937
ISBN 0-87857-275-9 (Hardcover)
ISBN 0-87857-274-0 (Paperback)

2 4 6 8 10 9 7 5 3 1 (Hardcover)
2 4 6 8 10 9 7 5 3 1 (Paperback)

Contents

Acknowledgments

Many people have helped with this project. Foremost are all of those people who wrote asking detailed questions which prompted writing the book. Owners of the houses featured herein have opened up their experiences to others in order to help them build better homes.

Gregg Torchio assumed responsibility for my architectural practice while I was writing the book. He also helped with actual construction and produced and refined several of the actual designs.

Alasdair MacAulay did research and technical editing for the book, making sure that what I was saying could be understood by the layman.

Frank Gilbert built one of the houses, helped with several others, and did all of the final drawings for the book.

Bob Dakin and Kevin Berry did the basic framing or other major portions of the work on seven of the houses. They also prepared detailed drawings and materials lists.

Bill Harper did research and development for windmills and alternate energy sources. He also helped with much of the construction.

Jeremy Blodgett did the basic photography. Finished houses were photographed by Gregg Torchio, Tom Pollack, and Alasdair MacAulay.

Many others have helped with construction mock-ups and production of the book itself. Special thanks to Linda Unson, Eric Seeward, Sue Baughman, Steve Newkirk, and Karen Schell.

Finally, Mike and Carol Stoner contributed their house and their experiences and also acted as my editors.

I am deeply grateful to all.

Introduction

This is a unique book which describes a very different way of building houses. Many people have written books about building your own house. Others have written about how to design solar-heated houses. While this book has elements of both, it is distinctly different from either.

A common theme among all of the housing books is that they are usually written by people who *design* houses, not by people who *build* houses. My aim is to set before the layman a logical construction sequence which will "demystify" the many tasks and trades of building. You see, building is not all that difficult.

When I was six years old, my father let me dismantle a chicken coop and use the lumber to build a tree house. Since we lived in an area with few trees large enough for a tree house, I built a structure somewhat similar to a bridge which spanned three trees. Just how I accomplished this with no construction knowledge or experience in the use of tools is still a bit of a mystery. If I could build a tree house at age six, there is no reason why any reasonably competent adult cannot build his own house.

Every one of the houses shown in this book was under construction during 1979, so all of the techniques and ideas suggested here are thoroughly tested and up to date. The truly unique feature of these houses is that they use traditional building materials in a way which makes them safer, stronger, and easier to build. No one idea means much by itself, but a combination of them produces significant savings in time and materials. Drawing from my extensive background in commercial building, I have combined principles normally used in metal industrial buildings with traditional post and beam framing to create an easy-to-build structural shell. High-quality, commercial-grade sealants and coatings not usually found in residential construction enable the beginning carpenter to make economical installations of sheets of fixed glass. These same sealing materials make possible simple, easy-to-build doors and windows by eliminating complex joinery otherwise necessary for weather protection. Special finish materials and installation techniques permit the use of locally milled, rough-sawn lumber instead of using great quantities of fuel to transport lumber hundreds of miles.

In addition, these integrated designs make use of every inch of space and use all materials in the most efficient manner. It is not coincidence that they cost a lot less to build than conventionally designed houses. They also cost very little to heat and cool and virtually nothing to maintain.

Within the last few years America's growth rate in productivity and research and development has declined so that we are now competing with Great Britain in both areas. In fact, Japan has assumed the role of the highest-paying country in the world while the United States is rapidly slipping out of the top ten (we are number six at this writing). Japan, Germany, France, and Italy are all pushing ahead of us. Greedy businessmen and unions have milked the economy dry. The policies of maximum profits and maximum wages regardless of consequence are taking their toll. The United States has been left years behind in such basic technologies as steel and automobile production. The severe energy shortages now in the offing will aggravate the situation.

Our housing industry is sick. It has been hit by

the triple whammy of a high rate of inflation, low rate of productivity, and stifling and inconsistent regulations. Costs have escalated so wildly that only a small fraction of families can afford the $70,000-plus cost of a new home. It would appear that the situation is going to get much worse, forcing most people to give up the dream of owning their own home. Even during the course of writing this book, costs have risen drastically. Remember that the prices I quote reflect those of early 1979, and should be adjusted accordingly.

Two years ago, when I wrote *30 Energy-Efficient Houses . . . You Can Build,* I predicted this development. It has taken a bit longer than I anticipated, but it is now upon us. In my other book, I offered several plans for sale and indicated that I would consult with potential homebuilders on their problems. I really didn't envision thousands of letters, many with multiple pages of detailed questions. Many people asked for variations of the plans. Most were planning to build for themselves and frequently wanted larger houses than I had included in that book, although the plans for my basic Volkswagen house have been very popular.

It is obvious to me that people want detailed information, so that they can do their own work and thus bring the cost of a home back within their financial means. This book is my response. In it you will find step-by-step directions for applying the unique cost- and energy-saving techniques which I described in my earlier book.

In order to break the existing pattern of dependence and put an end to the erosion of competence, citizens will have to take the solution of their problems into their own hands. They will have to create their own "communities of competence." Only then will the productive capacities of modern capitalism, together with the scientific knowledge that now serves it, come to serve the interests of humanity instead.

Christopher Lasch
The Culture of Narcissism: American Life in an Age of
Diminishing Expectations
W. W. Norton, 1978

A selection of eleven owner-built houses is presented herein, incorporating those features which were most popular with my correspondents. Nine of the houses are of my own design; most of them were heavily modified by their owner-builders. Two were designed by other architects for owners who had read my book and wanted to follow my design principles. The majority of the houses I designed were built in the Northeast within a 200-mile radius, so I was able

to supervise and photograph readily. Three of them are in the Midwest and one, a pole house, is in the South. Many of the owners visited and corresponded with each other, and some actually helped each other with the construction of their houses. In this way, they were able to learn from the experiences of others, avoid mistakes, and share research on materials and construction techniques. With so many houses going up at once, some mistakes were made. I will relate pertinent ones so that you will know what to avoid.

My mail indicated that people were attracted to the traditional saltbox shape, but wanted a larger version with a greenhouse (*everyone* wanted a greenhouse) and a carport, garage, or shop. Consequently, I went back to the drawing board and devised a basic saltbox-style house with several variations. As I am writing this, five different versions of this house are under construction. Three of these houses are presented in detail in Part III. The working drawings at the back of the book represent the best ideas and details from the five designs distilled into one set of working drawings. Detailed materials lists and specifications are provided in Part IV.

The basic house is designed to be built for $20,000 to $35,000, exclusive of land and site development. The price will depend upon the version selected, the sources and quality of materials, and the amount of work the owner does. The costs of the other houses range from a low of $8,000 for the basic Volkswagen house with a floor area of 900 square feet to a high of $65,000 for a luxurious three-story house with 2,400 square feet of floor area. I must emphasize that your costs will vary depending upon how much work you do yourself. In the lowest-cost house, all labor was donated or performed by the owner; in the highest-cost house, all labor was hired, although the owner arranged subcontracts and purchased all of the materials.

Unlike conventional tract houses, these houses are designed with a major wall of each house facing due south to take maximum advantage of the sun for heating without adding significantly to the cost of the structure. This means that careful site selection is important. I think you will find the extra effort well spent.

I am very careful to use ecologically sound materials for my houses. Except for rare instances, I avoid aluminum and plastics completely. Aluminum refining consumes vast amounts of inefficient electrical power; most plastics are petroleum based. Other metals can almost always be substituted for aluminum, and the use of plastics is limited to piping, caulking, and glazing where their performance and low cost justify their use. My construction palette consists of locally harvested wood, stone, used brick, and galvanized or terne roofing. All of these materials are used in somewhat different fashion than in common construction practice. These special methods have been devised with the beginning builder in mind and have been carefully tested by the group of people who built the houses shown in this book.

One of the most vexing problems for the owner-builder is estimating quantities and prices for materials. Special attention has been given to this aspect of building. Since a large portion of my mail comes from Canada, I have tried to include Canadian resources wherever possible. As a reference tool, I include extensive listings from Sears, Roebuck and Co. catalogs. They are available everywhere in the United States and Canada and provide a standard of reference for tools and construction items. Since Sears is the world's largest retail merchandiser, prices are usually very low, and if you shop carefully, their merchandise can be a real bargain.

In many cases, you will want to think twice about buying from Sears, though. If you live in a small community, supporting local merchants may be vital to the economic health of your town. The money you save buying at Sears could come very dear. It will pay to look over the catalogs and specific items which I recommend before shopping locally so that you can have a standard of comparison. In some remote areas, the only way to get merchandise is by mail, and, in this case, Sears can be indispensable.

Your involvement in the actual construction process can vary considerably depending upon your available time, budget, and native abilities. Just acting as your own contractor without doing any of the construction labor can save 20 to 30 percent of the cost of a house. By doing all or most of your own labor, you can save well over 50 percent of the cost of having the house built by a contractor. The personal satisfactions of making your own decisions as you go along can be greatly satisfying. If you do your own work, you can feel free to experiment or reconstruct something until it pleases you. If you hire a workman and don't like the results, financial pressures may force you to leave the work unaltered. Even if you feel you must hire a contractor, these designs have so many cost- and energy-saving features that you can still save money; that is, *if* you can locate a conscientious contractor.

Generally, these houses rely upon wood heat as a backup for the sun. My basic design also has provisions for a small gas- or oil-fired furnace if your bank insists. I don't recommend it, but in some cases a furnace may be the only practical solution. In case you are concerned over my use of wood as both a construction material and a fuel source, rest assured. An estimated 80 percent of the ground area of the Northeast is now covered with forest, up from only 20 percent a hundred years ago. There are some potential shortages of commercial timber coming up, but this is due to poor management by timber farmers and the federal government rather than to real shortages.

One problem which I can't fully solve with this book is the "code problem." Building codes give lip service to safety, but are usually written to protect property values and to establish construction techniques as law to reinforce the status of the contractor/engineers who write the codes. There are so many different building codes and jurisdictions in this country that it would be futile to try to meet all of them. The saltbox house is designed to meet the requirements of the major, widely accepted codes. However, if your community passed a zoning ordinance or code amendment which requires a very large house, you may be stuck. Several years ago, I authored a chapter in a book by Eugene Eccli, *Low-Cost, Energy-Efficient Shelter,* which gives specific details of dealing with codes and code officials. This book has chapters by specialists in several construction fields and is well worth reading.

While I tend to regard many code restrictions as repressive and unnecessary, I wholly support reasonable code provisions on fire safety. In fact, I feel that most codes don't go far enough in this area. It may come as a surprise to you that the leading cause of adult deaths in this country is not cancer, heart disease, or automobile accidents—it is *fire*. Extensive use of wood-burning heaters by a generation unaccustomed to proper safety precautions has accelerated a trend.

The houses in this book have been designed with fire safety as a primary consideration. Most are constructed with a brick or slate floor set in a sand bed installed directly on grade. This leaves no possibility of sparks starting a fire in a floor. Chimneys are of masonry and are freestanding in the center of the houses where they absorb heat from a stove. Suspended floor structures are of heavy timber construction with a 2- or 3-inch deck forming finish floor and ceiling. This type of construction is classed as "fire-resistant" by many codes. The heavy beams will just char in a fire, and there are no hidden cavities to conceal a fire. Attics and basements which are the most frequent starting points for a fire are eliminated or used directly as a part of the basic living space. Six-inch-thick exterior walls are framed horizontally with 2X6s set at 2-foot centers, providing superior thermal performance as well as a fire stop every 2 feet. Conventional vertical studs create spaces which act as small chimneys to spread a fire. My roofs are usually of metal to prevent any possibility of a roof fire being started by sparks.

No amount of precaution can offset human complacency or carelessness, however. Make sure that you keep all combustibles away from stoves, clean your chimney frequently, have adequate fire extinguishers, and most important, decide what to do in an emergency *before* it happens.

Building your own house is a labor-intensive undertaking. Before you start, make sure that you are up to it. If you get help with the basic frame and some finish work, it should take you three to four months of diligent, full-time work to complete the basic saltbox. If you just work on weekends, it could take a year or more. Costs of houses are rising much faster than the general rate of inflation, so all of your hard work will be time well spent.

One major key is to do your homework well. If possible, spend a couple of months lining up references, materials, and labor. A well-organized job with all the necessary materials and workmen on hand at the proper time is a joy. Otherwise, the project can drag on interminably and will get discouraging. If you don't do your homework, it is all too easy to be browbeaten by your workmen into doing things their way. Knowing what you want and how you want it done will give you the confidence to issue direct, concise orders. Make sure that the chain of command is established and that one person always gives instructions. Also, make sure that the instructions go directly to the person performing the task. All too often, the "boss" forgets vital instructions. If you do a really good job, maybe you'll get so enthused that you will go into the business, as several of my former clients have done.

I hope this book will give you the information and motivation to enable you to snatch an important part of your life (housing) away from the technocrats who would make you pay dearly for the privilege of owning your own home.

GOOD LUCK!

Part I

Preparation for Building

Chapter 1

Energy Sources

As an initial step in planning an energy-efficient home, you should examine your entire lifestyle for areas in which you waste energy. Figure out how you can cut down on this energy use. Transportation is one of the greatest areas of energy waste in our society. It has been estimated that over 50 percent of the cost of supermarket food is attributable to the costs of transporting the goods to the market. Since I advocate moving out to the countryside where you can grow your own food, much of this waste can be eliminated. But what of the ever-rising costs of gasoline? Does it make sense to be remote from your place of work? It does only if you have an efficient car which gets good gas mileage. You can save a great deal by growing your own food and harvesting your own firewood, but it is very easy to squander the savings on inefficient vehicles.

The automobile industry whines that it is impossible to make more efficient cars without staggering capital investments. What Detroit really means is that they don't have engineers who are skilled enough to design them. Not one gasoline engine made in this country can meet emissions standards without a catalytic converter. The unleaded fuel which these monstrosities require consumes more raw oil in refining, so that the true mileage of these cars is much worse than advertised. Every major foreign car maker who sells cars in this country offers at least one engine which doesn't require one of these expensive, fuel-wasting gadgets. How much longer are we going to be content to be second-rate?

Wouldn't it be great if we could have lightweight, efficient cars and trucks which got 60 miles to the gallon? Maybe what we need is a light, efficient power plant which can produce power without all of the mass of belts, external gadgets, leaky gaskets, and radiators we've become used to. With advanced technology, it should be possible to produce such a vehicle weighing only about 1,000 pounds. Of course, Detroit executives assure us that such a car is a fantasy.

Actually, it is not a fantasy, but a regular production vehicle designed in 1936. At this writing, over eight million have been produced. The car I described is the legendary Citroen 2CV. It has an advanced two-cylinder engine much like a BMW motorcycle. The engine is so precisely machined that it can be assembled with no gaskets whatsoever and so durable that there is virtually no maintenance required. Strangely, making such a fine product is a good way to go out of business. Citroen nearly did fold but was saved by the 1973 oil shortages which caused demand for their superefficient car to blossom all over the world. Recent profits have set records. Citroen is planning to invade the United States market with an updated version of the 2CV, called a Visa. Watch

These cars, designed in 1936, get 60 mpg. Eight million have been sold.

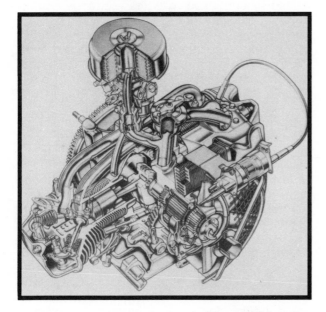

Citroen 2CV engine.

for it. In the meantime, Hondas, Subarus, and Volkswagen Rabbits seem to be the best bets.

Electricity

One major concern in selecting a location for an energy-saving house will be a source of electricity. Our nation has become excessively dependent upon electricity as an energy source for doing an incredible array of tasks. Power companies like to spout endless strings of lies. One of the choice ones is that electricity is 100 percent efficient. They use this line to force electric heat down the throats of unsuspecting homeowners, and are helped along by very obvious advantages of electric heat such as cleanliness, flexibility, low initial installation cost, and easy zone control. The rub is that generating plants are very costly and, including transmission losses, 30 to 35 percent efficient. Also the dirt and pollution which you don't have in your house are dumped

elsewhere — out of sight, out of mind. In certain limited situations, electric heat is an ideal *supplemental* heat source. But too often it becomes the quick, easy heat solution.

In Chapter 11 I discuss means of heating with electricity which are vastly more efficient than the usual baseboard heating units which the power companies tend to push. The power companies got themselves into very serious trouble years ago by basing all of their financial planning on an exponential growth curve. Tax benefits from continuous expansion and the revenues from an ever-increasing consumer base were projected far off into the rosy future. Finite supplies of fossil fuels and dangers of nuclear power plants were forgotten in the rush for expansion. Now that continual expansion is no longer viewed as inevitable, the companies are in real trouble. Drastically rising electric rates must pay for past expansion plus present and future high costs of imported fuels.

It has occurred to me — and to a number of other people — that we in the electrical industry have spent a lot of time and energy explaining rationally the potential ill consequences of energy shortages when the real issue is not rational. It's fear, an emotional set which is being stimulated by people who, frankly, may understand better than we do how to get people's attention. . . .

I think we should recognize that what the American people are being urged to accept is not an alternate energy system, "soft" versus "hard," but a completely different way of life that is pictured as simpler, healthier, more harmonious with nature, and less exploitative of resources. And the lever which is being used to move people towards this lifestyle is fear. . . .

We cannot combat this fear purely by documenting how irrational, unsupportable, or containable it is. Instead, I think we should clarify for people how fearful are the alternatives to moderate energy growth and economic expansion.

Thomas A. Vanderslice, Senior Vice President, Power Systems Sector of General Electric Company

I think all members of our society have a moral obligation to fully oppose Mr. Vanderslice and his ilk in their assumptions that more consumption is better. According to the Department of Housing and Urban Development we use two to three times the power per capita of other industrialized nations. Simply using power efficiently doesn't mean that our economy has to grind to a halt. If other countries with even higher standards of living (say Sweden) can get by with 40 percent less energy use per capita, why can't we?

In my own community, we are embroiled in a controversy with the mighty Consolidated Edison Co. which supplies New York City. Since New York City has passed a moratorium on any additional electric generating plants, Con Ed plans to seize enough property to build two generating plants plus rights-of-way for 765 KVA lines into New York City.

Over thirty years ago, my grandfather had a similar confrontation with a power company, although on a much smaller scale. He spent many thousands of dollars trying to prevent the power lines from ruining much of his beautiful farmland; of course he lost. He vowed never to connect to the power even though it was within sight and free connections had been offered him in attempted reconciliation. This resulted in my growing up in a household with no electricity. We lived a very comfortable life without electric power and many of the techniques which we used are equally applicable today. Two of the houses in this book have no external source of power and I will combine my experiences with theirs to show how power consumption can be drastically cut or eliminated.

Running water is considered a necessity in our society, and to have running water in a house often requires an electrically powered pump. Even though they usually don't require electricity, all major codes require a minimum plumbing system. This means that you can, by code, figure out other ways of getting water to the house without using electricity. On my grandfather's farm, springs were quite common. It was easy to construct a concrete cistern and divert the spring into the cistern. This was done in the 1920s; running water had been installed long before the power lines came along. We did have to be careful in long periods of dry weather or the cistern could be drawn dry, but otherwise it worked in a very trouble-free fashion. The two houses in this book without commercial power use other approaches to obtaining water. The various possibilities are examined in detail in Chapter 6.

Refrigeration

Another major domestic necessity commonly requiring electricity is refrigeration. It is a heavy consumer of electricity, usually number one in households which avoid more obvious excessive electrical uses, such as cooking and resistance-type space and water heating. Many people don't know that refrigerators that don't require electricity are made. If it were not for the recreational vehicle industry, they probably would not be.

Back at the dawn of commercial refrigerator manufacture, a company named Servel patented a unique refrigeration system with no moving parts, somewhat similar in concept to the Stirling engine. Heat is applied within a completely enclosed system, causing a phase change in a refrigerant. The gas thus created is passed through cooling coils and absorbs heat from the interior of the box, recondensing into a liquid and starting the cycle over again. A gas flame is used to heat the refrigerant in the Servel system. There is virtually nothing to wear out and very little to malfunction. Hence, used Servels are prized, particularly in remote areas that have no commercial power sources. Early models used no electricity; later ones had ice makers, interior lights, etc.

Unfortunately, American tastes changed much more rapidly than the design of the Servel. Large refrigerators with automatic defrosting and giant combination refrigerator-freezers were the rage. The very last Servels, made in the early sixties, attempted to meet this market, but by then the company had lost most of its dealers and much of its market. Enter the Whirlpool Corp. who bought up the Servel rights and the leftover inventory. For a few years, Whirlpool marketed an improved "bigger and better" gas refrigerator, but it was too expensive and was shortly dropped. (Repair parts for both Servel and Whirlpool gas refrigerators, such as door gaskets, handles, and thermostats are still available from Whirlpool Corp.†)

Somehow the marvelous concept of the Servel refused to die. Whirlpool sold the rights to Arkala Industries which now makes very efficient gas air-conditioning units which use the same foolproof system as the refrigerators. They are described in Chapter 11. Arkala sold the Servel rights for home refrigerators to Norcold Co.† Norcold manufactures a wide variety of equipment for recreational vehicles, including gas refrigerators. The foreign rights to the system were sold off several years ago and imported (expensive) refrigerators and freezers using natural gas, bottled gas (propane), or kerosene are available from Lehman Hardware and Appliance.† See *30*

---

†The address of this and other manufacturers and associations so indicated will be found under "Addresses of Manufacturers and Associations" in Part IV.

Energy-Efficient Houses for other ideas for reducing energy consumption for conventional electric refrigerators.

The real beauty of this system is that, like the Stirling engine to which it is related, the power source is external and in the form of heat. Theoretically, the heat can be supplied by any fuel — gas, wood, kerosene, electricity, or even the sun. Focusing collectors are readily available; they can produce very hot water which can power the refrigerator or, in more direct applications, focus directly on the refrigerator unit itself. Experimenters have set up units which produce refrigeration directly from the sun, but since so few of these direct absorption-type refrigerators exist there are no commercial versions available. Bottled gas or kerosene units seem the best solution for those remote from power lines.

Small, efficient generator; trade name: AquaBug.

Other Appliances

The recreational vehicle and camping industries have spawned some fine, efficient appliances and lighting fixtures which run on bottled gas. They also make available many devices which use 12-volt DC current, most of them very modest in their consumption of energy. For those interested in energy conservation these items are a must. Many recreational vehicle stores carry expensive lines of appliances. In contrast, Sears, Roebuck and Co. and J. C. Whitney both have

extensive lines of recreational vehicle equipment at reasonable prices. J. C. Whitney markets such goodies as an efficient 12-volt quartz-iodine lamp, a 12-volt, remote-mounted conversion compressor for refrigerators, and a full line of three-way refrigerators which operate on 12-volt DC, 110-volt AC, or bottled gas. These latter units may be of special interest if you plan to run the main power lines to your house at a later date or if you plan a very limited wind system.

In Chapter 9, I discuss lighting designs which produce maximum light from minimum wattage. If you are going to use any alternate power system, this is very important, so think out window, skylight, and light fixture placement carefully. Also examine all energy-consuming appliances to see whether they can use an energy source other than electric power.

Alternate Electrical Energy Sources

After you've reduced your electrical requirements to a bare minimum, how do you supply this power? A wind system is the most logical answer, but those have limitations which I'll discuss shortly. For a very minimal installation, you can start with a 12-volt, battery-powered system which can be fed by wind at a later date. How do you charge the batteries? There are three approaches which I have found successful. First is simply to take the batteries somewhere where there is 110-volt power and hook them to a charger. If you regularly commute to work, this could be easily accomplished.

The second solution is easier and just a bit more expensive. It involves attaching a second or third battery to your car or truck. This is very commonly done on recreational vehicles, and a shop which specializes in this type of installation can readily accomplish it for you. Do not be fooled into thinking that you are getting this power free, though; your car's engine is doing the extra work to generate the power to charge the batteries. You may have to go to the expense of installing a bigger alternator or generator to handle the extra load. Also, you should buy expensive deep-draw batteries. The ones used in automobiles are designed to maintain a constant charge, and deteriorate rapidly if they are repeatedly discharged. Automobile batteries will work for you on a short-term emergency basis, but get good batteries for the long term.

The third and least advisable means of charging your batteries is a generator. American-made generators, except for the very expensive industrial models, are noisy, consume lots of gas and oil, and require almost constant maintenance. There is a very small Honda generator on the market which does do a nice job of charging batteries. It is model no. E400, costing under $400.

For a very lightweight portable generator, I recommend the AquaBug, which produces 300 watts at 110 volts and 12 amps at 12 volts. It is available from AquaBug International† and costs about $300.

Wind Generators

Before you get too enthusiastic about wind power, make sure that you are located to receive enough wind to make a wind machine practical. If you are in a borderline area, you will either have to cut consumption or increase battery storage capacity. People who have wind-power systems learn to regard electric power as a commodity which can be used up just as a jug of water; it's a very healthy attitude. If you are remote from power lines and in an area of low wind velocity, you should check on the developments of the Norelco Stirling-powered generator which I describe in Chapter 11. It is set up for 12 volts, but you may have to get on a long waiting list.

In my book, *30 Energy-Efficient Houses,* I briefly discussed wind generators and recommended the prebuilt Kedco generators or the plans for these machines. My feedback from readers as well as my own recent experiments indicate that you are better off buying the prebuilt unit. Unless you are a trained machinist with access to a full machine shop, building your own wind generator is a frustrating and expensive proposition. The Helion plans for the Kedco unit are very, very complete and detailed. Unfortunately, the unit is quite sophisticated and many specialty materials such as high-strength metals and special bearings are required. Also, a truly expert welder must assemble the hub to assure safety. A poorly balanced or poorly welded wind machine can disintegrate, causing instant death to anyone in the path of flying debris. For this reason, I would strongly urge you to buy a fully assembled wind generator such as Kedco, Enertech, or a rebuilt Jacobs unit.

If you really want to experiment on your own, there is one refined, safe design on the market which is worthy of your consideration. Some years ago, Bill Sweeney of Princeton University devised a modern version of the old Mediterranean sail-type windmill. He applied modern aerodynamic design to the old mills and created a

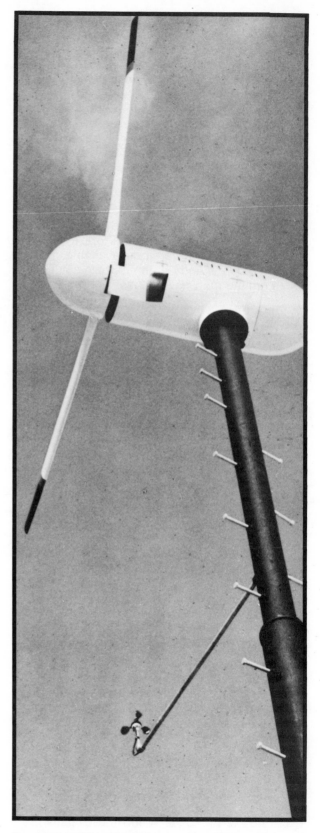

Enertech 1,500-watt wind generator. This generator and the Kedco unit are two of the best new wind generators on the market.

very low-cost, sophisticated design which is relatively easy to build. His design was taken over by a large American firm and refined and thoroughly tested in preparation for production. Production plans were dropped when it was discovered that the sails would disintegrate in winds over 110 miles per hour.

I do not feel that this is a fatal flaw as the sails are easy to furl and such winds are rare and usually give advance warning. Excellent, easy-to-follow plans are available for this windmill from Flanagan's Plans, Box 891, Cathedral Station, New York, NY 10025. They are specifically designed with the amateur builder in mind and do not in-

---

There can be no civilization without progress, no progress without ideas, no ideas without books. . . .

Norman Cousins
Saturday Review

---

volve any welding. The plans call for various high-strength aluminum alloys, stainless steel pop rivets, stainless steel cables, and specialty thrust bearings for the drive train but the necessary specialty parts are available from Flanagan's Plans at reasonable cost. Plans for the windmill itself are $25; tower and electrical system, $15; a full set of materials for the machine itself is $600;

and the fabricated sails and lines, $150. All parts are available individually in case you want to order yours locally and just get a few specialty items from Flanagan's Plans. These plans are some of the clearest I have ever seen. Others are available for other items of interest, such as greenhouses and furniture. Write to the company for a current listing.

The Princeton sailwing is by far the easiest windmill to build that I have seen. I tried to design my own last summer and quickly discovered that even highly rated machine shops had difficulty in performing accurate welds, following directions, and the like. Also, finding proper materials out in the country was a serious problem. For those with further interest in homebuilt wind machines or for those who want to experiment, the developer of the Kedco/Helion wind generator has written two excellent books. The first, *Simplified Windpower Systems for Experimenters,* is available from Helion Inc., Box 445, Brownsville, CA 95919. Highly technical plans for a wind generator are also available from Helion Inc., at $15 a set. The best reference work for the homeowner is now out of print; check your nearest large technical library. It is *Wind Power for Farms, Homes, and Small Industry,* by Jack Park and Dick Schwind, prepared a few years ago for the Energy Research and Development Administration in Washington, D.C. As is usual with government documents, it's very difficult to find.

Chapter 2

Financing and Site Selection

Before you begin building, you have to find a building site, and before you buy a site you have to figure out how you're going to pay for it. This chapter discusses several options for financing your land and construction costs and talks about what to look for in a building site.

Financing

Many people have realized that a house is an almost perfect hedge against inflation. Therefore, banks are overextended with housing loans and tend to be very, very choosy when providing mortgage money. There are two diametrically opposed means of coping with the "bank problem."

Eliminating the Bank

The first, easiest, and cheapest solution is to avoid using the bank at all, or at least to limit your borrowing to a small personal loan rather than a large mortgage. With the current interest rates, you are paying more in interest than you are actually borrowing. However, the staggering inflation rate does mean that you will be paying back the loan with dollars which are worth much less than they are presently. If your source of income

is such that it will keep pace with or exceed the rate of inflation, you may want to proceed and take a substantial mortgage. But what if you can't afford to give the bank all of that money, and you still want your new home? Should the economy reach the crisis which seems imminent, repaying a mortgage may become difficult or impossible.

This book directly addresses the problems of acquiring reasonably priced housing. If you are willing to make some sacrifices and invest lots of hard work, you can build a house for very little money. Building a very simple, basic house, using many recycled materials and doing a major portion of the work yourself, it is still possible to construct a comfortable house for less than $10,000. A full-size American car or four-wheel-drive truck now costs that much!

Saving Money

Go on an extreme austerity budget. Aim to save several thousand dollars per year. Four of the houses featured in this book were built entirely from savings and hard work. The extremes of inflation may discourage you into thinking that savings are impossible. However, consider that most of the expense incurred in our society is based on buying goods which we don't really need and paying others to do things which we can do ourselves. Food, clothing, shelter, and transportation are considered the basic necessities. If you are willing to examine these aspects of your life and make some adjustments, many savings are possible!

For instance, grow all, or part of, your food. A recent *Wall Street Journal* article described how extremely wealthy residents of a Boston suburb were successfully raising pigs, chickens, and even a cow in their yard, much to the consternation of their neighbors! Gardens are once again becoming popular with everyone, particularly with adverse weather conditions and unions pushing fresh produce costs to unaffordable levels. Just using common sense in buying can save a lot. Co-ops and stores featuring unbranded merchandise are two very good ways to save a third to a half of the costs of buying at a conventional store. Buying produce in quantity in season and drying, canning, or freezing it for later consumption also saves a lot.

Avoid buying anything on credit and throwing away interest money. Try checking thrift shops, garage sales, and community newspapers for items you feel that you really must have. Wealthy people and even middle-class people are constantly discarding excellent-quality merchandise either because they have grown tired of it or, in the case of autos and the like, because it needs some repairs and they would rather not bother fixing whatever is wrong. According to Hertz, it costs over $4,000 to drive a full-size, new American car 10,000 miles a year. This includes indirect costs such as depreciation and insurance. I drove my $100 Peugeot over twice that far (22,000 miles) last year for just under $1,000. It handles well and can travel easily over all the back roads to my numerous clients. Furthermore, it is a very comfortable, advanced, front-wheel-drive car. It's not very pretty and I do have to worry about eventual breakdowns, but the savings have been incredible. It is a sad reflection on American industry that to get a car like this, one has to look to the import market.

Budget

One way to almost guarantee savings is to establish a budget. If nothing else, keeping a budget will get you into the habit of keeping accurate records, a vital part of doing a good job on your house. To set up a budget, take all checks, bills, and other records from the previous year and sort them into categories. Next, establish major

categories of expenses and record the actual amounts which were spent each month. Many items purchased with cash will have to be estimated. Once you have a rough idea of your actual expenditures, rewrite the budget, establishing what you believe to be the minimum possible figure for each item. It may help to further break the budget down into weekly or even daily items. Make sure that every member of the family studies the budget and is aware of its implications and the reasons for the attempted savings. Many people who have had a serious calamity befall them have suddenly discovered that they can actually make do with much less than they thought they could.

Dealing with the Bank

For those busy people who do not feel that they have the time or skills to build for themselves and will therefore have to borrow money from a bank to hire others, I have designed the basic saltbox. There are alternate plans for various parts of the house, but the basic design is aimed at bank acceptability while still using passive solar design. It is just large enough and has the potential for incorporating all of the things which conservative banks want in a house. Banks want something they feel they can sell on the conventional housing market, not a "white elephant" with which they may be stuck for years. They usually want three bedrooms, or at least three rooms which can function as bedrooms. One and a half to two baths are considered a minimum. Laundry facilities and some sort of automatic heat are minimal features for the bank. Banks usually don't like extreme or unusual designs, although mortgages were obtained for two of the most unusual shown in this book.

I had the good fortune to be able to interview the vice-president of one of the major banks in this country; he offered some sage advice for owner-builders. First, present the bank with very thorough documentation of everything. They will want details and proof of your financial situation. Copies of income tax records are usually golden. Banks do not look kindly upon rough sketches on the back of a napkin. They will want a full set of reasonably detailed working drawings, and a breakdown of costs for all of the different trades for the house. After they have satisfied themselves that your credit is sufficient for them to consider your loan, they will investigate further. For $4, you can obtain your credit rating from TRW Credit Rate, 20 Just Rd., Fairfield, NJ 07006.

Two different sets of appraisers will look over

your project. First, a land appraiser will check your property to see if it is worth what you paid for it. In many cases, it will have appreciated and be worth more. Many banks will apply the value of your land toward the required down payment for a mortgage. The bank will almost certainly require title insurance for your property, and it's a rather good idea in any case. What if you don't actually own your land, or have just made a few payments on the property? If the bank feels that you have a valuable piece of property, you are still in good shape. It may be advantageous to you to transfer your loan on the property to the bank as a part of your mortgage. State regulations and individual banking practices vary on how this can be handled. Check into the matter carefully with several banks. Remember that a mortgage spans a considerable number of years. A tiny fraction of a percentage point of interest can add up to a substantial sum of money.

Contractor of Record

Bank attitudes toward owner-builders vary considerably and are changing rapidly. Traditional banking practice was to give an automatic NO!!! to anyone attempting to build his own house. Since costs have escalated so wildly, more and more people are doing all or part of their own building. This has put great pressure on banks to abandon their traditional restrictive attitudes toward do-it-yourselfers.

It is a good idea to feel out the bank with some questions before you get too far along. If your bank is negative, it's usually easy to set up a Contractor of Record. In effect, you are being hired by the contractor to build your own house. It may take some looking to find the right contractor, and you may want to hire him as a consultant to help you locate subcontractors and maybe do some of the major construction such as the foundation and/or shell of your house. Many of the houses in this book were built in this manner. If you give the contractor some of the work to make it worth his while, he will be much more willing to help out with the bank. It's also very comforting to have someone to fall back on for advice or help in case you get bogged down with the job. The contractor's fee for helping you should be clearly understood before you start. An agreement should be drawn up and precautions should be taken to protect both parties. You should get contractors' insurance so that the Contractor of Record will not be responsible for your actions. Contractors' insurance is readily available at reasonable cost.

Be very careful with your estimate. Banks don't like expensive finishes which they don't feel add to the sales value of the house. Examples of items which have caused us trouble are copper and cedar shake roofs, large greenhouses, a swimming lane in a greenhouse (mentioned as part of the reason for rejecting the house), and cedar siding. All or most of these items would probably have been acceptable if the houses had been very large and lavish, but all of them were compact, two-bedroom houses. The bank's rationale was that the materials were undoubtedly nice and did indeed increase the value of the house, but at the same time would make a small house difficult to sell because the sale price would be too high. Great logic! This doesn't mean that you can't plan to use quality materials, particularly if you are doing a lot of your own work so that you can afford them. It does mean that you shouldn't put them on the copy of the estimate which goes to the bank. For instance, you may submit to the bank an estimate from an electrical contractor when you know that you will be doing the wiring yourself. With the money you save, you can afford cedar siding, but your estimate for the bank will show the siding as pine.

Payment Schedules

Bank troubles do not necessarily end with the granting of your loan. A particularly ugly facet of bank loans is known as a "payment schedule." On first glance, this will probably seem reasonable, and you are likely to dismiss it as routine. Don't. Banks are extremely conservative at doling out their money. Most payment schedules are heavily weighted in the bank's favor. They pay you relatively small amounts of money for the first stages of construction which are actually the most expensive. In this way, the bank assures themselves that all materials have been paid for *before* they give out any money. Since you are waiting for that money to pay for the same materials, an impasse is at hand. Some banks are very reasonable about payments, but they are the exceptions. The usual practice is to split the payments into four or five stages as follows:

First payment: foundation, basement floor, road, septic system, and well.

Second payment: shell of house, including doors, windows, and finish roof.

Third payment: rough wiring and plumbing, drywall, and exterior finishing.

Fourth payment: finish wiring and plumbing, cabinetwork and appliances, heating system installed and tested, and interior painting and finishing.

Since installation of the well and septic systems may be something over which you have little control, the bank is usually flexible about which payment contains these items. Some banks in my experience have been very fair about the whole project; others have created nightmares. The money bind usually occurs at the end of payment two. This is a very expensive stage, and, typically, banks drastically underpay this amount. Post and beam construction aggravates this problem because much of the work which you are doing will also serve as exposed finish work which the bank doesn't want to pay for until later. There are three ways of combating the payment deficit problem.

First, buy most materials on credit and lean on the creditors until the bank pays. This is the typical "big business" way of handling the matter and just one more reason why our economy lags. Sometimes, you have no other alternative. If you are forewarned of this problem, you can talk to the bank and possibly arrange some short-term funding (of course at high interest rates), but don't be shocked when you apply to the bank for $7,000 and they give you $4,000. Or maybe you can set aside some savings or make other arrangements.

Wisdom consists of the anticipation of consequences.

Norman Cousins
Saturday Review

Banks use several different schemes for making construction payments. If they arrange a separate "construction loan," at a higher interest rate, they are more generous with their payments. If you are actually getting a portion of the final mortgage moneys, they may be quite tightfisted. Make sure that you discuss all possible options with the bank before you execute any documents.

Alternate Financing Methods

No matter how much shopping you do, you may find that you still can't find a bank willing to take a mortgage or that the high interest rates and various closing costs will push the cost of a mortgage out of your budget range. Since this is a nationwide problem, various alternate financing plans have been developed.

Tax-Free Bonds

Government bodies are taking advantage of their tax-free status to issue bonds for housebuilding. Typically, these bonds have an interest rate of about 8 percent as opposed to 11 percent-plus for commercial mortgages. There are two rubs. First, one has to live in a community or governmental jurisdiction which is offering the bonds. This will probably, but not necessarily, limit you to living in a metropolitan area since most of the places offering these bonds are cities, although a few scattered county governments have also issued them.

The second problem involves tax losses. The reason that the bonds are such a bargain is that the government agencies are exempt from taxes. Banks have to pay taxes. It is possible that these bonds are unfair competition to the banks. More important, they deprive the federal government of rapidly increasing amounts of tax revenue. It is a distinct possibility that Congress will act to plug this loss of income.

Second-Trust Deeds

Even if you live out in the country, you may be able to take advantage of this form of financing. In this arrangement, you are actually borrowing another individual's savings. Second-trust deeds are arranged through mortgage brokers who get two parties together. The laws which permit these trusts make it easier for an individual to foreclose on a mortgage, so they are an attractive way for an individual to invest his money. This is an obscure method of financing and there are very few brokers who can arrange them. Two who do handle them are: American Investors Management, Inc., P.O. Box 3074, Reno, NV 89505 and Metropolitan Mortgage Company, 2244 Biscayne Blvd., Miami, FL 33137.

Another way to obtain money for building is to buy enough property so that you can split off a building lot and take a mortgage on that lot. This can also serve as an emergency hedge in case you get into a financial bind during construction. Always watch your finances carefully during construction, though. Almost everyone tends to get carried away and get into the "most expensive is best for my house" frame of mind. Many little extra expenditures can mount up into one huge extra sum of money! Since our basic saltbox is designed to be added to in stages, you may want to start without the greenhouse or carport and add them when you have the money.

Records

Business failures of professional contractors are notoriously frequent. Make absolutely sure that you keep accurate records. A small, spiral-bound notebook should be carried at all times to record expenditures and other business transactions for your house. Make a note of exactly what was agreed upon with subcontractors and when. At the end of each week, transfer expenditures and major decisions into a second permanent ledger book so that you will have a second record in case you should lose your notebook. Lumberyards, hardware stores, and other building suppliers are frequently lax about sending you all of your bills. Sometimes bills come along months after you purchase the items. Keep track of all of your bills, even though this is difficult when you are tired from a week of hard work, trying to keep the house on schedule. Rather than let finances get out of date, get someone to help with them. Almost all other problems facing the owner-builder can be solved by study and hard work, but finances have to be a day-by-day activity or you can quickly get into serious trouble.

Taxes

Your records are vital for substantiating tax deductions. In addition to such obvious deductions as interest payments and sales taxes, Congress has passed a new tax incentive for energy-conserving items such as solar water heaters and windmills. Your maximum credit is $2,200, and since it is direct credit it is very valuable. Passive devices such as solar greenhouses are not allowed as credits, although guidelines for passive solar deductions are under consideration at this writing. Several states have already enacted their own tax incentive programs for energy conservation, and many other proposals are in the works. Check with a tax consultant before you build. Some simple changes could make you eligible for additional benefits.

Selecting a Site

Commercial developers like to cite the drastic rise in land costs as one of the major factors in the escalation of sale prices for the average house. It is true that tracts close to urban areas, suitable for subdivision into small, level lots, have increased in price astronomically in recent years. If one is willing to do a bit of hunting and live just a bit further away from it all, real bargains still exist, particularly for rugged terrain. For example, the most expensive and least expensive pieces of property in this book are both within 100 miles of New York City. Both cost the same amount of money. One is 62 acres; the other only 1½ acres. Both are located on rural back roads, and have views from south-facing hillsides. The expensive one is located in a development; the inexpensive one far away from civilization.

The legal and administrative cost of dividing a piece of property into a number of smaller lots is high and always passed on to the new owners. Try to find a piece of property of medium size and buy the whole tract. If you can find someone else to buy a portion, you may be able to get your lot for very little money. Many people are suffering from the combined effects of inflation and rising fuel costs; keep your ear to the ground. Rather than lose his farm, a farmer may be willing to sell or lease you a small tract of unproductive land which might be perfect for a passive solar house. Developers, too, are feeling the pinch. A client persuaded a local developer to sell just one lot on the edge of a proposed development at less than half of the proposed cost of lots in the final subdivision. This particular lot fronts on a paved road and would have been difficult for the developer to fit into his final scheme. The client heard about the dilemma from the surveyor for the property.

Self-Sufficiency

When looking for a piece of property, keep in mind the possibility of using materials directly from your site for building your house. Old stone foundations, brick chimneys, stone walls, and nice stands of timber are things to look for. If the property is steep and remote, these materials may be regarded as worthless and not increase the sale price. If you are planning to grow your own food and cut your own timber for fuel and lumber, five to ten acres is a suitable-size tract. Many people who write to me are concerned, as I am, that the economy may collapse completely and we will need to be as self-sufficient as possible. Many occupations may preclude living in a remote area. Most of the sites in this book are quite remote, yet all of the owners but one have regular jobs which require daily travel to work.

Location and Lifestyles

Before you make the leap and move out to the country and spend great amounts of money and effort on a house, you should consider your values and lifestyle and make absolutely sure that this location is for you. This is another reason

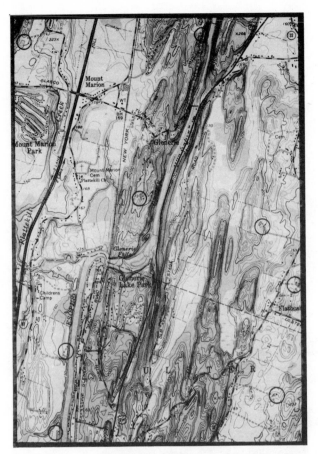

Remote roads lead to nice house sites.

ing which I have done. The encircled areas indicate back roads with abandoned houses or other interesting features, such as a pond or water frontage. Typical highway maps only show the three major north-south roads on this map as if none of the rest exists.

Even if none of the back roads results in a direct find, you will get a view of the countryside which is much different than that which is gained by traveling the superhighways. In this case, the New York State Thruway cuts right through the center of the map, yet the areas surrounding it are very rural except for one tiny housing development at center left.

Commercial real estate agents rarely list the sort of property which I have been discussing. You will have to ferret it out on your own and hunt up the owners. Local stores, neighbors, post offices, and the county tax office are sources of information. Sometimes a No Hunting or Trespassing sign on adjoining property will be signed. You can look up the deed and see who is listed as an abutter. Then, of course, you still have to talk the owner into selling.

Leasing

Maybe he doesn't want to sell, as the property has been in the family for generations, but he still isn't planning to use the land. Try to lease a building site. This is a new concept which is rapidly gaining popularity due to the drastic rise in housing costs. Commercial developers are jumping on the bandwagon and using land leases as a way to cut total sales prices and make their houses available to lower-income families. The lowest-cost Volkswagen house was built on leased property.

There are two common types of leases. In the first case, you take a long-term lease, say fifty or a hundred years, and the land reverts to the original owners or their successors at the end of the lease. In the second case, commonly used by developers, the land is yours at the end of a thirty- to forty-year lease. In reality, you are just making very extended time payments on the land. Farmers are quite used to using leases either to gain additional crop acreage or to obtain additional income from their own unused property. These are usually short-term leases of two, five, or ten years. Since farmers are used to the concept, try advertising in local farm journals and rural weekly newspapers for a piece of property to lease. One client reported 27 replies to just one ad.

why subdivisions are so expensive. Most people like neighbors and conveniences such as supermarkets right at their fingertips. It takes a special breed to live away from it all. Even if you will be very happy with solitude, what about your children? Several of the owners in this book don't have children, so the problem doesn't come up. Give it serious consideration. Remember that children have a herd instinct and want to be with their friends after school. Teenagers, in particular, can want to go six different places in just one evening. They are not likely to be tolerant of alternative energy systems, long muddy roads, no telephone, and the like. If there are a few neighbors within walking distance, some of these difficulties may be overcome.

Finding your ideal piece of property may take quite a lot of hunting. It can be great fun, though. In the ten years I have lived in this area, I have spent many happy hours exploring and hunting for abandoned houses, interesting property, and beautiful places. A good way to start your search is to order a set of U.S. Geological Survey maps of your area from USGS, Washington, DC 20244. The one shown here is an example of the explor-

Placement of Your Home

Before you buy or lease, study the property carefully to see if it provides an ecologically suitable site for a house. The examples in Part III will give you an idea of how some of the houses in this book were sited to best take advantage of site conditions. Ideally, the house should be located on a hill with a slope facing nearly due south. Entrance can either be from above to the north (least desirable, but quite feasible) or below from the south. In many cases, you will want a view to the south unobstructed by roads. An eastern approach is also possible. West is probably the worst, incorporating hot summer sun and cold winter winds. A windbreak of evergreen trees is desirable. South and east can either be clear or have deciduous trees to provide summer shade and winter sun. To do this just right these trees may have to be planted. If at all possible, take a look at your proposed property in the dead of winter to check sun angles. Charts and gadgets are available for calculating them, but there is no substitute for actually seeing what they will do in the field.

An Example

Just at the start of this winter, I rescued an abandoned house from ruin by buying it, along with fifteen inaccessible hillside acres. Because of the difficult access, and the house which was considered a liability due to its poor condition, the property had gone begging. The house was built by Bavarian immigrants sometime in the middle of the last century. A realtor friend of mine told me about the house some years ago, saying, "It's a perfect Alex Wade house. It does all of the things which you advocate."

And indeed it does. Built into a south-facing hill-

Built in the late 1800s, this house demonstrates many features of passive solar design. Large, south-facing windows trap sun, and a solid north wall keeps out winter wind.

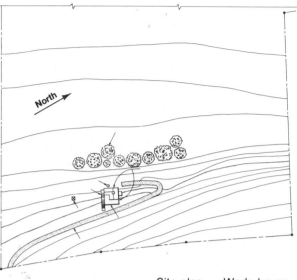

Site plan — Wade house.

side, lots of stone mass, small ground area, three stories, no windows on the north or west, extensive glass on south and east; in short, it's almost a textbook case of passive solar design elements. It also has post and beam framing with solid decking, horizontal girts for framing, and a cedar and cypress exterior. It's almost as though I had been there guiding the builders.

Since the site is so well planned, I've included a site plan here with significant features noted. This plan shows a nice solution for the conditions which are created when the hillside slopes in such a way that the main axis of the house can't be north-south. In this case, the house faces southeast; and due south is almost exactly at 45° to the slope of the hillside. In case you can't face your house exactly south, this site plan suggests alternatives. (Remember when looking at property to take a compass along. Also take a look at the bottom of your USGS map. It gives you the declination of true north from magnetic north, varying by 10 to 15° depending upon where you are located.)

Just as the Bavarians did, you will need to take into account wind angles; sun angles; and locations of windows, walks, and drives. I look out my window to see my distant neighbors' futile efforts to clear ice off their north-facing walk and driveway while my incredibly steep drive and steps are kept clear by nature. In fact, the whole other side of my road is a flat, treeless plain, inhabited by little boxes all with their big picture windows, drives, and walks in beautiful north shade. The winter winds sweep snow down off the mountain

where it lands right on their doorsteps and driveways. I think a great deal of it originally lands on *my* driveway, but the wind pattern is such that it doesn't stay there. If possible, observe your property carefully in winter before starting to build.

Site Plans

A typical site plan has lines (called contours) which indicate the slope of your land. These lines indicate the shape of the surface of a section of land by representing it as though it were intersected by a horizontal plane at set intervals, usually 5, 10, or 20 feet. Closely spaced lines indicate a steep slope; widely spaced ones a gentle slope. The USGS maps are stocked for all areas of the country. They are made from aerial photographs and are usually quite accurate, even if made at a very small scale.

If you need an accurate contour map for your property and don't want to pay a surveyor a steep price for the labor-intensive job of surveying one in the field, a very usable map can be made by enlarging a section of a USGS map to the same scale as the map which shows the boundaries of your property. If you don't understand the map, you can make an easy model of it by simply cutting out layers of cardboard to the same shape as the lines on the map and gluing the layers together. Site plans and aerial photos are included for a few of the houses to show you by example how site maps work and how to properly site a house. A couple of relatively flat sites are not included as they add little information.

The desensitization of the twentieth-century man is more ·than a danger to the common safety. It represents the loss of impairment of the noblest faculty of human life - the ability to be aware of both suffering and beauty; the ability to share sorrow and create hope; the ability to think and respond beyond one's wants. There are some things we have no right ever to get used to.

Norman Cousins
Saturday Review

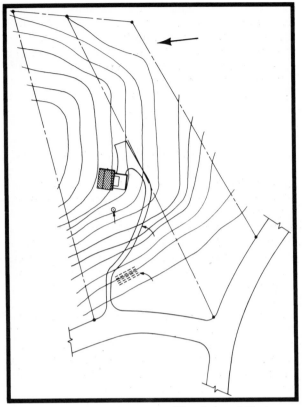

Site plan — Lillio house.

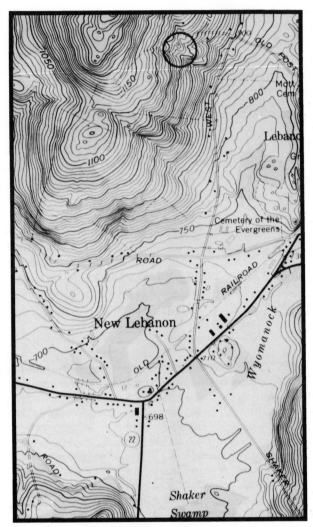

Site plan — Gilbert house.

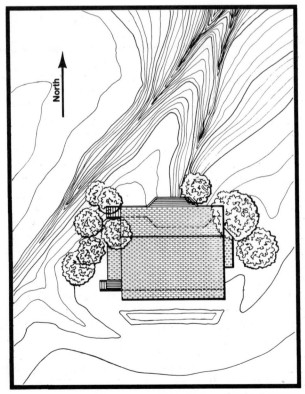

Site plan — Caddell house.

Aerial view of the Jones house.

Aerial view of the Lillio house.

Aerial view of the Tompkins house.

Aerial view of the Laskin house.

Chapter 3

Materials

Salvaged Materials

The potential for saving money on materials is almost unlimited. The limiting factors are the time and effort which you have to spend in hunting up the materials and transporting them. Despite recent downturns, ours is still a throwaway society. Urban renewal still destroys acres of good buildings at a time, and the countryside is dotted with abandoned, crumbling buildings. The small town in which I live is having a feud with two property owners whose abandoned structures are deemed eyesores. No one wants the materials from the houses even if the houses were torn down and the materials free for the taking. But then again, our economy is so depressed that no one is building houses in the immediate area. The real rub seems to be that no one will assume responsibility for cleaning up the sites after the houses are demolished.

Since this type of situation is rather common, it presents a golden opportunity for the owner-builder. You may have to post a bond to guarantee your work, but it should be worth it. Windows, doors, plumbing fixtures, and brick are very valuable items which can be obtained either directly from old buildings or from salvage yards. Be careful though; fancy salvage yards near large cities often charge more than the materials are worth new.

Native Materials

Materials such as stone and wood may be found right on your own land. If you buy a large piece of land with the idea of harvesting wood for heating, you can cut your own trees for the lumber you need for a house. In the easiest and most costly version of this scenario, you hire someone to cut the logs, take them to a sawmill, and have them cut into posts, beams, and boards for your house. This will save a third to a half of the cost of buying roughcut lumber direct from the sawmill. You may also be able to arrange a trade with the sawmill owner — your logs for his finish-cut materials. Check your sawmill out closely, though. Measure some of the material stacked in the yard for uniformity of cut. It takes good equipment, properly aligned, and a bit of skill to make uniform cuts.

Sawmills

What if your property is very remote from a commercial sawmill or you are on a rock-bottom budget? There are quite a number of portable mills on the market which have the major advantage of being able to come to the trees, which can save a great deal of energy in transportation and may save you time. The simplest of these mills is just a jig for a chain saw which enables you to make

The Savichs bought these fixtures used and had them resurfaced.

several different clients. It is the Sperber portable mill which costs over $500, but which is well worth it. With any of these mills count on wearing out many chain saw blades and probably at least one chain saw.

Conventional-style sawmills built small enough to be portable are another possibility. Bellsaw makes a widely advertised, inexpensive unit which requires quite a bit of setup time, but is of good quality. For a truly fine saw which will actually outperform big commercial mills, look into the Mobile Dimension Saw. It is delightfully portable and, like chain saws, the machine itself travels along a track, thus making long, large timbers easy to cut. It is powered by a Volkswagen engine and has three blades, so it cuts a complete board with each pass of the saw. The price is prohibitively high ($6,000) unless you plan to go into business with the saw (as one of my clients just did). These mills are becoming very popular

Mobile Dimension Saw — lightweight, portable unit that cuts a complete board at one pass.

controlled cuts of timbers and boards from logs. This is not an easy method; lots of hard work and at least a couple of months will be necessary to cut the lumber for a small house. Use this type of rig to cut posts and larger timbers, as they require much less cutting than smaller-dimension lumber. Thin boards are the least productive use for the chain saw mill.

Basic chain saw mills are available from Sears for less than $50. I would not attempt to use them for a whole house. A very fine, professional-quality chain saw mill has been recommended to me by in the United States and Canada as they can readily go to the remote sites usually passed over by commercial lumber cutters. A list of owners who cut for hire appears under "Commercial Sawmills" in Part IV.

Free Materials

Some materials may be completely free. An excellent example is used utility poles. One of my clients who is an executive with Ma Bell points out that most members of the Bell Telephone System as well as many power companies give away surplus poles. In some cases, they will actually deliver them to a site just to get rid of them. If you are building a pole house or garage, you may be able to get your foundation and basic posts absolutely free. Policies vary from company to company, and you will have to take potluck on what is available at the time you make your request. Utility poles rarely wear out; they get damaged by storms and vehicles and more frequently are replaced by larger poles to carry a greater number of lines or increase road clearance.

Keep your eyes open and be patient and flexible about materials if you can. One of my clients made a floor from old stone paving blocks which were being discarded. Others have used scrap and rejects from insulation plants; short-end cuts of oak flooring; timbers from old barns (everyone wants barn siding, but timbers go begging); and random board flooring, parquet flooring, and carpets removed from a posh corporate headquarters during an unnecessary remodeling. All of this takes time, and you will need a means of transporting your materials.

Damaged Materials

Great buys are available to those who are willing to accept materials which are slightly damaged, discolored, or otherwise unsuitable for sale at full market price. Lumber, if improperly stored, may have watermarks or damages from strapping, or may have turned gray from exposure to weather. Many lumberyards will sell this material at half-price or less. You will have to go to the work of refinishing the lumber, but if you have the time, this material is a bargain.

Masonry materials are brittle and particularly subject to damage. Concrete blocks with chipped corners or superficial cracks or casting defects are sometimes available for the taking from concrete block manufacturing plants. Precast concrete planks are also available as rejects. One of

This rack enables long pieces of wood to be carried on a short truck.

my clients used a damaged concrete septic tank for a cistern. Keep a sharp eye out for items such as windows with a piece of clouded Thermopane, plumbing fixtures with a minor chip, and the like. If you see something of this nature, make the owner an offer for substantially less than the posted price. You may get lucky.

Transportation

If you are going to be hunting around for materials, an economical means of transporting them is a must. Older American trucks are usually the best buys, but do basic checks such as a compression test before you buy. Dodge and Ford trucks with six-cylinder engines are my preferences. Jeep trucks need a bit too much maintenance, but last forever, particularly four-wheel-drive machines. They also tend to be higher priced initially.

If you want a new truck, the foreign ones are the only trucks with modern, efficient engines. They hold their value well so that you can get rid of them at the end of the job and still get most of your money back. Toyota, Mazda, Ford Courier, and the Dodge Colt are the top choices. Avoid Datsun and Chevy Luv. If you need four-wheel-drive, the Subaru Brat or station wagon is best. These vehicles are among the most durable, economical, and useful made anywhere in the world. Since load space is short, a top-mounted lumber rack is highly recommended if you are going to do much of your own hauling.

If you buy property out on a remote road, you will probably have to forget about a big American car. They are designed for use on city streets and superhighways only, and are at their very best sitting perfectly still in a dealer's showroom. Poor road clearance and outdated chassis design with old-fashioned rear-wheel drive make them unsuitable for unpaved roads or driveways.

Wholesale Suppliers

Maybe you don't have the time or inclination to chase around hunting materials or to mill your own lumber. There are still some fine options to being taken by your local lumberyard. There are several large building materials supply houses located throughout the country who handle a large range of building products at reasonable prices. You can order directly and take advantage of wholesale prices.

Two of the top companies are the Fingerle Lumber Co.[†] and the Pease Lumber Co.[†] Both will ship to most north-central and northeastern states. These are the only two with which I have had personal contact — very favorable experiences in both cases.

Whether or not you buy from these outfits, their free catalogs are invaluable sources of informa-tion, providing a good idea of what items are available and of reasonable prices for materials. Either of these firms will ship a whole truckload of building materials to your site if it is located within their shipping area. Fingerle in particular has the following items which are difficult to find elsewhere at reasonable prices: seasoned Douglas fir timbers up to 8X8 inches by 42 feet long; end-matched 2X6 and 3X6 wood decking; cedar sidewall shakes; wood-framed sliding glass doors (for less than half the price of Andersen windows); wood-framed screen doors and combination storm-screens instead of the energy-wasting aluminum junk usually stocked by neighborhood lumberyards; good-looking, real wood entrance doors; solid-core flush doors and real, 6-panel white pine interior doors; very low-cost wood window sash; galvanized ribbed steel roofing; and other items too numerous to mention.

Figuring Quantities of Material

The most difficult problem with materials, even after you locate them at a reasonable price, is in determining the proper quantity of materials to order. Even professionals have their difficulties

All the lumber for the entire house delivered on a flatbed trailer.

†The address of this and other manufacturers and associations so indicated with be found under "Addresses of Manufacturers and Associations" in Part IV.

with this aspect of building. It's virtually impossible to determine just how much material might be miscut, damaged, stolen, or otherwise lost in the shuffle. The beginner on a budget will usually try to order just exactly the right amount, only to find that he always comes up short. In Part IV, I include specifications and a very detailed materials list for the basic saltbox. I have declined numerous requests for materials lists for my houses in the past because I didn't want to narrow the choices by following a definite set of materials specifications and limiting the homeowner to the exact materials on the list. Since this is a very basic house, I have relented this time and included a detailed list.

But what if you change some of the materials on the list, make extensive modifications to the house, design your own, or build from some other set of plans? Then you will need to know how to figure quantities for yourself.

Lumber is calculated by the board foot which represents a rough piece of lumber 1 inch thick by 12 inches square. Thus a 2X6 has 1 board foot per foot of length; a 2X12, 2 board feet per foot of length; a 2X4, two-thirds of a board foot per foot, and so on. (Calculations are always made on the *nominal* size of the board, which is the size as it comes from the sawmill, not the finished, planed size.) Milling tongues and grooves, shiplaps, or other special cuts, to the edges of a board reduces the actual amount of coverage but the board feet which you pay for remains the same.

For example, if you were to use roughsawn 2X6s for a floor deck, the number of board feet would be simply twice the actual floor area. However, if you get planed decking with tongue-and-groove edges, you need to multiply the floor area by 2.4. If you have longer spans and use 3X6 decking, you will have to multiply by 3.6.

Prices for lumber are usually quoted per 1,000 board feet, abbreviated MBF. Unfortunately, the waste due to planing and milling is only the beginning. Many times the area to be covered will not work out exactly to the length of the boards which you order, resulting in much more waste. And then you will always get a certain number of boards which have defects or severe warpage, discolorations, damage in shipment, and the like. The deck for our basic house is calculated for exact lengths of decking. If you can order the exact length, order 10 percent extra for waste; otherwise 20 to 25 percent should be allowed for waste. Main timbers can usually be ordered exactly to the quantity desired. Just to be safe, I always order at least one extra of each size; you

will always find some good use for them. Some suppliers will let you order extra material and return the excess for credit.

For tongue-and-groove siding boards, I find that adding 25 percent to the board footage comes out just about perfect. Figure the total exposed area of the house, deduct the square footage of major glass areas, but don't deduct small vents. Then figure the board footage required and add 25 percent. For board-on-board roughsawn siding, add 40 percent. With any of the sidings, if you order a bit too much you can always use the extra as interior paneling; ordering too little can be a disaster. In the case of roughsawn, take delivery in the spring for use in the fall, if possible. Winter-cut wood dries much faster than summer-cut wood does.

In ordering concrete, calculate the exact number of *cubic feet* which you need and divide by 27 (this gives you cubic yards). Add 10 percent and then round off to the nearest half-yard above that figure. Some concrete suppliers will only sell full yards, so you may need to order extra. Plan ahead and figure something useful to do with any excess and, if necessary, make a simple form for a walk or stoop. Most concrete suppliers charge a substantial penalty for small quantities, so check your figures carefully. If you are pouring a concrete slab, for instance, the tiniest, unnoticed dip can eat up a yard of concrete in a hurry. If you figure you need 4 inches of concrete on a large slab and it actually takes 4½ inches, the overrun can be several yards. In my experience, beginners and experts alike always tend to underfigure.

Brick floors are very easy to figure. Normal bricks have a nominal face size of 4 inches by 8 inches. If you use this size brick, figure 4½ brick per square foot of floor area. If you are buying new brick, you can use this figure almost exactly. If you buy or salvage used brick, look them over and add a reasonable amount for chipped, broken, and odd-size brick.

When ordering miscellaneous items such as nails, always buy 50-pound boxes. Similarly, paint, stain, and preservatives should be ordered in 5-gallon units, caulking in full cases, etc.

Plumbing, Heating, and Electrical Supplies

In many areas of the country, these supplies are a supreme headache. You are forced to buy at inflated prices from "hardware" stores because the large wholesale plumbing and electrical suppliers used by commercial plumbers and electricians commonly refuse to sell to the homeowner. There is an easy way around this dilemma if you plan ahead. Sears has very complete lines of plumbing, heating, and electrical supplies, but you may not think so if you examine the Sears large, general catalog. The bulk of these items is to be found in one of Sears' "specialty" catalogs, called the *Home Improvement Catalog,* identified as *Catalog KY* (1979) or *Catalog LY* (1980).

You will also need the current large Sears catalog as they feature the more commonly ordered items in their "big book" and don't repeat everything in the *Home Improvement Catalog.* Also invaluable are the Sears installation booklets and free consultants. For each of the three trades — plumbing, heating, electrical work — there is a booklet (it costs 50¢) which provides some of the most comprehensive instructions I have ever seen. These are: *Plumbing Planning and Installing* (42 G 9997); *Simplified Electrical Wiring* (34 G 5428); and *Central Heating and Cooling* (42 KY 9998).* For both heating and plumbing, Sears will completely lay out your system, do a detailed materials takeoff, and figure the cost of your system for you at no obligation. If you actually order the materials, they will supply very detailed installation directions for your particular system. Of course, you can use the materials list supplied with the basic house plans in Part IV, but if you want to make major modifications or build another house it will pay to keep this special service in mind.

One major financial consideration to be aware of when buying these materials (as well as tools and appliances) from Sears is that the company offers a Commercial Account for buyers of large quantities of material. They will give a discount of 10 to 15 percent off the catalog prices depending upon the quantities which you order. Commercial Account offices will be found hidden in the back of Sears stores in large cities. They are much slower than ordering through the catalog, so plan well ahead. Deliveries are usually direct to you by truck in one large order and this can be very handy. I used a Sears Commercial Account with good success on one job which I contracted.

If you are short on cash, Sears also has a financial plan for home improvement materials, tools, and appliances which enables you to get a loan of up to $2,000 for these items. You cannot use this plan in combination with the Commercial Account, which requires payment within thirty days, but it's good to know about if you haven't quite been able to raise all of the money you need for your house.

If you decide to deal with local suppliers for your supplies for mechanical trades, make a detailed list of items needed and approach them with the complete list of materials for your entire job. In this way, you will stand a better chance of being able to deal with them and might even get a professional discount. Use your Sears catalog to check prices, though. A proper discount should give you prices from 5 to 10 percent lower than the catalog prices for stock items such as wire and piping.

Scheduling and Delivery

Two big headaches for the beginning builder are scheduling and delivery of materials. Sometimes you can expedite matters by doing pickups of materials yourself. Whatever you do, order them as far as possible in advance of when you actually need them. No matter what a supplier promises in the way of delivery, *don't believe him.* Play it safe; if you need something in October, tell the supplier you want it in August and maybe you'll get it in November.

---

*Since I make frequent reference to Sears items by catalog number, an explanation of their numbering system will insure that you are able to order the correct merchandise after the current catalogs become obsolete. The catalog numbers are divided into three parts: the first one- or two-digit number indicates the department; i.e., Plumbing and Heating is 42, Electrical 34, Tools 9. The second one- or two-letter code identifies the specific catalog and the date of its issue. The main fall and spring "big books" have one letter; i.e., *Fall and Winter 1979-80* is G, *Spring and Summer 1980* is K, and so forth. Specialty catalogs have two letters; the first indicates date of issue and the second the type of catalog, i.e., HT is the 1979-80 *Tool Catalog,* LY is the 1980 *Home Improvement Catalog.* Usually the Sears department and item numbers remain the same, while the catalog letters are changed to indicate the type of catalog and year of issue.

The last four- or five-digit section of the catalog number is the item number itself and will actually appear on the nameplate as part of the serial number. On the nameplates, the first part of the catalog number is replaced by a three-digit code which identifies who made the item for Sears. A power saw will appear in the general catalog as 9 G 1096; in the *Tool Catalog* as 9 HT 1096; and the serial number will be 315.1096, indicating that the Black & Decker Co. (315) — or some other major tool company — made the item for Sears.

Catalog numbers and some merchandise are different in Canada; however, tools and basic appliances appear to be identical.

Deliveries by commercial trucking lines or UPS to a remote site can be difficult to arrange and may be impossible. Warning: Don't pay for it until it arrives *undamaged.* With one major truckload of materials, you can usually make very careful arrangements in advance and it will work, particularly if the load represents a lot of money, but forget about getting paint or caulking delivered. The smart thing to do is to pay a local businessman such as a gas station to accept materials for you. Try to find a business close to your site which is also in an easy-to-locate spot on the highway. In this way, you can arrange deliveries in care of the business and not have to worry. I have done this several times, always with good success.

Always remember when dealing with a materials supplier that he will tend to give better service if he thinks you are good for more than just one order. It may pay to stretch the truth a bit and imply more orders from yourself or neighbors. If the supplier thinks you are building a prototype for a development, the service can be great. I ordered all of the glass for six of the houses in this book from the same supplier. Needless to say, the service was excellent. If you can locate others in your area who are building for themselves, combined orders can frequently save time and money.

Security

Ordering materials ahead of time does pose one major problem: theft. This has become so routine that insurance companies refuse to insure anything at a building site except the building itself for fire. Keep large, valuable items securely locked up, and take smaller valuables home with you. If items are stolen from your home, insurance will usually cover them. Better still, have someone camp out at the site until expensive items are all in place. A long, remote, rough driveway can be quite discouraging, but don't count on it. Two chains or cables securely locked across the drive can be a powerful deterrent. Place one at the main road and a second far enough away not to be visible.

Caulking

While I generally recommend all natural materials, there are certain specialty items which make things vastly easier for the beginner. The most useful is Mono caulking. It enables the beginner to make very simple wood joints, basically gluing the materials together with the caulking compound. Professionals frown upon this, having usually had very bad experiences with the cheap caulking compounds which are available at the local lumberyard or hardware store.

Whatever you do, don't be tempted to buy any of these. Order a case of Mono directly from Tremco Mfg. Co.[†] It should be used for setting all glass, greenhouse glazing, and sealing *all* construction joints in your house. See Chapter 10 for detailed instructions on its use.

Liquid neoprene is another very versatile material. It can be used for a wide variety of flashing and sealing operations other than its primary use as a roofing and decking top coat. Again, it is a special-order item. Other, newer silicone and urethane coatings claim to do the same job, but I have used the neoprene for over twenty years and I know it holds up properly.

Plastic Glazing

For greenhouse glazing and skylights, I recommend the acrylic plastic commonly sold under the Plexiglas trade name, although much of the material for sale is not Plexiglas. If you do buy the brand name, *don't* let anyone sell you type K (brown lettering on paper covering). It is made by a cheap, inferior process and is optically wavy; furthermore, it is sold for the same price as type G (blue lettering) which is far superior. If you want full-spectrum light transmission, order Plexiglas UV.

I install the Plexiglas with Mono caulking to make very inexpensive skylights and greenhouses. See Chapter 15 for precautions and limitations and installation instructions.

Many specialty items will be described as we go through the actual construction phases of our basic house. Time and effort spent in locating materials can really pay off. The front page of a recent local paper had pictures of a house built by a young couple entirely by their own labor. The materials for the house cost less than $5,000. They credited Ken Kern (author of *The Owner-Built House*) and Rodale Press for enabling them to build by themselves for so little money. The house was based upon a design of mine from *Low-Cost, Energy-Efficient Shelter.*

Chapter 4

Library and Tools

Reference materials and tools are of vital importance to the beginning builder. Study this chapter and the tools list in Part IV carefully and start collecting references and tools well in advance of the date you are starting construction.

Library

The most important basic tool for your house construction is an adequate library. If I were to cover every possible aspect of construction and every suitable material in this book, you would be faced with an expensive, several-volume monster which would repeat much information which has already been well covered. I have confined myself primarily to giving detailed directions for building my special cost-saving post and beam frames and special finishes which are not usually described elsewhere. I offer hints for the basic trades and try to steer you clear of some of the more serious construction pitfalls. Beyond that, I suggest that before you actually begin construction, you assemble a personal library including all the information relative to building your house. Look for large, expensive books at your local public library; photocopy relevant material instead of buying the entire volume. Throughout the book I have tried to recommend sources of information which are free or low-cost, clear, and to the point.

Codes

The first item you should obtain is a copy of your local zoning or building code, as well as any special local plumbing and electrical codes. If you are in an area where the codes are strictly enforced, these will have great bearing on everything else you do. Sometimes local codes are lengthy and expensive to buy. A great bulk of the information in a building code relates to commercial and rental structures. If the code is very expensive, copy or take notes on the sections which apply to single-family houses. Ordering information for any of the nationally recognized codes can be found inside the front cover of the building code.

Carbon monoxide, an odorless, colorless gas, kills, not by poisoning but by asphyxiation. It suffocates its victim by displacing oxygen in the blood. . . . If you ever got a headache from the fumes of heavy traffic, you experienced the fist symptom. The others, in ascending order or danger, are: nausea, vomiting and dim vision, severe headache, weakness, dizziness and collapse, coma and convulsions, depressed heart action and respiration, and respiration failure.

Family Safety,
published by the
National Safety Council

Codes and Their Jurisdictions

BOCA (Basic Building Code): Building Officials and Administrators International — in use in midwestern and some northeastern states.

National Building Code: American Insurance Association — used in a few eastern states.

Southern Building Code: Southern Building Code Congress — used in southern states; where else?

UBC (Uniform Building Code): International Conference of Building Officials — used in western states, particularly California.

Catalogs

I mentioned Sears catalogs in Chapter 3. At the minimum, you should have the current Sears *Tool Catalog* and the *Home Improvement Catalog*. The large main catalog for the current season will also help. For a really complete listing, also look over the off-season catalog (they are published twice a year as *Spring/Summer* and *Fall/Winter*).

The following catalogs of hard-to-find tools are also valuable.

Brookstone Tool Catalog
Brookstone Co.
127 Vose Farm Rd.
Peterborough, NH 03458
Free. Hard-to-find specialty tools.

Craftsman Catalog
Craftsman Wood Service Co.
2727 So. Mary St.
Chicago, IL 60608
50¢. Exotic and cabinet woods and tools.

Silvo Tool Catalog
Silvo Hardware Co.
107-109 Walnut St., Dept. PS9-1
Philadelphia, PA 19106
$1. Power tools and hardware.

Tool and Hardware Catalog
U.S. General Supply Corp.
100 General Place
Jericho, NY 11753
$1. Power tools and hardware.

Woodcraft Catalog
Woodcraft Supply Corp.
313 Montvale Ave.
Woburn, MA 01801
$1. Fine hand woodworking tools.

Order a copy of a catalog from a wholesale building materials supplier. This will give you an idea what the real prices of building materials should be and how much of a markup your local supplier is tacking onto your bill. It can also be a strong bargaining point. My two favorites are Fingerle Lumber Co., 108 E. Madison St., Ann Arbor, MI 48104 and Pease Lumber Co., 900-T Laurel Ave., Hamilton, OH 45023.

Manufacturers' Brochures and Directions

Most manufacturers of building materials will furnish these free or at a very nominal charge. Very detailed instructions are available for many trades such as drywall, roofing, and others. The California Redwood Association and like trade associations are especially prolific in their distribution of free information on the use of their materials. The American Plywood Association[†] has several very detailed free pamphlets. They are: *Plywood Encyclopedia, Form X505; Plywood Residential Construction Guide, Form Y505;* and *Engineered 24 Framing and Plywood, Form P420.*

Sweet's Architectural Catalog File provides you with a central information source for most major manufacturers in this country. It is about twice the size of the *Encyclopaedia Britannica,* so you can't carry it around handily. *Sweet's* files are published annually by McGraw-Hill Information Systems and distributed free-of-charge to major contractors and architects. Most public and school libraries are not likely to have a set, but technical libraries for large universities or construction trade schools will have a copy. Manufacturers' inserts for *Sweet's* files are standardized 8½-inch by 11-inch brochures, usually available as free reprints.

Get your hands on the large *Sweet's* files (they also publish a much less common light construction and industrial construction file) and go through sections which are of interest. These files will be of great help if you want the very latest information on technical products such as so-

---

[†]The address of this and other manufacturers and associations so indicated will be found under "Addresses of Manufacturers and Associations" in Part IV.

lar-assisted heat pumps, new types of commercially available solar collectors, and others. If you are not on a tight budget, you can also find sources for exotic tiles, brick, marble, doors, woodwork, and cabinetry. These files are fun to look through just to see the wide variety of products available to the construction industry. *Sweet's* has a national "buyline" toll-free number for manufacturers' regional addresses and phone numbers — 800-255-6880.

If Henry Ford had had to worry with safety regulations, we wouldn't have automobiles.

Walter Creitz, President, Metropolitan Edison Company, Harrisburg, Pa.

Reference Books for Building Trades

Most of the housebuilding books which try to describe every construction process wind up giving sketchy descriptions of many different trades. Buy books giving solid information on each trade. Sears has a number of such books. In addition to the 50¢ books on plumbing, heating, and electrical work which I mentioned in the last chapter, they have many free instruction booklets for various specific tasks, as well as a complete line of Easi Bild construction books by Donald R. Braun. The latter are quite variable in quality, apparently depending upon Braun's experience with the task at hand.

I recommend the following:

Installing Submersible Pumps	39 LY 7312	Free
Installing Plastic Pipe	39 LY 7479	Free
Building Storm Sash and Screens	39 LY 7312	Free
#668 Bricklaying Simplified	9 LY 2915 H	$2.50
#617 Concretework Simplified	9 LY 2915 H	$2.50

The latter two are Easi Bild books and are available from Sears under the catalog number noted plus the book number preceding the title. They are also available from Easi Bild Directions Simplified, P.O. Box 215, Briarcliff Manor, NY 10510. Most of the other titles in this series are artsy-craftsy or not applicable to building a new house.

Use of Tools

Most books about using tools are hopelessly outdated or overly technical. Two which I find useful are *Hand Woodworking Tools*, by Donald M. Kidd and Louis J. Siy, and *The Complete Book of Home Workshop Tools*, by Robert Scharff. I also highly recommend *Methods and Materials of Residential Construction*, by Alonzo Wass, a Canadian author. It is one of the best all-round house construction books I've ever seen. Another low-cost general information source on standard wood framing and finishing techniques is L. O. Anderson's *How to Build a Wood-Frame House.* This is Anderson's most recent work and reflects his excellent research for the U.S. Department of Agriculture.

The Sears books on plumbing and heating, listed in Chapter 3, will do very well as the complete references for those trades. For electrical work, Sears leads you by the hand nicely for actual installation, but doesn't explain enough about code requirements for you to understand a complete system. H. P. Rictor's *Wiring Simplified* has been the bible for years. It is updated with each change in the National Electric Code and makes the perfect companion to the Sears booklet. It is available at most electrical supply stores or from the publisher.

If you follow the structural designs on my plans exactly, you shouldn't need to make any calculations concerning the design of the structure. Due to the extra-thick wall and roof construction, all members are considerably oversized for any snow- or wind-loading conditions likely to occur within the United States. Should you have occasion to design something special involving long spans or pole construction, or if you get into a dispute with a contractor or building official over almost any aspect of wooden construction, you can find the basics covered in one primary reference. If you need to hire an engineer for any of your timber-design work, make sure that he has this book. Engineers are trained in school to ignore wood, so you may have to do some educating. The book is *Timber Construction Manual,* by the American Institute of Timber Construction. While it is too technical for general use, it can be very handy to wave at an insurance inspector who claims that heavy timber construction isn't fire resistant or a building inspector who claims that pole buildings aren't safe or questions whether you can embed pressure-treated poles directly into the ground. The appendix of the book includes complete specifications for treating timbers against decay, grading standards for structural and laminated timbers, and other detailed specification material.

General Reference Work

Architectural Graphic Standards, by Charles G. Ramsey and Harold R. Sleeper, which now costs over $50 and is strictly a library item, takes the structural design material described in *Timber Construction Manual* and presents it in a series of simple, easy-to-read tables. This is one of the few sources of beam-sizing information for post and beam construction. Architects and contractors will have one if your local library doesn't. This huge volume is frequently referred to as the "architects' bible." While it doesn't give you step-by-step directions, it does provide explicit details for all aspects of commercial and residential construction including such basics as an assortment of layouts for efficient bathrooms and kitchens. Practically every imaginable building technique and material is presented with complete and accurate dimensions and details.

Color and Interior Design

The scope of this book does not permit me to go into details of interior decoration, and the costs of color printing prohibit extensive color plates. For superb examples of both, I delve a hundred years into the past. The Swedish craftsman/painter Carl Larsson wrote and illustrated many books on interior design, the best known of which is *Ett Hem (A Home),* written by Lennart Rudstrom and republished in recent years. A nice selection of Larsson's color prints which illustrate his use of wood, color, and interior design is found in a paperback book, *The Paintings of Carl Larsson,* by David Larkin.

Lifestyle

If you are planning to move from an urban area to the country, particularly if your aim is self-sufficiency, be prepared for many changes in your way of life. This will be particularly true if you move out beyond public utilities and strive to make it on your own. For those who desire some guidance, help comes from a rather unlikely source — the U.S. Department of Agriculture.

Their new book, *Living on a Few Acres* (001-000-03809-5), is available from the Superintendent of Documents, U.S. Government Printing Office, Washington, DC 20402 for $7. Someone very different from the typical bureaucrat wrote this book. It's nice to know that our tax dollars occasionally do something useful.

Safety Precautions

Since a larger number of people are now heating with wood and are not familiar with basic wood heat safety, I strongly recommend the new book *Wood Heat Safety* by Jay Sheldon.

Passive Solar Energy

Passive systems provide one of the easiest and least expensive means of obtaining useful heat from the sun. Because this system has received less attention than the more glamorous "active" systems, accurate design criteria are difficult or impossible to find. A new publication by Ed Mazria, *The Passive Solar Energy Book,* is an excellent reference. Finally, in one source, one can find information on the basic parameters necessary for designing a passive structure. The book is highly technical and sometimes difficult to follow, but it is absolutely tops as a design guide.

Periodicals

Intensifying energy shortages have created a flood of publications. A real bargain is *Solar Heating and Cooling* magazine (Box 2106R, Morristown, NJ 07960). It is only $8/year (7 issues) and explores a wide variety of solar applications.

Solar Age magazine is the original pioneer, but quite expensive; $20/year (12 issues, SolarVision, Inc., Church Hill, Harrisville, NH 03450).

Harrowsmith magazine is a Canadian publication and my personal favorite periodical. The advertisements alone are worth the cost of a subscription; $10/year (8 issues). The magazine deals with alternate lifestyles with very frequent articles on solar systems and innovative housing (Camden House Publishing, Ltd., Camden East, ON K0K 1J0 Canada).

Tools

Most would-be homebuilders tend to underbudget and overbuy tools for their house. The techniques I advocate make it possible to build without buying much expensive equipment. In many cases, expensive items can be rented rather than bought. Most people who are interested in building their own house already have many basic tools on hand. Some people just want tools that will get them through the job. Others want better-quality tools. Many owner-builders get so much enjoyment out of building their own houses that they want to get into the business for themselves. Other people are interested in having the best tools and equipment available regardless of price. For these people I've included some recommendations for many "state-of-the-art" items.

For purposes of discussion, I will divide the tools into three categories: gasoline-powered machines, electric hand tools and accessories to go with them, and hand tools. You will notice that I didn't include any shop or bench tools. These require very great capital investments and are not necessary for the type of construction details which I advocate. Also, they are difficult to transport to a building site and present almost insurmountable security problems. One of my clients lost a $600 radial arm saw the first week of a job.

Gasoline-Powered Machines

Since these machines are very expensive, they should be rented or borrowed. One tool I'd recommend, however, is an exception to this rule. The chain saw, while not actually a construction tool, is very necessary on many sites for a variety of tasks. If you plan to cut your own firewood, you will need one anyway. My two favorite brands are Poulon and Stihl. Various guides for using chain saws as a tool for cutting lumber are available, but generally this is not a good idea. Clearing land is tough work for a chain saw and it is usually best to have two around in the event that one gives out.

The most basic gasoline-powered tool required on most jobs is the generator. These are notoriously undependable and noisy; if at all possible plan ahead and get electric service installed so that you have permanent power — only, of course, if you are going to install a permanent electric system.

If you plan a "house-raising" for the frame of your house before power is run in, you will need either two small (1,500-watt) generators or one big (2,500- to 3,000-watt) generator. The big Honda (cat. no. E2500) is a super machine. It will do nicely as a backup unit for wind power or can

charge batteries for 12-volt use with its built-in battery charger. See Chapter 1 for other options.

Honda E2500 generator — quiet and durable. Low gas consumption.

Most tool rental firms have only 1,500-watt generators for rent. Generators in particular take a real beating, so always test them before accepting one. I recommend having two generators on the job because if one breaks, you can still make progress with the other. This is particularly crucial on a remote site.

Posthole digger — saves considerable time and labor.

Another very useful tool is the gasoline-powered posthole digger. If you need to set your own temporary power pole or dig for a post-type foundation in hard soil this is indispensable. Again, most rental shops stock them.

A newly introduced piece of rental equipment which takes the place of a noisy generator is called the Juicemaker, which is manufactured by the Dynamote Corp.[†] It is basically a high-quality, rechargeable battery pack which is charged on line voltage and then transported to the jobsite. No noise, no fumes, no gasoline; just a bigger electric bill. Only a few rental firms are stocking this unit, but it's well worth looking for.

The last item is only useful if you are on a very low budget or at a remote location. It is a cement mixer. It is much easier to order ready-mixed concrete, but for very small quantities, such as an isolated footing or mortar for a chimney, hand mixing is probably easier. Again, check to see that it works properly before renting it.

Locating a Rental Firm

Since you will probably need to lean on a rental firm quite a bit for essential heavy-duty tools, it will pay to do some research. First, check the Yellow Pages of your phone book. Also double-check with the Rental Equipment Register, 410 Lowell St., Lynnfield, MA 01940 or 2048 Cotner Ave., Los Angeles, CA 90025. Visit the rental shop as soon as possible. Look over the tools. Are they fairly new and kept clean and presentable? Check the gasoline motors on self-powered tools. A good rental supplier will have high-quality engines on his tools. Honda, Kawasaki, and Wisconsin Robin are the quality engines. Stay away from machines with lightweight aluminum engines of American manufacture.

Electric Hand Tools and Accessories

You can go wild and wreck your budget by buying too many — and the wrong kind — of electric hand tools if you are not careful. Most American companies now make overpriced, plastic junk which is liable to break quickly and for which repair parts are virtually unobtainable. In the olden days, companies like DeWalt and Porter Cable made fine power tools. Those companies have been absorbed or have faded from the scene. Other well-known companies are using their once-esteemed names on plastic toys for the hobbyist.

Dynamote Juicemaker — an advanced, rechargeable battery pack.

For medium-quality, low-cost tools, Sears' Craftsman line is almost unbeatable. Always buy the model at or near the top of the line, though. Sears tools are not of better quality than other brands, but they are cheaper and are guaranteed for one year. When a tool breaks, you can return it and demand a new one — immediately. Other tool companies provide a guarantee, not a replacement, and if you are on a budget and a tight schedule, Sears' policy can make all the difference. A brush fell out of a brand-new, very expensive Rockwell circular saw this summer and it took half the summer to get a replacement.

People on a rock-bottom budget should check around on the lower back shelves in the tool department at the local Sears. Sears very quietly rebuilds returned tools and sells them for about half the price of a new tool — with a 90-day guarantee. It's possible to buy a top-of-the-line, rebuilt Sears Craftsman circular saw for $35 to $40.

The Milwaukee Electric Tool Co. is one of the few major American tool companies that has resisted the temptation to make toy tools. All of their tools are first class, hence no bewildering arrays of skillsaws — just two excellent ones. The first is an offset, worm-gear-driven saw similar to the Skil but a bit lighter without the excessive current draw of the Skil. Their heavy-duty contractor's saw is a real gem. It is a lightweight, nicely balanced 7¼-inch saw with every feature one could want. Unlike some other expensive saws, it adjusts quickly and easily, its baseplate is accurately square, and, most important, it has a good, easy-to-see base guide for accurate cuts.

Two other Milwaukee tools well known among professionals are the Sawzall reciprocating saw and the Holehawg right-angle, ½-inch drill. The abilities of both are legendary. Large, reputable tool rental houses will have both. These machines are very useful for working in close quarters and making large holes for piping and wiring. Unlike most other tools, they can make virtually flush cuts in very tight quarters. Beware of imitations from other manufacturers; they are not of the same quality and do not perform well. Sears makes a cheap reciprocating saw which is worthless — it is the only Sears tool I have returned and for which I have asked for a refund.

Milwaukee also makes a couple of hand tools which are worth buying if you hunt up a Milwaukee dealer. A simple handle which holds all of the Sawzall blades for hand cutting, cat. no. 48–08–0400, will do duty as a metal-cutting saw, keyhole saw, and drywall saw. Milwaukee also makes an industrial-duty hacksaw which will make absolutely flush cuts and has a superior blade-tensioning system with no little parts to get lost. It also has a storage compartment for spare blades. All Milwaukee tools work on AC or DC, an important feature for people with alternate power sources. The company makes an assortment of fine, 12-volt, battery-operated tools. Don't confuse these with the plastic toys by Rockwell and Skil which are only suitable for drilling tiny holes in thin sheet metal or plastic.

For those who want professional-quality tools without paying premium prices, I suggest Makita tools. This Japanese company is blanketing the country with high-quality, reasonably priced tools. Professional post and beam framers use Makita tools simply because there is no competition. Makita makes such mind-boggling items as a 16-inch circular saw, a 6-inch hand planer, a mortising tool, and hundreds of other items too numerous to mention. They, like Sears, make all sorts of jigs, benches, and accessories to make their tools more useful. You will see some of these tools in use on the houses in Part III. The real gem for the owner-builder is the Makita circular saw, model no. 5801B, a magnificent tool.

Circular Saws

Whatever make of tool you choose, your electric circular saw (skillsaw) is your most basic tool. Good ones can sometimes be found used. When buying, check the following features to make sure that your saw is useful for the life of your building project. It's a real waste of money to buy a second saw three-quarters of the way through construction. Make sure that your saw has a 7-inch-diameter blade (7¼-inch is preferable). It should have a powerful motor, 1¾ to 2 horsepower. All bearings should be ball-, roller-, or needle-type. Brushes should be the readily accessible, external type. Adjustments should be quick and easy, preferably on the front of the saw. Drive gears should be either helical or worm-drive for durability. Brushes and the trigger switch, and for beginners, the cord, are three items which may have to be replaced. It is wise to have extras on hand, particularly if you buy a used saw. Only buy a used saw if it is cheap, a major brand name (Skil, Black & Decker, Rockwell, or Milwaukee), and you have time to dismantle it and replace any worn parts as need be.

The top-of-the-line Sears circular saw has a very important safety feature — an electronic brake. When the switch is released, the field current reverses, stopping the blade instantly. Black & Decker makes a saw with a similar feature, but it is quite expensive. The Skil company, which deserves credit for inventing the hand power saw in the first place, makes finely constructed top-of-the-line saws which are a favorite of contractors. Avoid anything under about $80 and stay away from their gear-driven saws with the offset blades. These are very heavy duty saws which consume large quantities of current (they will bog down a small generator), and are heavy and awkward to use.

Sears markets a gadget which will turn any skillsaw into a very accurate bench saw somewhat similar to a radial arm saw. This is the Craftsman miter arm, cat. no. 9 GT 1715 1N. It has parallel rails which can be adjusted to any angle and per-

Makita model 5007B7 circular saw.

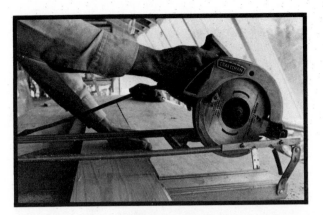

Sears — 9 GT 1715 1N miter arm.

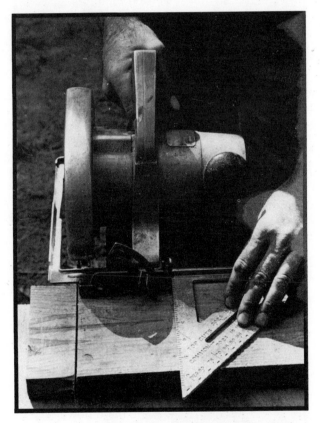

Swanson Speed Square.

home at night. Since the miter arm is inexpensive and permanently attached to the bench, it is unlikely that it will be stolen. It is particularly useful if you have to make a number of pieces exactly the same length.

For ordinary framing cuts, the beginner can achieve greater accuracy by using a guide for his skillsaw. Sears makes a slightly cumbersome one, cat. no. 9 GT 1719. There is also a really fine saw guide called a Speed Square made by Swanson Tool Co.† and available from the company or from Woodcraft Supply Corp.† It comes with a complete instruction booklet and is very useful for angle cuts such as stairs and rafters. Either of these guides will enable you to make quick, accurate cuts in the field.

The only other power tool which is a real must is an electric drill. I recommend either Sears cat. no. 9 GT 1148 or Makita model no. 6510LVR. Both are top-quality, variable-speed, reversible ⅜-inch drills. For the budget-minded, get the Sears cat. no. 9 GT 1143 at about $20. It should get you through the job, but that's about all. Good ½-inch drills are very expensive and are used infrequently, you should rent one if you need it; ¼-inch drills are usually toys.

Other Tools

Various other tools can be a big help, but are not really a must and could be rented. In order of

Makita model 6510LVR variable speed drill.

mit the saw itself to make accurate cuts at any angle to the vertical. This unit has two big advantages over a radial arm saw. First, the cutting motion is away from you rather than toward you, making it much easier and safer to use. The second feature is that the miter arm automatically clamps your work in place, important for both accuracy and safety. The disadvantage of the miter arm is that it takes time to set up. If you follow my advice and build a workbench, you can leave the miter arm permanently installed and take the saw usefulness, I suggest a router, useful for cutting accurate grooves, shiplap joints, and the like. If you plan to build your own windows, doors, or cabinets, this gadget can be a real help. Sears cat. no. 9 GT 1747 or Makita model no. 3608B are the best buys. Both are heavy-duty, 1-horse-power units. The Sears gets the nod here as it is cheaper and has a built-in light, a very important feature which no other commercial routers have. A hand planer can be useful for working with roughsawn wood and in cabinetmaking. I like the Sears cat. no. 9 GT 1732 or Makita model no. 1900B. The Sears is a bit cheaper, but the Makita has optional carbide blades which are much more durable.

If you do fine finish work, a belt sander is a must, and you should have a big one with a 4-inch-wide belt and a dust collector, such as Sears cat. no. 9 GT 1176C or Makita model no. 9401. The Makita is much more durable, but also more expensive. Another tool which I have found to be very helpful for the beginning carpenter is a rotary disk sander, the type generally used by auto-body shops. It is not very good for fine finish work, although with a fine disk it provides a credible

finish. I have found that when working with roughsawn wood and heavy-timber construction, it can serve as a combined replacement for the planer and belt sander mentioned above. It can be very useful for taking just a tiny fraction of wood off a beam to make a perfect fit. With a coarse disk it can take off a lot of wood in a hurry. The construction of this sander gives it a reach which the other tools don't have. I have found it exceptionally useful when used as a stationary

Makita model 3608B router.

Sears 9 GT 1747 router.

Makita model 1805B planer. This is the big Makita 6-inch planer, which is used for planing large timbers. The Makita 1900B, which I recommend for homeowners, is similar but smaller.

tool. Just turn it on its back and lock the switch in "On" position. This is a great way to take off just a bit of end grain. It is very difficult to saw a tiny fraction and a hand plane or planer will tend to split the wood. A rebuilt grinder can be had at Sears for about $60 if you are lucky. For a new unit, I recommend either Sears Craftsman, cat. no. 9 GT 1156 (1-horsepower, single-speed — for woodworking you don't need extra power or multiple speed) or Makita model no. 9607BL. The Sears model is much cheaper.

No matter what make of tools you use, Sears is an excellent place to order saw blades, router bits, sanding belts, and fiber-backed sanding disks for a rotary sander. Never try to use paper — it self-destructs immediately and is useless. Sears is also an excellent source for commercial circular-saw blades. They have very cheap carbide-tipped blades which are excellent for framing, as well as disposable framing blades. Saw blades get dull very quickly under heavy use and can be a real nuisance to get sharpened. *Plan ahead.* The carbide blades are about $7.00 each, the disposables, $1.50. You won't come within miles of that at your local hardware store, or at your Sears retail store, either, for that matter. These bargains are hidden away in the special Sears *Tool Catalog* which you must order. Even if you don't buy any Sears merchandise, this catalog will give you a thorough, comprehensive listing of most commercially available tools and a rough idea of a low price for them.

Other worthwhile catalogs which show much more exotic and expensive tools than Sears carries are available from Brookstone Co.†, Woodcraft Supply Corp.†, and Craftsman Wood Service Co.† (no relation to Sears). These companies deal in fine-quality (usually imported), tools for special purposes. If you plan to go further in the business or do fine cabinetwork, check these firms out. In addition to tools, Craftsman deals in exotic woods. See listing under "Library," earlier in this chapter, for addresses and prices.

Carbide-Tipped Cutting Edges

Most high-speed power tools with cutting edges such as circular saws, bench saws, drills, routers, and planers are available with blades which are tipped with silicone carbide. Since this material is considerably harder than even the finest-grade steel, it holds an edge much longer and usually does a much better cutting job. Not only do dull steel edges produce a ragged cut, but they cause rapid wear on the tool itself and cause the tool to consume excessive amounts of elec-

tricity. Get a carbide-tipped blade or blades at the start of the job. Framing, particularly with rough-sawn, green lumber, chews up blades in a hurry. The extra costs of buying and sharpening steel circular saw blades are not worth the trouble. Either buy disposable steel blades or get one of the Sears carbide framing blades.

Cheap carbide blades tend to have very few teeth, as carbide is quite expensive, and they will make relatively rough cuts. Usually this doesn't matter if the framing is concealed. Be wary if you are using recycled lumber. Just one nail will ruin a carbide blade; carbide is brittle and will disintegrate if it hits a nail. Unless you are doing a lot of

Sears 9 GT 1176 C belt sander.

Makita model 9401 sander.

very extensive finish cabinetwork or acres of wood paneling, an expensive carbide finish blade is probably a waste of money.

For *any* work requiring production of a good number of pieces, spend the extra money for carbide. This is particularly true for router bits. In this case, steel ones aren't worth buying.

Hand Tools

There are so many different hand tools with various uses that I could write a whole book on just this subject. In Part IV, under "Basic Tools," I give a list of common hand tools which I feel are necessary for construction of your house. In this section, all I can do is discuss options, advantages, and drawbacks of various items.

You should have one steel tape measure for layout purposes, longer than the longest measurement of the house. These are non-spring-loaded and wind into a case with a crank. They are also expensive. Sears makes a 50-foot version, cat no. 9 GT 39001, for about $10. Other brands are much more expensive and will have minimum use. Borrow one if you can. For general construction measurements, the real pros use a high-quality folding wood rule. Usually, these are a bit much for a beginner to handle. Stanley makes a great tape measure called the Extender, cat. no. 33408C, a wide, rigid tape which can be pulled completely out of its case and used as an 8-foot measuring device or extended to the desired length. Other commercially available tapes are virtually all spring-loaded with locking devices. They are very prone to breakage, but very handy. If you buy one, make sure that you buy an extra tape blade. Get a ¾-inch-wide, 20-foot-long tape for maximum versatility. Again, Sears Craftsman is a best buy, particularly in view of the year's guarantee. The Craftsman locking tapes have an all-metal case and a superior locking device, located so that it can be used without changing hand position. Others are more awkward to use. If you keep them clean and dry, tapes will last much longer.

A good, well-balanced hammer is vital. Beginners tend to make two mistakes when buying hammers. They buy too light a hammer and buy a curved-claw instead of a straight-claw hammer. Professional framers use hammers with a 28-ounce head. These are too heavy for the beginner. Buy a 20- or 22-ounce hammer with *straight* claws (curved claws are frequently useless because they limit the use of the hammer for nail.

pulling in corners and tight spots). The quality professional tool here is Estwing. The readily available models have blue plastic handles. The top-of-the-line model has a laminated leather handle, and is available from Estwing Mfg. Co.[†] For the budget-minded, get a Sears Craftsman cat. no. 9 GT 38273. A smaller, 12- to 13-ounce cabinetmaker's hammer is useful for finish work, but not a necessity. Specialty hammers are made for laying brick and shingling roofs. These are usually available at mason's and roofer's supply stores and are only necessary if you are doing slate work or brickwork.

Handsaws are somewhat of a rarity on construction sites these days. If you must work without electrical power, they are vital. A Swedish saw called the Bushman Boardsaw is an excellent time-saver for framing if you have no power. It has coarse teeth which cut on both forward and backward strokes. To make starting a cut easier, the first few inches of the saw have fine teeth. The saw handle is shaped so that it can be used as a 90° and a 45° square, making a very versatile all-in-one cutting tool. Another useful tool is a fine-tooth cabinetmaker's saw. This has a rounded end with teeth on the curve for making plunge cuts. I have a Swedish Sandvik saw which has served well. Both are available from Brookstone Co.[†] and Woodcraft Supply Corp.[†] For regular, full-size handsaws, the English-made Spear and Jackson is top-quality, followed (distantly) by American-made Disston and Craftsman. Only buy the top-of-the-line with taper-ground teeth. If you use a skillsaw with a miter guide, a fine handsaw is a waste of money.

Ladders are a very necessary tool. Everyone should own a good, rugged, wooden stepladder. Larger extension ladders can be rented. If you do your construction in proper sequence, you will have little need of one. If you buy, steer clear of cheap aluminum ladders. The extension section tends to stick and the ladders can actually break in two under a heavy load (one did on one of the jobs this summer). Also, many people have been electrocuted on aluminum ladders. Fiberglass ladders are the best, but expensive, and usually must be special-ordered. Also, they tend to bounce which may be disconcerting. If you rent, try to get a heavy-duty aluminum ladder, as that is probably the best choice you'll be offered.

See Part IV for a complete listing of required tools, most of which are well known and do not require detailed discussion. In the various chapters detailing construction, I will describe in detail the use of some of the tools and options to the use of expensive power tools.

Chapter 5

Contracting and Contractors; Construction Tips

Almost anyone can order his or her own materials and learn enough skills to save substantially on the labor costs for a house. Much of the savings can be squandered, though, if the job isn't organized properly. A contractor charges from 25 to 40 percent of the cost of a new house for doing the organizing. This figure includes his overhead for such things as an office, estimator, bookkeeper, tools, equipment, telephone, insurance, taxes, and usually a substantial profit. The housing industry is notoriously disorganized and inefficient. It is very easy for a contractor with large, fixed overhead costs to lose money if factors beyond his control, such as regulatory or scheduling problems, delay a job. Consequently, he adds a hefty markup to each job so that the profitable ones can balance out the disasters.

Contracting

Since you do not have the large, fixed overhead and are not trying to make a profit, you are in an excellent position to save a substantial portion of a contractor's fee. In so doing, though, you are taking on a very tough job. Obviously, the smaller and simpler your house, the easier your task will

be. Whatever you do, don't allow yourself to be rushed. Since you are inexperienced, you will need more time to prepare for your job. Also, a contractor may have several people who perform the functions which you are planning to do alone.

If you have the flexibility, try to schedule your job off-season. In the northern and central portions of the country, this means starting construction in the fall instead of early spring or summer as is usually the case. By doing this, you will avoid having to compete with professional contractors for subcontractors and workmen in their busiest season. Also, in most parts of the country, fall is a relatively dry season, making construction easier. If you schedule construction properly, you can have the shell of your house enclosed before severe winter weather. Then you can either take your time and perform mechanical and finish trades yourself, or hire subcontractors from a relatively large pool of unemployed workmen.

Critical Path Method

Building a house is an amazingly complex process. You must carefully establish a sequence of
(continued on page 46)

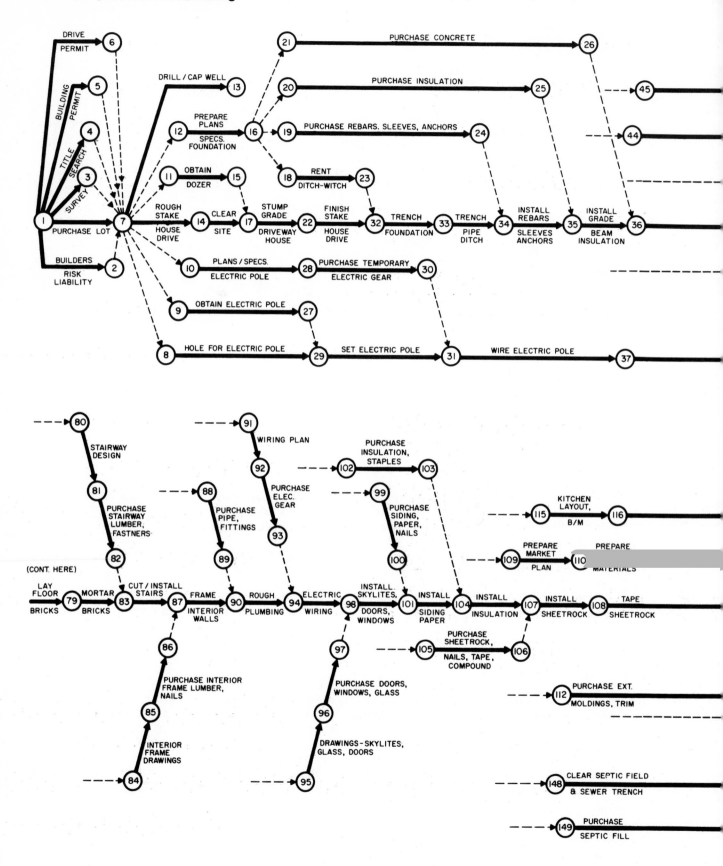

Critical Path Method

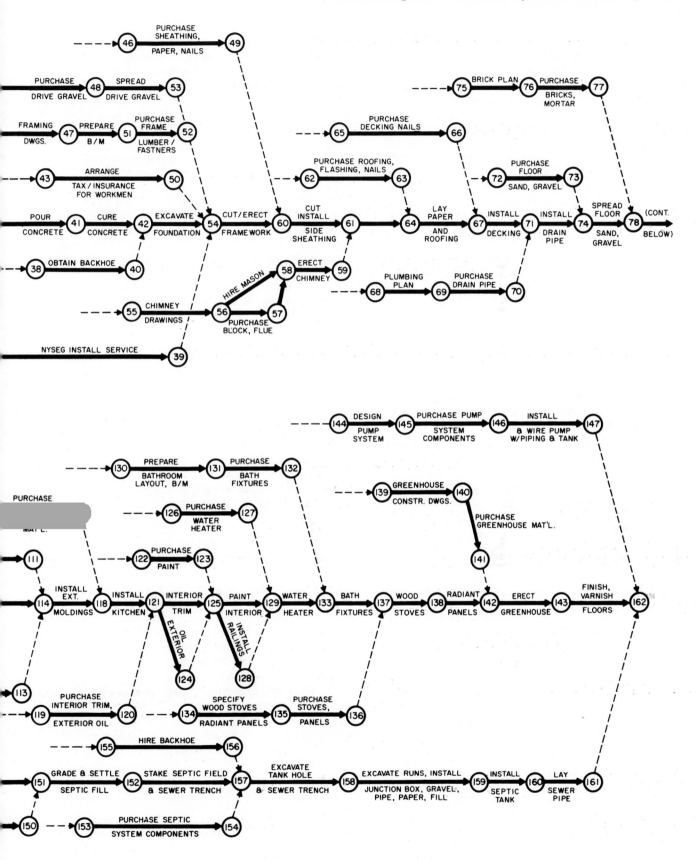

events and then allot priorities to the most significant ones. Large firms who do commercial building use a method called the Critical Path Method (CPM) to identify by number all of the different items of work which must be performed on a job. Estimated times required to perform the individual tasks are assigned to each number on a chart. All of this information is entered on a diagram which indicates at a glance which item will cause a bottleneck if delayed beyond a certain date. On the CPM, each item is assigned two dates — the earliest it could be performed and the latest it can be done without holding up the rest of the job.

The United States has 6 percent of the world's population and uses 60 percent of the world's resources.

John McPhee
Encounters with the Archdruid
Farrar, Straus and Giroux, 1971

On large projects all of this information is fed into a computer so that problem areas can be quickly identified. For a small project, it is unnecessary to go to all of this work. One of my clients went to the time and effort to do a CPM for the basic house. I reproduce it here for your guidance. Don't be alarmed by its complexity; it describes every possible event during the course of construction. It just may bring you down to earth as to how much work is involved in building your own house.

Whether you use the actual diagram or not, the list of items of work which have to be performed is quite valuable. Study the list carefully and sort it into three categories: (1) items which must be subcontracted (work by others); (2) items which you intend to do yourself; and (3) optional items which you might do if you have the time. You should start immediately doing research to find subcontractors for category 1.

Selecting a Subcontractor

Most really good subcontractors have little need to advertise, so you are not likely to find them in the Yellow Pages or listed in local newspapers. A very good way to locate subcontractors is to make periodic visits to various construction sites to see who is doing the plumbing, electrical work, masonry, framing, etc. Also, do some investigation through customers of a very reputable general contractor in your area. You could even

approach the contractor directly and ask for references from people for whom he has built houses. Check with them to see what quality work was done and who the various subcontractors were. If the general contractor himself checks out very well, you may even want to hire him to do the foundation and shell for you. Obviously, he won't be interested in doing this in his busy season, but he might take the job if he needs fall or winter work. See the Gilbert house for a description of how this can work.

If you don't have any luck with finding contractors through clients, try some commercial supply firms who deal mainly with professionals. A concrete plant may provide some names of masons and concrete formwork contractors; electrical and plumbing supply houses should know electricians and plumbers; a sawmill operator should know local carpenters familiar with roughsawn lumber. If all else fails, the local bartender probably knows most of them.

The most important aspect of judging a contractor is his work, the final results, but other things are also important. Did he show up when he promised to? Was the work completed on schedule? Was he responsible in handling money? Did the owner make changes during the course of the job; how were these handled? All of these considerations can affect the job. Contractors and carpenters, like auto mechanics, do not have to have licenses, so be wary. Anyone, regardless of skill or training, can claim to be a carpenter.

Remember that each subcontractor may have several jobs going at once. Obviously, the jobs for regular employers are going to get priority over your work. Try to find out what other work the contractors have going, and get an estimate of when they will be free to start your job. If you have some flexibility, let them know this, as it may affect their price. In any case, keep in touch fairly frequently. Rather than bothering them at home when they are tired, take a run by the job where they are working; you might learn a lot. Is the job well organized, reasonably neat, and tidy? If it's a mess, you should think twice. But if it's too tidy, this may indicate high prices and an obsession with organization over actual work. Take a look at vehicles and equipment. Again, extremes are a warning sign. Ratty or scanty equipment may indicate a poor businessman. All new equipment and fancy vehicles indicate high prices.

Make sure that all subcontractors have liability insurance and sign a contract (see Part IV for a suggested form). Otherwise the federal government might hold you liable for withholding tax, Social Security, etc. Before you make final payment, you should secure a release of liens from all contractors (see Part IV for a sample). This assures you that they have actually paid suppliers and workmen. If you are furnishing materials and there only is one workman, the release of liens is quite simple.

One technique which has worked well for a number of my clients is to work along with workmen as a helper. In the case of wiring and plumbing, you can get the professional to check layout with you and then you can drill holes, mount outlet boxes, and do other routine items, leaving actual wiring and piping to the pros.

Many people have a tendency to get a bit too friendly with their workmen. Keep your distance. This may sound a bit hard-hearted, but if you get to be good friends, you may start to overlook poor workmanship. Contractors are notoriously poor businessmen, and due to long off-season periods they tend to hang out at bars a bit more than they should. Consequently, you may get hit up for advances against work not yet performed. Be prepared to say no, or to advance no more than a small sum.

Proper site preparation and work conditions are imperative if you are going to get good work out of your workmen (and yourself, for that matter). A storage area for materials close to the construction site but still removed from the actual work area is important. Make sure that all snags are removed in any clearing operation; workmen carrying heavy timbers don't need obstacles to trip over. Rugged, heavy-duty sawhorses are a must for starting work, as are tarps for covering finished work. Just as soon as the shell is up, the work area should be moved inside to the large

This 16-foot-long workbench provides efficient work space for two people; a fluorescent light and shelf over the top would increase efficiency.

living room area. A sturdy 4-foot by 16-foot workbench should be constructed with a shelf and worklight over it. This gives adequate area for two people to work at once, and the shelf provides a good place for hanging and storing small tools where they will be handy. Another shelf under the table is also useful.

Power for Construction

If possible, get temporary power installed immediately. Some contractors and electricians have temporary poles for rent which are all set up and ready to go. This is much cheaper than having an electrician set up a temporary service which then has to be discarded. For safety, make sure that you use GFI-type (Ground Fault Interrupter) breakers. These are particularly important when working outside with power tools. These are expensive, but you have to have them for the permanent breakers for bathrooms and any outside receptacles anyway, and can use them there. If the panel box on the rented pole doesn't have this type breaker, exchange the breakers immediately (almost all boxes have snap-in breakers) but make sure that you buy the same brand — some are not interchangeable.

If you must use a generator, select a location for it 35 to 40 feet away from the house, preferably behind a mound of dirt to block sound. If necessary, construct a baffle between the generator and the work area from nailbase sheathing. In this way, some of the noise of the generator will be blocked. The noise makes communication difficult, and drives every one wild after a few hours. Run a line to the house using 12/2 Romex.

Communications

If you have the power run in, by all means install a phone. It will more than pay for itself, particularly for amateur builders (put a lock on the dial or you may wind up with some very strange bills). If you can't get a phone, try to have a friend or a local answering service take your calls and call in every day at noon and at the end of the day. In this way, deliverymen and subcontractors will have a way to get messages to you. If you spend long hours at the house site without a phone, there may be very long periods when you can't be reached.

Roads

If you have selected a remote country site, an

access road can be a real problem. Heavy concrete trucks and loads of materials can quickly demolish a light-duty road, or even an asphalt driveway if the weather is very wet. If possible, schedule materials delivery when the ground is either dry or frozen solid. For light-duty use with good, front-wheel-drive vehicles and intelligent drivers, a lightweight gravel driveway may be adequate. In certain types of clay soils, gravel just disappears and reapplications can be a bi-yearly event.

Even though it is costly, it will pay to construct a proper roadbed. This means installing a base of heavy stone 12 to 18 inches thick, over which layers of finer stone and gravel are placed. It is an expensive proposition, but the only way to build a proper road. If you install the thick base course before construction starts, the heavy trucks can compact it for you.

Take a careful look at watercourses before you select a route for your driveway. Particularly if you build a heavy permanent base, you may be blocking natural drainage, and you will have to install large, expensive culverts to divert the water. Many state highway departments will require a culvert where your driveway intersects the main road. Other states and counties may require that all or part of the driveway be paved with asphalt or concrete. This is very expensive and unnecessary. Check carefully before you buy. A common requirement which isn't all that expensive is to pave the first 10 or 15 feet so that gravel or other loose driveway materials are not spread out on the main road by snowplowing.

Architectural Graphic Standards has detailed layouts for drives and roads. It also shows standard, widely accepted methods of construction. Study it carefully before you spend any money on a driveway.

Miscellaneous Details

As you saw on the CPM, building a house requires careful coordination of many diverse trades and materials. You will have to quickly learn to establish priorities and to pace yourself. When doing repetitive work, set up your work area so that you can work most efficiently. If at all possible, set up close to the spot where the materials are actually to be installed so that the least amount of time is wasted moving back and forth for measurements and installation. Keep the site cleaned up at all times and people will work more efficiently. Store tools neatly at the end of the day; all valuable tools should be taken home at night. Or stay at the site as long as valuable tools and materials are still vulnerable to theft.

One of my clients bought a dilapidated house trailer and installed one of his carpenters in it. It was very useful in the bitter winter weather which followed, as an office, meeting place, and warm-up spot. At the end of the job, he sold it for more than he paid for it — the ultimate in low-cost fringe benefits.

Part II

Building the House

Chapter 6

Water Supplies and Waste Disposal

While other systems in a self-sufficient house are required for comfort or convenience, a good, unpolluted water supply and a safe, efficient means of waste disposal are vital for a healthy existence. People who live in or near major population centers have been lulled into a false sense of security by city water and sewer services. City water is commonly drawn from frighteningly polluted sources, and sewage is often dumped right back into the very same body of water. Although moving to the country enables you to exert a degree of control over your water and sewage systems, there are many potential problems to avoid and decisions to make.

Oil is only one natural resource in short supply. Supplies of fresh water are fast becoming a critical problem. Our wasteful society is rapidly depleting natural water sources. In many places, the water table is dropping at an alarming rate. Government studies show that several wide areas of the country are on the brink of very serious water shortages. The situation in New York City is so serious that the U.S. Army Corps of Engineers is proceeding seriously with plans to divert the PCB-laden Hudson River to supplant the city's dwindling water supplies from pristine upstate reservoirs.

When you consider that health officials routinely refuse permission for individual families to use spring water, even if it tests as safe, you begin to realize just how difficult health standards can be. Large municipalities and government agencies typically furnish your water from any source they choose, safe or not. The individual is required to conform to a narrow, frequently arbitrary, set of standards for both water supply and waste disposal. Let's examine the various possibilities, so that you have an idea of the choices available.

Sources of Water

There are three sources of water. The first is water collected from rain or melted snow and usually stored in reservoirs for cities or cisterns for individual houses. The second source is surface water, a river or lake. Shallow wells and most springs are fed from surface water. The third source is groundwater which seeps down through many layers of rock and becomes thoroughly filtered in the process. A deep-drilled well is required to tap this water source; in most parts of the country, it will be considered the standard water source by the authorities.

In some parts of the country, the water table is so deep that drilled wells are prohibitively expensive or even impossible. In other areas, underground mineral deposits may make the water unusable. In these areas, as well as in places where access for a drilling rig is difficult, one must examine water sources carefully.

Where supplies of pure, drinkable water are very short, it is common to provide separate water supplies for different functions. Of the water used in a normal household, only a tiny fraction is actually consumed. If you are in an area where safe water supplies are difficult to obtain, you may want to consider hauling small quantities of water for drinking.

Testing

Most health departments and many banks will require that you have your source of drinking water tested. These tests are usually performed for a nominal fee by a county lab or a private lab approved by the county, and reveal the presence of harmful bacteria — not dangerous industrial chemicals or pesticides. These can easily be present, particularly if you live near a heavily industrialized area or use water from a cistern or shallow well. Special testing for trace minerals and heavy metals is available for $25 from the Soil and Health Foundation, 222 Main St., Emmaus, PA 18049.

Cisterns

Cisterns are used to store water for later use. They are common in dry areas of the world where the water table is prohibitively deep. Sources of supply for cisterns can be roof catchments, natural springs, or tank trucks. The cisterns themselves can be constructed of precast concrete, poured concrete, coated steel, or fiberglass. Precast concrete tanks are durable, but heavy and expensive to buy and transport. Try to locate a slightly damaged tank which can be repaired. You can build formwork and pour your own tank, but this is a lot of work and transportation of the necessary concrete may be difficult. Coated steel tanks are cheap, but don't last. Large fiberglass tanks are a good bet as they are durable, reasonably priced, and easy to transport. The Sears *Farm and Ranch Catalog* has suitable tanks; they can also be ordered from Raven Industries, Inc.†

Any cistern must have an access hole for clean-ing and suitable inlet and outlet connections. For use with rainwater, the cistern must have a filter to remove airborne debris. The accompanying diagram shows a 4,000-gallon concrete cistern with a built-in sand filter. For use with water supplied from tank trucks or underground springs, the sand filter can be eliminated.

Great care must be used when selecting a spring as a water source for a cistern. As with any water supply source, it must be located uphill from any possible source of contamination. Also, examine the watershed area carefully for anything which might cause trouble. Even if your water source tests as drinkable, most health departments will require regular testing to insure purity. This can be expensive. Some health departments will require chlorination to insure purity; others prohibit home applications of such substances. Check first before you plan a cistern. Since springs and cisterns are unfamiliar territory in most parts of the country, you should do some additional reading if you plan to use either or both. Two excellent sources are *Manual of Individual Water Supply Systems* by the U.S. Environmental Protection Agency and E. G. Wagner and J. N. Lanoix's *Water Supply for Rural Areas and Small Communities.* The latter book is out-of-print; check in a large technical library or try to obtain it through an interlibrary loan service.

Shallow Wells

A shallow well draws water from the water table by means of atmospheric pressure. If one removes the weight of the atmosphere from a column of water, it will rise to a theoretical level of 34 feet (sea level). For practical purposes, 25 feet is about the limit for drawing water up from a shallow well. A shallow well pump, whether hand- or power-driven, is located aboveground at the top or side of the well (any offset from the top of the well must be included in the 25-foot maximum distance). Several methods are used to excavate a shallow well. The oldest is to just dig a hole in the ground and line it with stone or brick. This is rarely done nowadays; it is considered unsafe and should not be used as a source of water for human consumption because it is too easily contaminated by surface water.

Another method of producing a shallow well, common in areas of extensive layers of soft soil, sand, and gravel, is the driven well. In this

---

†The address of this and other manufacturers and associations so indicated will be found under "Addresses of Manufacturers and Associations" in Part IV.

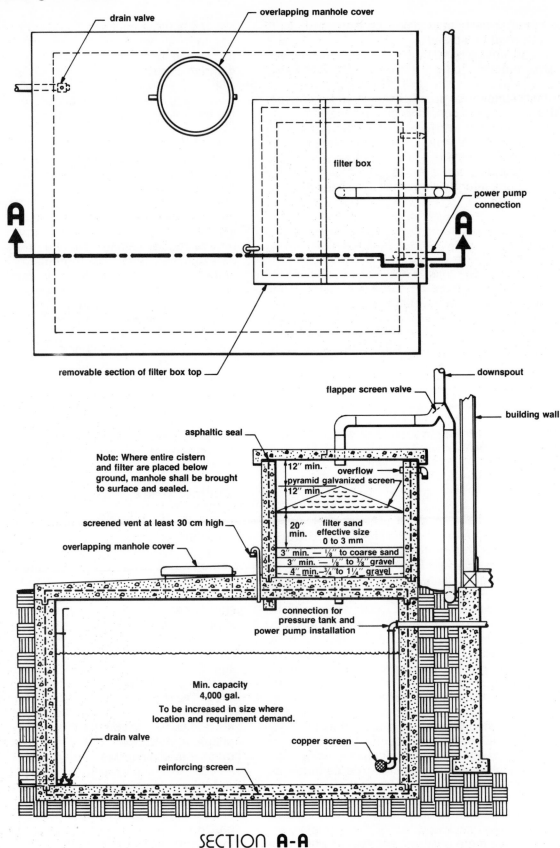

drain valve

overlapping manhole cover

filter box

power pump connection

A

A

removable section of filter box top

downspout

flapper screen valve

building wall

asphaltic seal

Note: Where entire cistern and filter are placed below ground, manhole shall be brought to surface and sealed.

12″ min.

overflow

pyramid galvanized screen

12″ min.

screened vent at least 30 cm high

20″ min.

filter sand effective size 0 to 3 mm

overlapping manhole cover

3″ min. — ⅛″ to coarse sand

3″ min. — ⅛″ to ⅜″ gravel

4″ min. — ¾″ to 1¼″ gravel

connection for pressure tank and power pump installation

Min. capacity 4,000 gal.

To be increased in size where location and requirement demand.

drain valve

copper screen

reinforcing screen

SECTION A-A

Cross section of a 4,000-gallon cistern with sand filter.

method, a perforated, hardened-steel well point is attached to a piece of pipe and driven into the ground until it penetrates the water table. Additional pieces of pipe are then attached to the top as it is driven further into the ground. The perforations allow water to seep into the pipe. This is a particularly easy "well-drilling" method for the do-it-yourselfer, but it usually produces limited quantities of water and is limited to areas of the country with suitable soils. A watertight concrete pad must be poured around the top of the well pipe to prevent penetration of groundwater.

Another method of producing shallow wells is boring. A hand- or machine-powered auger is used to drill a hole in the ground, just as one drills in wood. The well is then lined with steel well casing or clay tile and a concrete plug poured around the top. This type of well is difficult to close against groundwater contamination and is prohibited by many health departments.

Deep Wells

Deep wells are the standard acceptable source of water in most areas of the country. To get a deep well dug requires a contractor with a very large, cumbersome drilling rig which drills a 4- to 6-inch-diameter hole down into the deep layers of water-bearing rock. An expensive steel casing extending through the soil and 10 feet into the rock must be used to prevent surface water and soft layers of soil from getting into the well.

Two wells of exactly the same depth can have vastly different costs, even if drilled by the same contractor. Drilling charges for a rotary well-drilling rig will vary from $6 to $10 per foot. Well-drillers usually charge $10 to $12 per foot for installing the steel casing. You can see that a well which requires a lot of casing can cost a lot more than one which has bedrock at or near the surface of the ground. Because a well-drilling rig, a big, cumbersome device mounted on a large truck, is awkwardly balanced and quite top-heavy, drillers usually require a hard-surface, prepared roadway before drilling your well. Be prepared to meet this criterion or find another water source. I know of one family who transports their water for almost a mile because the well-driller wouldn't come near their proposed house site. Older well-drilling rigs frequently used percussion-type bits rather than rotary drills. These machines are not as versatile, but the rigs are more compact and lighter which may make them a better bet for a remote site. Since the machines are less expensive and may be fully

depreciated, the well-drillers who use them sometimes charge less for their services.

Feasibility and Location of Wells

The cost of a well and the availability of water are two of the most chancy items involved in building in the country. Check with future neighbors about their water supply before buying a piece of property. The depth of water tables and the availability of water is usually fairly consistent throughout an area. In some regions of the country where water is difficult to locate, property is sold with a clause of purchase subject to drilling a successful well. Usually, the well-drilling cost is borne by the prospective purchaser or split between the buyer and seller with a clause in the sales contract that he doesn't have to buy if there is no water. Wells in many areas frequently have a heavy sulphur or iron content which makes the water unacceptable to many people. Also, be on the lookout for contamination from oil, gas, and dangerous chemicals.

The actual *location* of a well on your property can pose problems, particularly when house siting itself is critical to receive ample sunlight. The well must be uphill from the waste disposal area; authorities disagree as to the exact distance, but 150 feet is a reasonable separation. If you plan to use a spring or cistern as a water source and some alternative means of waste disposal, you may alleviate some of the problems, but study the situation carefully before you make a final decision. Further information on well-drilling can be found in *Water Well Handbook* by K. E. Anderson. Another good book is *Water Quality and Treatment: A Handbook for Public Water Supplies* by the American Water Works Association.

Producing, Transporting, and Pressurizing Your Water Supply

Once you have a spring, cistern, or well, you are faced with the problem of lifting the water to ground level, transporting it to your house, and pressurizing it for use in a modern plumbing system. Ideally, this can be done with little or no outside energy supply. Many ingenious solutions have been developed over the centuries for pumping water without using electrical power, but most have fallen into disuse in an era of cheap, plentiful power. Since an electric well pump consumes a very significant portion of your house's electrical use, elimination of an electric pump can save quite a bit of energy, particularly important if you depend upon some sort of alternative electric supply. Let's examine the options.

Gravity

A gravity system is the simplest and easiest water supply that I know of. There are very few situations where this system can work, but where it can, it is absolutely foolproof and uses no power or mechanical devices of any sort. It will only work if you are using a spring or cistern as a water supply source and have a good fall between your cistern and the house. My grandparents installed such a system early in this century. It is still in use. One of its drawbacks is that some modern appliances which require high water pressure won't work with this system. You can install a small booster pump for use when the appliances are in operation, or eliminate them.

Hand Pumps

The old standby method of pumping water is by hand. Many people are unaware that hand pumps can be connected to a pressure tank to provide a normal, pressurized water system. To use this system, you need to buy a "force pump." These differ from the more common and less expensive lift pumps in that they have an air chamber which is put in compression as the water is brought to the surface, allowing the water to be expelled under pressure on the next pump stroke.

As I mentioned earlier, a pump can only lift water about 25 feet, so you will probably need to order a deep well pump. These have a brass cylinder which is suspended in the water in the well; when the pump operates, this water is drawn to the surface. This is unlike a shallow well pump which merely provides suction at the well's surface. For a shallow well with an ample water supply, the shallow well pumps are cheaper, but usually not as rugged. The major pump supplier for the United States is the Heller-Allen Co. of Napoleon, Ohio. A complete line of these pumps is handled by Cumberland General Store.[†] This firm dedicates itself to providing merchandise for self-sufficiency, stocking all manner of hand-powered and horse-drawn farm equipment, windmills, windmill towers, and the like.

Windmills

Unlike the highly technical, high-speed wind generators, windmills used for water pumping are simple, fairly low-cost machines. Since they

A homemade windmill of the Mediterranean type, with an improved sail design.

operate at relatively low speeds, balance and safety are much less critical than with a wind generator. Water storage is also easier and cheaper than storing electricity. Cumberland General Store stocks the Heller-Allen force pumps with a windmill pumping rod attached. By using this pump with a windmill, you can have an economical water system which uses no electricity. In areas of erratic winds, you can use the hand pump to pressurize the system during calm periods. If you are on a very tight budget, you can install a windmill force pump, pressurizing the water by hand initially, and add the windmill at a later date.

Multibladed farm windmills can be bought used in many parts of the country. Try to find a Baker mill if you can; the firm is still in business and parts are still available for most models. New Baker mills and towers are available from Cumberland General Store if you can't locate them used.

For those with a construction bent on low budgets, a water-pumping windmill is a relatively easy project. The photograph shows an updated version of the Mediterranean-type sail windmill. The shape of the sails has been changed from the traditional triangle to a more efficient aerodynamic shape, but otherwise this is the same basic machine which has been in use for centuries. We built one from salvaged automobile parts this past summer. Tensioning of the rigging cables for the machine is a bit difficult; otherwise, it's an easy project. The sails do have to be replaced periodically, but this is a relatively easy job. For further details on this design, contact the New Alchemy Institute, P.O. Box 47, Woods Hole, MA 02543. Their publication, *Journal of the New Alchemists,* vol. 6, gives details on sailwing-type, water-pumping windmills.

History is an accumulation of error.

Norman Cousins
Saturday Review

An inexpensive water-pumping windmill which pumps water by using an air compressor is made by the Bowjon Co. This means that the windmill itself can be mounted up to ¼ mile away from the top of the well.

Hydraulic Rams

A hydraulic ram is a type of pump powered by the action of falling water. Basically, it uses the energy generated by falling water to lift some of the water to a storage tank above the original source. The building or other area to be supplied with water is then gravity-fed from the tank. This system is more commonly used for irrigation and livestock watering systems than for household water systems, but it is a possibility. Remember that this system does not deliver *all* of the water from the water source. Minimum requirements for using a ram are a 3-foot fall in altitude and a flow rate of at least 3 gallons per minute. The water can be raised about 25 feet for each 1 foot of the fall. The flow rate must be substantial, or the output will be minimal. A medium-size hydraulic ram costs about $200. Detailed information can be obtained in Booklet 9641 from Cumberland General Store ($1). Another commercial source is Rife Hydraulic Engine Mfg. Co.[†]

The hydraulic ram is an almost magical power source, and there is virtually no maintenance involved with the machine. A special double-acting ram can be used with an impure water source such as a stream to pump two-thirds of the pure

water from a spring or cistern up to a storage tank. If you have the special conditions which permit the use of a ram, by all means get one.

Jet Pumps

Jet pumps are old standbys, standard until a few years ago. The pump is mounted aboveground and can be adapted to a variety of well depths, depending upon its configuration. It is less noisy than the old-fashioned piston-type pumps, but still noisy enough to need to be isolated. The pump uses a "jet" nozzle to create a venturi effect which sucks in water from the well as water from the pump is forced through the jet. In its simplest form, this type of pump is used for shallow wells and the jet is attached directly to the end of the pump housing. Moving the jet down into the well greatly increases the lifting capacity. A single-stage, deep-well jet pump is useful for depths up to 110 feet. A multistage jet pump has a maximum depth of 260 feet. These pumps are

This photo of a water-pumping mill by Bowjon shows the compressor at the intersection of blades. (Photo courtesy of Bowjon.)

not very efficient, but they are low-cost and durable, a good pump for a shallow well. In deep wells with a heavy sand content, a jet pump is much more durable than the more desirable submersible pump.

Submersible Pumps

Submersible pumps are the current "standard of the industry." They are the most efficient pumps you can buy and are good for wells up to 500 feet deep. They consist of a long, stainless steel cartridge which has a pipe, electric cable, and hoisting rope attached to the top end. The whole assembly is dropped down the well and submerged. The pumps are quiet and dependable, but fairly expensive. Since they are at the bottom of the well, they are protected from freezing, and they don't require any space inside the house.

Until recently, a three-wire, 220-volt electrical supply system was standard for these pumps. Recently, all of the major companies have introduced simpler, less expensive, two-wire versions. The major name brands are Goulds, Meyers, and Sears. The pumps can be installed by a commercial pump dealer, the well driller, the plumber, or the homeowner. The normal charge is $700 to $1,200 for supplying and installing a pump. The price will vary, increasing as the well depth and pump size increase.

Installing a submersible pump is an easy job for the homeowner. I would strongly recommend that you do the work yourself so that you will know how the pump is installed in case of an emergency. The Sears booklet, *Installing Submersible Pumps* (39 LY 7476), is a valuable tool, no matter what make of pump you choose.

The only special skill needed to install a pump is the ability to prepare the well casing to receive the pump outlet. In warm climates, the piping can be run out the top of the well casing. In cold climates, a hole should be cut in the side of the well casing below the frost line for the outlet supply pipe to your house. Into this hole you insert a brass gadget called a "pitless adapter" which permits the pump to be lifted from the well without disconnecting any piping.

Try to locate a wholesale supplier in your area from whom to purchase supplies, or buy them from Sears. A ½-horsepower, 220-volt submersible pump is about $200 from Sears. In case this sounds very cheap when compared to the commercial figures above, bear in mind that you need many other expensive materials to complete the installation. Heavy-duty piping and electrical cables, a pitless adapter kit, and a pressurized storage tank are major items which are required to complete the installation.

Storage Tanks

An important energy-saving feature for any water system which uses an electric pump is a captive-air pressure storage tank. This tank has a rubber diaphragm inside which keeps the water under constant uniform pressure. Conventional steel storage tanks use trapped air at the top of the tank to supply pressure. Using the captive-air tank permits the use of a smaller tank to supply the same capacity of water. These tanks also decrease the operating frequency of the pump, saving electricity and prolonging the life of your pump. If you eliminate automatic, water-consuming gadgets, you can lower the pressure so that the pump will run less often, saving even more. The standard 42-gallon tank with its pressurized diaphragm replaces an 80-gallon conventional tank and will fit neatly under a standard kitchen counter top.

Waste Disposal

One reason that our water table is dropping so rapidly is that we waste a great deal of water. The flush toilet, automatic washing machine, and garbage disposal are major culprits. Garbage disposals are among the worst culprits. They grind up otherwise useful compost and flush it down the drain where it rapidly clogs conventional septic systems. As the systems begin to fail, health departments become more and more conservative in their sizing requirements. Many areas have actually doubled the area requirements for the disposal fields due to these premature failures.

But as the possibilities of serious water shortages begin to sink in, the regulations are rapidly changing. Many areas of the country now require installation of toilets which use a maximum of 3½ gallons of water per flush. All major manufacturers now market these toilets, but you may have to special-order them. Some health departments now look favorably on various types of composting toilets which use no water at all. All of this is a dramatic change from just a few years ago when one small company made water-saving toilets and composting toilets were automatically disapproved. Since most people will use a conventional septic system, I describe it first.

Septic Systems

A septic system consists of a large concrete, steel, or fiberglass tank (I recommend concrete) with internal baffles to allow sludge to settle to the bottom of the tank. The inlet to the tank is connected to the house sewer; the outlet, to a drainage field which typically consists of 200 to 300 feet of perforated terra-cotta tile or plastic pipe. Clay soils, shallow bedrock, and very steeply sloped sites can make septic systems difficult or impossible to install. The size and type of septic system is determined by a test called a percolation (perc) test. This is done by digging a 24- to 36-inch-deep hole and repeatedly filling it with water to determine the rate at which your soil can absorb water. As a part of the perc test, health departments may require an additional test hole to determine how much soil cover there is over bedrock. If you have either a very slow absorption rate or shallow rock, the authorities will make you transport fill and install an aboveground septic system. The accompanying drawings show such an aboveground system. Conventional septic systems are constructed in exactly the same way except that the trenches for the perforated pipe are excavated directly into the ground.

A standard system, installed by a contractor who specializes in them, usually costs $1,000 to $2,000 depending upon the region of the country, soil conditions, and local regulations. Difficulties can double or triple the cost. If you avoid a garbage disposal, pump the sludge out regularly, and use water-consuming appliances carefully, a septic system will last a lifetime. The sludge *must* be pumped out at intervals. If it is allowed to build up and overflow into the perforated pipes, it will clog them, ruining the system. This means that the entire disposal field has to be abandoned or dug up and replaced. It will pay to oversize your septic tank (use a 1,000-gallon minimum) and have it pumped out at least every three years. If you follow these directions carefully, your septic system should last indefinitely.

Since more and more equipment rental firms are renting excavating equipment, you may be able to install the system yourself. Do not attempt to install any but the simplest, basic system. If you can protect the tank from vehicle traffic, a fiberglass tank will be easier for the beginner to install than a concrete tank. Under no circumstances should you use a steel tank. Rent a transit or builder's level to make sure that the whole system slopes gradually away from your house. A suitable slope is ⅛ inch to ¼ inch per foot. Aside from sloping the piping properly, the job just in-

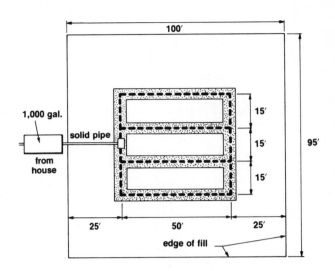

Plan of aboveground-type disposal field.

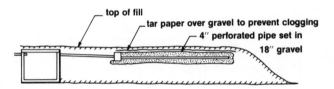

Section through disposal field.

volves excavating and backfilling. Final covering of the tank and piping should be done by hand; keep the main weight of any heavy machinery off the piping and tank. It could push them out of level or crush the disposal piping. A good reference book is *Septic Tank Practices* by Peter Warshall. Also, check your local health department regulations carefully. Most health departments will require that they inspect the system before you cover it. Some others will only allow specially licensed contractors to install the system. Check before you dig.

Waterless Toilets

Composting toilets or toilets which do not require the use of running water are gaining increasing favor with ecologically minded individuals. Three of the houses in this book use such toilets and other owners would have used them except for a New York State law prohibiting their use except on an experimental basis. The saltbox plans show a variation which permits the use of the Clivus Multrum, the best-known of these toilets. The Clivus Multrum composts naturally with no additional power, except for a small vent fan.

Composting Toilets*

Make and Type	Cost	Size and Capacity	Notes
CLIVUS MULTRUM Clivus Multrum USA 14A Eliot St. Cambridge, MA 02138	about $2,000	45X101X68h 3–10 persons	Large and expensive. Slow start-up and problems with initial liquid buildup. Best known and widely used.
TOA THRONE Enviroscope, Inc. P.O. Box 752 Corona del Mar, CA 92625	about $1,300	39X66X55h 5–6 persons	Similar to Clivus, but not as well tested. End product must be composted 6 months before use.
MULLBANK Recreation Ecology Conservation of U.S., Inc. 9800 W. Blue Mound Ct., W Milwaukee, WI 53226	about $900	24X42X32h 6 persons	Wastes must be manually distributed by mixing arm. Popular model; uses heater. Waste must be composted 6 months.
ENVIROLET Santerra Ind. 1081 Alness St. Downsview, ON M3J 2J1, Can.	about $800	25X33X25h 4 persons	Very similar to Mullbank. Easy servicing. Waste claimed pathogen-free.
BIO-TOILET Bio-Systems Toilets, Corp. Ltd. P.O. Box 539 Hawksbury, ON K6A 2G8, Can.	about $600	24X40X35h 3–4 persons	Similar to above units. Available in nonelectric model.
MAINE TANK Maine Compost Deer Isle, ME 04627	about $500 plans $15	various sizes available	Homebuilt unit of poured concrete; excellent design. Design can be varied to suit individual needs.
CLIVUS MINIMUS McGill University Montreal, PQ H3A 2T5, Can.	about $150	40X98X80h 3–10 persons	Similar to commercial Clivus. Constructed of concrete block. Plans available on an experimental basis from McGill University.
COMPOST PRIVY Farallones Institute 15290 Colemen Valley Rd. Occidental, CA 95465	about $125 plans $2.50	various sizes available	Plans are readily available; likely to be rejected by local health departments.

*For further reading and information on selecting and maintaining a composting toilet, I recommend the book *Goodbye to the Flush Toilet*, edited by Carol Stoner. It also has detailed drawings on several homebuilt toilets including the Clivus Minimus. Another excellent book which describes many low-cost, ecologically sound means of waste disposal is *Sanitation in Developing Countries* by Arnold Pacey.

The Clivus Multrum is quite large which can make it difficult to situate in a house. Its competitors tend to be smaller and easier to install. Most of them require electric heaters, forced agitation, or other outside power sources. The factory-built Clivus Multrum in the Stoner house has worked perfectly so far. The unit is expensive (about $2,000 at this writing), and since it is made of petroleum-based fiberglass, costs will undoubtedly continue to rise. If the basic contours of the Clivus tank are followed, a toilet can be homebuilt. Plans for a similar unit, the Clivus Minimus, are available on an experimental basis from McGill University (see Composting Toilets, above). A similar plan is available for a homebuilt composting toilet called the Maine Tank.

Bill Caddell built his own toilet, but he used overlaid plywood (Duro-ply by U.S. Plywood is a common trade name) and a neoprene/Hypalon coating for waterproofing. His homebuilt has not been in service long enough to say that it is a success. Other people who have tried to make homebuilt composting toilets have met with varying success. Some have been total disasters.

Other Types of Dry Toilets

Of course, the old-fashioned privy is an inexpensive, safe method of waste disposal. In recognition of water shortage problems, many areas have reversed their codes and permitted its use. Privies must be tightly constructed to be sanitary; many are not. For this reason, health departments tend to disallow them. The Farallones Institute has devised and thoroughly tested their own composting privy which can be built for about $125. Plans are available from Farallones Institute. (See Composting Toilets, opposite. This table shows the sizes and prices for the major manufacturers of composting toilets.)

Greywater Disposal

One very significant problem with the use of composting toilets or privies is the disposal of the remaining wastewater from the household (known to engineers as "greywater," a term used to describe all water other than that discharged by toilets). It may contain various contaminants, including some which can be dangerous. Many health departments require a standard, full-size septic system just to dispose of greywater. Others will allow much smaller versions of the standard system or the use of sand-bed trickle filters. Since the decomposing of wastes in a standard septic system generates heat, septic systems do not freeze. Greywater systems can freeze, however. For this reason, trickle filters are easily clogged, and you will need to use care, particularly with kitchen grease. I strongly advise the installation of a grease trap under your kitchen sink. This is a small, cast-iron box with internal baffles somewhat similar in design to a shrunken septic tank and is installed flush with the floor under the sink. It is usually required for commercial restaurants. Grease traps must be cleaned periodically, but will keep your sand filter clean and in good operating condition.

A very workable disposal system for greywater can be made from two 55-gallon drums and some perforated pipe. This system can be used outside in moderate climates. In areas where the frost line extends below 2½ feet, the system should be placed within the greenhouse. The saltbox plans in Part IV show how this can be done.

Chapter 7

Layout and Foundations

Layout

The layout of your foundation is one of the most crucial steps in building your house. When you selected your exact building site you did a rough stakeout of your house to establish orientation, window location, and the like. Make absolutely sure that you have the correct location before proceeding further.

A transit or builder's level will greatly simplify the layout procedure. Try to borrow or rent one (rental is about $12 per day). Both instruments are basically similar to a small telescope mounted upon an adjustable tripod and swiveling 360°. A baseplate is marked in degrees so that accurate 90° corners can be established. A bubble level built into the top of the telescope permits you to set the instrument dead level for accurate readings. A tripod with adjustable legs makes the leveling process much easier on rough terrain. A transit is a more expensive and precise instrument which also has provisions for reading angles so that it can be used for survey work on slopes. A good-quality builder's level is quite acceptable for your needs, though.

The procedure for the layout of the basic saltbox house is as follows:

1. Set the instrument directly over one of your preliminary corner stakes.

2. Level the instrument and drop a plumb bob from the center of the instrument to the top of your stake. Put a small nail in the top of the stake to mark this point.

3. With a tape, measure along the long wall of the house 36 feet. This should give the approximate location of your second corner stake. Drive a stake with a nail in it at this mark, measuring 36 feet to the nail.

4. Check this line with a compass to make sure that the orientation of the south face of the house is what you had planned. (Caution: Kids love to play with stakes; they may have moved your rough layout stakes.)

5. Move the transit, set the second stake with a plumb bob, sighting on the nail as before, and set the baseplate at 0°. (If the baseplate isn't adjustable, read the angle.)

6. Turn the instrument 90° and establish a direction for the sidewall of the house. Stretch a tape from the first stake along the line so that you can see it in the instrument. Establish the distance and set a

third stake with a nail at 26 feet. Now you have set two sides of the house at 90° to each other.

7. Measure off the other two sides of the house and set the fourth stake. Since the basic form of all of the houses is a square or a rectangle, you can do this without resetting the instrument.

8. Measure both diagonals of the rectangle. If the measurements are within 1 inch of each other you did a good job. If not, start over.

9. Leaving the transit in place, set offset stakes and stretch strings along the sides of the house as shown in the diagram of the foundation layout. The offset stakes are required so that you can dig for the foundations and still be able to find the exact location of the stakes.

10. Measure along the sides of the house and determine the placement of the intermediate line of stakes. Set offset stakes for these positions.

11. Back to the transit. Using either a survey rod or a tape measure, check the height of the sight line of the telescope from the ground. Make a sketch of the house showing the location of all the stakes. Leaving the transit locked at level, swing it around so that you can read a height on the rod or tape measure at each post location. Record all the readings on your sketch. If you have a level site or if your excavator did a good job on your rough excavation, all readings will be approximately the same. If there are significant differences, you will have to recheck the level after you dig for the foundation. You should establish a permanent reference of the level mark on the offset stakes so that you don't have to rent the transit again.

Alternate Method

What if you are miles out in the country with no access to a transit? With some string, a tape measure, a 50-foot length of clear plastic tubing, and some water, you can accomplish the same thing — with just a bit more patience.

1. Put a nail in one of the preliminary stakes.

2. Measure 36 feet along the long wall in the direction of the second preliminary stake. Set a nail in the stake at 36 feet and check direction with a compass as before. Adjust line if necessary.

3. Stretch a string along the 36-foot wall, setting offset stakes as before. Measure off 9 feet from stake 1 toward stake 2 and mark this point.

4. Stretch a second string from the first stake to the *approximate* location of stake 3. Measure 12 feet along this string from stake 1 toward stake 3. Now stretch a tape between the marked points on the two strings. Swing the second string around until the distance between the two marked points is 15 feet; you have established a right-angle triangle. Skip to steps 7 and 8 above. If you kept your strings absolutely tight you should do almost as well as if you used the transit. Alternately, construct a right-angle triangle to the dimensions shown in the sketch, and use it to set the strings to the proper angle. Repeat steps 9 and 10.

11. Fill the plastic tubing nearly full of water. Eyeball the house site and pick what you think to be the high corner. Adjust the water level in the tubing so that you can mark a point on one of the offset stakes at the high point. Mark the level on the plastic tubing.

12. Have someone else move the other end of the tubing around to each of the other corner stakes. Since water will seek its own level, you can mark each of the other stakes and establish an accurate reference point. You can purchase a ready-made package of this apparatus from Hydrolevel† for about $15.

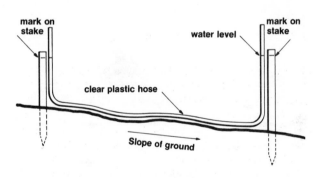

A clear hose filled with water can be used to establish a level point.

Frequently, a device called a line level is used for the operation described above. It is simple and quick, but can be wildly inaccurate. If you use a line level, observe the following precautions. First, check it by placing it on top of a high-quality framing level which you know to be accurate. Second, place the line level at the *exact* center of the line to be leveled. Third, pull the line as tight as possible. Fourth, check all around the house and if you are lucky, you will come back to your starting point. If not, get plastic tubing.

---

†The address of this and other manufacturers and associations so indicated will be found under "Addresses of Manufacturers and Associations" in Part IV.

This rigid tripod is only good for level ground; for uneven terrain use an adjustable tripod.

Foundations

Several different types of foundations are used on the houses in this book. Since there is only one pole-type house, I will describe that foundation in the Pole house in Part III.

The first foundation was used on the Volkswagen house. It is very low-cost, was quick and easy to install, and has performed excellently. It is just as applicable to the basic saltbox as it is to the Volkswagen house. One major reason for using this foundation was a completely remote site which made transportation of heavy, conventional masonry foundation materials difficult, if not impossible.

Since this is a post and beam house, all of the loads are carried by the posts and none by the walls. On the exterior, we embedded pressure-treated 6X6 posts (#6 treatment) directly in the earth, extending below the frost line. (Since we were on a very limited budget and pressure-treated posts are rather expensive, we spliced them to untreated posts aboveground, as shown in the photos.) Between the treated posts, we installed horizontal framing members made up of two pressure-treated 2X6s fastened together in an L-shape as shown in the detail. These foundation members were cut to the required length to accurately locate the posts.

Before installing the framing members, a narrow trench was dug all around the foundation as deep as was practical, ranging 2 to 4 feet below floor line. Two-inch-thick foil-faced urethane insulation board faced with 1/4-inch-thick cement-asbestos board (marketed by Johns-Manville under the trade name "Transite") on the outside

Foundation layout (from left to right).

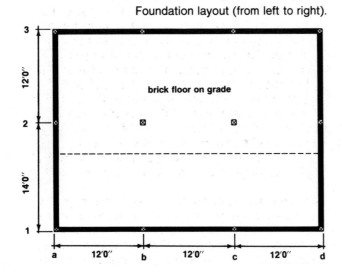

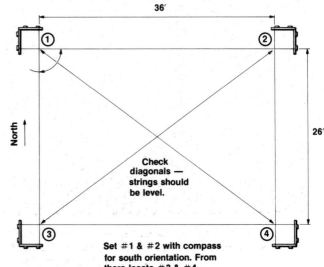

Set #1 & #2 with compass for south orientation. From there locate #3 & #4.

Splicing an untreated post to treated foundation post.

Pressure-treated post embedded directly in the earth.

was inserted in the trench. The weight of the sand fill and masonry floor inside the house holds the board tight against the treated framing member (see detail). This is the type of detail which will get you in trouble with a conservative building inspector. However, if your house is remote enough to have trouble transporting concrete and masonry, it may also be too remote for a building inspector.

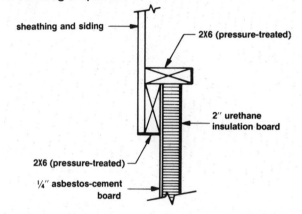

L-shaped sill made from 2X6s for Volkswagen house.

Concrete is an energy-intensive material; costs are rising and shortages are developing. As an option to concrete foundations, many contractors have started using pressure-treated wood foundations which are just framed up with treated framing lumber and covered with plywood (see the Stoner house). I believe that system which we developed for the Volkswagen house is much more durable as well as cheaper than the all-wood foundation. If you are using a large central chimney as shown in our plans, I would use a concrete pad underneath the chimney and the

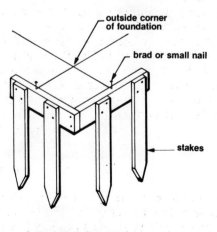

batter board, 2' to 4' long, offset from corner so string can be removed and replaced

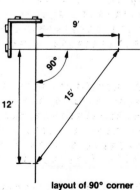

layout of 90° corner
Alternate — use large wooden square made from lumber using 3-4-5 multiples.

This rigid insulation board will be held in place by the weight of the floor.

two inside posts. These inside posts carry double the weight of any of the exterior posts and will need the extra bearing area of the concrete footing for soft soil conditions in many parts of the country. Also, it is very easy to pour the footings for these two posts as an integral part of the chimney foundation. For the small amount of concrete involved in this footing, you can job-mix your own concrete.

Five of the houses shown in this book use a poured concrete "grade beam" as shown on the working drawings for the basic saltbox. If executed properly, this foundation can be very economical, quick to install, and also used to store

heat for the house. If done poorly, it can be a major headache. The grade beam foundation is just starting to be used, so many contractors and building inspectors will be completely unfamiliar with the technique. Two very important criteria are to have a uniformly stable soil and a skilled excavator with a machine with a very narrow bucket. If your soil is filled with heavy roots and large boulders, it will be impossible to dig accurately and a block foundation may be best.

The technique is to dig a narrow, accurate trench 8 inches wide by about $3\frac{1}{2}$ feet deep. The outside line of the trench should fall exactly under those strings which you set for the layout. The great majority of excavating contractors are not sufficiently skilled or equipped to dig this sort of a trench. If you know just what to look for, though, you may find someone. Electric and telephone companies frequently subcontract buried lines to outside contractors. Since they are usually laying lines on someone else's property, they want to keep damage to a minimum and the contractors are usually equipped with machines with capabilities for digging narrow trenches.

Standard backhoes can be had with small buckets, but they are unusual. Check to see if anyone in your area has one. If not, try to locate a Melroe Bobcat or a Ditch-Witch. Both are likely to be used by underground line installers. The Bobcat is the better of the two, particularly with rocky soil conditions. If you have a fairly soft soil and lots of available labor, you may want to hand-dig the trench. It's lots of work, though. Be careful if the soil is soft; if it is, the trench may cave in on you.

After digging your trench, proceed as follows:

In this house, the top of the south wall is considerably above original grade so that aboveground forms are necessary for the grade beams. Uncut sheets of plywood were used for forms so that they could be reused for the siding.

Concrete exerts tremendous pressure. Corners must be thoroughly tied and braced as shown in photo.

1. Build a box around the outside perimeter of the foundation with 2X6s, preferably 12 and 14 feet long so that they can be reused economically. Set the top of the box level with your finish floor line. Set the inside face of your 2X6s to the outside foundation lines of the house.

2. Line the outside face of your trench with 2-inch urethane insulation board in 4X8 sheets placed horizontally. Trim where necessary to clear any obstacles at the bottom of the trench. Now set another box of 2X6s on the inside face of the trench. The top of this box must be level with the outside box. Tack spacers spanning the two boxes so that they are a uniform 8 inches apart all around the foundation. (Spacers should be no more than 2 feet apart.) Spacers should either be drilled to position anchor bolts or placed so that they miss them completely. (See anchor bolt plan in working drawings for locations.)

3. Embed sections of plastic pipe in the trench at appropriate points to provide sleeves for water service, sewer line, and underground electric service. Option: Dig under foundation after pouring for these services.

This well-braced form is the work of professionals. Yours needn't look so neat, but it gives you some idea of what's required.

Framework tied at corner with steel strapping.

If your soil is relatively easy to dig, running services under the foundation is the easy way; if not, install the sleeves. Most of the sleeves which I have seen installed by amateurs got pushed out of place by the concrete. The safest way to make a sleeve is to cut through the urethane insulation board with a hole saw and install a piece of plastic pipe which extends through the formwork and is embedded in the earth until after your pour. This also makes a watertight seal if you have troublesome groundwater.

Concrete is a tricky material. If properly mixed and cured, it is capable of developing very great strength; however, precautions are necessary. Excessive amounts of water weaken concrete noticeably. Add just enough to get the material to pour into the formwork properly. Typical construction hacks always add lots of water to "make it pour easily," so be prepared to fight on this one. Extremes of heat and cold are disastrous for concrete. In hot weather keep it covered with burlap, and wet it down several times a day for at least three days. Rain is actually beneficial, unless the concrete was just poured.

Freezing weather is another serious problem. Concrete which is allowed to freeze loses most of its strength. Chemical additives which prevent freezing can be used, but they also weaken the

Allow the concrete to "cure," and then remove the forms. Note the exterior urethane insulation board.

concrete. The best bet is to try to avoid subfreezing weather. (Concrete will be okay down to about 25°F. as it is massive and generates heat in the curing process.) If you must pour in very cold weather, build an enclosure over the concrete and supply heat. I once built a brick chimney in very severe weather with just a tiny electric heater and a simple sliding enclosure.

Concrete in relatively thin vertical forms will develop air pockets unless it is agitated after it is placed in the forms. For a small pour, it can be stirred with a steel or wooden rod; for larger jobs, rent a professional concrete vibrator. Finally, remember that concrete is very heavy. Make sure that your forms are very strong, and provide adequate access by means of a solid roadbed for a concrete truck.

The standard foundation in most parts of the country is precast concrete block set on a poured concrete footing. This is a perfectly acceptable foundation, but uses more material than is really necessary. My primary objection to this type of foundation is that it disrupts much more soil than other systems. It dates back to the days of unlimited resources and cheap materials.

However, using concrete block is your easiest way to build a foundation. Just hire a foundation contractor or mason, and he will do all of the work with little trouble on your part. Masons are notorious for making dimensional mistakes. You should do your own layout, or at least check the mason's layout carefully. Also check carefully for proper elevation and height of the top of the foundation. In my many years of experience with contractors and commercial and residential buildings, this is a very frequent problem: the excavator makes a mistake and then the mason

If you engage a contractor for your foundation, it should look like this; if not, ask why.

Tell the concrete contractor to bring a long extension chute. Shifting tons of setting concrete across your site in a wheelbarrow is no joke.

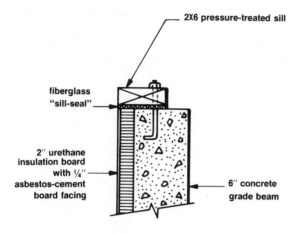

— 2X6 pressure-treated sill

fiberglass "sill-seal"

2″ urethane insulation board with ¼″ asbestos-cement board facing

6″ concrete grade beam

Sill detail for saltbox house.

cores of the block 4 to 6 feet apart, depending upon the stability of your soil.

In areas of seismic activity, landslides, or other soil problems, you should engage a professional to design the wall for you. See if you can persuade him to do it on a consulting basis. Just a rough sketch will be enough for you to build a simple wall. Try to avoid using 12-inch concrete block. They are heavy, expensive, and the masons charge much more for laying them than the extra 2-inch thickness would warrant. You are much better off from a cost standpoint using 10-inch block and adding extra reinforcement. This is the sort of practical application which typical engineers don't understand. They will look it up in a table, select 12-inch block, and give no thought whatsoever to cost.

compounds it. Then all sort of frantic adjustments are made to compensate for the errors.

Several of the houses in this book use block foundations and, except for the Pole house, any of them could be adapted to the standard block foundation. Laying masonry is tricky and something I would not recommend for the beginner. One of the houses in the book does have a block foundation laid entirely by the owners; it is very successful; a professional job in all respects. It took a very long time, though. There are several good books on do-it-yourself masonry but, in this case, the owners took a course in block laying at the local trade school.

Concrete block does not have nearly the strength of poured concrete. If you are in a heavy soil with a fully buried wall, you may be better off with a concrete foundation. For the basic saltbox house, an 8-inch-block wall is satisfactory. The top course should be set back on the inside to a 6-inch course so that the block won't show at the floor line. Use extra-long (12-inch) anchor bolts set in concrete so that the 6-inch course is solidly tied to the 8-inch blocks.

If you have a foundation wall enclosing a living space, use a minimum of 10-inch block and install steel reinforcement. Dur-O-Wall wire reinforcement should be installed in the horizontal joints at every other course. For vertical reinforcement, use #4 (½-inch diameter) steel reinforcing rods. Fill the cores of the block solid with mortar around the rods. Place the rods in the

Concrete vibrator quickly forces out air pockets in large volumes of poured concrete.

When laying out your foundation walls, make sure to allow for insulation on the *outside* of them. You would be amazed at how difficult this idea is to get across to contractors. On one of my jobs, a contractor even deliberately backfilled around a foundation omitting the insulation which he knew was supposed to be installed (it was sitting right in front of him). "That architect is crazy. What do you want to insulate the ground for?" was his response to other workmen who asked why he left out the insulation. Of course, his real game was to get paid twice for the excavation work. At least one state has made it illegal to construct an uninsulated foundation. See Chapter 10 for insulation details.

Chapter 8

Rough Framing

The rough framing described in this chapter has been carefully coordinated with the materials list in Part IV. Note that there are some differences in the final set of plans enclosed in the back of the book and the plans of the three houses pictured elsewhere. The plans in the back are a composite with the best features of all three houses. Also, there are two framing systems (one with heavy timbers and one laminated from stock lumberyard material) and two roof-framing systems. One standard roof-framing system uses conventional plywood sheathing and is suitable for a variety of roofing materials. The other is designed specifically for ribbed metal roofing and eliminates the plywood. Check the optional sections of the materials lists carefully so that you know which materials to order.

Framing the Walls

Before starting with the framing, double-check your foundation for square and level. If your diagonals measure within 1 inch of each other, your foundation is close enough to square for you to proceed. If not, you may have to set the sill plates so that they overhang the foundation a bit to help true up your foundation. Also check for level. In an open plan such as this, 1 inch end to end or 2 inches diagonally will not be noticed, but you should note it and compensate for same.

(continued on page 75)

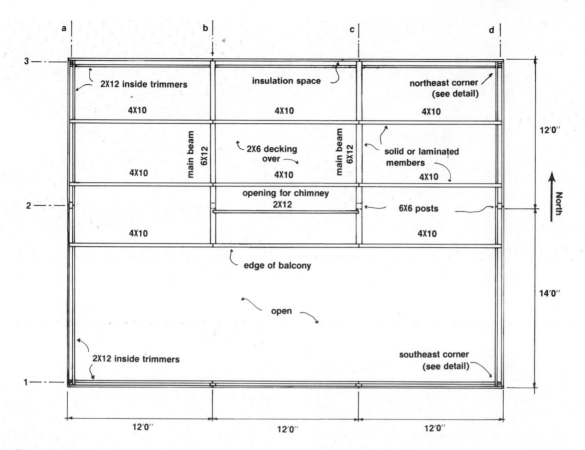

Framing plan.

The above plan shows the location of all the posts and framing members which support the second floor. A numbered and lettered grid enables you to locate each piece exactly. Study the drawings on the next few pages carefully, and locate each piece on the plan. Regardless of the type of framing system which is used, the perimeter members at the outside walls of the house consist of box beams made up of 2X12s. This permits full insulation of the outside walls. The inside members which support the 2X6 decking can be made of either laminated or solid wood. Solid members are shown on this plan. It may help speed construction if you build a scale model frame from balsa wood before starting with the actual frame.

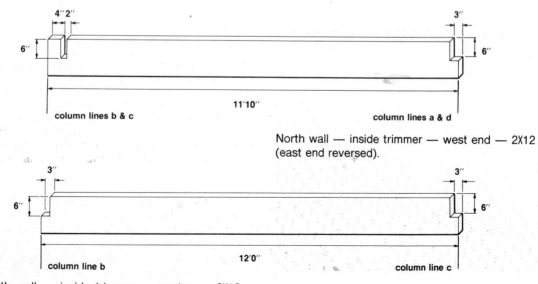

North wall — inside trimmer — west end — 2X12 (east end reversed).

North wall — inside trimmer — center — 2X12.

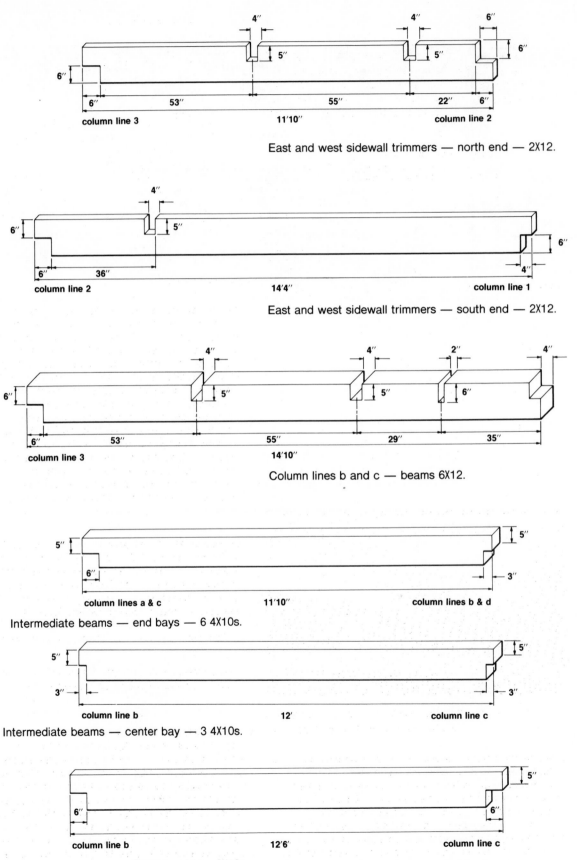

4″   4″   6″

5″   5″   6″

6″

6″   53″   55″   22″   6″

column line 3   11′10″   column line 2

East and west sidewall trimmers — north end — 2X12.

4″

6″   5″

6″

6″   36″   4″

column line 2   14′4″   column line 1

East and west sidewall trimmers — south end — 2X12.

4″   4″   2″   4″

6″   5″   5″   6″

6″   53″   55″   29″   35″

column line 3   14′10″

Column lines b and c — beams 6X12.

5″   5″

6″   3″

column lines a & c   11′10″   column lines b & d

Intermediate beams — end bays — 6 4X10s.

5″   5″

3″   3″

column line b   12′   column line c

Intermediate beams — center bay — 3 4X10s.

5″

6″   6″

column line b   12′6′   column line c

Chimney girt — 2X12.

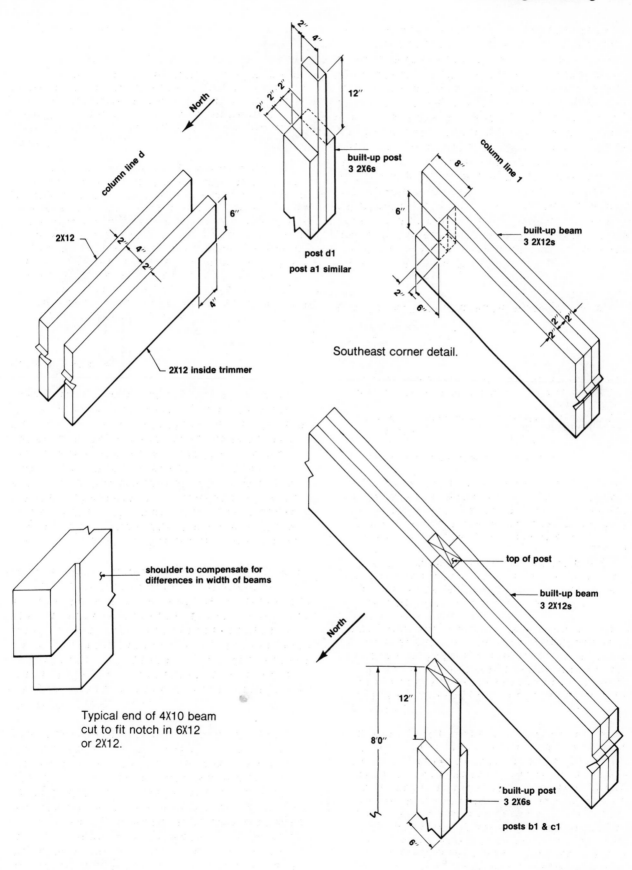

North

2'' 4''

12''

2'' 2'' 2''

built-up post
3 2X6s

post d1
post a1 similar

column line d

2X12

6''

2''
4''
2''

4''

2X12 inside trimmer

column line 1

8''

6''

built-up beam
3 2X12s

2''

6''

2'' 2''

2''

Southeast corner detail.

shoulder to compensate for
differences in width of beams

top of post

built-up beam
3 2X12s

North

12''

8'0''

built-up post
3 2X6s

posts b1 & c1

6''

Typical end of 4X10 beam
cut to fit notch in 6X12
or 2X12.

South wall — intermediate post.

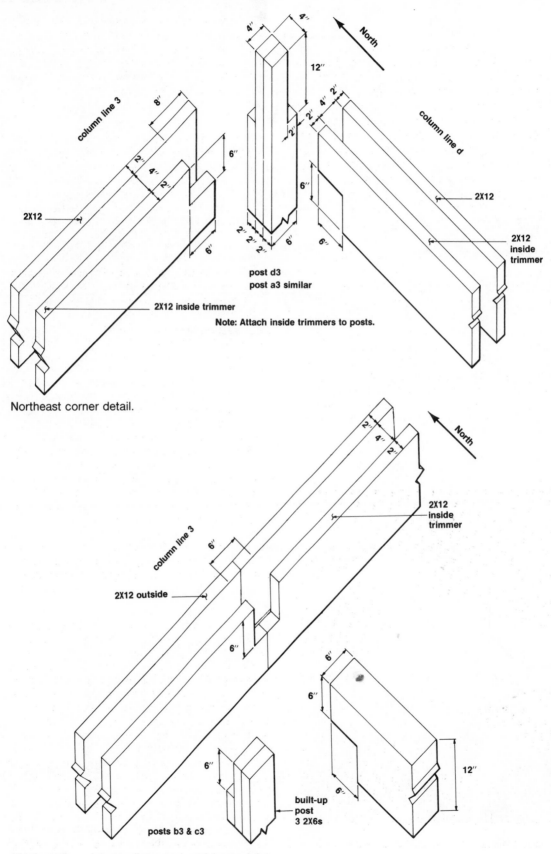

North

4"
4"
12"
2"

column line 3

8"

2X12

2X12 inside trimmer

6"

2"
4"
2"

6"

2"
2"
4"
2"

column line d

2X12

2X12
inside
trimmer

6"

2"
2"
2"
6"
6"

post d3
post a3 similar

Note: Attach inside trimmers to posts.

Northeast corner detail.

North

2"
4"
2"

2X12
inside
trimmer

column line 3

6"

2X12 outside

6"

6"
6"

12"

6"

6"

6"

posts b3 & c3

built-up
post
3 2X6s

North wall — intermediate post and beam joint.

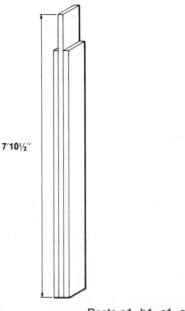

7'10½"

Posts a1, b1, c1, and d1.

Overlapping trimmers in place, viewed from outside (above) and inside (below) the house.

Overlapping trimmers at corner post, viewed from inside the house.

If you're using a solid post, this is the way you notch one end.

An out-of-level foundation will cause you more work but is not terribly serious. The length of the first-floor posts must be adjusted to compensate for the unlevel condition. I recommend renting a transit and shooting the levels for the second floor if you have a real problem with your foundation. Within limits, the brick floor can also be adjusted for an out-of-level condition. Since the foundation wall and the framing members are of the same thickness, the baseboard trim will cover any exposed foundation wall which would result from leveling the floor.

Proceed as follows:

1. Set the pressure-treated (green) 2X6 sill plate flush with the outside of the urethane insulation board. Locate the holes for the anchor bolts by setting the plate in place on top of them and hitting them with a hammer. Drill from the bottom where the anchor bolts marked the plate. After installing a fiberglass or rubber seal under the plate, set it in place with nuts and washers.

Set the sill plate on the foundation.

Brace the post thoroughly.

Set the two south corner posts.

Set a string to align the posts.

2. Prepare the two corner posts for the south wall from three 2X6s as shown. Set the two posts in place and align the outside faces with the outside corner of the treated plate (if roughsawn framing members are used, the inside face will overhang by about ½ inch). Anchor the post to the plate with perforated framing anchor plates. Set the posts vertical in both directions by use of a plumb bob, *not a level*. Even though a plumb bob must be offset and takes a bit more time, it is much more accurate than a level; a level can be badly "off" due to warpage in the post or an inaccuracy in the level. Use a level if you must, but check at various points along the post. Brace the post thoroughly with diagonal braces nailed high up the post and to the sill plate.

3. Set a nail in the upper outside corner of each post, and stretch a string between them. This string will give you heights for the intermediate posts and ensure that your roof line is straight. Measure from the plate to the string, and fabricate the two intermediate posts. Set the posts and brace them.

4. Fabricate three laminated beams as shown, and set the beams in place on the posts. Check that the tops of the beams align with the string; if not, adjust seat cuts on intermediate posts so that beams set level. Make absolutely sure that this wall is plumb and level. It is your reference point for the roof framing.

Set the three laminated beams on the posts.

Set the beams in place, bay by bay.

Move to the north wall, and repeat steps 1 through 4.

Use a "come-along" to make the joints tight.

Set the main beams in place.

5. Move to the north wall of your house and repeat steps 1 to 4. Note that the inside faces of the beams are cut differently to receive the intermediate beams which support the balcony.

6. Stretch strings along the east and west walls to establish the height for intermediate posts. Fabricate posts to the necessary height. Note that laminations are always parallel to direction of the beam, in this case at 90° to those of posts on the north and south walls. Plumb and brace these posts.

7. Fabricate, but do not assemble, exterior trimmers. These trimmers are used as patterns for the layout for your interior beams at column lines 2 and 3.

8. Lay out and cut the interior beams. Note: These beams may be either solid or laminated of stan-

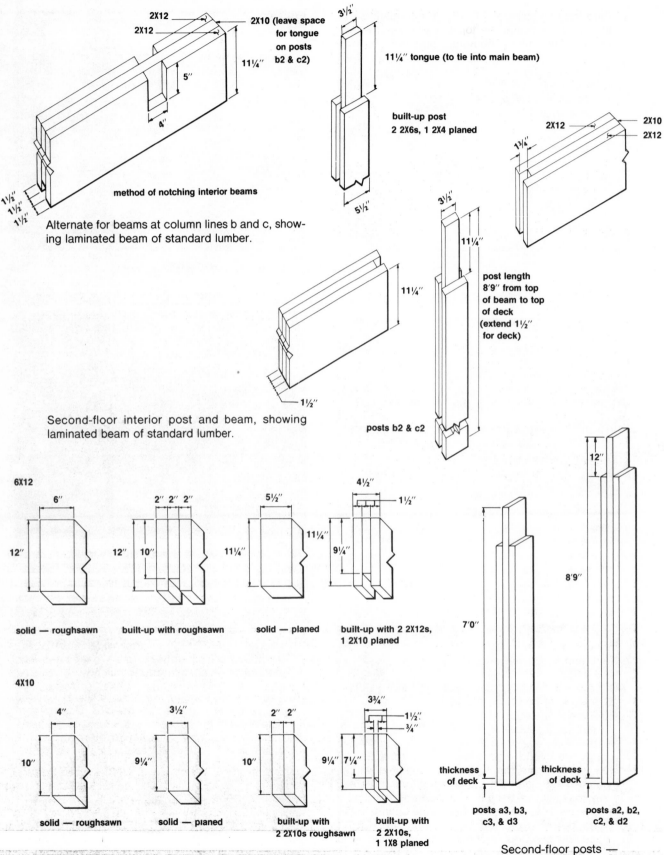

2X12
2X12
2X10 (leave space for tongue on posts b2 & c2)

11¼″
5″
4″

3½″

11¼″ tongue (to tie into main beam)

built-up post
2 2X6s, 1 2X4 planed

5½″

2X12
2X10
2X12

1¾″

1½″
1½″
1½″

method of notching interior beams

Alternate for beams at column lines b and c, showing laminated beam of standard lumber.

3½″
11¼″

post length 8′9″ from top of beam to top of deck (extend 1½″ for deck)

11¼″

1½″

posts b2 & c2

Second-floor interior post and beam, showing laminated beam of standard lumber.

6X12

6″
12″
12″

2″ 2″ 2″
10″

5½″
11¼″

4½″
1½″
11¼″
9¼″

solid — roughsawn

built-up with roughsawn

solid — planed

built-up with 2 2X12s, 1 2X10 planed

12″

4X10

4″
10″

3½″
9¼″

2″ 2″
10″

3¾″
1½″
¾″
9¼″ 7¼″

solid — roughsawn

solid — planed

built-up with 2 2X10s roughsawn

built-up with 2 2X10s, 1 1X8 planed

8′9″
7′0″

thickness of deck

thickness of deck

posts a3, b3, c3, & d3

posts a2, b2, c2, & d2

Different types of beams.

Second-floor posts — conventional roof system.

dard framing members. If solid, a 4X5 notch is cut all the way through the top of each beam where shown. If laminated, the notch is cut only through the outside layers of 2X12 before assembly. Caution: Knots weaken a beam considerably and should always be placed so that they are in the upper portion of a beam where they are compressed by the bending of the beam.

9. Stretch strings from the intermediate post on the west wall to the intermediate post on the east wall (a2 to d2). Cut the intermediate posts which flank the chimney wall. If laminated posts are used, these should be made up of one 2X4 and two 2X6s with the 2X4 in the center extending up into the main beam as a tie. Set the posts in place, measuring carefully, then brace them solidly.

10. Set the perimeter beams at the east and west walls (column lines a and d) and the main balcony beams at column lines b and c. Make sure that all beams are parallel with each other. Now measure for the nine intermediate 4X10 beams which finish the balcony framing. Start at one end of the house and move to the other. You will never be able to get an absolutely tight joint, and the house will tend to "grow," so cut each beam about $\frac{1}{16}$-inch short of its actual required dimension. These beams can be solid 4X10s of either roughcut or finish timber or two 2X10s laminated on either side of a 1X8 or two roughsawn 2X10s laminated together. The actual width of these beams will variously be 4 inches, $3\frac{1}{2}$ inches, $3\frac{3}{4}$ inches and 4 inches. The 4-inch roughcut beams are apt to vary in width from beam to beam. If all of the notches in beams at column lines a, b, c, and d are cut a bit small, each 4X10 can be trimmed down a bit in width for a very professional-looking fit. No matter what the width of the cuts, the 5-inch depth is constant. Always measure this exactly from the tops of the beams so that the top surface will be uniform for flooring.

11. Set the beams in place one bay at a time. The beams must be dropped into place uniformly. If one end is allowed to drop in ahead of the other, the beam will bind and refuse to go into place. Check the size of all cuts carefully before going to the work of hoisting your beams into place. Remember that cuts can taper in either direction, so check *all* measurements. After all beams are in place, but before fastening, check to see that all joints are tight. If necessary, wrap a rope around the ends of the frame, and pull together with a come-along. After the frame is tight, strap across the tops of the beams with perforated framing plates, and toe-nail the intermediate beams to the main beams from the top so that the nailing doesn't show. Double-check all of your bracing to see that the structure is still true and plumb. You are now ready for the second-floor deck.

Deck

Decking should be purchased in 16-foot lengths if at all possible. Before starting to install the decking, sort it carefully, sighting along its length for straightness. Also sort out damaged or badly cut pieces. Badly curved pieces can be cut in half and installed in two pieces. All cut ends should fall *over* the support, not between. Some yards stock end-matched decking in random lengths (they have tongue-and-groove joints on the ends as well as the sides). It will work well provided you stagger all the joints. Make sure your decking is 1½ inches thick. Some yards sell thinner decking as 2X6.

Decking should be either nailed through the tongue with 16d cement-coated sinkers (these are very necessary to prevent squeaks; special-order by exact size and type from your lumber-yard) or surface-nailed with 10d cut nails, two per bearing. Snap a line across the deck with a chalk line for these, and align them so that they look neat. Nailing with the 16d nails through the tongue requires good accuracy to prevent marring the edges of the decking. If your nailing leaves something to be desired, use cut nails through the surface instead.

Owner-builder Pat Morris, installing his decking with a pipe clamp.

Proceed as follows:

1. Cut all posts for the second floor (eight are required, cut to lengths shown). The decking is cut around them and it's easier to set them in place as you go. Toe-nail the posts into the beams below, taking care that the thickness of the decking will hide the nailheads.

2. Start laying decking from either column line 1 or column line 4. Use scraps of decking to pound each piece in place for a snug fit. If necessary, use pipe clamps, using scraps to protect the tongue. Good decking won't require this. When you get to the second row of posts, stop and set them in place. Continue until the balcony is complete. Remember the cutout for the chimney. Damaged decking can be used in this area, cutting out the damaged or warped portions and using the shorter lengths on either side of the chimney. Continue with decking until the balcony is complete.

Roof Framing

Cutting out rafters tends to be scary for the beginner. If you have done your framing for the bottom of the house accurately, the roof framing is a breeze. It is simply a matter of placing a trial rafter along the side of the building with its top set to the desired slope. The required notches in the rafters or beams are marked on the side of the trial rafter by drawing around the part of the support beam which projects into the rafter. Before you make your rafter pattern, you should double-check all posts to see that they are in alignment.

In the following instructions, I describe two very different roof-framing systems step-by-step. In the first, the rafters are run conventionally from peak to eaves with intermediate support beams along column line 2. The rafters for the front of the house must be a minimum of 22 feet long and are expensive and heavy. This system is quite conventional, and the rafter spacing is ideal for our heat-collecting skylights. Roof sheathing of ½-inch plywood is used.

The purlin roof-framing system was designed for my Volkswagen house with the idea of reducing costs to a bare minimum. The framing system is turned 90° so that the rafters run parallel to the 36-foot dimension of the house. In this system, the support beams are installed along column lines b and c. The support beams are notched over the posts in similar fashion to rafters, but this is only required for two beams, not nineteen rafters as in the conventional framing system. Hollow boxbeams are used for these main sup-

ports. Support beams aren't needed at column lines 1, 2, and 3, but the structure has to be thoroughly braced to keep the posts in alignment until the shell is complete. The roof rafters for this system are only 12 feet long and are square-cut at their ends, making installation easy for the beginner. The system is ideal for a Sheetrock ceiling, as the two support beams break up the ceiling into three 12-foot bays, eliminating the need for taping cross-seams. Additional blocking must be installed for skylights. The framing is designed primarily for ribbed metal roofing so that expensive plywood sheathing can be eliminated. If you want to use this framing system because it is simpler and easier to install, you can still cover the rafters with plywood and use any roofing materials which you desire.

Installation of Conventional Rafters

Proceed as follows:

1. Install the beams at column lines 2 and 3 in similar fashion to the beam installed at column line 1.

2. Recheck column line 1 for plumb and adjust as necessary.

3. Check and brace column lines 2 and 3.

4. Set strings along column lines 1, 2, and 3 and take measurements between the strings at the posts. Make any adjustments necessary to bring the three lines parallel with each other. Brace securely so that the posts can't move out of alignment.

5. Stretch a chalk line along the outside face of the support beams at column lines 1 and 2 along the line where the bottom of the roof rafter should rest. Mark the beams with the chalk line.

6. Nail temporary support blocks across the outside of the ends of the beams. Set your trial rafter in place, checking to see that the overhang and ridge points are lined up correctly. Mark for cutting where the beams ends intersect the rafter. These cuts are called "seat cuts" or "bird's-mouths."

7. Remove the rafter and cut the notches. Now set it in place up on the beams next to the support blocks to see if it fits properly. If not, try again. Our rafters are oversized to accommodate heavy insulation, so they will have plenty of strength with notches cut both sides if you make a mistake. When you have the rafter properly fitted at one end of the house, slide it along the roof to see that the other three sets of columns are in proper alignment. (It may be easier to take it down from the roof and put it back up at the other three locations.)

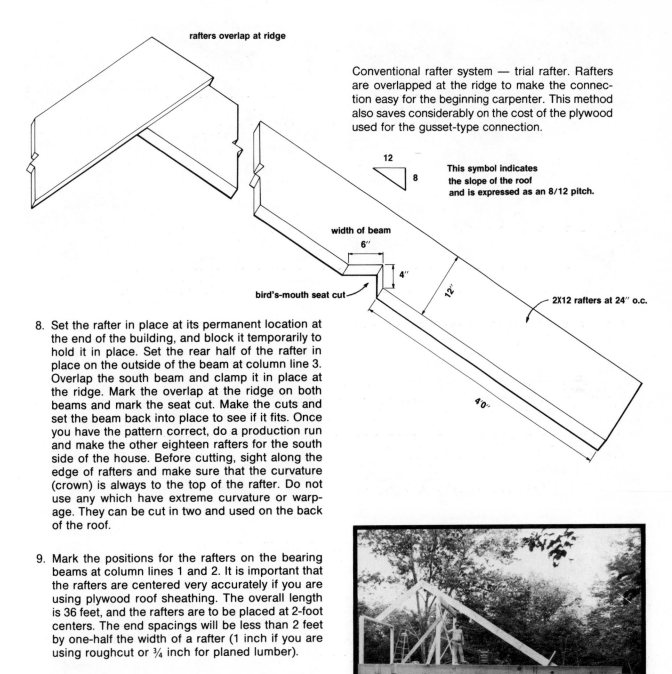

rafters overlap at ridge

Conventional rafter system — trial rafter. Rafters are overlapped at the ridge to make the connection easy for the beginning carpenter. This method also saves considerably on the cost of the plywood used for the gusset-type connection.

12
8

This symbol indicates the slope of the roof and is expressed as an 8/12 pitch.

width of beam
6″
4″
bird's-mouth seat cut
12″
2X12 rafters at 24″ o.c.
4′0″

8. Set the rafter in place at its permanent location at the end of the building, and block it temporarily to hold it in place. Set the rear half of the rafter in place on the outside of the beam at column line 3. Overlap the south beam and clamp it in place at the ridge. Mark the overlap at the ridge on both beams and mark the seat cut. Make the cuts and set the beam back into place to see if it fits. Once you have the pattern correct, do a production run and make the other eighteen rafters for the south side of the house. Before cutting, sight along the edge of rafters and make sure that the curvature (crown) is always to the top of the rafter. Do not use any which have extreme curvature or warpage. They can be cut in two and used on the back of the roof.

9. Mark the positions for the rafters on the bearing beams at column lines 1 and 2. It is important that the rafters are centered very accurately if you are using plywood roof sheathing. The overall length is 36 feet, and the rafters are to be placed at 2-foot centers. The end spacings will be less than 2 feet by one-half the width of a rafter (1 inch if you are using roughcut or ¾ inch for planed lumber).

10. Now set all of the front rafters in place, toe-nailing them to each bearing from both sides with 10d common nails.

11. Now move to the back of the house. The back rafters are offset by the thickness of a rafter so that they overlap the front rafters at the ridge. The starting rafter is set inside of the front rafter. If no carport is used, all of the rafters can be cut to the same pattern. If the carport is used, the rafters at the center of the house will be longer and have a second seat cut similar to the front rafters. You may want to finish enclosing the main house in a hurry and build the carport later. If necessary, the rafters can be spliced at column line 3.

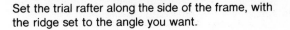

Set the trial rafter along the side of the frame, with the ridge set to the angle you want.

12. If you want to install the carport roof with the main roof, it will be necessary to set two posts and a beam for bearing. Since the loads are light, we used two 6X6 pressure-treated posts buried 4 feet in the ground. A beam of three 2X12s is set on top of the posts. Check to see that the beam is level and parallel to column line 3. Make a pattern for these longer rafters in similar fashion to the other rafters. Cut the rafters and set them in place.

Once you have the pattern for the roof rafters, do a production run.

Be sure to center the rafters accurately, then set them in place.

Run rafters from peak to eaves in the conventional way. This system does not require a ridge board but does require a solid connection between north and south rafters. On the first house shown, we used plywood gusset plates to make this connection.

Once the front rafters are in place, install the back rafters, offsetting at the ridge. These rafters were actually installed in one piece, but proved awkward to handle. See trial rafter diagram for the overlap detail.

13. After installing the roof section for the carport, continue installing the short rafters to the end of the house. Note that the last rafter overlaps the framing on the outside of the building. Take a scrap piece of rafter and make a seat cut for column line 3 and nail the block to the inside of this last rafter. The seat cut should be omitted in the rafter itself. By offsetting the rafters in this fashion, we make the ridge connection very easy.

If you have bad weather approaching, you will want to continue as rapidly as possible to enclose the roof. If not, I advise turning ahead in this chapter to the section on "Sidewall Framing" and framing up the sidewalls. It is much easier to install the top of the siding from inside the house than from a scaffold or ladder outside the house.

Back roof rafters, conventional framing.

If you put in your horizontal girts now and install siding you can use the inside of the girts as a ladder, and simply hang over the eaves to install siding and trim at the roof. This is essentially a technique for beginners, but can speed up the siding and trim for everyone.

If you do not install siding before the finish roof, your next operation will be to sheath the roof. Roofing boards used to be used for this, but are now so expensive that plywood makes more sense. If you can get 1X8 or 1X10 boards at salvage in good condition, I would highly recommend them instead of plywood. Install them on the diagonal for improved strength. This is very important, as the plywood on a steep roof considerably strengthens the structure. Individual boards placed at 90° to the rafters aren't very strong and should not be used.

Installing Plywood Sheathing

Before you start, check the plywood. It must say that it has exterior glue or you shouldn't use it. Exterior-grade plywood is better, but is quite expensive. The usual sheathing-grade plywoods are marked Interior/Exterior Glue. Even if put together with exterior glue, you shouldn't let the plywood get wet. Also, use solid lumber around the edges of your roof. Plywood tends to disintegrate when constantly exposed to the weather (at least the cheap grades used for sheathing do).

Before starting to install the plywood, the fascia boards should be installed. Install fascia board of the same depth as the roof rafters on the north and south sides (the 36-foot-long ones) of the house. Note that I cut the rafters at a very simple 90° on the ends. This not only looks better than the standard vertical fascia, but it makes cutting and fitting easier and allows you to use the same width roof trim all around the building. Rather than use the typical ½-inch or ¾-inch trim boards, I use regular 2-inch nominal framing lumber. This costs about the same as the higher grades of finish wood, but is heavier, more resistant to warpage, and looks better because of its extra thickness. On the sloping sides of the house (east and west) the fascia board should be blocked out with blocks made of 2-inch-thick lumber top and bottom so that it projects beyond the siding. Now we are ready to start installing the plywood.

Plywood should always be installed with the long dimension of the sheet spanning across the framing members. Since our basic house is 36 feet long, it will require 4½ sheets per row, if you use the conventional rafter layout. Always stagger the joints of any plywood sheathing. Cut the last sheet exactly in half and use the half-sheet to start the next course. Start and end the plywood at the ends of the basic house framing, leaving the tops of the fascia boards which we added exposed. If you are in a real hurry to get a roof over your heads, you can leave the east and west fascias off until you finish with the sheathing.

It is quite possible that your roof is slightly out of square or that even the plywood itself may not be cut accurately. Lay the first two rows of plywood cautiously, nailing only the corners without driving the nails home. This way if something doesn't fit, you can make adjustments without wasting expensive plywood. The most likely problem is that some of the roof rafters will be bowed so that the plywood seams don't land on a rafter. If you have just tacked the sheets, you can easily pull some nails and push the rafters into alignment.

Plywood is exceptionally weak at the long edges of the sheet. For maximum strength, when full bracing is required, install nailers between the rafters to support all edges of the plywood. This isn't necessary unless you are using the neoprene roofing system described in Chapter 15. For other roof finishes, I recommend plyclips, small H-shaped pieces of metal which slip over the adjacent edges of plywood sheets between supports to keep the sheets in alignment. After placing the first row of plywood, set a plyclip in place on the edge of the first row at each midpoint between the rafters (eighteen clips). When the second row of plywood is installed, the sheets are slipped into the clips, thereby preventing any tendency for the unsupported edges of the plywood to move up and down and damage roofing materials.

Finish laying the plywood for the south side of the roof. The plans show a full 4-foot by 8-foot skylight which saves one sheet of roof sheathing if you want to leave it out as you go. If you fill in the skylight space and plan to cut it out later, watch nails so that they won't be in the way of sawing the plywood.

After one side of the roof is finished, immediately nail the sheets at 8 inches on center over all supports, and cover with tar paper or 6-mil plastic sheeting. Plywood doesn't like rain and must be thoroughly protected. Temporary coverings have a marked tendency to blow off, and strips of lathing should be nailed around all edges of the roof to prevent wind from removing the material. Thin metal disks which act as washers under the nailheads to hold the tar paper in place are usually known as "Chinese money" or roof washers by lumberyards. They work very well out in the center of the roof, but not for holding the edges. If you are in a dry climate where rain is extremely unlikely, you can omit this step.

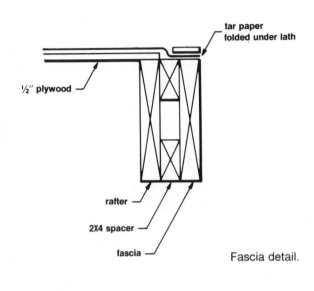

½" plywood

tar paper folded under lath

rafter

2X4 spacer

fascia

Fascia detail.

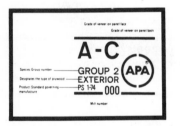

Typical sheathing-grade plywood.

Finishing the Roof Edges

Remember that you still have to add strips to the fascia boards to bring the tops flush with the plywood and to protect the edge grain of the plywood. Note that the strips on the north side have to be cut to different widths than at the east and west ends. This is because the framing is offset by one rafter to allow the rafters to overlap at the ridge. The north and south edges of the roof are trimmed with a ¾X¾-inch strip to cover the plywood edge and provide an extra projection so that water doesn't run down the fascia. For maximum durability, coat these strips and the fascia with clear Cuprinol before installing the strips. These strips can also be used quite effectively to tightly secure the edges of the tar paper if you have to use it as a temporary roof surface.

Stagger the joints in the plywood as it spans the rafters.

Half-lap the plywood.

Plyclips add strength to the edges that don't have nailers.

This photo by David Howard shows his preferred system of putting up the siding before enclosing the roof.

The fascia board is made of standard framing lumber.

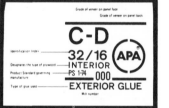

Typical finish plywood.

To make the main beams easier, I have designed them to be made up from standard framing lumber instead of heavy solid beams.

The procedure for this system is as follows:

Installation of Alternate Framing System

The system just described is very easy to install, but the long rafters on the south side command a steep price and the cost of the plywood roof sheathing is also substantial. In working on the Volkswagen house, which uses part of the same basic framing system, I looked for a way to reduce the costs of the premium-length rafters and eliminate the expensive plywood. Pole barns and prefabricated metal industrial buildings both use a V-ribbed galvanized roofing which is designed to serve as sheathing and roofing all in one. To use this system, one must run the roofing supports perpendicular to the pitch of the roof — this is the key to saving costs. Instead of nine support beams running the length of the house, I have four main supports running front to back. Instead of 10-foot and 22-foot rafters, all are a uniform 12 feet long. Except for the four main beams, everything is lighter and easier to handle.

1. Posts at column line 1 do not get beams placed on top of them (the first-floor section of column lines 2 and 3 and the balcony are framed exactly as before). The four posts along column line 1 on the first floor as well as the eight posts on column lines 2 and 3 on the second floor are made of three 2X6s, but the posts are turned 90° to those on the first floor so that they can be notched to receive the roof beams.

2. Set one row of posts in place temporarily to make a pattern. The row in this case is set from front to back. Let's start with posts b1, b2, b3 or column line c (these posts can be braced more securely than the end rows). To start, laminate two 2X6s together without driving the nails home. Leave the tops square-cut. Now set these three posts in place temporarily. Double- and triple-check them for accurate location and to be sure that they are plumb. These are going to be used as a pattern; a mistake could be costly.

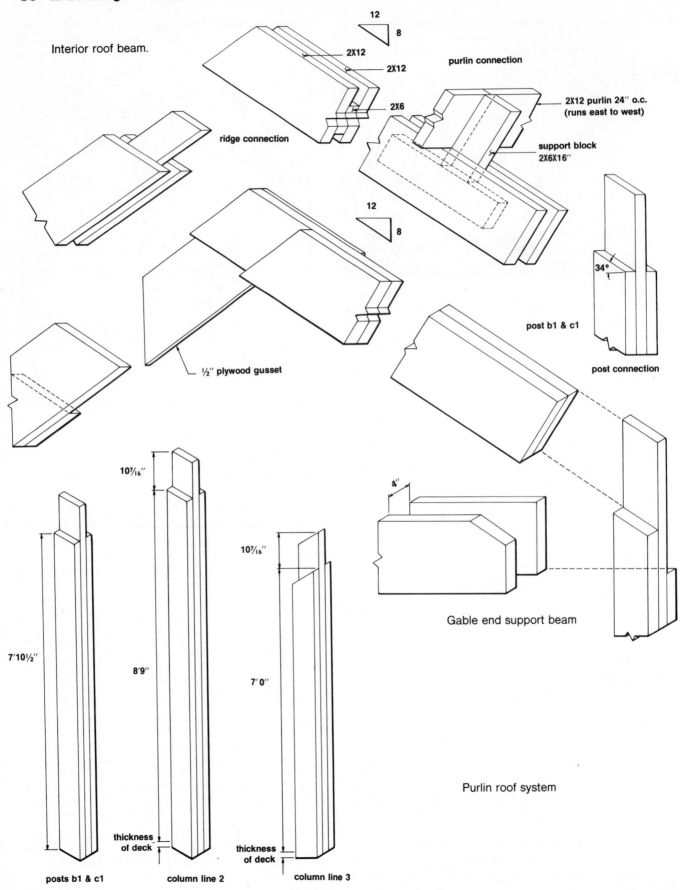

Interior roof beam.

2X12

2X12

2X6

ridge connection

purlin connection

2X12 purlin 24" o.c.
(runs east to west)

support block
2X6X16"

½" plywood gusset

post b1 & c1

34°

post connection

Gable end support beam

4"

Purlin roof system

10⁷⁄₁₆"

10⁷⁄₁₆"

7'10½"

8'9"

7'0"

thickness
of deck

thickness
of deck

posts b1 & c1

column line 2

column line 3

3. Take a 24-foot 2X12, two C clamps, and two blocks of wood. Mark the heights shown on the plans for the bottom of the beams on one side of the posts and stretch a chalk line along this line. Clamp temporary bearing blocks to the sides of the posts with the tops accurately aligned with the chalk line. Set the 2X12 in place and check the angle. Nail or clamp it temporarily in place. Mark the point where the top intersects the post with a pencil.

4. In similar fashion, set a 10-foot 2X12 at post b3. (If a carport or garage is desired, column line 4 must be set, and a 24-foot rafter is also used on this side. This portion is shown as an option in the working drawings in Part IV.) Establish the proper ridge point, and clamp the two beams together, letting them overlap at the ridge. Check very carefully to see that the front and rear roof slope are the same. It should be an 8/12 pitch. Double-check all heights and clearances.

5. Now mark the position of the rear 2X12 on post b3 and b4 if you have a carport/garage. Mark the overlap at the ridge. Mark the longest intersection for the front beam and the shortest for the rear beam as shown in the drawing. The center member of the beam will overlap and make a solid connection. Dismantle the beams and posts, leaving them in their relative positions and marking the pieces so that you know where they came from.

6. Now make up the remaining pieces. Twelve pieces of 2X6 are required for each row of posts. Cut six to the height of the chalk line and six to the height of the pencil mark. Assemble the posts. The posts at column lines a and d are made with two long pieces toward the ends of the building and one short piece on the inside face. The posts at column lines b and c are made with a long piece in the center flanked by a short piece on either side.

7. Set the posts permanently in place, checking that they are all plumb and parallel. Stretch strings along the bearing points for the main beams at lines 1, 2, and 3 to make sure that they are level. *Do not* make any adjustments to column line b; now shim or cut column lines a, c, and d if necessary to level bearing points. Do not worry about 1/4-inch variance from post to post. A large hump or a sag in the middle of the structure will be noticeable, particularly at the ridge, but an out-of-level condition from to back or end to end will not be noticeable; 1 1/2 inches should be maximum for a corner-to-corner variation. Of course, you would like to have the structure perfect, but sometimes you have to do the best you can. On this size house, this is a very reasonable tolerance.

8. Cut roof beams to the pattern. Prepare six 2X12s to the pattern for the south side of the roof. Nail a plywood gusset to the north end of two of them. Nail gussets on opposite sides. Set the two end beams in place with the gussets away from the inside of the house. These will be used to support the rear section of these beams. Measure the front overhang, and check the position of the ridge before spiking the beams to the posts. Tightly stretch a string between the bottom corners of the two end beams. This is your guide to make sure that all four main beams are in alignment. Now set the four center 2X12s, one at a time.

9. Repeat the operation, preparing the six pieces for the north side of the house. The two end beams are installed first, nailing the plywood gusset into the ridge end of the north-side beam.

10. Cut one end of a 4-foot-long piece of 2X10 to the same angle as the ridge splice. Nail it in place between the overhanging ends of the 2X12s so that it acts as a support for the north-side beams. Set the two remaining north-side beams, one piece at a time. Very thoroughly fasten all connections using exact size and number of fasteners shown on plans. Add a second layer to the beams at column lines a and d, overlapping the joint in the opposite direction. Set the second layer on the north side first, and let the south side butt the underside of it. Anchor this second layer with twelve 2 1/2-inch #8 lag bolts installed from outside.

11. Slip a 2X4 up into the hollow space between the 2X12s at column lines b and c. Slide it up so that it makes a 2-inch reveal to match the bottom of the 2X10 which we installed to lap the beams at the ridge. Nail very securely with 16d finish nails. This member adds considerably to the strength of these beams, so don't omit it.

We are now ready to install the roof rafters. Except that they are not called "rafters" in this case. When the supporting members are run perpendicular to the slope of the roof, they are called "purlins." Depending upon the climate where you're building, amount of insulation needed, and your budget, you can use 2X8s, 2X10s, or 2X12s for the purlins. Since they are all the same length and square-cut on the ends, they are quick and easy to install.

Starting at the ends of the overhangs, mark off 2-foot intervals for purlin spacing. The purlins over column lines b and c have a butt joint and will have a tendency to overturn, due to the force of gravity. The ends of the roof are held by the fascia board and don't need additional support. In this case, we put the slot between the 2X12s to work. Cut some short lengths of 2X6 scrap into 16-inch lengths. Slip them into the slot projecting at 90° to the slope of the roof, and nail securely with 16d finish nails, aligning them so that the bottom side (downroof face) of the purlins will rest on them. Now, install the purlins, spiking them into the top of each 2X12 member of the main beams. For more reinforcement in areas with heavy snow loads, see the working drawings in Part IV.

You are now ready to install ribbed metal roofing or plywood over the purlins. While this system is more difficult to describe and may sound more difficult than the standard framing system, it is actually much easier and less costly. In addition, we improve the insulation capabilities of the house by eliminating all heavy beams on the exterior. In this way, all portions of the exterior walls can be heavily insulated.

Sidewall Framing

Now that we have the roof on, we can tackle framing the walls. In the roof, we just turned rafters into purlins by changing direction. In the sidewalls, studs which run horizontally between posts are called "girts," again a term used in pole buildings and commercial construction. These are so easy as to require little explanation. If you've gotten this far successfully, you are almost home free.

The working drawings for the basic saltbox house show exact dimensions for the girts. They have been carefully spaced to allow standard 4X8 exterior sheathing to be anchored to them. They also permit quick, easy installation of vertical board siding inside and out and greatly increase fire safety and insulation effectiveness by creating a horizontal barrier every 2 feet. They are simply toe-nailed to the posts in horizontal position, measuring carefully so that your spacing is accurate. A 2X6 girt spans 12 feet nicely. Do not try to go further than that without a vertical member in the wall.

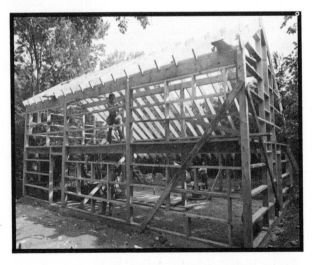

Toe-nail 12-foot 2X6s for horizontal girts.

If you change the window sizes and locations, make sure that you follow the same spacings for your girts. Chapter 12 shows how a window can be framed right into the girt system without wasteful double members.

Sheathing

The last operation of the framing is installing sheathing. Three materials are normally used: CDX-grade plywood, so-called "nailbase" insulating sheathing, and 1-inch tongue-and-groove blue Styrofoam insulating sheathing. The sheathing performs three functions.

First off, it braces the structure. Post and beam houses need a lot of bracing, and only plywood does this well. (Traditional post and beam houses have diagonal braces mortised and tenoned into all the connections; this is a prohibitively expensive solution.)

Second, sheathing provides extra insulation. Styrofoam is the winner here. It does so superbly, but is quite expensive. You may be gilding the lily. Plywood has little insulating value. Nailbase is made from asphalt-impregnated vegetable fibers (read cornstalks) and adds slightly to the wall's insulating value. Conventional builders use nailbase with plywood reinforcements at the corners.

Third, sheathing provides a weathertight base for siding. The Styrofoam is weathertight and the other two provide a base. Tar paper (added expense and time) needs to be used to ensure a weathertight wall over plywood or nailbase. Some people tape or caulk the joints between panels as a substitute for tar paper.

The ideal material has not as yet been developed. In Chapter 10, I explain that all sides of the house don't need the same degree of insulation or weather protection and that you should use different sheathings to suit the orientation of the particular face of your house. Since the south faces of my houses have very large glass areas, I recommend plywood for this side in all cases (a table in Chapter 10 gives recommendations for various winter conditions). One 4-foot-wide band of plywood set vertically at the corners will give very adequate bracing for our basic house. If you use all Styrofoam, use perforated steel braces which are sold to be used with the system. They are nailed diagonally across the framing members before the sheathing is installed.

Apply the plywood sheathing to the corners first to
brace the structure.

Chapter 9

Electrical Wiring and Plumbing Systems

These trades have a great deal in common. They use expensive raw materials which are potentially in short supply. The systems are usually installed in an inefficient manner, leaving considerable room for improvement. And both are expensive trades which are not all that difficult if you study them carefully. Even if you don't actually do the work, study the systems, and plan them as efficiently as possible.

Electrical Service

Your first task is to get power to your house. Underground main service lines are more aesthetically pleasing, but a good bit more expensive and waste energy. An overhead line, since it is surrounded by air, stays cooler and thus more efficient, so that a smaller wire size is required. Another reason that underground service is so costly is that the power companies usually make *you* buy the underground cable, while they furnish the overhead variety.

If an overhead service is used, locating the point of connection to your house can be a problem. Codes require a minimum of 14 feet under the cable so that vehicles can pass under it safely. Actually, the phone company gets mixed up in this one by requiring that their lines be 2 feet

away from the electric lines and insisting on putting their lines below the electric lines, reducing the actual clearance to 12 feet. If you go overhead, you will have to either attach the wire to the house high up on a gable end, or stick an ugly and expensive pipe mast up through the roof.

There can easily be a conflict. If the site dictates that the house be oriented a certain way to take advantage of the sun or for other reasons, there may be no tall portion of your house on the side nearest the power pole. If you have to set an extra pole (at your cost) or put a mast on the front of your house, it may make sense to use a direct-burial, underground cable.

Power company regulations concerning who pays for what poles and lines vary considerably. Some pay for no poles at all and will just wire to your house if it is close to the street or their source of power. More typically, they will set just one pole and bring the lines to your house, provided it is within a certain distance of their closest line. Treated poles 35 feet long (the minimum size required by most power companies) will cost several hundred dollars apiece. Prices vary quite a bit in different parts of the country, but they are expensive everywhere.

In addition to expenses for poles and/or lines, you will have to have a "temporary" service installed for construction and then dismantle that service and install the permanent one. Prewired poles are available for rent by electrical contractors. The alternative is to buy the materials for the temporary service and have the service installed on your own permanent pole. Then, when the house is nearly complete, you have to dismantle the temporary service and move it to the house; a wasteful procedure. The small panel used for temporary service must be discarded; sometimes it can be sold. An electrical inspection is required for the temporary service before the power company will connect it. This can take several weeks.

The attractive alternative to these wasteful practices is called a trailer service and is intended for use with house trailers. In installation, the meter socket and main disconnect switch are permanently mounted on the pole, and a cable is run back up the pole and then through the air to the house. The power company may not like it, but there's nothing to prevent you from saying you are going to put in a trailer and then changing your mind.

Officials of our local power company actually pointed out this loophole to me. One of my clients had a driveway of insufficient width to meet power company requirements for them to run the cable all of the way to the house (most companies require 20 feet minimum width). The power company suggested that we have a pole installed with a trailer service and then run our own cable to the house.

You can also sidestep the required inspection of the house by putting in a trailer service. In the case of a temporary service, the power company will require that the building have two more inspections, one of the rough wiring and another of the completed job, before they make final connections. If a trailer service is installed, they consider you finished after the service is inspected. *Note:* I definitely do not recommend that you avoid inspection if you do your own work, but since it is not required, you could have your work checked by a reputable electrician instead of the electrical inspector. Or if you hire an electrician to do your work, you can eliminate some of the wasteful extravagances required by the code, provided you can make him understand the economies which you wish to make.

Planning the Electrical System

Before starting to plan your system, read H. P. Rictor's *Wiring Simplified,* the generally accepted bible. Most lumberyards and large electrical sup-

Some codes will insist upon a "correct" number of outlets. For walls with large areas of glass, a floor outlet may be the answer.

ply houses will have it. It describes the requirements of the National Electric Code which is universally used. Sears' *Electric Wiring Handbook* is also a fine reference.

Unfortunately, the code was sponsored by the big power companies and is left over from the "more is better" era. Based upon the theory that the average household will have hundreds of plug-in gadgets and lights, the code requires an excessive number of outlets and dictates the maximum spacing. You are even required to put outlets in unlikely places such as along a full-length glass wall where there is no space for them (they make you install them in the floor). A 60-ampere main service used to be considered adequate, then 100-amp, now 200-amp. For a careful, energy-conserving household, a 30-amp service would probably be more than adequate. Most places will require a minimum of a 100-amp service; others require bigger services, and of course if you have any major items with resistance heat, you should install the larger size. Bear in mind that the wire size and panel costs increase considerably as the capacity is raised. Be wary of power companies who require an extra-large service if *any* electrical heating devices are installed. It may be that you will want to wire for the devices, but install them later, after the electrical inspection.

When planning your house try to avoid electrical devices with resistance heaters or large compressor loads. These include electric ranges (most professional cooks use gas), electric water heaters (somewhat like trying to heat water with a candle), electric clothes dryers (use sun, gas, or a Laundromat), central air conditioners (use fans, ventilation, a gas-powered chiller, or high-efficiency, portable units). In some areas of the country, central electric air conditioning or a heat pump may be the best solution. In this case, you will need to have a larger service. A 100-amp service will do nicely for our basic saltbox, but the regulations will assume that you have many energy wasters and you may have to install at least a 200-amp service.

The location of the service panel within the house is very important. It should be as centrally located as possible to minimize lengths of wiring runs. It should also be easy to get to in case of an emergency. In case of fire, it should be located near an exit so that the main switch can be tripped on the way out of the house. The code is strict about the distance of the panel from the outside wall: if it is further away than 6 feet, you have to install an extra main breaker. This is a very silly provision, and can be troublesome if you are on a tight budget.

After determining the location of your main panel, lay out electrical outlets (receptacles) where you think they will be of most use to you. Then add enough extra outlets to meet code provisions — (one per wall minimum, no more than 10 feet apart or 3 feet from an opening. The code and good practice dictate a separate circuit for heavy current users such as refrigerators or freezers, and any 220-volt devices will require separate circuits. The kitchen must have at least two circuits feeding wall outlets in addition to the refrigerator outlet.

An excellent recent code provision requires ground-fault protective breakers for all wet areas and all outside outlets (The code doesn't require outside outlets — yet.) A maximum of ten outlets (eight is better practice) may be connected to a standard 20-amp breaker using #12 wire. A standard 100-amp panel has spaces for twenty of these breakers; 220-amp, 2-pole breakers use up two spaces. Use #12 wire with a ground rather than the usual #14. It is slightly more expensive, but not significantly so, and — more important — #12 has less current drop and will make your appliances work at peak efficiency. You are also allowed more outlets per circuit when you use the heavier wire.

Try to make your electric runs within the core of

the house; avoid putting wires through the outside wall as is common practice. My suggested layout on the standard saltbox plans is designed to keep all wiring out of the exterior walls. The only exceptions are the main service cable and wiring for outside lights and outlets. Raceways are shown for the few areas where outlets are required by code to be in the exterior walls.

Indoor Lighting

The codes are much less restrictive on number and placement of lighting fixtures than outlet placement. Ceiling fixtures usually give off very poor-quality light and should generally be avoided. Recessed lighting fixtures are a particularly inefficient light source. All advantages of the reflectivity of the ceiling surface are lost by burying the light source, and recessed fixtures are fire hazards when installed in an insulated ceiling. Even in an uninsulated space, heat buildup shortens bulb life considerably. Finally, you are wasting money on a tin box with reflectors which wouldn't be necessary in a surface light. When

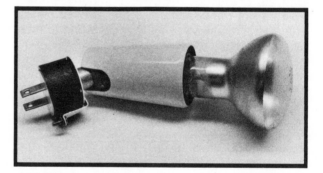

For recessed or spot lighting, the Par bulb gives most efficient lighting.

you do use a fixture where the bulb is recessed into the housing, buy a type which uses an efficient Par-type reflector bulb (similar to an automobile headlight).

My favorite lights are very inexpensive, and employ simple, white, porcelain sockets with globe bulbs. If these are placed so that they can reflect light from two adjacent walls and the ceiling, they will supply over double the light of a recessed fixture of the same wattage.

A large-size, 60-watt Globelite bulb, made by Duro-Lite Lamps Inc.,† has low surface bright-

---

†The address of this and other manufacturers and associations so indicated will be found under "Addresses of Manufacturers and Associations" in Part IV.

ness and less heat buildup than conventional bulbs. It is more expensive initially, but also lasts longer because it runs cooler. For people who don't like the appearance of the porcelain socket, Lightolier makes a simple, inexpensive socket in chrome (cat. no. 40847) or in brass (cat. no. 40818). Another favorite low-brightness bulb which can be used exposed is the tubular appliance light. They come in 25- and 40-watt sizes in

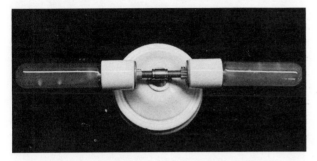

Tubular appliance light and double-ended socket.

clear, frosted, and white. An elegant, double-ended socket permits these bulbs to be used exposed and look quite handsome. They are a good alternative to fluorescent lights for people who don't like fluorescents but still want to conserve energy in lighting.

Efficient Light Bulbs

The standard 40-watt fluorescent bulb is the most efficient, readily available light bulb. It produces just about the same light output as a standard 100-watt incandescent bulb. Do not even consider buying the cool white or daylight bulbs. Numerous scientific studies have shown that these bulbs are deficient in areas of the light spectrum which are vital to one's health.* When ordering standard bulbs, buy warm white or deluxe warm white bulbs. One expensive bulb, Vita Lite, made by Duro-Test Corp.† and Duro-Test Electric Ltd.†, comes very close to duplicating the effects of sunlight; it is much more effective than the common gro-lites and is also reputed to be quite beneficial to health. It is widely used in hospitals and places where exact color rendition is necessary. The diagrams show the relative spectrum outputs for three types of light.

The same company is just completing a new production facility for manufacturing a spectacularly efficient incandescent bulb, the Duro-Test low energy bulb. This bulb has a special inside coating which bounces heat back to the filament of

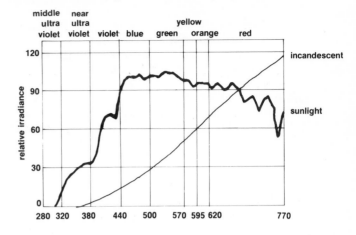

Incandescent light vs. sunlight.

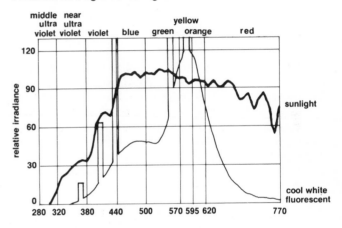

Cool white fluorescent light vs. sunlight.

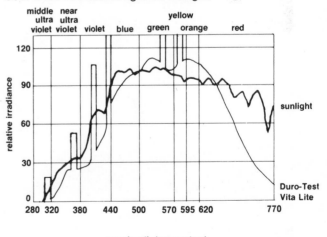

Duro-Test Vita Lite vs. sunlight.

the bulb, increasing its efficiency and length of life so much that 100 watts of light output are achieved from only 40 watts of power input. The

*Richard J. Wurtman, "The Effects of Light on the Human Body," *Scientific American,* July 1975.

bulb requires very exotic technology to produce and has been regarded as impractical by General Electric and Westinghouse who together make almost three-quarters of the light bulbs in this country. Since they also make various sorts of generating plants, they have little incentive to make efficient light bulbs. General Electric once did some widely publicized research into reducing the life expectancy of its flashlight bulbs because they lasted longer than the batteries.

The Duro-Test low energy bulb is initially only manufactured in the one 40/100-watt size and is sold at a premium price. It is well worth the extra cost in energy savings, and will be particularly useful if you are planning an alternate energy source for your house.

Lamps

Do not overlight! Our houses and buildings tend to be very greatly overlighted, a carry-over from days of endless cheap power. It is much better to have soft, overall lighting with an adjustable source directly over your work area. Even local light sources have widely differing efficiencies. For instance, a table lamp with a 150-watt incandescent bulb produces slightly less light on the work surface than does an adjustable fluorescent with two 15-watt bulbs. A hanging light with a reflector over a dining table gives much better lighting than a chandelier which wastes light by throwing it in all directions. Lamps also can be

A hanging light with a reflector can utilize a low-watt bulb to great effect.

A low-watt bulb gives good light with the Prestolite lamp.

versatile and provide light at different locations, saving on expensive permanent wiring. The Prestolite lamp (made by the Prestolite Co.[†]) shown here uses only a 40-watt bulb, yet gives plenty of light for reading. It has a keyhole slot on the back so that it can be easily moved.

Closet lights are required by code to be enclosed and recessed for safety. This can make them expensive. The code doesn't say that you have to have closet lights, though. The easy solution is to use full-height doors so that the room light lights the closet. Every extra electric outlet saved is money in your pocket.

Outdoor Lighting

You have seen the jump in efficiency between fluorescent and incandescent lighting. Mercury-vapor lights are a similar improvement over fluorescent, and sodium-vapor is yet another step up the ladder. Expense rises with efficiency. A 250-watt mercury-vapor light costs about $40. A 70-watt sodium-vapor light which gives much more light is over $100. If you have a small area to light and use the light sparingly, a standard 75- or 150-watt floodlight will give plenty of light and can be used in a swivel socket, the whole setup costing about $15. Of course, if you plan to light a wide area or need to leave the light on for long periods, the mercury or sodium lights may be a good buy.

Wiring Tips

H. P. Rictor's *Wiring Simplified* and Sears' *Simplified Electrical Wiring* (34 G 5428) give specific requirements and general directions for wiring your house. These are quite detailed and generally self-explanatory. Over the years, I have picked up several special techniques which are worth sharing.

The old-fashioned, pot-metal outlet boxes with the rattling clamps inside are a disaster. Use the new plastic ones. Make sure that you get Slater S-18r boxes. These are perfect rectangles, making cutting finish materials to fit quicker and easier. They have built-in nails for attaching to studs, and, finally, they have marks on the side so that you can make them project from the wall just the right amount to be flush with the finish wall surface. Electricians are very sloppy when they install boxes.

Buy good professional tools for stripping wires. You will need a squeeze-type cable sheathing stripper, and a good, automatic-type wire stripper. This tool is a bit expensive, but vital for the beginner since it not only cuts the insulation but removes it from the wire, all in one quick operation. It also has a gauge so that you can strip to the same length each time.

I recommend that beginners use screw terminals and push-in connections wherever possible. Loose connections can cause arcing and start a fire. Switches and receptacles are available with clamp-type connections — there is a hole in the back, and you simply strip the wire and push it into the hole. In the olden days of high quality, electricians joining two wires twisted them together, soldered the connection, and covered the joint with a layer of rubber tape topped off with friction tape. Nowadays, a plastic "wire nut" with inside threads is used. You have to have a bit of practice to twist several wires together and make them hold securely. If the connections are not secure, you could start a fire. Practice carefully on some scrap wire before starting the final connections. Better still, use the screw terminal wire nut shown in the picture. It makes a perfectly tight connection like the solder joints of the past.

Take your time and do a neat, professional-looking job. Even though the wires don't show, the electrical inspector will be skeptical if your work looks messy. Finally, take the cover to your electric panel home and put it under lock and key. A fairly long period of time elapses between initial installation of the panel and final installation of

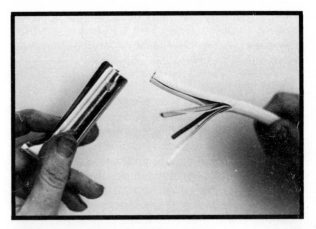

Squeeze-type cable sheathing stripper.

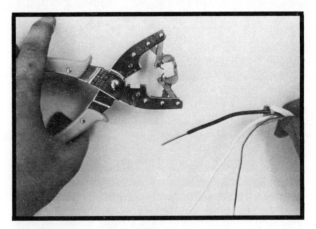

These automatic wire strippers clean wire in one movement.

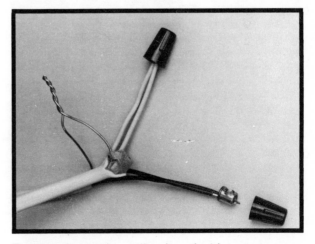

The two-piece "wire nut" makes electric connections quick and simple.

the cover. Covers are not very big and tend to get thrown out with the trash. They are *not* available separately from the panel except as a very special-order item (figure six months to a year waiting time). If your electrical inspector is a real stickler, he may not sign off your job until the cover is in place. One client had to buy a whole new panel just to get the cover so that he could move into his new house.

Rough Wiring

Begin your rough wiring by mounting the main service panel. If you have located it within 6 feet of the outside wall where your service enters the house, it will contain the main breaker for the house. If you are remote from the outside wall, you will have to install a separate main breaker near the point where the cable enters the house. Before you mount the panel, reinforce the wall so that the panel can be securely mounted in place.

Study your circuits carefully so that you know where to remove the knockout plugs from the panel. Most panels have the knockouts on all sides to provide maximum flexibility. The large feeder cables are designed for top or top/side entry. You will find concentric knockout rings at these locations. Remove them one at a time, starting with the smallest, until you have the required size for your cable. These are tough steel and difficult to remove. It is easy to lose your temper and knock out too many of the concentric rings. The electric codes require that all openings in the panel be blocked. If you make a hole you don't use, you will have to buy a special cover to close the hole to pass inspection.

Well-designed boxes make wiring quicker and safer. This is a Slater S-18r.

Wires entering and leaving the box must be clamped tightly and have a bushing to protect them from metal edges. Formerly, this was done with cumbersome, screw-type clamps. Plastic squeeze-lock connectors have largely replaced these. For safety, the code requires that wires be stapled in place at the ends of a run where they enter a box. If they are not run through a stud at 24-inch intervals, they must also have intermediate staples. Previous codes required metal clamps in the outlet boxes. Now a staple just outside the box is acceptable.

Before inserting wires in any of the boxes, strip off the outside sheathing so that it will just enter the box. About 3 inches of wire are left projecting out of the front of the box. When all wires are installed, the wires are loosely rolled and pushed into the box. The main service cable should be connected from the meter socket to the main panel (most power companies furnish the socket for their meter). The cables for low-amp service are fairly light and easy to handle. For larger services, they are stiff and very difficult to bend. Make sure that your cables are positioned so that they make a straight run into the lugs on the panel and meter, especially if the service is larger than 100 amps. Nothing is quite so impossible for the amateur as to try to make a 90° bend in a 2/0 heavy cable and then try to coax it into a screw terminal.

The main service requires a ground rod or grounding to a cold-water pipe if you have an underground metal pipe service (not as common as they once were). Standard ground rods are 6 feet long and are supposed to be driven at least 4 feet into the ground. If you have bedrock, a hole must be drilled in the rock.

For our simple saltbox house, I have shown a basic wiring layout which shows how a 100-amp service should be installed and how the circuits can be installed in the most economical manner. Use it only as a guide, as everyone will have different electrical needs and should draw up their own requirements. This layout is designed to meet the 1978 edition of the National Electric Code. Some localities and power companies add their own requirements to the code. Check before starting work.

Finish Wiring

The purpose of the rough wiring inspection is to approve wiring so that walls can be enclosed. Most commercial electrical contractors don't return to the job until all of the interior wall finishes are in place. I strongly recommend that the beginner immediately proceed with finish wiring, except for installation of fixtures. In this way, he or she can see all wires and trace them down if there are any conflicts. You can find out in a hurry if you left anything out. Also, if you wait a couple of months, it is very hard to remember where wires go and how you intended to connect them.

When executing the finish wiring be very careful that you never interrupt the white wire. It is the ground and your protection. Be careful not to reverse the polarity of the wires. Outlets are easy to wire, as they are always marked "black" and "white." Switches for fixtures, if wired in the usual fashion, require careful connection. Usually the feed wire is taken to the light socket and then a two-conductor wire is run back down the wall to the light switch, in effect breaking the connection of the black wire to the fixture. To keep the color coding correct, a piece of wire with two black conductors should be used for this purpose. Since standard cable is colored one black and one white, make do by connecting the black feed wire to the white switch leg wire. Then at the switch, connect the white wire to the incoming leg and the black wire to the outgoing leg or "On" terminal. Back at the fixture, connect the black and white wires as usual.

An alternate and sometimes more efficient (and rarely used) method of switching the fixture is simpler and much easier for the beginner to understand. If the switch is placed so that it is in the path of the feed from the panel to the light fixture, the cable can be run through the switch box, breaking only the black wire at the switch. This is theoretical since it is a bit awkward to do physically unless the fixture is very close to the switch. This method is good for lights very close to the panel and for the last light in a circuit. Remember that you are connecting the wires in the fixture box to a switch directly, so you can't use them as a junction box except for other lights that are to be controlled by the same switch.

Relays

Lights which are controlled from several locations or from a very remote location waste a lot of wire and are quite expensive. Three-way (control from two locations) and four-way (control from three locations) switches are difficult for the beginner to wire. Low-voltage relays which greatly simplify the wiring are a good solution. The relay is mounted at the fixture to be switched, and light-gauge bell wire with two conductors is run to any number of remote points.

The same basic idea is available in a wireless system. A small console controls and dims lights and appliances at up to sixteen locations. A separate remote control can operate the main control from 30 feet away with no wires. This unit will allow you to eliminate switches from exterior lights and control them from one or two variable points within the house. The device is manufac-

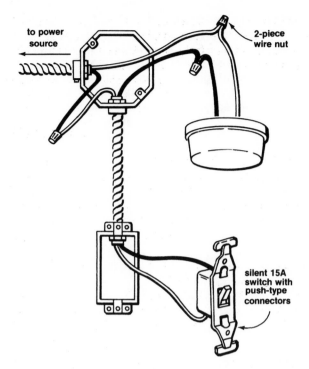

Wiring a light switch — standard method.

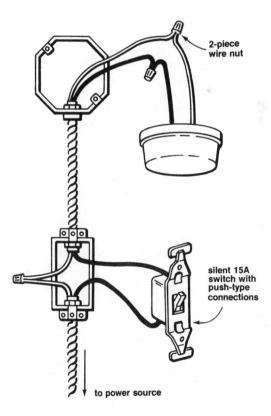

Wiring a light switch — alternate method for a light at the end of a circuit.

tured by Potter-Bromfield and sold under various trade names. Sears markets one of the systems; cost is about $100 for a master unit and four remote stations. If you are doing your own wiring on a tight budget, the cost might be a bit steep. However, if you hire an electrician or the outside lights are really remote, you would save money.

Safety Equipment

As I mentioned, the code will require ground-fault protection on all circuits feeding potentially wet areas. It will also require at least one smoke detector. I recommend one for each level of your house. Honeywell makes the best units that I have seen. Buy a combination smoke and heat-rise detector and get an electrically operated unit with a battery backup. These are the most expensive, but well worth it.

If you use bottled (propane) gas, install a leak detector. Propane is very heavy, and a leak builds up rapidly. This is why there are regulations against enclosing propane tanks. Natural gas isn't nearly as dangerous, but a detector is still worth consideration. They cost about $30.

Checkup

When planning your electrical outlets, rethink your plans carefully. This is the last opportunity that you will have to make any changes economically. Walk through the house and mentally open each door. Which way does it swing or slide, and where do you turn on the light? Where are you putting major heavy pieces of furniture? Will the outlet be buried behind the furniture? Mark all proposed locations for wall and ceiling outlets on the framing. Now, go back and count them. Do you really need that many? Think of the outlets as $25 to $35 each (the amount an electrical contractor charges) or $10 (your materials cost), and see if you still want the same number. Remember that the code mandates many of them. Most lights and switches are at your discretion, though.

Planning the Plumbing System

Plumbing is much easier than the electrical work, since it isn't spread out all over the house. At least it shouldn't be if you do a good job planning. The standard materials for a plumbing system these days are copper supply pipes and PVC (white or beige) and ABS (black) plastic waste

pipes. Since copper is in critical supply and getting more expensive by the day and plastic is petroleum-based, it will pay to make the plumbing system as small and compact as possible and still meet code and bank requirements.

Unlike the electrical codes which are standardized with local modifications, plumbing codes are a jungle. If you are in a big city where unions helped write the code, you might be required to use lead and cast-iron waste pipes and threaded brass supply piping. The more outlandish codes are widely ignored because of the impossible costs of meeting them. I have included two detailed plumbing layouts for the basic saltbox

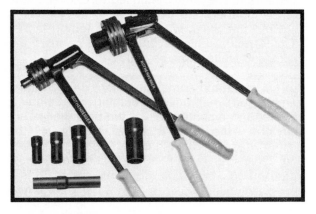

The Rothenberger expanding tool.

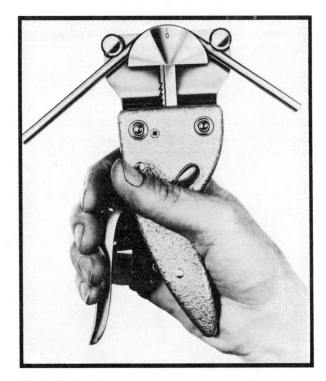

Hand pipe bender.

house. One shows a fairly conventional plumbing layout with two water-saving flush toilets, automatic washer, and space for an additional half-bath if required. This layout should meet all but the most unreasonable regulations. All fixtures are placed back-to-back around a center core which lines up from floor to floor. Every possible economy has been made to allow the least amount of expensive materials to be used in this system.

The alternate system assumes that you have maximum leeway in the design and execution of your system. I show a Clivus Multrum and a minimum piping system with a small drain field for the greywater. Both systems show an alternate solar water-heating system.

If you design your own system, keep the layout as compact as possible. Start the layout from the point where piping leaves the pressure tank or where it enters the house if you don't have a pressure tank. Install a valve and a main drain with provisions for draining the water out of the house. Now, gradually slope all piping upward from this low point. Avoid low spots which can trap water.

This layout gives you the option of quickly and easily draining the pipes in winter. If you go away

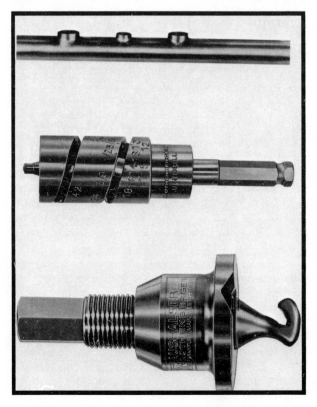

Tee cutter.

for a period of time, you won't need to depend upon an automatic heating system or expensive electric heat to keep pipes from freezing. Turning just two valves will do the trick. Traps must also be drained or filled with antifreeze. Even if you don't design or install your own system, have your plumber follow these simple procedures for your protection.

Materials

All plumbing supplies are expensive. While nothing you do can reduce the prices, it is possible to reduce the amount of costly raw material actually used. A compact basic layout results in further savings in materials by reducing pipe size. Current piping systems are sized larger than necessary. Ironically, many locations require flow control devices to be installed at the fixtures to cut down the rate of flow. The same thing can be accomplished by using smaller-size pipe, saving quite a bit of copper and money. For most applications, ⅜-inch copper tubing will work as well as ½-inch, particularly if you eliminate automatic water-using gadgets.

However, do not reduce the size of the supply to the hot-water heater. The hot water has to travel much further as it goes into the tank and then back to the point of use. This is particularly true of the roof-mounted solar water heater. My piping diagrams show where different sizes should be used. Follow them carefully.

In addition to saving money by reducing the size, switch from rigid copper piping to flexible copper tubing. By doing this, you can eliminate most of the expensive, troublesome fittings which have to be sweated together and are potential leak points. Since the fittings are subject to considerable stress, they are heavier and hence more expensive than regular piping. Tubing is regularly used for these applications in other countries where plumbers eliminate expensive couplings by expanding one end of the tubing and inserting another piece of tubing into it. Expander tools and lightweight tees for this system are available from the Rothenberger System.† A tubing bender is also necessary; it will prevent the tubing from flattening out as it is bent. In case your code prohibits the use of flexible tubing, regular rigid tubing can also be bent with a tubing bender and expanded as described. I know of no code which would prohibit this procedure.

Do not reduce the size of your piping if your area has exceptionally hard water; the minerals in hard water tend to build up sediment in the piping. In this case, use ½-inch tubing, with ¾-inch for the supply to the hot-water heater. By reducing the piping size, switching to flexible tubing, and eliminating most fittings, you can reduce the amount of copper used by more than 40 percent, a significant amount, as copper gets more expensive by the day.

Plastic drainage piping has virtually displaced all other materials for waste piping because it is so

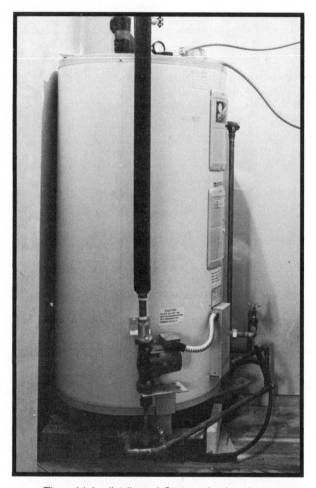

The widely distributed State solar heating system is the basic source of hot water for the Prices of Ann Arbor, Michigan. Here you see the hot-water storage tank and the roof collector.

easily installed. While there is no current shortage, prices are rising due to the oil content of the pipes. If you use a composting toilet or privy, the waste system becomes much simpler and expensive 3-inch waste lines can be eliminated. In fact, if you eliminate automatic machines which discharge water rapidly, you could use a 1-inch-diameter waste line quite satisfactorily. Of course, your local plumbing inspector will have heart failure, and you can only do this if you aren't supervised by a code.

Whether or not you are supervised by a code, all drainage systems require traps and venting for proper operation. Most traps are designed to be connected to 1½-inch pipe, so it isn't a good idea to reduce below this size. See my piping diagram in the working drawings for proper venting connections. The vents are designed to relieve atmospheric pressure on the system; you have to punch two holes in a can of liquid to be able to pour it properly for the same reason. The vent also discharges sewer gases. Notice that I have increased the pipe size to 3 inches at the roof, even on the minimal system. This is necessary because vapors will tend to freeze above the roof in cold weather and can sometimes clog a small pipe. Also, most standard roof flashings are made for 3-inch pipe.

Alternate Materials

Copper and oil shortages may become serious enough to force you to find alternate materials for supply and waste piping. None of the alternatives are easy, but they do exist and materials are readily available. Before the use of copper and plastic, galvanized steel and cast-iron piping were commonly used. Galvanized steel pipe is used for supply piping and for 1½-inch runs to the main vent stack. Connections are made by laboriously cutting and threading piping to the exact lengths required. Assembly requires starting at one end of a system and moving to the other. A union has to be used any place where the piping must be disconnected.

Cast-iron waste piping used to be a nightmare requiring tamping hub-type joints with oakum and pouring molten lead into the joints. New cast-iron piping systems use a simple neoprene gasket. Cast-iron pipes still must be cut to length which is difficult and requires a special tool which can be rented if necessary. These materials are difficult to use and are probably best left to professionals, if indeed you can find professionals who can still use them.

An alternative which *is* very much within the range of skills of the beginner is to use salvaged copper pipe. Normally, this stuff is sold for scrap because it is in short lengths and usually has all sorts of fittings soldered to it. The tubing expander which I mentioned earlier is the key to using this pipe. Wherever practical, heat the pipe, remove the fittings, and reuse them, particularly the tees. Then take the remaining pieces and connect them by expanding the ends. Leftover fittings can be sold for scrap. Use a tubing bender for bends, and avoid having to clean and trying to reuse the ells. Flexible copper tubing is much easier and quicker, but you may not be able to buy it.

Hot-Water Heaters

With a well-insulated house which requires a minimum quantity of heat, you can wind up paying almost half of your utility bill for hot water, particularly if you have an electric hot-water heater. True, your bill may not be high, but it is still possible to reduce it. Dishwashers and automatic washing machines require 160°F. hot water; for other uses, 120°F. water is satisfactory. It may be desirable to eliminate the machines or install a demand-type booster heater right at the machine. That way, you are not overheating a large tank of water for occasional use by these machines.

The basic saltbox is designed to use standard, commercially available solar collectors* on the south face of the chimney. These systems are expensive, but the federal tax credit makes them worth serious consideration. The breadbox-design, direct solar water heater shown in the working drawings is ideal for this location, but the tax credit would probably be disallowed if the government checked up on you. They only like expensive, gadget-ridden solutions.

Take a good, careful look at this heater design. It has other applications. The basic reason for the horizontal double-tank design is to make most efficient use of the limited amounts of heat which can be captured from the sun by this unit. If you are in an area where electricity is your only practical hot-water source, this design is much more efficient than most commercial heaters. The horizontal tanks do not stratify as much as vertical tanks, allowing you to draw more hot water from

the same size tank. The additional tank and the special piping system prevent the rapid cooling of the hot water from incoming cold water.

The tank can be located at the back of the balcony above the second floor in the same location as I show the storage tank for the commercial solar system. Do-it-yourselfers can assemble one of these tanks from standard parts available at wholesale plumbing supply dealers for less than the cost of one of the so-called "energy-saving" water heaters now available. As a bonus, you get more hot water at less cost. Buy the low-density, high-efficiency, screw-in-type heating elements, and put one near the outlet of each tank. Set the temperature control for the input tank about 6°F. lower than the output tank so that it will work as a preheater. Insulate with 12 inches of fiberglass or its equivalent on all sides.

In summary, I strongly recommend the breadbox heater design as it uses the least amount of critical materials and will be very durable. If you use a commercial system, make sure you buy from a well-established dealer and get a guarantee for at least five years. The electric heater is a good compromise and can be used as a backup storage tank for a nonfreeze-protected collector system. Much of the complexity of the commercial systems involves heat exchangers and freeze-proof loops. By combining the two systems, you simply shut down and drain the collector in freezing weather, avoiding the use of potentially dangerous chemical solutions and inefficient heat exchangers.

Sprinkler Systems

No, this is not something to keep the grass green, but a very serious and thoroughly effective means of fire protection. Sprinkler systems are widely used in commercial buildings, almost never in private houses even though insurance companies grant substantial discounts to buildings with sprinkler systems. But as of this writing, not one occupant death due to fire has been recorded in a building with a functioning sprinkler system. If you are quite remote from a fire station, the insurance savings could pay for the system in just a few years, and you might even consider eliminating the fire insurance completely. Most of the damage to your house would be water damage to the contents if a fire did start.

---

*A list of recommended manufacturers will be found under "Recommended Efficient Appliances and Equipment for Energy-Saving Houses" in Part IV.

Sprinkler systems require rows of piping with sprinkler heads mounted at intervals. Our basic house is ideal for a sprinkler system, and I show an approved one on the working drawings as an incentive for you to install it. The sprinkler system requires a 120-gallon storage tank at the top of the house: use the one installed for the hot-water heater. The interconnection is tricky and slightly complicated because the sprinkler piping should be protected with antifreeze — it is not an installation for an amateur. At the very least, it should be made under the supervision of a trained sprinkler system installer. A similar-size system cost some neighbors about $2,000, including the tank.

Plumbing Fixtures

Used fixtures are an excellent idea if you can find what you want at a reasonable price. They are becoming increasingly popular and more expensive. I covered them thoroughly in *30 Energy-Efficient Houses.*

New fixtures are very expensive. Kohler, Crane, and American Standard are top-of-the-line and quite expensive, particularly Kohler. Buy them used unless you are a real stickler for design and quality. Sears and Gerber offer very low-cost fixtures of reasonable quality. My favorite low-cost fixture is an elegant little slab sink from Sears which costs less than $20. Sears faucets are very ugly. Gerber makes decent-quality, inoffensive-looking faucets. Sterling Faucet Co. of Morgantown, West Virginia, sells nationally distributed, well-designed faucets at a reasonable cost. Speakman is the quality line in standard faucets, Delta in the lever-type, single-control models.

Piping Installation

Sears' booklet *Plumbing Planning and Installing* (42 G 9997) which I recommend highly, tells you almost everything you could want to know. Here are a few special tips not found in the manuals. First, never assemble anything until you have completed cutting and fitting the entire system. Let it sit for a few days and wait until you have all of your fixtures before soldering the copper or solvent-welding the drain lines. Make all piping cuts square and neat; file all burrs off both the inside and outside of the piping. Use a tubing cutter for copper and a fine-toothed handsaw for plastic. Thoroughly clean both mating surfaces of the piping with emery cloth, and apply flux or plastic pipe cleaner. Don't handle the joint. Grease or oil from your fingers may cause an area not to bond. Assemble the pipes with a twisting motion to coat both surfaces evenly. Use a Mapp gas torch rather than the conventional propane torch for a hotter flame and perfect joints in copper pipe; wipe excess solder off quickly.

If you take your time and clean everything carefully, you are unlikely to have any leaks and can be very proud of your job. Sometimes leaks take a while to show up. On commercial jobs, plumbers use a pressure test. On a home system, you can reset your pump pressure switch a bit higher than normal (no more than 10 pounds or you may damage something). Run the water to start the pump, and close the faucets so maximum pressure is obtained. Do this at the beginning of the day, *not* at the end. Never leave a newly installed system pressurized overnight. You may find a leak the hard way.

Chapter 10

Insulation and
Weathersealing

Insulation has become one of the biggest consumer hypes ever. Since the passage of insulation tax credits, the country has been overrun with sleazy salesmen playing every con game in the book to fleece the public. There is now a bewildering array of insulating materials on the market. None of the products available are perfect, no matter what you may be told. Every major insulation material has some serious drawback, and those with the highest insulating value have the most serious drawbacks. Conflicting claims and an almost total lack of official standards makes buying insulation a nightmare. Study this chapter carefully so that you know how much insulation to use and where to use it.

Proper insulation is vital for using natural forces to temper a house instead of depending upon large quantities of fossil fuels. Many firms use tricky figures to estimate a "payback" period which is the theoretical period in which you offset the extra costs of insulation by a saving in fuel costs. Since fuel costs are impossible to predict accurately, this is nonsense. Obviously, as time goes on, there will be less and less fuel available at higher and higher prices. It certainly will pay you to use the maximum amount of insulation which you can afford.

Factors to Consider

There are three very important factors to consider when deciding how much insulation you need. These are where you live, which way your house faces, and the actual part of the structure to which you are applying the insulation.

Where you live determines the climate which is basic to your insulation calculations. Unless you are lucky enough to live in a climate which is temperate year-round, such as southern California or Hawaii, you should use a minimum of insulation as follows: walls and floors, R-20; roofs, R-30. The R value is the resistance to heat flow of a given material and is widely cited in insulation ads. For instance, fiberglass, the most common insulation, has an R value of 3.5 per inch, giving it a theoretical value of 19 for standard 6-inch batts ("6-inch" batts are only 5½ inches thick). I say "theoretical," because the actual installed values of insulation rarely, if ever, work out to agree with engineer's calculations.

A second major factor which is usually completely overlooked is the orientation of the house. Since most houses in this country are scattered into housing developments with maximum use of land area as the prime criteria, no one has considered the effects of exposure to weather in the selection of economical quantities of insulation. Anyone who has ever traveled to areas where permafrost occurs can attest to the effects of shining sun on the south side of buildings. I will never forget waking in the morning to look out of a train window at a whole row of tilted houses in northern Norway. The sun warms the south face of the buildings and the adjacent ground so much that the permafrost starts to melt and the foundations on the south side of the buildings settle noticeably.

This is quite significant in that we make assumptions about the depth of frost lines and thickness of insulation as though the conditions on all four sides of a house were exactly the same. They aren't. On my houses, I use extra insulation on the north and west faces. Not only is less insulation needed on the south face, but the depth of the foundation can be reduced on the south side since the frost doesn't penetrate as deeply as on other exposures. In our area, the frost line is usually about 3 feet down at the coldest period of the winter. At the time when the radio was reporting 37 inches as the frost line, I dug a test hole next to the south-facing foundation wall of a new, but unheated, building which is buried in a south slope. The frost had penetrated only 10½ inches. The "Insulation Requirements" table in this chapter gives my recommendations for insulating different exposures of a house based upon the number of degree-days for your area.

Foundation Walls

The third factor in choosing an insulation is dependent upon where you are planning to apply the material. The exterior surfaces of foundation walls should be insulated in all areas where the ground freezes in winter. Masonry conducts heat out of a building readily, so don't skimp here. The standard material for use on foundations is rigid urethane insulation board.

These boards are flammable and give off toxic fumes when burned, so they should always be covered with a layer of ¼-inch-thick cement-asbestos board. A piece of heavy-gauge galvanized sheet metal or aluminum can also be used as a covering, but it is not as durable. If a thick insulation board is used, a metal flashing must be used to protect the top edge of the boards where they project beyond the siding.

Again, consult my insulation table for recommended thicknesses and location of urethane in-

This foundation wall shows three layers of protection: cement-asbestos board, urethane insulation board, and vapor barrier.

sulation board. Do not use any other material for foundation insulation. Do not use this material in exposed locations in the interior of the building due to smoke hazards.

Sidewalls

Sidewalls can be insulated with a wide variety of materials discussed in detail later in this chapter. Good workmanship is very important here. Most insulation materials are porous and will permit air to leak through them. If the inside and outside skins of your exterior walls leak air, much of the value of the insulation is lost. If large areas of the exterior wall are occupied by wood framing, as in standard 16-inch-on-center stud-frame construction, more heat is lost. (Wood, although a fairly good insulator, is not nearly as effective as most commonly used insulating materials.) Contrary to the old wive's tale, heat does *not* rise, but flows uniformly from an area of high temperature to an area of low temperature. Concealed areas such as foundations, floors above crawl spaces, and blocking between floor levels are frequently overlooked when installing insulation. The various types of insulation which are blown or

Exterior-applied urethane insulation board should be protected with metal or asbestos sheeting.

foamed into place are particularly susceptible to human error.

Roof Insulation

Except in rare instances, I would only recommend fiberglass as a roof insulation. A full discussion of the use of fiberglass in roofs is found later in the chapter. My houses are designed to use the material in very heavy blankets placed directly between the roof rafters. In mild climates, I would consider the use of a rigid urethane insulation board placed over a solid wood roof deck. This is a common solution for resort houses in warm climates and does work well in that it gives you the advantages of a structural wood deck while providing insulation. It does not provide enough insulation for northern climates, though.

Vapor Barriers

Tightly sealed, well-insulated buildings can have serious problems with accumulations of vapor in walls and roofs. Old houses which have had foams and other loose materials "blown in" frequently experience peeling paint and eventual deterioration of structural members due to accumulation of vapor in the walls. In about ten years, we should see many of those lovely old houses which were ruined by tacky aluminum siding and blown-in insulation starting to deteriorate from the effects of a tight vapor seal being applied to the outside wall surface. Alcoa Aluminum Co. promotes this tight seal as an actual advantage but has been restrained by the Federal Trade Commission from promoting their aluminum siding as an insulating material.

The condensation problems which occur in your walls are best illustrated by noticing how moisture condenses on the inside of glass in a warm, occupied room. At some point inside your walls, any moisture present will reach its "dew point" and condense into water droplets within the insulation. This moisture considerably reduces the effectiveness of the insulation and promotes decay of the wood framing members. Fiberglass and blown-in cellulose are particularly susceptible to these problems. With these materials you should use a continuous sheet of 6-mil polyethylene as a vapor barrier. Foil-backed Sheetrock also works well, provided it is installed with a mastic and all electric outlets are sealed. Make sure that *all* joints in any vapor barrier are airtight, particularly around electric wiring. Better still, use raceways as recommended by the federal government and keep the wiring from breaking the integrity of the insulation and the vapor barrier (see Chapter 9). The paper or foil backing normally found on fiberglass insulation is not a satisfactory vapor barrier unless it can be sealed airtight with duct tape.

Wall Insulation Materials

The following materials are commonly used in insulating walls of houses. They are listed in order

To prevent dampness seeping into the wall, use a vapor barrier of polyethylene.

of desirability. Note that the first material (blue Styrofoam) is normally combined with the fourth (fiberglass) when insulating walls. The two Styrofoams use petroleum bases in their manufacture; fiberglass requires considerable quantities of fuel to produce, but derives its raw materials from plentiful natural resources.

Closed-Cell (Blue) Styrofoam Board

This material is usually made with tongue-and-grooved edges in 1-inch, 1½-inch, and 2-inch thicknesses. The R value is 6.5 per inch. It is applied over the outside of the framing members of the house and serves to provide a good weather-tight seal. It has the further advantage of transmitting small amounts of water vapor so that while it shuts out cold effectively, it still permits the wall to breathe and prevents condensation problems. The matched edges and ends permit the insulation boards to be installed rapidly with little or no waste. It works well when combined with 6-inch-thick fiberglass, as the dew point is moved out to near the face of the Styrofoam.

Styrofoam is not affected by moisture or freezing and thawing, but it is affected by ultraviolet light (sunlight), so it must be covered within two to three weeks with siding or other protective material. It is also flammable and produces toxic fumes when burned. It will not ignite until a very high temperature is reached, though, so it is reasonably safe to use on the exterior of the house underneath the siding. Since it completely covers the framing members, it considerably reduces conductive heat losses through them.

This material is fairly expensive and illustrates very well how insulation can be used selectively on the differently exposed walls of your house. Use the 1-inch-thick material on the north and west faces of your house in moderate climates (to 5,500 degree-days). Other walls should be sheathed with insulating sheathing (see below) or plywood. The "Insulation Requirements" table gives proper combinations of insulation and recommended thicknesses for various climates.

Insulating Sheathing

Insulating sheathing, or nailbase, is a cheap material which can be used in place of blue Styrofoam as a base for siding for mild climates or on exposures of your house which do not require the extra insulating capacity of the closed-cell Styrofoam. Its insulation value is slight, but it does protect the exterior surfaces of the studs and improves the overall insulating value of the wall. If the joints between panels are sealed with duct tape or caulking, and they should be, air infiltration into the wall will be prevented.

These boards are made of compressed wood or vegetable fibers impregnated with an asphalt compound. They are widely marketed by Celotex and Homosote and until recently were the standard sheathing material. See Chapter 8 for a discussion of the properties of this material when used as a structural bracing element.

Open-Cell (White) Styrofoam Beadboard

This material has an R value of 4.5. It is very similar to the blue Styrofoam mentioned earlier, but slightly less efficient and considerably less expensive. Unlike the blue closed-cell Styrofoam which is manufactured only by Dow Chemical Co. in a few central locations, this material is made by many companies. The secret of its widespread manufacture is in the composition of the boards themselves. The raw material is loose Styrofoam beads. Small firms purchase the beads from any of several national manufacturers. At local plants, they are transformed into large billets by means of heat and pressure. Then they are cut up into boards of desired size and thickness. Normal boards are either 2X4 feet or 4X8 feet and 1 to 6 inches thick. Usually, only thin boards are stocked by lumberyards.

If you are planning to use this material to insulate a whole house, order directly from the manufacturer. Check the Yellow Pages of your nearest large city under "Insulation" for a manufacturer. If you order direct, the costs are about the same as for fiberglass of similar insulating value. Major advantages of Styrofoam are that, unlike fiberglass, it can be fitted very tightly and that it breathes slightly, thereby eliminating the need for a separate vapor barrier. It also makes a fine base for an interior plaster finish which is much superior to Sheetrock.

There are drawbacks to Styrofoam, but they are relatively easy to combat. First, you will have to go to the trouble of tracking down a supplier and arranging to special-order the material if you want to insulate a whole house at reasonable cost. Second, exposure to sunlight will very rapidly cause disintegration of the material, so it must be stored in darkness and covered with a protective material within a few days after installation, or it will begin to decompose. This is much more critical than with the blue closed-cell Styrofoam. The blue color is actually caused by the addition of an ultraviolet inhibitor to the basic insulation mix.

Styrofoam must be covered with a fire-resistant material such as plaster or Sheetrock, at least ½-inch thick. (For a first-class Sheetrock job, I recommend the double-layer system described in Chapter 14.)

If you are using my post and beam framing system with horizontal girts, order your Styrofoam cut to fit between the 24 inches-on-center girts. It should also be made to the full thickness of the wall, i.e., 5½ inches or 6 inches. If you lay up the girts and the Styrofoam together it is easy to get a tight fit. Cutting should be done with a straightedge and a very fine-toothed handsaw. As an alternate, you can score the boards with a serrated knife and break them, but this technique only works with thin sheets.

Fiberglass Batts or Rolls

This is the old standby, the standard of the housing industry. It is the most readily available insulation, and, if installed properly and in sufficient thickness, it will do a fine job. In order to get sufficient insulation into your walls in most areas of the country, you will need to use 6-inch wall framing. Since the houses in this book are designed to take advantage of longer spans of 2X6 framing, this thickness of fiberglass works well.

A problem with fiberglass is that it is porous and loses a great deal of its value if either the interior or exterior skin of the house is not airtight. My system of horizontal framing members helps reduce air flow through the material, thereby improving its efficiency. On the north and west walls of your house, fiberglass should be used with Styrofoam sheathing to prevent moisture from freezing within the insulation and drastically reducing insulating value. The action of the sun on the east and south walls tends to dissipate the moisture, and the Styrofoam isn't necessary unless you are in an extreme climate.

All of my house designs use 2X12 rafters to allow for wide spacing of support members and plenty of depth for 12-inch fiberglass roof insulation. I recommend this insulation for all but the mildest climates. Many areas with mild winters have extremely hot summers, and this insulation will help prevent heat buildup. One 12-inch layer of fiberglass is cheaper than two layers of 6-inch or one layer of 8-inch plus one layer of 4-inch. Sometimes you may have to use two layers because of supply problems. If you do, remove the vapor barrier from the top layer; it can cause problems.

Fiberglass is also made in 6-inch-thick, friction-fit batts. In this case, a separate vapor barrier is applied over the entire ceiling surface. The friction-fit material is slightly wider and will fill the space more tightly. Be very careful not to compress fiberglass when installing it. It is designed to insulate by means of air spaces between fibers, and

Insulation Requirements

Degree-Days	Foundations[1] (recommended thickness in inches)	Walls[2] (recommended thickness in inches)				Roof[3] (recommended thickness in inches)
		North	South	East	West	
7,000+	4	2+6	1+6	2+6	2+6	12+2
6–7,000	3	2+6	6	1+6	1+6	12
5–6,000	2	1+6	6	6	6	12
3–5,000	1	1+6	6	6	6	10
3,000−	0	4	4	4	4	10

1. Foundation insulation to be foil-faced rigid urethane insulation board.

2. Sidewall insulation to be tongue-and-grooved blue Styrofoam (first digit) plus basic wall insulating material as selected by owner (second or only digit). Basic insulation can be a variety of materials as discussed in this chapter. In extreme northern climates, where Styrofoam is not readily available, double-thickness wall construction is frequently used, with two layers of 2X4s or 2X6s to accommodate heavy fiberglass insulation.

3. Roof insulation should be fiberglass. Extra digit indicates rigid urethane insulation board applied over roof decking.

compressing it reduces its insulating value. For this reason, it is a poor material to use for filling small cracks. Use a spray foam or caulking for that purpose.

Since the roof is heavily insulated, I do not use a conventional vent slot at the eaves. Most roofs with comparatively poor insulation tend to melt snow off the upper portions of the roof and form ice dams at the eaves. The air introduced into the roof cavity to prevent ice dams considerably reduces the performance of the insulation. I do provide a ridge vent to allow any slight accumulation of moisture to escape.

Moisture accumulation can cause severe problems in conventional construction because of the combined effects of poor insulation, low roof slope, and inadequate vapor barriers. Follow the instructions in the section about vapor barriers earlier in this chapter to the letter. If you don't, you will have condensation and might have to add eave vents, thereby reducing the value of your insulation. Never use recessed lighting fixtures in an insulated roof space (if your house has any, remove them immediately). They create a serious fire hazard and are an inefficient light source; they also reduce the value of your insulation and vapor barrier. If possible keep *all* wiring out of the roof cavity.

Installation of fiberglass is done in a different manner in walls and roofs. When fiberglass is installed in walls, it should be recessed ½ inch behind the face of the studs to reduce conductive heat flow through the walls. Foil-faced insulation or foil-backed Sheetrock also reduce conductive losses, although both are not needed. The foil-backed Sheetrock doubles as a vapor barrier and saves time and cost of installing a separate one.

Attach the sidewall insulation by stapling the flanges to the *sides* of the studs, not the face. For a top-quality job, nail furring strips over the stapled flanges to insure tight contact with the studs. If the fiberglass is used for ceiling, roof, or floor insulation, the flanges can overlap the face of the framing members. Make sure that the paper or foil backing is facing *toward* the heated area. Many contractors have made the mistake of installing insulation on a suspended floor structure with the vapor barrier placed away from the heated space. Think ahead and install the insulation before you put down your floor deck.

Fiberglass, like Styrofoam, is difficult to cut. Here too, I have found that a fine-toothed saw does the best job. A serrated knife also works well. Measure carefully so that the fiberglass completely fills the space without being compressed. It is a severe irritant; I recommend both goggles and a face mask. A quick hot shower with a cold rinse immediately after installing the fiberglass will help alleviate irritation. Scrub your hands thoroughly.

Cellulose Fiber Fill-Type Insulation

This insulation is made of shredded paper (cellulose) fibers which have been fluffed up and protected from rodents and fire by adding boric acid. At least you hope that's what has been added. This excellent material has two drawbacks. First, there is a serious shortage of boric acid. There just isn't enough manufacturing capacity at the moment to supply all the boric acid necessary. Other chemicals which are toxic, corrosive to metals (electric wiring), and which impart only color, but no flame retardancy, are frequently added to the raw material.

The situation is further complicated by the fact that preparing cellulose fiber insulation requires little or nothing in the way of special manufacturing equipment, making it a natural backyard enterprise. There are no uniformly enforced standards or inspections, and using this material can be a risky venture. Since it is about 30 percent better as an insulator than fiberglass (R value–4.5/inch) and recycles otherwise wasted resources, it should be a major contender in the insulation industry. But it will be 1981 before new boric acid plants will be able to meet all of the demand. Until then, I urge extreme caution when using this material.

If you use cellulose fiber insulation, send actual samples of the material to a testing lab before blowing it into the walls. A trained applicator must install it to the proper density so that it will not settle within the wall cavities. A good vapor barrier is essential, and the material should be kept away from all possible sources of heat such as recessed light fixtures, heat ducts, flues, etc. Make sure that your installer has been in business for at least three years, get several references, and visit his jobs to check them out personally.

Urea-Formaldehyde Foam Insulation

One more step up the ladder in insulating effectiveness (R value–5.5/inch), but regrettably, also one big step up in potential troubles. A quick look at the specifications makes this material look like the most ideal of all insulating materials. It is reasonably priced, waterproof, rodentproof, and completely nonflammable. In fact, since it releases water vapor when heated, it can even retard the spread of fire. For this reason, I have used it many times in the renovation of older houses, and all these installations have been very successful.

Urea-formaldehyde was developed in Europe almost twenty years ago and is widely used there as a standard insulating material. Regrettably, the same fly-by-night contractors who have moved into the cellulose insulation business have also invaded the urea-formaldehyde application scene. Installation of this material is a complicated process requiring extensive training, expensive equipment, and very careful monitoring of temperature, humidity, and chemical proportions. It is a much less forgiving material than cellulose. Any slight deviation from proper specifications can result in improperly cured foam which at best will shrink and crumble and at worst release such strong formaldehyde fumes that it has to be removed from the walls. Other countries prevent such problems by requiring strict licensing and training programs.

Problems due to incorrect formulations have been so severe and so frequent in this country that the material has been outlawed in several places, and many reputable dealers have been driven out of business due to the mistakes of their untrained brethren. Since a 2 percent solution of formaldehyde is lethal, a small goof can create a dangerous situation. The raw chemicals used are very weak, nowhere close to 1/10th of 1 percent, but an incorrect concentration of them makes a house uninhabitable due to irritation of the mucus membranes.

Some people are sensitive to the very slightest amount of formaldehyde and experience headaches and nausea when exposed; this would be present even if the material were installed properly. Various common construction adhesives contain the same chemicals. These include plywood, prefinished paneling, parquet flooring, plastic laminates (Formica and its cousins), flush doors, and urethane varnishes. People with a sensitivity to formaldehyde will also be bothered in a house which has a high concentration of these materials. A small house trailer insulated with urea foam and paneled with plywood with flush doors and glittery Formica causes many people to have headaches and nausea for reasons other than the obvious aesthetic ones.

Properly installed urea foam is such a good insulator that it makes the exterior walls feel warm to the touch and allows the room to be kept at a lower temperature than would otherwise be comfortable. In view of the above dangers, if you still want to use this material, I would advise the following precautions. Deal only with a certified dealer supplying Rapco Foam, who has been in business for at least five years. Rapco Foam is manufactured by Rapco Foam Inc.,† formerly Rapperswill Corp. Always use a tight vapor barrier between the living space and the wall and a porous material (almost any commonly used sheathing except plywood) as the exterior skin. Never use the material as an attic insulation or in thickness greater than 5 inches. Greater thicknesses or installations on horizontal planes such as floors or roofs can result in curing problems. If you use it in my 2X6 framing system, I recommend that you set the vapor barrier back from the inside face of the studs to reduce the thickness of the insulation. Check with other homeowners who have had urea-formaldehyde installed by the same contractor to make sure that they have had no problems. Properly installed, it will give off less fumes than the common or garden variety prefinished sheet paneling. It will also do a superior insulating job.

Other Insulations for Special Applications

The previously listed insulations are all of those in common use for large areas. You may have some special circumstances which require other insulations. Cavity walls, particularly if they are constructed of a rough material such as stone, need a waterproof insulation which can be poured into them. Vermiculite and perlite are granular insulations which are excellent for this purpose, although they are about 30 percent less effective than fiberglass and vastly less effective than urethane insulation board which can be used if you install it as you build the cavity. The granular insulations are rather cheap, so you can build a bigger cavity and still have a well-insulated wall.

Sprayed urethane insulation is an excellent means of sealing and insulating at the same time. It must be covered with a fireproof material to prevent fire. *This is imperative; make no exceptions.* It has to be installed by a professional with extensive equipment and is normally used only

†The address of this and other manufacturers and associations so indicated will be found under "Addresses of Manufacturers and Associations" in Part IV.

for commercial installations. If you are building a house with large areas of masonry wall, this can be a cost-effective way of obtaining insulation and absolutely perfect waterproofing all in one shot. Even though small areas of the insulation on the outside of your house don't pose a serious fire threat, they must still be covered to prevent ultraviolet degradation from the sun.

Small containers of aerosol-type sprayed ure-thane foam are being marketed under the trade names Certainseal and Instafoam. They are widely distributed by hardware stores and lumberyards and are heavily billed as caulking materials, which they simply aren't. They are impossible to apply neatly and are only useful for concealed cracks. Also, the spray units don't work unless the container is at or above 70°F. and the surrounding air is above 55°F. This limits usefulness during winter construction.

If weather conditions are suitable, however, these small cans can save lots of grief later. Keep a sharp eye out for gaps in your insulation blanket. Make a thorough check of the entire building shell with a flashlight on a dark night before installation of final interior and exterior skins. Have a helper on the inside mark all insulation gaps for remedial work with either the spray can or other insulation materials. In this way, much later weathersealing can be eliminated. A good, high-quality tube of Mono caulking compound costs about $3; a can of urethane spray about double that. The spray equals about ten tubes of caulking in volume and will adhere tightly to most construction materials. Even though it isn't really a caulking material, its use in sealing cracks at the rough framing stage will pay off handsomely later when you don't have to spend days caulking your house to make sure you have the minimum of air infiltration.

Insulation for Glass

Double and triple glazing have become the popular methods of preventing excessive heat losses through glass areas. This is an expensive solution, and since glass transmits heat readily, even three layers of it lose a lot of heat. In Chapter 13 I have described various insulating shades which can be used to cut down heat losses effectively. Various homeowners have used sheets of Styrofoam beadboard which are fitted over their windows at night. The Styrofoam boards are a cheap, easy solution, but pose a fire hazard and are difficult to store.

Despite limitations, these aerosols are handy for concealed leaks and cracks.

Zomeworks[†] has devised two rather highly publicized insulating devices worthy of note, both available from Zomeworks. The first is called Beadwall and makes use of the Styrofoam beads which are used to make the open-cell insulation described earlier. The beads are treated with a flame-retardant and antistatic agent and pumped into the void between two panes of glass to provide nighttime insulation. In the daytime, the beads are pumped out of the void and stored in a canister. The operation is controlled by a simple manual switch or can be automatically activated by the sun.

A second device, called a Skylid, is used to insulate skylights. It consists of a series of insulated louvers which are automatically operated by gas-filled canisters attached to the edges of the louvers. The action of the sun drives the gas back and forth between canisters on opposite edges of the louvers, thereby opening and closing them. These are expensive but great for remote skylights or for automatic operation if you are away from home for extensive periods.

Weathersealing

The old adage concerning the chain and its weakest link comes to mind when one seriously upgrades the quality of insulation in a house. No longer is the heat loss through walls, roof, and floor the major heat loss which requires replacement heat. Instead, infiltration of unheated air assumes a leading role in calculating the amount of heat required to maintain the desired inside temperature. It's almost impossible to seal a house completely, and, since man requires oxygen to survive, we are lucky that complete sealing is that difficult. But we can and must do a better job than the typical contractor if we are to conserve a maximum amount of heat, and heat with the sun supplemented by small amounts of backup heat.

Every possible joint between two adjacent materials which penetrates through the exterior wall should have a sealant applied. Sealants work much better when they are applied during construction rather than as an afterthought as in conventional construction practice. This practice is a direct result of the negative influences of construction unions. Union workers are generally too incompetent to be able to perform more than one task well, so caulking and sealing is assigned to a separate trade brought in after all other work is completed. The workers proceed to smear messy beads of caulking all over everything so union ''laborers'' can come along and try to clean up the mess.

Shortly after World War II when modern architects invented the glass box with its ''curtain walls,'' they made a nasty discovery: *they leaked!* No conventional caulking or sealing materials could provide more than a temporary solution; one quick weather change was enough to cause most conventional caulking materials to crack and separate. A wide variety of heavy-duty elastic caulking compounds was developed to solve the problem. Most work very, very well. They are called ''elastomeric'' materials and remain flexible and sticky for years and withstand repeated seasonal movement of construction materials without cracking or separating.

Unfortunately, these special qualities were achieved at a high price. Most of the materials are completely unsuitable for use by the homeowner. In order to achieve their special adhesive and elastic qualities, chemists combined materials which must either be mixed from two components (as in epoxies), applied under pressure with a compressor, or which have extremely toxic or flammable solvents. Since high-quality caulkings are so special, nothing in the caulking line which you will find for sale at your hardware store or building supplier is worth bringing home. The products which you do find there crack almost

immediately, particularly if applied to something which moves a lot, such as roughsawn lumber.

Fortunately, there are a couple of materials on the market which bridge the gap between the worthless junk at the hardware store and the mixing and application problems of most industrial/commercial sealants. The first is called Mono caulking compound. It is a very sticky, acrylic-type sealant which performs well at modest cost. It has two minor drawbacks. It has an unpleasant smell until the solvent has evaporated, and it

Infrared scanner graphically demonstrates heat-loss points of the house. (Infrared photo courtesy of AGA Corp.)

must be warm (80 to 90°F.) to be applied properly. The smell goes away after a few days, but don't store a whole case of the stuff in your living room, your friend's office, or the back of the van. Heating can be accomplished by setting it in warm sunlight, hanging a light bulb over it, putting it on a warm car radiator, or storing it close to a heat source such as a woodstove. Heating is imperative, as the material must be warm to even come out of the caulking tube. It must also be warm to stick properly.

Applying any caulking material correctly is tricky. First cut the tip of the plastic nozzle off at a 15° angle. A smooth, clean cut is important or the material will not flow properly. Break the inner seal with a long nail or wire. (The caulking gun listed in "Basic Tools" in Part IV has built-in cutters.) Apply gentle pressure to the trigger until the material is just ready to come out of the spout. Hold the spout against the joint to be sealed in such a way that the front end of the angled nozzle just makes contact with the surface. Move the gun along the surface rapidly, applying uniform pressure to the trigger of the caulking gun. This is a technique which has to be learned, so buy some junk caulking at the hardware store and practice a bit first. Professionals tool their caulking material into the joint for a tight seal by running a mason's jointing tool or a similar tool along the surface of the joint after the caulking has been applied. Recheck your job carefully as most elastic caulking will settle into a crack, sometimes leaving voids.

Surface preparation is vital to a good caulking job. The material to be caulked must be clean and dry, and the cracks shouldn't be over 3/16-inch wide. If possible, apply the caulking before assembling the materials. For wide cracks (greater than 3/16 inch), partially fill with a backing material before applying the caulking. The best material to use is a compressible foam backer rod called Ethafoam, manufactured by Dow Chemical. You will have to talk a glass supplier out of a small quantity of it, as it is only sold in 250-foot rolls. If you can't get any of this material, cut some strips of foam rubber. The backup material should be forced well into the joint to allow plenty of room for the caulking. A good joint is almost square, that is, of equal width and depth.

Mono caulking compound is available at large glass installation companies and masonry supply houses. Check the Yellow Pages in your nearest large city. It comes in cases of thirty tubes in several colors; you will need most of a case for a typical house. The material can be ordered directly from the manufacturer, Tremco Mfg. Co.[†]

If you are located on the East Coast, another fine caulking material, Gacoflex, is available from Gates Engineering Co.[†] It is a neoprene rubber caulking compound which is every bit as good as the Mono; however, distribution is very limited and as far as I know it is available in black only. The solvent is extremely flammable, so be careful. I would not recommend its use on any job where an open flame or cigarette smokers are present. It is used as a component of the roofing system I describe in Chapter 15, so you may want to order the caulking along with the roofing materials. Unlike Mono, the neoprene can be applied straight from the tube at any normal temperature without difficulties.

Silicone caulking is widely touted as a superior material. It is good, but not nearly as good as the two preceding caulking materials. Also, from usual sources of supply it is outrageously overpriced. The solvent used in the material is a severe irritant and somewhat dangerous. Silicone is made in a clear formulation which makes it invaluable where two pieces of clear material such as glass or Plexiglas must be butted together as in the breakfront-design greenhouse. Do not be tempted to use it elsewhere, though. The solvent is dangerous and the profit margin over 400 percent per tube.

Testing

Even the most careful and thorough workmen may miss some spots in insulating and sealing a house. If you did all of your work yourself, paying very careful attention to detail, and your house heats easily, you may skip this step. However, if you hired contractors to perform the work or just to install insulation, you should arrange to check their work.

Infrared photographic scanners are coming into wide use to check on heat losses. Unfortunately, they are extremely expensive and getting a reasonably priced scan by a reputable firm can be quite difficult. In our area, we have access to an AGA scanner, one of the best. Write to the AGA Corp.[†] for the name of a firm using the scanner in your area. These produce direct color images which graphically pinpoint your problem areas.

An older, less-expensive system is marketed by Barnes Engineering.[†] This is a somewhat more primitive system. It takes more time and care to interpret, but the results have been excellent for me. Again, write for a listing of firms which use this equipment.

If anything, the scanner business is more of a racket than installation of insulation itself, so avoid any door-to-door salesmen like the plague.

There are other companies which make scanning equipment, but these are the only two well-established ones which I would recommend. Costs range from about $40 for the Barnes scan when done as a part of a group of houses to about $250 for a very detailed individual scan with the AGA system.

For the dedicated do-it-yourselfer who has just a bit of electronics knowledge, there is a simple device called a temperature differential thermometer with which you can check the envelope of your house for heat leaks. Parts for the gadget cost less than $15. It is a very simple, battery-operated, solid-state device with a temperature sensing probe attached. It can work either inside or outside the house and simply registers a fluctuation in heat level. It does take a lot of time, but you can accurately pinpoint a leak and check every conceivable leak spot on your house inside and out. The device has an adjustable zero-scale meter which reads to the right for higher temperatures and to the left for lower temperatures. When you are through using the device as a leak detector, it can be simply converted to a permanent electronic thermometer.

For complete circuitry and construction details, see *Popular Electronics,* September 1978. This device will not do as good a job as the scanners, but it would be useful for low budgets or in remote areas.

An assembled version of the device is available at about $40 from Enertron Corp.† but I find the cost spread between parts and finished product a bit steep. A Barnes scan as a part of a group is about the same price and a lot less hassle.

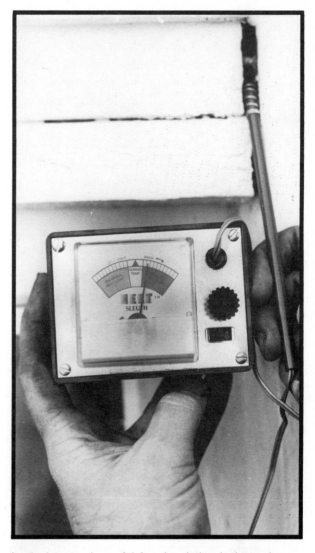

Leak detector is useful for pinpointing leaks and drafts.

Chapter 11

Heating and Cooling

If you have built one of my compact houses, insulated it to the standards suggested, and provided thorough weathersealing and insulating covers for openings, you now have a house which can be heated or cooled at minimal cost. With supplies of fossil fuels rapidly dwindling, it is imperative for all of us to reexamine how much fuel we are using and what the source of this fuel should be. The time has passed when we can continue to use inefficient electrical power for heating and cooling and for other household purposes for which more efficient sources are available.

The most obvious heat source is the sun. A properly oriented house with south-facing glass can easily heat itself on even the coldest winter day and is capable of retaining much of that heat at night if the house and glass areas are properly insulated. Of course, the sun doesn't shine all of the time, and in winter daylight hours are considerably reduced. In some bleak northern areas, the sun rarely shines at all. Most active means of storing heat from the sun are too cumbersome and expensive to be considered by the budget-minded builder. Fortunately, nature has its own method of storing energy from the sun. It is called a tree. While other forms of energy are finite, trees grow quickly and can easily be re-

planted. It has been estimated* that the United States has enough excess tree growth to directly supply half of the heating needs of the nation. That's half of all existing houses, most of them poorly insulated.

Ten years ago, it was impossible to find a new woodstove in this country. Those who heated with wood had to content themselves with antiques. Now there are so many manufacturers that the choice is bewildering. High-quality, very expensive imported stoves have been brought into this country in ever-increasing quantities. Just about every small manufacturer with excess shop space and welding equipment has rushed a stove onto the market. Standards are virtually nonexistent. Safety is widely ignored. Meaningless "lifetime" guarantees are bandied about. New stoves and gadgets are promoted every week. Each day brings me several letters from confused people asking what they should do about heating their houses. The same mail frequently brings ingenious solutions to heating problems.

Wood heat has some considerable problems other than stove quality. Unless the wood burned is very well seasoned hardwood, it produces un-

*Marilyn Pelo, ''Old-Fashioned Energy,'' *New York Times Magazine,* February 11, 1979.

114

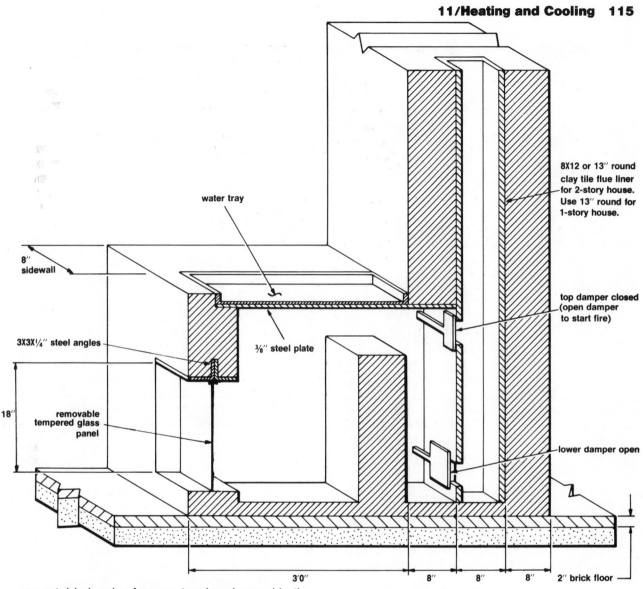

water tray

8X12 or 13″ round
clay tile flue liner
for 2-story house.
Use 13″ round for
1-story house.

8″
sidewall

top damper closed
(open damper
to start fire)

3X3X¼″ steel angles

⅜″ steel plate

18″

removable
tempered glass
panel

lower damper open

3′0″   8″   8″   8″   2″ brick floor

Perlberg's fireplace — brick baffle extracts heat
as in a Russian fireplace.

acceptable levels of creosote when burned in the popular "airtight" stoves. Older woodstoves did not have this problem; they burned their wood rapidly with hotter fires, consuming most of the volatile chemicals which produce dangerous creosote. Busy families do not like to have to add wood to a fire every couple of hours, never mind the excessive consumption of wood itself. We desperately need a medium ground between long-burning and hot fires. The obvious solution is to provide a means of storing heat from a vigorously burning (clean and efficient) fire to be used at a later time.

Masonry Walls

My basic house design for this book shows a masonry wall which surrounds the woodstove and stores a maximum of heat from it, somewhat in the same fashion as the European-style "Russian fireplace." The principle of this type of fireplace

is to bend the exhaust fumes from the fire through a series of convolutions so that maximum heat is extracted and held within the masonry to be radiated back to the living space long after the actual fire has gone out. Bill Caddell's house has a Russian fireplace which he has built himself. It is so difficult in this country to get a reasonably priced mason who can even build a straight foundation wall that I hesitate to recommend a Russian fireplace, even though they are quite efficient and will keep a house warm for several days. The Perlberg house has a primitive version of a Russian fireplace (detailed above) which is simple enough for the average mason to build without too much difficulty.

Front view of the Perlberg fireplace.

Russian Fireplaces

A finely detailed set of drawings for several different variations of the Russian fireplace is available from Timeless Products, Inc., P.O. Box 143, Roxbury, CT 06783 for $10. These drawings show the same basic design combined with a variety of open fireplaces and provide for incorporating a cooktop, oven, and a domestic hot-water coil. This is quite a setup — heating, cooking, and hot water all in one. Now all you have to do is build it.

Russian Fireplace Construction Tips

Constructing a Russian fireplace is a serious venture. If not properly built, there is considerable danger of fire or carbon monoxide poisoning. The firebox of a Russian fireplace is a high-

Frank Gilbert employs brick for thermal mass around his woodstove.

The Weso tile-faced stove — a high-quality, high-efficiency import. (Photo courtesy of Weso.)

heat appliance, and its construction is highly critical. The mason who builds it should be thoroughly familiar with high-temperature fireboxes and their construction. A mason who has had experience building commercial kilns is ideal. Expansion of the firebrick liner is quite critical, and space must be left between the firebrick liner and the surrounding brick casing. Otherwise, the high temperatures will cause the outer enclosure to crack, causing a dangerous condition. If possible, allow the masonry to set up for several months before using the fireplace. Build in the early spring for use the following winter if at all possible.

Since the convoluted flues of this fireplace extract heat by slowing the flow of exhaust gases, an airtight flue is vital. Leaks in the flue section could result in fatal doses of carbon monoxide.

Russian-style fireplace — a complex structure, but it does get maximum amount of heat for fuel used.

This particular design has access doors in the flues for cleanout. I recommend sealing them airtight with Silverseal and breaking the seal at cleaning time. I also strongly recommend the use of a gas detector for carbon monoxide leaks. One such detector is made by Romar Alarm Systems.[†]

Stove and Masonry Combinations

You can achieve the same effect by surrounding a conventional cast-iron woodstove with masonry. Don't try it with a steel stove, as you are likely to cause the stove to overheat and warp. The masonry absorbs quite a lot of heat from the stove and redirects it to the room. It also makes the stove much safer, particularly if there are small children in the house. The stove should be run wide open with a very hot fire until the masonry has heated up; then the vents are closed down to preserve the coals.

In case you don't want to build a masonry wall or Russian fireplace, or if you have an existing house and want some of the heat storage/safety

A gas detector is a valuable safety device.

†The address of this and other manufacturers and associations so indicated will be found under "Addresses of Manufacturers and Associations" in Part IV.

The Sturgis system reclaims a great deal of heat that would otherwise be lost.

This steam system was designed and built by the owner. It generates and recondenses steam in an enclosed cycle.

benefits I have mentioned, there is a solution — the tile-faced stove. They are expensive, but very efficient and burn coal, an important consideration if you are in an area with little available wood or are too busy to deal with obtaining and storing wood. This stove is a high-quality German import which meets very exacting industrial standards unknown in this country. It is much nicer looking than most cast-iron stoves, and a tempered-glass door allows a view of the fire. These stoves are sold in this country under the brand name Weso and are distributed by Ceramic Radiant Heat.[†]

Fireplaces

Everyone likes an open fire, so there has been much attention given to fireplace efficiency. The first step is to make the basic size and shape efficient, as in the Rumsford fireplace. I gave details for the Rumsford in *30 Energy-Efficient Houses.*

All sorts of gadgets such as glass doors, tubular heat exchangers, and improved versions of the old Heatilator-type fireplace are being marketed. Most of these items are vastly overpriced and not very efficient. The typical loose-fitting glass doors and lightweight heat exchangers are not worth buying. There are three fireplace systems which I can recommend highly, however. They all have the capability to store heat for long periods of time and radiate it back to the house.

The first of these is a complete fireplace unit marketed by Sturgis Heat Recovery, Inc.[†] Paul Sturgis discovered that local masons could make a mess of critical portions of his heat recovery system, so he is now marketing the unit himself.

The second system was designed and built by the illustrator for this book, Frank Gilbert. It is connected directly from his fireplace to his hot-water-heating system. Frank has heated an entire sprawling ranch house from his fireplace for the past five years. The local gas company couldn't figure out why the Gilberts were using so little gas, so they hired private investigators to snoop around to see if they were secretly bypassing their meter and stealing gas to heat their house.

The third system is somewhat similar to Frank's but uses steam instead of hot water. The steam generator and a radiator are mounted right above the fireplace. With this system, a standard-size fireplace puts out about as much heat as a small furnace.

These three systems are generally better-suited

to large houses than to the ones shown in this book. If you want to retrofit your present house, or if you want to build a large house, these systems are well worth considering. The Sturgis system is available directly from Sturgis Heat Recovery. The other two units can easily be homebuilt; detailed plans are available for $15 from Smallplan, Box 43, Barrytown, NY 12507.

Wood and Coal Stoves

In conventional woodstoves, it is best to stick to the best-known, most widely distributed brands. I recommend the domestic Vigilant (smaller brother to the famed Defiant) by Vermont Cast-

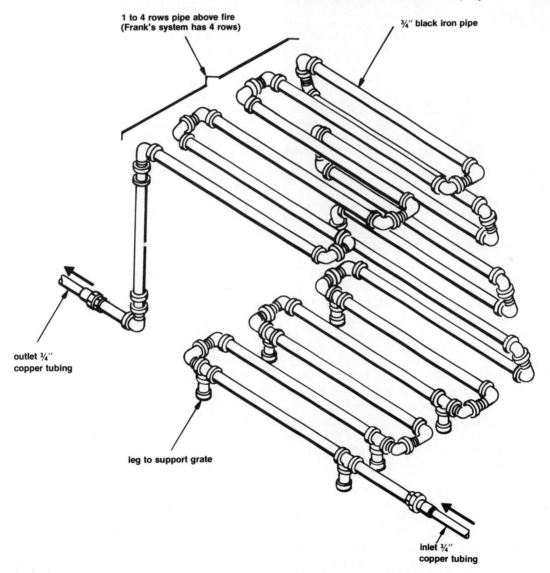

1 to 4 rows pipe above fire (Frank's system has 4 rows)

¾″ black iron pipe

outlet ¾″ copper tubing

leg to support grate

inlet ¾″ copper tubing

Fireplace heat exchanger designed by Frank Gilbert. (For details for interconnection to a standard boiler, see *Popular Mechanics*, October 1974.)

Le Petit Godin.

ings or the imported Jøtul #118 (smaller Jøtuls have a small firebox which is difficult to load). Either of these stoves can be installed with the long side parallel to and very close to the central masonry wall. Do not use the rear heat shield on the Vigilant, though. And do not buy any stove constructed entirely of sheet steel. The door(s) and door frame, at least, must be made of cast iron to prevent warpage. Steel stove makers will point out that cast iron cracks, but a reputable stove company such as I recommend will provide a replacement.

Coal or brickette stoves may be the answer for some parts of the country. There are three which I heartily recommend. All of them burn wood, but are primarily intended as coal burners. Le Petit Godin, made in France, is by far the best looking. One of my.clients bought it for looks alone, but I was amazed at its capabilities. The second stove, the Quebec Heater, is similar, but less expensive and ornate. Both stoves must be top-loaded with

logs set vertically, but they will accept 24-inch logs. (Don't buy any stove that will not accept wood at least this long.) The third stove is a comparatively ugly American model, the Atlantic kitchen heater. Atlantic just dusted off the dies for their 1930s-style modern heater, which is basically the firebox from a standard wood/coal kitchen cookstove made as a separate unit. All of these stoves are fire-brick-lined and have coal grates. They are primarily designed to use coal, but can burn wood easily in a pinch. Heat output from coal is quite adequate for a basic house. The stoves don't burn as well if stoked with wood, and the firebox is so small that wood will burn for only a relatively short time.

Other Types of Heating Units

For areas of moderate climate with a lot of sun, only a small amount of supplemental heat may be required. Building a flue and buying a woodstove can cost as much as a couple of thousand dollars. Spending this kind of money is silly if you don't need the capacity. Low-output heaters burning various fuels can be used instead. I stumbled onto one Japanese import by accident. Some friends who were searching desperately for a way to cut down on their $400-plus electric bill discovered a beautifully made Japanese kerosene heater called the Kero-Sun.[†] One of these heaters heats an entire, heavily insulated ranch house in moderate weather. The bill for kerosene is less than $50 per month.

These heaters are similar to the familiar English blue-flame heaters, only much more refined. Kerosene heaters are not noted for their safety, are difficult to fill without spilling fuel, and tend to give off fumes. The Kero-Sun has solved all of these problems very well. Unlike the blue-flame heater, the Kero-Sun is well balanced and difficult to tip. It has a full pan underneath to catch any spills. A safety shield slides over the burner if the heater is slightly jarred, much less upset. Ignition is electric (battery-powered), so exposed open flame is never encountered. A very clever syphon tube/pump makes filling the reservoir almost pleasant. The heater is very well constructed, easy to disassemble, and an excellent buy at about $120. Try matching that with any other heating system.

There are drawbacks. The heater only burns for a maximum of about twenty hours on a medium setting, meaning that you can't use it as a backup heating source for an unattended house. Second, under continuous operation, the wick needs to be trimmed about every five days. This takes about ten minutes, but requires disassembling the heater. I was so impressed with the heater that I bought one so that I could devote more of my time to writing this book than to chopping wood. It has fully measured up to expectations. If you have a large, older house to heat, there is a bigger brother at about twice the capacity and price. As with all devices employing combustion, it uses up oxygen and expels carbon monoxide. Though it uses an oil product as fuel, it does so very efficiently and is normally used in Japan with no venting of any sort. If you should choose to use it as a permanent heater, I recommend an outside vent and exhaust as shown on the working drawings.

Gas Heaters

The natural/bottled gas industry also has small heating units which can be used in a similar fashion to the Kero-Sun. Very small gas space heaters have been used for years and can be connected to an automatic thermostat to serve as an automatic backup to a passive solar system. Such a heater costs about $50 and can serve as a backup or even as the only heat source in a well-insulated house. It can be set up like the Kero-Sun heater and should be vented in the same way.

Some codes are very strict about the venting of gas appliances, so it will pay to check carefully before installing a heater such as this. Many codes require that all gas appliances be rigidly connected with black iron piping rather than the commonly used flexible copper tubing. Drastic increases in copper prices will soon make black iron cheaper. Should you install the system yourself, don't be tempted to use the flexible copper just because it is quick and easy. Copper is soft and can rupture unnoticed. The lethal explosion could also be quick and easy. Gas is dangerous and should be handled carefully.

Another gas appliance which is great for temporary auxiliary heat is the radiant gas heater. This heater has no actual flame. A porous ceramic element is ignited and gives off radiant heat. The process is very clean and does not produce any combustion fumes; however, it does use up oxygen. Since these heaters do not produce fumes, and hence do not have to be vented, they are frequently used as primary heat sources in trailers. Since they do use oxygen, an exterior intake is vital. These heaters cannot be connected to a thermostat; they are either on or off. They are made in 5,000 Btu. to 15,000 Btu. models and are inexpensive and versatile. The smallest models are made to accept a 1-pound propane bottle

and hence are completely portable. Since they are widely used by the trailer industry, the best sources for them are J. C. Whitney, Sears, or your local recreational vehicle dealer.

Radiant Heaters

Radiant heat has always been one of the most effective means of space heating. The sun streaming through a window provides *radiant* heat; the blast of hot air coming from a furnace register is *convective* heat. Radiant heat has been used since the days of the Romans who heated a stone floor by running hot-air ducts through it, allowing the heat radiated from the stone to warm the occupants. A person feels warm when in close proximity to a radiant heat source even if the surrounding air temperature is relatively cold.

Kero-Sun — an efficient Japanese import.

I have always been an advocate of radiant heat. Many years ago, I discovered some radiant glass panels made by Continental Radiant Glass Heat Co.‡ They are very heavy units and they have a fairly substantial convection component which limits their efficiency when placed on the ceiling (the most desirable location for radiant heat panels). A second-generation, improved panel is made by Aztech International Ltd.‡ Their radiant element is graphite sandwiched between layers of metal, with a sand finish that disperses heat better than a smooth surface. These heaters are quite unobstrusive and blend as they are right into a white ceiling. You can paint them with any color latex paint if you prefer. Aztech has capitalized upon the energy and cost savings of their units to create a brisk national market. Sears also markets these heaters.

A third company, TVI Corp.,‡ has now entered the field with substantial improvements in both efficiency and cost, using space-age materials to achieve an extremely lightweight panel. The basic panel is just a flexible film which can be bonded to any suitable substrate. When installed on a Sheetrock ceiling, for instance, it is completely invisible. It requires a very special adhesive and is a bit tricky to install; however, if you'd rather not fool with the flexible film, TVI also sells a standard, surface-applied panel similar to the products of the other two companies. This panel eliminates the heat-dissipating metal of the Aztec unit, thereby getting slightly better efficiency from the unit, and the low mass of the unit permits much more responsive controls to be used. The Aztec and Continental units are noticeably slow to heat up, causing some complaints from my clients.

I emphatically do not endorse the conventional use of electricity for heating. The typical baseboard electric heaters should be banned immediately. The radiant panels described above are 25 to 35 percent more efficient than the resistance heaters in the baseboard units, and in addition, the units can be placed where they warm people, not the outside wall. Even so, generation of electricity requires over three times the energy of burning the fuel directly to supply heat. Therefore, people who care will use even electric radiant heaters very sparingly. In some remote, treeless areas of this country, electricity is almost the only available source of energy, so in those areas, people have no choice. If you design your house to take maximum advantage of natural weather conditions and select very efficient electric radiant heaters, you can use a minimal amount of electricity. As a general rule, though, I would recommend these heaters only as a backup system for passive solar heat, primarily to satisfy stodgy bank officials.

One of the clients in this book split the cost of the panels with another. They switched the panels around so that the bank officials saw full installations in both houses. After the inspections, the heaters were divided so that they were used in bathrooms and bedrooms where the heat source was really needed.

Generators

The energy crisis has finally stimulated some long-needed basic research into problems of energy use. The North American Phillips Corp. (Norelco) holds the license for the much-touted, but undeveloped Stirling engine. The Stirling is an external combustion engine of very high theoretical efficiency. It works in somewhat the same fashion as an absorption-type refrigerator (see Chapter 16 and cooling section of this chapter). The automobile industry mumbles occasionally about using the Stirling for a future power source, but doesn't actually bother to try it. An American licensee of Norelco that has a pilot operation that is producing a Stirling engine power plant finds that they are noiseless and very lightweight and efficient compared to conventional generators. Initial production for the first two years is scheduled to be sold to Winnebago Ind. The unit will supply electricity, heating, and cooling for a large luxury recreational vehicle. Since this is an exotic new type of generator, the company hopes to be able to monitor the first units carefully until full production is achieved.

In theory, the external combustion engine can run on anything which produces heat, even the sun. The unit installed in the Winnebagos burns propane gas, but could be powered by almost any heat source. I must emphasize that the first units are prohibitively expensive and that production is very limited. It is very interesting that this alternate power source is being developed by a giant foreign company in collaboration with a tiny innovative American firm. One wonders what the giant American companies are doing.

Heat Pumps

In addition to the dramatic upsurge in popularity of criminally wasteful electric resistance heating

---

‡The addresses of these appliance manufacturers will be found under "Recommended Efficient Appliances and Equipment for Energy-Saving Houses" in Part IV.

in this country, there has been a parallel increase in the installation of central air conditioning even in areas where it really isn't necessary. In areas of moderate climate, other cooling methods can easily be used. Of course, if you are in a very hot area of the country, no amount of natural ventilation or evaporative cooling will make you truly comfortable. In areas which require substantial amounts of both heating and cooling, a heat pump is a reasonable answer.

Heat pumps have rather limited heating capacity in cold weather, so a solar-assisted heat pump is an attractive idea. Several systems are just being introduced to the market. I would be wary of them. The heart of a heat pump is a compressor. American companies make their compressors to the same abysmal standards as their small gasoline engines. Since the heat pump puts the compressor to heavy use year round, durability is a very serious problem. From many year's experience with large commercial installations, I have found that the Carrier Corp. in Syracuse, New York, makes much better quality compressors than most companies; they are also durable and quiet. (A worn compressor still works, it just makes a lot of noise and uses excessive amounts of electricity.)

Single-Unit Heat Pumps

The usual heat pump installation consists of two units, one mounted inside the house and the other mounted outside the house. Ideally, the unit should be in one piece for ease of installation and economy of wiring and piping. Sears has just introduced a one-piece unit designed for through-the-wall installation. It is ideal for our basic saltbox house built with a carport, and the central location of the utility core makes the installation easy.

Calculations for sizing a heat pump are quite complex and require either a very highly skilled engineer or a sophisticated computer program. The engineer will charge you more than the heat pump is worth. Sears will engineer the system for you provided you give them detailed information on the insulation, latitude, and orientation of your house. Sears will then feed the information into a computer and give you the necessary size unit. The computer isn't going to know anything about the passive solar heat buildup, but the cooling mode will be critical in most areas of the country where a heat pump would be suitable (4,000 to 4,500 degree-days should be the cutoff point). My basic saltbox plans show a ductwork layout for this system. With any heat pump system, get a

service contract and a minimum of a five-year guarantee on the compressor. Sears offers this; many companies don't.

Air Conditioning

In extremely hot summer climates people are really miserable without air conditioning and it has become accepted as normal in all very hot southern regions of the country. Heat pumps are less efficient than conventional air-conditioning systems when their primary use is for cooling, so therefore I do not recommend them for use in very hot climates. Westinghouse, General Electric, and all of the other biggies make cheap, energy-gobbling, portable air-conditioning units. For areas of extreme heat I don't recommend any of them. Spend some extra money and buy a permanent system.

The marvelous Servel refrigerator with no moving parts still lives on as a commercial/residential cooling system. This is a completely foolproof system which simply works by applying heat to a closed system, somewhat similar in principle to the Stirling engine. Again, the heat can be from any source. In the basic Arkala-Servel air-conditioning units, the heat source is natural or bottled gas. The use of gas instead of electricity for cooling is parallel to the use of wood instead of electric resistance for heating. Burning the gas directly at your house to power the cooling unit is much more efficient than burning it in a generating plant to produce electricity which then moves a noisy, inefficient compressor.

But what if you object to the use of gas or are in an area where gas is not available? Remember that I said the heat source could be anything. Unlike the Stirling engine in which solar heat is still experimental, Arkala-Servel has a fully tested solar air-conditioning system on the market. (The basic saltbox house has a large south-facing roof which is ideal for placing the collectors for this system.) You can approach the system several ways. First, you could buy the gas-fired system and at a later date add the collectors. Second, you could buy the basic compressor and add your own solar collectors, either homebuilt or commercially constructed. Or, you can buy the complete system from Servel. They will even include a water storage tank and a domestic hot-water system if you desire. This is not a cheap system, but neither is it the typical overgadgeted solution. The basic components are extremely well made, all parts subject to corrosion are constructed of stainless steel. The basic cooling unit is fully guaranteed for labor and materials for a

Panels for an air-collector system are built into a south-facing roof.

period of ten years. If a few other companies such as those located in Detroit would make such high-quality machinery, maybe our balance of trade wouldn't be so disastrous.

Fans

Prior to the widespread use of central air conditioning, large, attic-mounted fans were common in warm areas of the country. Gravity-type roof ventilators were also used. Both are rapidly coming back into use. Our basic house is vented through the central chimney wall. Others have gravity roof-mounted turbines or strategically placed vent windows.

These fans take advantage of the rapid cooling of the outside air which occurs in many parts of the country at night. Heavy insulation will help a great deal in keeping daytime summer heat out but will also keep the cool air out at night. Careful attention should be paid to window location, and some sort of fan system should be considered.

Remember that the north and east sides of the house will be in shade and will cool more rapidly. Air intakes should be located near the ground in this area of the house. Fans can be connected to ductwork to move cool air more uniformly.

Air-conditioning systems waste a lot of fuel by continuing to cool the house with an expensive compressor even after the outside air temperature has fallen well below the inside house temperature. If you have an air-conditioning system, you may want to interconnect a fan system which automatically shuts down the air conditioner and circulates cool outside air instead when the temperature drops to optimum levels. Sears markets such a system, but any competent heating and cooling company can make one up for you. In areas of very hot days with a sharp temperature drop at night, the system will pay for itself in a very short time. The same ductwork system which I devised for the single-unit heat pump can be connected to an outside fan if no air conditioning is desired.

Chapter 12

Masonry Floors, Heat-Storage Walls, and Chimneys

In recent years, masonry has become an expensive decorative material. (By masonry, I mean brick, although slate, terra-cotta tile, stone, concrete block, and pavers have similar properties and may be used to the same advantage.) Typical tract houses frequently have a silly little patch of brick on their fronts and if they do have a functional masonry chimney, it is tacked onto one end of the house. Masonry has unique properties of absorbing, storing, and transferring heat which are not widely recognized. It is a serious mistake to use these materials on the outside of your house where these properties can actually be detrimental.

Heat Storage and Transfer

Masonry is heavy and absorbs heat readily from any heat source, such as the sun, a woodstove, or excess room heat from any other source. It also transmits heat readily. Some of the more unscrupulous insulation manufacturers are fond of comparing their products to a brick wall. Since the brick is a notoriously poor insulator, they can show that 1 inch of their material is "equal" to 18 inches of *solid brick.* This brings us to the immediate conclusion that masonry should be avoided on the exterior of the house if at all possible. If it

Central fireplace and chimney prevent heat loss through the wall and provide a mass of masonry to store heat from the sun.

is employed in a foundation wall, it must be heavily insulated on the outside face (see Chapter 10). Contractors who use masonry as an exterior facing material find this concept very difficult to understand. For the same reasons, I always isolate the chimney from the exterior wall.

These same heat-transfer characteristics have important safety implications. People tend to think that since masonry materials are incombustible, they work effectively to protect surfaces from heat. The truth is that they transmit very high temperatures quickly and can easily start fires in combustible materials. A fine example of what *not* to do is the brick- or tile-veneered wood wall which one finds near many woodstoves. The masonry creates a false sense of security, and may actually conceal a fire until it is too late. Under normal conditions, the flue temperatures in a typical chimney are fairly low and quite safe. In the case of a chimney fire, intense heat is generated which can quickly penetrate masonry and ignite adjacent combustible construction materials. Heavy timbers do not burn readily, but all other construction should be separated from the masonry by at least one inch. All flues should be lined with flue liners made of dense tile. These very effectively resist intense heat which causes conventional brick and mortar or metal to deteriorate. *Never* use an unlined chimney.

The heat-storage capabilities of masonry can be quite subtle. To a human with a body temperature of 98°F., a masonry floor which is only 75°F. may feel quite cool to the touch, yet the floor may contain enough stored heat to keep the room warm for hours. Houses with large, south-facing glass areas can overheat in very sunny winter weather! Conventional wisdom is to limit or shade the glass areas to prevent this. Instead of shading the glass, I make use of the chimney to store heat and prevent living space from getting too warm. Since the warm air will rise to the ceiling in an open plan, I add an extra shaft to the chimney and pull the air down through the chimney with a fan. This causes the excess heat to be stored in the chimney for release to the house as the interior temperature cools at night.

Use a roller or a tamper to compact the underfloor fill.

Masonry Floors

After the post and beam framing system, this is the most significant difference between my houses and conventional builder's houses. If you ask a typical builder for a brick, slate, or tile floor, what you will get is a thick (expensive) concrete slab with the masonry set in a thin layer of mortar by a professional mason at $15 to $20 per hour. You immediately discover that the cost is prohibitive. Besides, the typical tract-house plan has a basement or crawl space which makes the masonry floor on grade impossible anyway. Basements and crawl spaces are very wasteful from both a construction and an energy standpoint and should be avoided where possible.

The most significant cost savings I achieve in my houses are from eliminating wasted space and installing the do-it-yourself brick or masonry floor. If you follow my directions carefully, these floors are a snap even for the rank amateur. Even if you don't involve yourself in any other aspect of the construction, lay your own floor. It will give you great satisfaction and save you a lot of money. Most "professional" masons are unfamiliar with this technique and will try to talk you into a more expensive installation. Steer clear of them, at least for the floor. If you must have someone else install the floor, let the carpenters do it following my directions. Firms experienced in landscaping will be familiar with this technique as it is sometimes used for exterior terraces.

Laying a Brick Floor

The first and most important step is to prepare the subsurface properly for the brick. The brick is laid directly on a sand/gravel bed which must be level and well compacted. If the house is at a high point of the land and sits on well-drained soil, there is no need for a vapor barrier. A coat of sealer on the floor surface after installation will keep any slight dampness from seeping through.

Stretch strings along the interior post lines at roughly 12-foot intervals. Set the strings level with the top of the concrete grade beam which was poured to be level with the finish floor surface. These strings represent the top of the floor. Before covering any underfloor piping make sure that it has been thoroughly tested for leaks. Fill the underfloor area with bank-run gravel or other fine, porous material (a hard shale or coarse sand will do equally well). Keep the fill about ½ to 1 inch below the average level of the bottom of the brick. The fill must be compacted with a roller or tamper, or the floor will settle.

Now, mix a lean cement mixture to install under the brick. This is made up of one part cement to six parts sand. Dampen it slightly to the consistency of damp sand. It should not have any tendency to stick together, but should feel somewhat wet.

Starting near the center of the floor at the intersection of two of the strings, begin laying the brick in the sand/cement mix. Lay a small section at a time. Running bond is the easiest to lay and the most forgiving of different brick sizes. The basket weave requires precise brick of uniform size. New brick pavers are best for this pattern. The herringbone must be checked carefully to see that it is straight, but otherwise it is easy to set. Unlike installing a conventional brick floor in mortar, you can carefully space the brick as you go to keep the pattern uniform. Perfectly uniform-size, new brick can be set tight together with no joint if desired. With used brick or if you want mortar joints between the brick, you will need to allow space between them. The usual joint varies from ⅜ inch to ½ inch in width to allow for variations in brick size. If necessary, sections can be lifted and reset, brick exchanged for color and texture, or damaged brick removed.

Continually check your floor to be sure that it is level. If you started even with the tightly stretched strings and keep checking with a level from that point out, you should remain level with no trouble. Brick at the edge of the pattern can be broken by chipping and breaking with a mason's hammer or scored with a masonry blade and then broken. The latter method is better if you are a beginner.

After laying the full floor, check it very carefully. Make sure that it is uniform by taking a long, straight board and sliding it in all directions. Slight changes in level probably won't hurt, but sudden dips and crooked brick should be avoided. You may also want to replace odd-size or off-color brick. Particular care and attention is called for when laying used brick; you may find you have bought all sorts of shapes and sizes. Check it over carefully before grouting the joints; after that, it's difficult to replace or change brick. A light first coat of the final finish will keep the grouting from staining the floor.

Grouting the Floor

Grout is the filler material between brick, tile, etc. The grouting technique which I use is called dry-packed mortar. It is a commercial technique normally used in large buildings. The less water you

add to concrete (up to a point) the harder it sets. In big steel buildings, the columns are set in place on steel plates and then leveled, with space left under the baseplates. This space is filled with this special mortar which is actually supporting the weight of the building. So don't let anyone (read professional mason) tell you this is an inferior way to set the brick. It *is* time-consuming, so it will be expensive if you hire someone else to do it.

First, mix a very rich, dry mixture of 1 part cement to 1½ parts sand and then dampen it as we did for the base course. Thoroughly wet down a small section of the floor. Bricks sop up water very quickly, so make sure they are wet, stopping short of flooding the area. Apply the damp mortar mixture to the joints with a trowel, pushing it into the joints between the brick. Take a scrap of plywood or another blunt object narrow enough to fit between the brick and tamp the mortar into place. Finish flush with a trowel or concave with a mason's jointing tool, depending on your aesthetic preference.

By following the instructions, the beginner can build a beautiful and efficient floor for little money. First, spread the dry mortar mix over the brick.

Then, tamp the mortar between the brick with a narrow scrap of wood.

Finally, sweep excess mortar on to the next section to be grouted.

Continue the floor, grouting small sections at a time, until it is complete. Wet down floor again, as brick will absorb moisture from mortar. Be careful that other construction does not get debris, sawdust, or other dirt into the cracks between the brick before you grout them. If you have an area of the floor which might have to be removed, use a less-rich mortar mixture. Sakrete premixed mortar can be used if you add ½ bag of cement to each bag of Sakrete. Your final floor will have dense, tight mortar joints and will cost much less than a conventional concrete slab plus brick. It also saves a lot when compared to the conventional suspended floor with a crawl space which dissipates heat rather than storing it.

Floors of Other Masonry Materials

Any masonry material such as slate, quarry tile, paving stones, concrete block pavers, or even homemade concrete tiles can be used to construct a masonry floor. The larger the units, the more important the base preparation becomes.

For very large units, wet the bottom surface before setting in the sand/cement bed. The sand/cement bed is vital for setting materials such as slate and quarry tile. Also, leveling of large units is more critical.

If you can't find masonry paving materials at a reasonable price, you can easily make your own. Build several small, 2-inch-deep forms as shown in the picture, and oil the inside surfaces. Fill them with a concrete mixture, and level off the top with a board. Now spread a layer of fine stones of a color which you find pleasing over the top of the form. Tamp them lightly into the concrete. After the concrete has hardened, but not fully set (about four hours), remove the cement from on top of the aggregate with a soft brush and water. Be careful not to overdo it, or you'll loosen the aggregate. Let dry and remove from the forms. Continue the process until you have enough paving material for the floor.

These pavers can easily be made up months before and stored. They are also useful for patios and walks if you use other materials inside. If you plan them for exterior use, make them 3 inches

This form is simple to put together, and it allows you to make small concrete slabs.

thick. For a nice variation, they can be made in a hexagonal pattern instead of in squares. Standard concrete tinting colors can be added to the concrete mixture if desired.

In some cases you may want to use a poured concrete floor for a utility room, carport, or garage. I do not recommend that a beginner attempt a full concrete floor slab, but small areas such as these are relatively easy to install. For a smooth finish, rent a power troweling machine.

Cleaning and Finishing a Masonry Floor

A 5 percent solution of muriatic acid, which is sold at most hardware and masonry supply stores, is the standard material for cleaning masonry surfaces. Don't let the mortar set too hard (about three days) before cleaning the masonry. Use a stiff, new bristle brush and lots of elbow grease. Light-colored brick and concrete pavers will require little work. Dark-colored, porous brick may require several applications to come clean.

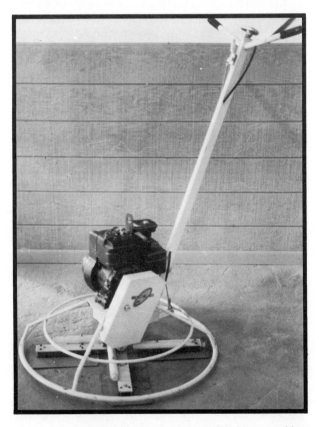

Power trowel — a cement-finishing machine.

A coat of polyurethane on the brick before grouting makes cleaning much easier. Wear rubber gloves and eye protection.

A terrazzo-grinding machine can be rented to put a smooth finish on bricks or concrete tiles. It will clean them at the same time.

There are a wide variety of finishes which are suitable for masonry floors. Some people prefer to leave them alone, but they will show grease spots or food spills on them. Butcher's paste wax, buffed into the surface, makes a nice finish. Commercial silicone waterproofing (use a clear 5 percent solution) will brighten the floor somewhat and keep water and grease out of the pores.

For the typical household with kids, animals, and lots of spills, a polyurethane finish just like on a wood floor is the most durable and makes mopping and cleaning a breeze. Test some of your paving materials with various finishes before you buy quantities of finish. It's a bit late after you have the floor down to decide that you want polyurethane varnish, but don't like the way it darkens the brick or slate.

Heat-Storage Walls

My basic house features an exposed masonry wall in the center designed to work in conjunction with a large skylight and a central heat source to store warmth in the daytime and reradiate it to the house at night. Its central location means that this heat source is accessible to every room in the house. At one end of the masonry wall is the heat-reclaiming flue described earlier and at the other, the flue or flues for woodstove, cookstove, furnace, or other heat source.

If you build this wall of concrete block with stucco, there are easy materials available for the beginner. Blockbond, marketed by Construction Products[†] and Benco Industrial Supply Co.,[†] is a bonding agent which allows the concrete block to be stacked by hand and then coated to hold them together. The block cores are filled with mortar reinforced with #4 bars. One of the houses in my first book, *30 Energy-Efficient Houses,* was built using this technique, and it worked well and has been completed for several years now. The stucco makes an easy-to-apply finish coat for the block wall. It is available from Dryvit Systems, Inc.[†]

[†]The address of this and other manufacturers and associates so indicated will be found under "Addresses of Manufacturers and Associations" in Part IV.

Masons at the Laskin house building a stone "veneer" around the block chimney.

A masonry chimney cap to prevent rainwater from combining with chimney soot.

While this method seems like a boon for the beginner, I would not want to recommend its use for exterior walls where soil pressure might put heavy stress on the walls.

Of course, you can hire a professional mason to build the wall for you. We used a wide variety of materials in the houses in this book. New brick, used brick, scored block, plain block, and stone were all used. In one of the houses, we had the professional mason lay up the chimney in block to get it in use quickly. Metal ties were left projecting from the block joints so that the chimney can be veneered with stone by the owners at their leisure.

Laying stone masonry is a vanishing art. Most masons charge two to three times as much to lay stonework as to lay brick, even when you furnish your own stone. For the beginner, laying stone is very tedious, but rewarding. The heat-absorbing wall in the picture is entirely constructed of native stone gathered on the owner's property. Notice how the recess allows the stove to fit into a niche in the wall for more efficient heat transfer to the masonry. Unless you are very lucky and find a really top-notch mason who charges reasonable rates, the only way to consider stone is to do it yourself.

Chimneys

In my basic house, the chimney has 7¼-inch round flues which can be easily laid up using standard 16-inch square chimney block lined with clay flue tiles. An 8-inch-diameter round clay thimble is used to connect the stovepipe to the clay flue tiles if a side entrance into the flue is used. In the photo of the stone fireplace, the flue connection is vertical, and a steel plate is cut to shape to make the connection between the stovepipe and the clay flue liner. When installing flue liners, always use refractory cement, and make sure that all transitions are smooth and even so that they don't tend to collect soot and creosote. Whenever possible, use round flues or ducts; air flow is much more efficient and cleaning is much easier.

For proper draft conditions and to prevent formation of creosote, chimneys should always be capped. Rainwater combined with soot creates a sticky mess which is hard to remove. One also needs ready access to the flue for cleaning, however. In the masonry cap shown in the picture, we provided a lift-out stone access plate directly over the flues for cleaning purposes. For a smaller chimney, I use a piece of slate instead of

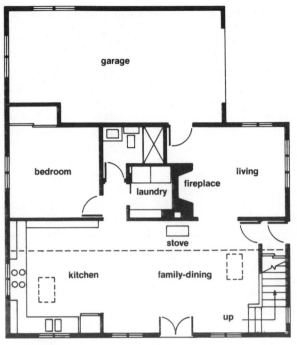

first-floor plan

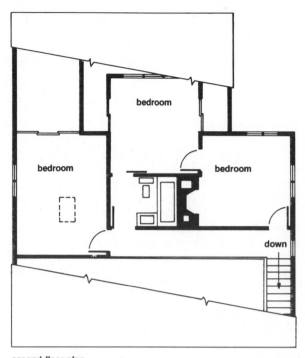

second-floor plan

Plans showing incorporation of heating stove and fireplace in one masonry column.

concrete. A removable cap can also be constructed of steel plate.

Any cap can be blocked on the side of prevailing winds to prevent downdrafts if necessary. I had to do this in my own house even though I have a very tall chimney with good draft. The house is located at the base of a mountain, and at times the wind comes roaring down the mountain and right down the chimney. This will restrict the draft and is not recommended unless you do have trouble. You will have to work this out by trial and error, but be ready to correct the situation if it does occur.

Whatever you do, make sure that the bottom surface of the cap is *flat*. The standard little conical stovepipe ''hat'' which is usually stocked at hardware stores should be illegal. It reduces the draft severely and causes rapid creosote buildup.

Dry, well-seasoned wood, a tight, properly capped chimney, and a daily hot fire will keep creosote buildup to a very minimum and cut down on the need for chimney cleaning. No matter how cleanly your fuel burns, you should always clean the chimney at the end of each season, and check it before using it in the fall. At least once a month, remove your stovepipe to check for creosote buildup there and clean as necessary. Even though I have isolated the chim-

This Rumsford fireplace draws air from outside and doesn't use up the oxygen in the house.

ney for safety, chimney fires are scary and can set roofs or woods on fire. With this in mind, be sure to install a spark arrester on top of the chimney, and don't burn any fires in very dry weather unless absolutely necessary.

Fireplaces

Many people also like to have an open fire. Unfortunately, the fireplace designs which are currently in vogue actually lose heat from your house. The working drawings show how our standard masonry column can be modified to accept both a heating stove and a fireplace, either on the first or second floor. The client who requested this modification installed the fireplaces on both floors. I gave details for Rumsford fireplaces in *30 Energy-Efficient Houses.*

The picture shown on the previous page shows a small Rumsford-type fireplace. It has a dampered opening directly to the outside and a tempered glass screen so that no room air is used for combustion or exhausted up the chimney. The fire screen is made very simply from a sheet of tempered glass. An airtight seal to the masonry is provided by using a bead of Silverseal, available in cans and caulking tubes from some woodstove dealers or direct from Industrial Gasket and Shim Co.[†] The gasket is made by first applying Vaseline to the masonry to prevent the Silverseal from bonding. Then a bead of Silverseal is applied to the edges of the sheet of glass where it overlaps the masonry. Finally, the glass is pressed against the masonry so that the Silverseal makes an airtight gasket. This screen costs about one-third as much as the commercially available variety and is airtight; the commercial ones aren't. Since special-size tempered glass takes several weeks to order, it may pay you to order an extra screen just in case you should break the original.

Chapter 13

Exterior Skin — Windows, Doors, and Siding

After the framing, the exterior skin is the most expensive and most important part of your house. If you purchase ready-made windows and doors, particularly from a local lumberyard, it is possible to spend $4,000 or $5,000 just for these items. Also, the construction joints around doors and windows are notorious leak points. You can actually do a better job and save a lot of money by building your own units. Even if you buy ready-made windows, there are ways to save substantially.

My special post and beam framing system with its horizontal girts allows great freedom in design and placement of windows. The standard cracker-boxes which the conventional builder builds are usually constructed with walls constructed flat on the ground and tilted up into place. This means that the exact size and placement of windows must be decided before the framing is even started. Door and window manufacturers establish "rough openings," the actual finished sizes of the outside of the door and window frames plus enough clearance added to allow for slightly out-of-square openings and sloppy measurements by carpenters. When the wall is framed, the carpenters use the rough opening dimensions to frame an opening for the door or window. Since these windows and doors

interrupt the actual structure of the stud wall, wasteful extra framing members are required at the sides and the tops of the windows.

Not only do these extra members waste labor and material, they also reduce the insulating value of the wall by displacing energy-saving insulation with more conductive wooden framing elements. Worse yet, the extra framing members and the narrow crack between the window and door frame and the structural members are certain to cause air leakage problems. If you use conventional preframed doors and windows, these joints can be sealed with sprayed urethane foam as described in Chapter 10.

A much better solution is to avoid the problem altogether by building your own doors and windows. You do not have to build the actual window sash yourself; these can be purchased ready-made. I use four different types of windows in my houses. All are easy to make and the savings are impressive. They all involve purchasing components such as insulating glass, window sashes, and hardware. Although building windows and doors in the usual way requires expert carpenters and takes a long time, my shortcuts allow even a beginner to turn out a creditable job. The secret is in knowing how to do it.

133

Windows

Before you start building windows, check the sizes and placement carefully. Walk through your house, and try to imagine final furniture placement. Take a chair along and sit in it to establish sight lines. Also think about your room layout and prevailing summertime breezes. Of course, you probably had windows shown on your plans, but it is very wise to think them through again to make sure that you are placing them where they will work best.

Casements

The casement window is the most popular with my clients and is also my personal favorite. This is probably because the window can be opened fully. Commercial casement windows are very expensive. This one if purchased from Andersen (I do *not* recommend them; this is for price comparison only) would cost almost $300 list. The materials-cost for my homemade casement is about $60.

Start your window by selecting a proper-size sash to make up the opening. The window shown is a double casement. A single one is easier to

build and costs exactly half as much. I use two 24-inch by 41-inch wooden sashes containing six 10-inch by 12-inch lights and costing less than $10 apiece from a standard millwork house. The window frame is made from standard framing materials coated with wood preservative.

Sort your lumber very carefully and choose straight, clear members. Thoroughly coat these members (and all other wood parts of the window) with clear Cuprinol wood preservative *before* assembly. Coat all cuts, drilled holes, and concealed areas.

Lay the sash out on a flat table and measure accurately. Build the top and sides of the frame from 2X6s, allowing 1/8-inch clearance at the top as well as between the sash. The sill is made from a 2X10. Since it will get the worst weathering, give it several coats of wood preservative. Instead of sloping the sill as is done in commercial windows, I bevel the portion of the sill which projects beyond the window with either a skillsaw or a planer. The skillsaw cut will have to be touched up with a sander or a hand plane. Make a 1/4-inch-deep saw cut 3/8-inch back from the overhanging edge on the underside of the sill. This is called a drip and prevents the water from running back the underside of the sill. (Make a cut of this na-

Excluding your labor, with these standard materials you can build a window for around $60.

ture on all overhanging surfaces to help keep out water!) This one sill does duty in place of several framing members and millwork pieces in a conventional window and stud wall.

Fasten the corners together with 3½-inch wood screws, thoroughly buttering the joint with Mono caulking before assembly. Cut stops from 1X3 finish stock (do not use roughsawn as weatherstripping will not stick). Stops are buttered with Mono and applied later with 6d finish nails. Allow a bit of clearance at the butt joints and fill with Mono. Apply ¼-inch by ¾-inch sponge neoprene

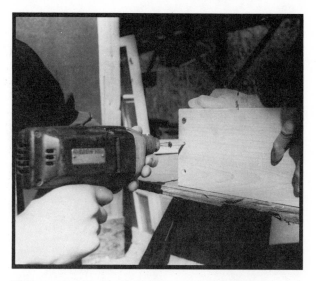

Use a variable-speed electric drill to install the screws.

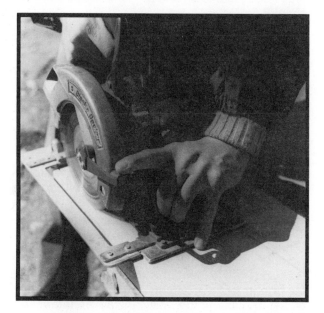

Contractor Kevin Berry shows the various steps in making your own windows. A ¼-inch cut on the underside of the sill prevents water seeping back into the wall.

Use a three-foot length of piano hinge, cut into six pieces.

Thoroughly coat all points of contact and screws with Mono caulking compound.

weatherstripping to the outside and inside face of the stops. Get this material from an auto supply store, not a hardware store, and use contact cement to make sure that the stuff stays put.

Now cut a 3-foot-long piano hinge into six 6-inch-long pieces, and screw them to the outside edge of the window sash. Space as shown. These hinges will keep the sash in perfect alignment and are very easy to install, as they do not require mortising to recess them into the wood.

The sash which opens first should have two cam-action handles. The other one gets flush bolts top and bottom. The meeting edges of the windows will have to beveled slightly with a plane. A 1X2 wood strip is attached to the sash which has the cam-action latches with screws and Mono. Apply a ⅛-inch-thick piece of weatherstripping

Space the piano hinges as shown here.

as above. An aluminum screen and storm sash complete the installation. See "Library" in Chapter 4 for do-it-yourself booklet, *Building Storm Sash and Screens,* 39 LY 7312.

If you want triple glazing, a sheet of ⅛-inch Plexiglas can be attached to the outside of each individual sash. Windows are held open by simple casement sash hooks or Ives sliding casement adjusters. All of the window hardware is surface-applied and does not require any specialist skills to install. It is not as sophisticated as the hardware on commercially available windows, but neither is it likely to break. It is also cheaper.

There are many other advantages over commercial windows. First, the window can be stained or finished in any way you choose. Most major brands come primed which means that you can't use a natural finish. Also, commercial windows are made for 4-inch stud walls and have to have specially ordered extension pieces or extra pieces added in the field; more extra costs and leak points. One of the most important differences between my job-built casements and the commercial ones is in the elimination of the center post in the double casement which obstructs the view when the windows are opened and can also pose a hazard in case of a fire. Many codes require that the minimum dimension of a window be 30 inches, effectively outlawing most casements. (This important requirement is widely ignored, however.) Finally, all ready-made

casements have the operating sash set flush with the outside of the wall. Tests have shown that heat loss is substantially reduced by recessing the glass several inches behind the outside of the house. Six-inch walls provide the thickness necessary to do this. My windows are set back to reduce heat loss, and of course the sash are better protected from the weather.

Should you want to install real operating shutters, there is also ample room for them. There is also plenty of room between the inside of the sash and the storm window/screen to accommodate the insulating shade which I describe later in this chapter.

Now that you have constructed the window, nail corner braces at two corners to keep it square while you are installing it in the wall. To install the window, first set the horizontal girt which is immediately under the window. Make sure that it is level and at the proper height for the top of it to receive the bottom of the sill. Also install a vertical stud at each corner of the window between the girt and the sill plate. Now apply two beads of Mono, near the edges of the girt in the area to be occupied by the window. Set the window in place, using the force of gravity to seal the window. Install braces from the top of the window to the floor to hold the window in vertical position. Cut and install blocking to attach the top of the window to the bottom of the perimeter beam. If the window is to be set with the head flush with the bottom of the perimeter beam, the top should be set in place first. Finally, install the intermediate girts and double-check the window for level and square. Now the stops can be permanently set in place in a bed of Mono.

Operating Sash

The other three types of windows are just variations of the above technique. The procedure for constructing the frame and installing it in the wall is essentially the same in all cases.

The second window type you can make is a large, multipaned, operating sash. The sash can be ordered in many sizes to suit your exact needs and taste. The photos show several variations. My favorite is the big window made from six 18-inch by 24-inch lights. This is also quite dramatic when made up of many very small panes. In the easiest version, it is attached with sections of piano hinge at the top (cut one 2-foot-long hinge into four pieces for a typical 4- to 5-foot-long window). The window is held open by casement hooks placed to allow for the desired opening, i.e., the higher they are placed, the wider the window opens. If desired, it can be hinged so that it swings inward, thereby opening fully. I recommend this option for hot summer climates where full ventilation is needed.

Another very easy method of operating the window is the pivot. As you can imagine, screening

This handsome six-paned window looks south from my desk.

Large, multipaned window, hinged from the top.

is almost impossible and this technique is widely used for industrial windows which don't need to be screened. If you are in one of those rare areas where screens are not necessary, it's a great way to hang a window. It is also a perfect choice for

For this window, a steel pin is inserted in the frame at either side, and the window rotates around it. This provides excellent ventilation, but is difficult to screen.

Multipanes like this can be found used, or made new by the homebuilder.

the wall between the living space and green-house. Commercial pivots are expensive and difficult to install; however, it's easy to make your own. A large spike works well. Set the sash in place in the frame, tacking blocks on either side so that it can't move. Locate the exact center point on either side of the window. Drill holes slightly smaller than the shank of a 20d spike through the frame and two-thirds of the way through the edge member of the window. Cut the spike off at the length of the holes you just drilled. Redrill the holes in the frame to the same size as the shank of the nail. Put a few drops of glue in the holes in the window sash. Drive the nails home and you have an exotic pivoting window.

Now cut stops for the window. These are a bit tricky. The bottom stop is placed inside and the top on the outside. The stops at the sides of the window cross over from inside to outside at the

This double-hung window is made up of used window sash, set in a new wood frame with steel side channels.

pivot point. The opening of the window is controlled by the angle cut on the stops.

Fixed Windows

The third window type is a common window seen in many of my houses, with a fixed rectangular pane (usually 46 inches by 76 inches) set above an operating vent. I use this size because it is the most common insulating glass size; it is made for sliding glass doors and is relatively inexpensive. Glass is an energy-intensive material, particularly tempered glass, and therefore expensive. The price of this lowest-cost unit has soared over the past three years from $48 to $90. Buy in quantity direct from the manufacturer, never from your local retail glass supplier, where markups of 100 to 200 percent are common. If you get together a whole order for your house, you can save a lot, even on custom sizes. Check with your supplier to see what his standard sheet glass sizes are, and use these sizes on any custom windows for minimum waste.

These windows are constructed just like the two preceding types except that there is an extra sill member underneath the fixed window. For vent windows under the fixed pane, buy a stock wood sash and hinge it top or bottom with a piano hinge as described for the casement windows. I had previously recommended the high-quality, low-priced Andersen basement vent. Unfortunately, Andersen caught on and revised the price so that people wouldn't be so eager to buy them instead of their more expensive units.

Double-Hung Windows

Many people still want the traditional double-hung window but very few manufacturers make them with authentic small panes. Instead, they are made of one large pane with a plastic grille tacked on to make them resemble the real thing! Most millwork shops can make standard double-hung sash in standard sizes, as there is a good market for replacement sash. Used sash is also frequently available. There are some good manufacturers who do make authentic double-hung windows, but the price is high and they have the same limitations as other commercial windows.

Fortunately, you can make your own rather easily. Double-hung windows are difficult to hang properly. They usually have awkward cords, pulleys, and sash weights or more modern spring balances which are difficult to install. All are prone to maintenance problems, and the windows tend to be loose and drafty or, alternatively, painted shut. A small company has come up with a very nice solution. Steel side-channels, which are weatherstripped and spring-loaded, allow the windows to slide easily and seal tightly at the same time. Cost is about $10 per window.

The channels are available from Quaker City Mfg. Co.[†] The same basic window frame which I show for the other windows is used along with one pair of new or salvaged double-hung sash. Quaker City includes detailed directions for installation. Apply Mono to the back of the channels before installing them. These same channels are excellent energy savers for remodelings as well.

Building your own windows and doors is a lot of work. You may not want to take the time or trouble. What are the alternatives? You can go shopping in salvage yards or try to find some windows in an old house. This method will appeal strongly to antique lovers. There is nothing quite so nice as having beautiful, handcrafted windows from another era in your home. The problem is, of course, that it's such a popular idea that many people are getting a small fortune for used windows. Lots of hard-nosed shopping can pay off if you have the time and perseverance.

Commercial Windows

What if you just want to go out and buy the windows? The Andersen Corp. spends an astronomical sum each year to convince people that their windows are top quality and super-weatherstripped. The truth is that they are of reasonably good quality, but vastly overpriced. Andersen has a complicated discount structure. The advertised ''retail'' price is a fake, designed to be discounted so that you think you are getting a good deal. For a small quantity of windows, 20 to 30 percent is a reasonable discount. For windows for a whole house, 40 percent is more like it.

The only reason for even considering these windows is that they are readily stocked in all parts of the country and can be obtained almost immediately. Avoid the plastic-clad lines. They are premium priced and constructed so that the wood can't breathe. Ultimately the plastic will disintegrate from the sun and the wood will rot. Buy the wood windows (you have to paint them as they already come prime-painted), and remove the ugly moldings from the outside. By doing this, you can recess the windows into the openings

and eliminate much of the area which has to be repainted. Build a separate frame around the window, in the fashion that we did in building our own from scratch. In this way the window can be weathersealed as you put it together rather than by caulking it later.

If price is no object, the Rollscreen Co. of Pella, Iowa, makes the windows Andersen would like you to think they make. These are absolutely top-quality windows, priced a bit above the Andersen ''retail'' prices with no discounts. It is nice that such quality still exists, but most people can't afford it. These windows can be special-ordered unprimed, but there is quite a wait. Pella windows come with such delightful features as concealed rolling screens and tiny operating venetian blinds between the panes of glass. Triple glazing is readily available. All at substantial cost.

The high-quality Marvin casement, made in America.

For those on more moderate budgets who still want a high-quality window, there is a nice compromise. This is the Marvin Window Co.[†] The company ships throughout the United States and Canada. All windows are made to order but unlike most companies who build to order, Marvin is fast. You can have anything you want made: unfinished windows, wide jambs of any dimension, specially sized and shaped windows, double-hung windows with real mullions. Marvin also makes wide casements which meet code requirements for exits. The premium-priced Case-

†The address of this and other manufacturers and associations so indicated will be found under ''Addresses of Manufacturers and Associations'' in Part IV.

Folding insulating shutter operates with a boat winch.

It can be left in a variety of positions.

This enables you to have partial shade in summer.

Shutter in fully closed position.

master casement windows are some of the nicest I have ever seen. They are mounted on sliding pivots so that you can clean both sides from inside the house and snap off of their mountings so that you can remove the whole sash. The lower-priced standard casements are of much better quality than the typical mass-produced units, at less cost.

Insulating Windows

Windows, even if they are very well weather-stripped and double- or tripled-glazed, are still a major source of heat loss (never mind the deceptive Andersen ads). Instead of paying a steep premium for double or triple glazing, there may be other, more cost-effective ways of insulating your windows. Glass is an extremely poor insulator; several layers are expensive and do not reduce loss as much as other devices.

Shutters

The old-timers who had no exotic insulation or means of multiple glazing had a simple solution for keeping heat from leaking through windows. It was called a shutter. They work very well, but someone does have to go outside to open and close them. Many people leave the shutters on the north and west walls closed all winter. Those on the south and east sides are opened to admit the heat of the sun in the daytime.

Many passive solar houses have inside shutters. The easiest ones are sheets of Styrofoam set in place on the inside of the windows. The Perlbergs use magnetic cabinet door catches to hold their panels in place. In my old house, I simply cut the panels for a loose friction fit. They work fine. The Styrofoam is not very pretty, does get dirty, and has to be stored someplace when not in the windows.

Many manufacturers have recognized the problem and jumped on the bandwagon with insulating shades or shutters. The best I have seen is manufactured by the Insulating Shade Co., Inc.[†] They are fairly expensive (around $3 per square foot) but do a fantastic job. If you face the shade with a decorative fabric, it can serve as curtains as well as insulation.

Shades

I prefer a much simpler solution. Merely install a standard light-tight shade in the wide space between the window sash and storm window as I show on the working drawings. Light-tight shades have a track at the sides and light seals at the top and bottom. Obviously, if they are impervious to light, they will also leak very little air. What makes them work especially well in this case is that they are creating two air spaces. Laminate a layer of reflective Mylar to the outside, and you have a super insulating window cover at very low cost. These shades cost only about $1.50 per square foot.

Doors

Doors are another very expensive item. A pre-hung exterior door complete with frame and hardware can cost $300 to $400 at your local lumberyard. A good top-of-the-line exterior door without hardware can be bought wholesale from Pease Lumber Co.[†] or Fingerle Lumber Co.[†] for $40 to $60 and installed in a job-built frame as we did with our windows. Homemade doors are also a possibility. See Chapter 14 for instructions for and photos of interior doors. Since all of these houses have vestibules, the exterior doors can be constructed in the same fashion. I gave instructions for fabricating insulated exterior doors in *30 Energy-Efficient Houses.*

The secret to easy installation of a homebuilt door is in the hardware. Again, the tricky mortise-type hinges and locksets make hanging an exterior door in the standard carpenter fashion difficult for the beginner. The early settlers used leather hinges which were simply screwed to the face of the door and frame. Primitive, but they worked. Surface-type locksets of many different varieties were also used. Fortunately for the amateur builder, many types of surface hinges and locks are still made. The most familiar hinge is

the ugly Stanley T-hinge which is usually made of galvanized metal. Stanley and other companies make several models of attractive surface-type hinges in brass and iron. Should you be hanging the door from one of the main structural posts, gate hinges are a good sturdy choice. These are much stronger than conventional butt hinges. Almost everyone has experienced doors with sagging hinges, stripped threads, and loose screws. Surface hinges apply most of their pressure at 90° to the direction of insertion of screws, thereby making stripped threads very unlikely. Using a framing member directly as a door frame means that lock and hinge screws can be much longer and will be less likely to split the frame.

Door Hardware

Locksets and dead bolts should always be surface-applied to insure maximum security. Mortised-in locksets take a big bite out of the door and weaken it significantly. If you buy a new door, specify that it not be prepared for hardware. Many of them now come predrilled for those inadequate "cylindrical" locksets. If you buy a used door that is already drilled, buy a Schlage lockset. Schlage invented this type of lock and all of the rest are inferior copies. I recommend using the old-fashioned Stanley black thumb latch with a dead bolt above it. Russwin and Yale make quality dead bolts. Look for name-brand dead bolts if you buy used locks.

If security is a problem for you, buy a Finnish lockset with a triangular key. The manufacturers offer a reward for anyone who can prove that these locks have ever been picked. Any maximum-security dead bolt should have a plate bolted through the door and a wrap-around striker plate. Before you go to such lengths, though, make sure that it's not easy to gain entrance through another part of the house, such as the greenhouse, thereby negating all of your efforts on the main door.

If you build a thick, insulated exterior door, be forewarned; dead locks can be ordered to fit any thickness door but standard locksets will not fit. Two of the houses in this book went through this hassle. For thick doors, stick to surface-applied hardware. I described exact construction details for exterior doors in *30 Energy-Efficient Houses.*

Many of the door-building techniques which I show for interior doors in Chapter 14 are suitable for exterior doors as well. None of them are insulated doors, but since all of my houses show air lock entries, insulated doors are unnecessary.

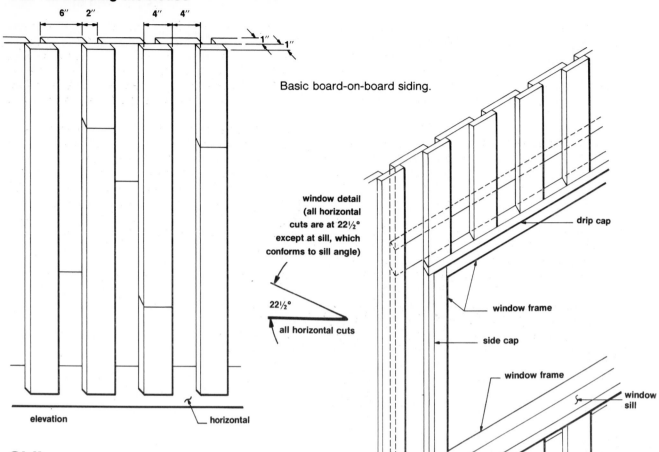

Basic board-on-board siding.

window detail
(all horizontal
cuts are at 22½°
except at sill, which
conforms to sill angle)

22½°

all horizontal cuts

drip cap

window frame

side cap

window frame

window sill

elevation

horizontal

Siding

After carefully installing all of your doors and windows, you are ready to install the siding. The framing system is designed for vertical siding; horizontal siding doesn't work. I recommend four different patterns of siding. Board and batten is the quickest and easiest. Shiplap is very tight but requires milling. Tongue and groove requires milling and shrinkage is critical; thoroughly dried lumber should be used. Board on board is the hardest to execute but the most handsome. Since it traps an extra layer of air under almost half of the surface area, it is the most energy-conserving pattern.

Your final decision will probably rest upon aesthetics and cost of the material. Most of the houses were sided in roughsawn green pine. Cedar, cypress, and redwood are also represented. The more expensive woods usually do not come roughsawn. If they are available this way, it usually means that they are "resawn," an incredibly wasteful practice that only American society could conceive. This means that finished, milled lumber is run back through a saw to get the desired roughcut look. Our local lumberyard is actually selling plain, square-edged, roughsawn pine boards, prestained and wrapped in plastic, for about ten times the price of unstained boards.

A major trick to installing vertical siding is to install it before the roof is sheathed. In this fashion, extensive scaffolding is avoided, and trim work at the eaves is easy and safe. The local contractors will all think you have lost your marbles, but you'll probably do a tighter siding job than they will. If your wood is very green, it may pay to wait and rent a set of pump jacks for installing the siding. Whenever you install the siding, seal the joint between the siding and the doors and windows as you go. Keep your tube of Mono caulking warm, 80 to 90°F., and apply it to the joint before installing the board. In this way you will have a weather-tight seal with no visible caulking.

Siding should be installed with hot-dipped galvanized nails. Many lumberyards will try to sell you a cheap imitation which is called galvanealed. Don't buy them. The galvanized nails have a rough, dull surface. Galvanealed are similar in color with a smooth surface. Aluminum nails can also be used, but they tend to stain natural finishes on redwood and cedar.

The board-on-board pattern is the only siding which requires special instructions. It is done in two distinct layers and should be executed as shown in the drawings. It is very important that the voids under the outer layer be closed top and bottom, or the siding pattern will cool the house in winter, not warm it. If it is necessay to splice two boards, bevel the horizontal joints so that water will not leak into the wall. Flashings must be installed as shown in Chapters 7 and 15 before starting the siding.

Shingles

For a relatively low materials cost (about 50¢/sq. ft.), you can have cedar shingles as an exterior finish. If you want a maintenance-free exterior and can't afford cedar siding, sawn cedar shingles cost about half as much but they are time-consuming to install. Roughsawn cedar shakes are also a possibility, but they are tricky for the beginner to install. Cedar sidewall shingles must be installed over plywood or wood plank sheathing. Clear and detailed installation directions, as well as descriptions of every possible size and grade of handsplit and sawn shingles are available from Red Cedar Shingle and Handsplit Shake Bureau.†

Cedar shingles should not need maintenance during your lifetime. If you dip them in clear Cup-rinol before installing, the shingles will weather to a uniform light brown color, eventually bleaching toward gray, instead of the dark brown and black that some people find objectionable.

Plywood Sidings

As I have noted previously, plywood is a very efficient way to use wood. Until recently, variously patterned plywood sidings were popular with builders. Intense foreign demand has sent plywood prices skyward, considerably negating the economies of using this material as a siding. However, if you are in a relatively warm climate where the plywood can do double duty as sheathing and siding, it may still make economic sense. It goes up very quickly, so it can save quite a bit of labor cost.

Standard plywood sidings are manufactured in fir, cedar, and redwood, with a variety of grooves. Redwood and cedar plywoods have become so expensive that you might as well use the real thing, i.e., solid boards. I recommend that you use roughsawn fir plywood, ⅝-inch thick with no grooves. The manufacturers charge about 50 percent more for the grooves which make the plywood resemble planks. The grooving operation costs virtually nothing but actually weakens the plywood and makes it less weatherproof. I recommend installing 1X3 roughsawn battens at 16 inches on center. The battens hide the plywood panel joints and give the siding more depth than do the recessed grooves. Also, the battens make the plywood joint at floor levels very unnoticeable. Grooved patterns are always a mess when used on houses of over one floor unless one changes plane or pattern at the floor line. A pigmented Cuprinol stain makes a good finish for this siding.

Chapter 14

Interior Finishes, Trim, Cabinets, Shelves, and Painting

The interior finishes of your house establish its character; this is where you can really begin to see your home take shape. Most builders' houses come with acres of Sheetrock trimmed with ugly clamshell moldings surrounding flush doors made of high-grade cardboard. The austere nature of these finishes is offset by Masonite fake paneling, gaudy kitchen cabinets, brightly colored carpeting, and plastic tiles. You can have a much more handsome interior at considerable savings in labor and materials if you go at the job properly. Contrary to popular notions, you do not need to be an expert finish carpenter to do a very credible job of finishing off the interior of your house. Even if you have all of the work done, many of these ideas will save money while producing a high-quality interior.

Planning Your Finishes

The post and beam framing system and the use of masonry floors on grade in my basic house construction eliminate much of the work required in finishing the interior. When selecting interior finishes, keep fire safety and lighting in mind. Many people tend to overdo the use of wood as an interior surface. Post and beam framing already provides a rich backdrop of wood. Any additional wood should be used sparingly. Keep wood construction well away from all heating and cooking appliances.

Light-colored reflective surfaces will cut down on the need for expensive artificial lighting. Plaster or Sheetrock should be used in small bedrooms and on walls where it can reflect light from south-facing skylights and windows. Good places for wood paneling are stairs, halls, and bathrooms where lighter finishes would soil quickly. Sloping ceilings are an excellent place for wood paneling, since large ceiling areas make Sheetrock application difficult for beginners. The location of lighting fixtures should be carefully coordinated with your finish selection so that you get maximum efficiency from your fixtures.

Wall Finishes

I advocate the use of three basic wall finishes. Plaster is a great favorite and is surprisingly easy if you know how to go about it. Sheetrock seems to be universally hated, but is the standard finish of the industry. If you know how, you can do a much better job than the commercial contractor. Roughsawn paneling can make a very attractive finish if you treat the joints so that shrinkage

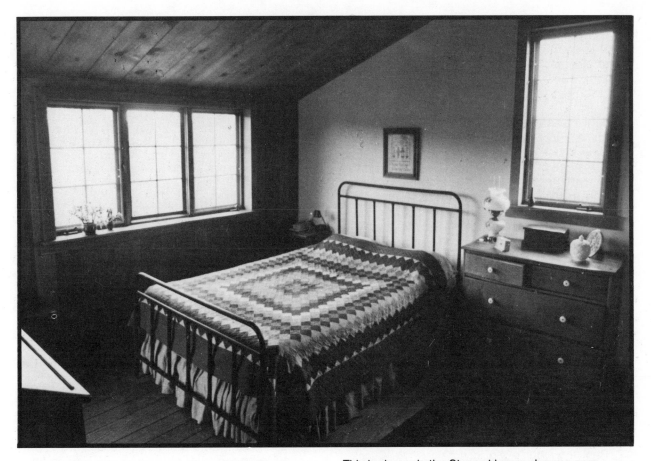

This bedroom in the Stoners' house shows a carefully considered balance of wood paneling and Sheetrock.

doesn't show. Kiln-dried, V-jointed commercial paneling in cedar is easy to install and makes a waterproof bathroom finish at less cost than tile.

A major key to the easy, inexpensive installation of finishes lies in the basic framing. Rather than add expensive and difficult-to-fit trim later, use the basic framing members of the house as the finish frames for doors and windows. Either roughsawn or finish lumber can be used and if it is selected carefully, it makes a fine-looking job. My very first house, built over twenty years ago, used this system. I devised it due to the limitations of an extremely low budget. It works very well, saves a lot of money, and the frames are actually stronger than if they were made in conventional fashion.

Plaster

Plaster makes a beautiful wall, but commercial plasterers are a dying breed. Fortunately, if you plan your job properly, it can be easy. Anyone who has ever attempted to patch a hole in an old

plaster wall will probably throw up their hands in horror. Believe me, applying new plaster is much different.

Ceilings and corners require a great deal of skill, but flat wall surfaces are almost a breeze. Plan your work carefully so that you don't have to turn corners or apply plaster to ceilings and you can have a fine do-it-yourself plaster finish for less than the cost of hiring someone to install Sheetrock. If you plan to use plaster as a finish, extend your door and window casings by about 2 inches so that you have a surface to plaster against. By doing your framing this way, you avoid adding extra trim at a later date. If you do have to turn a corner and there is no exposed post, install a wood trim piece. Apply the final finish coat (stain, paint, oil) to all surfaces abutting the plaster *before* starting work. Then cover the surfaces with masking tape.

Your plaster will have a natural, light gray, rough finish when you apply it. It will not need any additional finish. After a period of years, you can paint the plaster. Of course, if you want it some color other than light gray, you should paint it while the masking tape is still in place on the trim. I must emphasize that the result is not a typical smooth, white plaster finish, but a rough sand finish. The smooth, hard, white finish is difficult to achieve and requires years of practice.

To begin plastering, you must have a surface on which to apply the material. If you have initially planned to use plaster, you may have used Styrofoam insulation and wire mesh. If not, you must apply gypsum or metal lath to your walls before starting to plaster. If you do not have projecting jambs at doors and windows, a special metal plaster stop (Milcor 66SF) can be installed with the gypsum lath.

Applying Plaster

Several of my clients have done their own plastering using David Howard's directions. Here is an expanded version:

1. Use a perlite-base plaster in 80-pound bags. Gypsolite, Litemix, or Structolite are common trade names. For a whiter plaster (perlite is a medium gray), add 2 buckets of Stipple to each bag of mix.

2. Rent a 5½-cubic-yard concrete mixer. Check it over carefully before accepting it.

3. Use high-quality tools — a good plastering trowel costs about $10, a good hawk about $8. The latter can be homemade provided you do a good job.

4. Check your bags of plaster for a batch number. The plaster must be fresh or it will turn brown and crack. Test a small quantity of plaster from each batch number. If the plaster hardens rapidly and starts to turn brown, return it and get your money back. Make absolutely sure that you test each batch as the dealer may have old stock on hand.

5. Never apply plaster when the inside temperature is less than 50°F. Keep temporary heat on at night in cold weather until the plaster has cured. If it freezes on the wall, it is ruined.

6. Clean all tools and the mixer thoroughly after each use. Also clean at the end of each batch.

7. If you are using Styrofoam as a base, you must also apply small-mesh chicken wire as a reinforcement. Staple the mesh tightly to the studs with ¾-inch staples.

8. Plaster has the right amount of water in the mix when it's a bit soupy and will readily squeeze out through your fingers. Let the plaster set for thirty minutes after mixing, then apply.

9. Two coats of plaster are usually sufficient. Start at the edge of the wall to be plastered. Put a line of plaster on the edge of the trowel, and press into the side of the post or wood trim at the perimeter of the wall. Start in an area which isn't exposed, say in a closet or under a counter. Always cover a full wall at a time on the finish coat.

10. Let plaster set for about thirty minutes, then smooth it lightly with a trowel. Let it set for two hours, and when just slightly hard, smooth off the high spots with a trowel. This will result in a rustic, but uniform finish.

11. In hot, dry weather, spray a light mist of water on the wall surface each hour for the first three or four hours. This will prevent too-rapid drying and cracks.

12. In summer weather, the plaster may begin to harden in the wheelbarrow. Add a bit of water to restore the original consistency. (You will need a wheelbarrow to transport the plaster from the mixer bucket to the work area.)

Sheetrock (Gypsum Board)

Sheetrock is a universally used trade name for gypsum plaster manufactured in rigid boards. It comes in two basic types, waterproof (green color) and regular. Standard thicknesses are ⅜-inch (used in cheap tract houses), ½-inch (standard), and ⅝-inch (used where a one-hour fire rating is required, as in commercial exitways). Standard sheets are 4 feet wide with tapered edges along the length of the sheet, and vary in length by 2-foot increments from 6 to 16 feet. Eight-foot-long sheets are most commonly used. Our framing system is designed to allow horizontal application of longer sheets, thereby eliminating a great deal of work.

Before starting to install Sheetrock, examine your walls carefully to make sure that you have framing members behind all ends and edges of the sheets. This is a common error. If you are planning a Sheetrock finish, you should look ahead and make sure that all blocking is in place *before* installing your insulation.

A vapor barrier is vital to keeping moisture out of your walls and insulation. Styrofoam insulation doesn't need an extra vapor barrier, but one is vital if you use fiberglass or cellulose insulation. Some Sheetrock is manufactured with a foil backing laminated to the board and it makes an excellent vapor barrier, provided it is installed without breaks in its surface. This means installing it with a mastic at seams and sealing all penetrations of the wall such as electrical outlets.

Better still, use surface wiring and eliminate any breaks in the Sheetrock.

In addition to providing a vapor barrier, the foil improves the thermal performance of your wall. If you don't use the foil-backed Sheetrock, which might have to be special-ordered in some parts of the country, use a 6-mil vinyl vapor barrier applied to the full inside surface of all exterior walls and ceilings. Use as large a sheet as practical, and carefully seal all joints with duct tape, an aluminum-color, heavy-duty tape used by heating contractors to make airtight connections in metal ductwork. It is useful for all sealing operations, as it is a high-quality material designed for permanent installation.

Good Sheetrock installers use Sheetrock screws rather than nails. Nails frequently work their way out of the framing as the house dries out, requiring renailing and respackling of the Sheetrock.

Spackling is a particularly difficult operation for the beginner. You may want to hire a professional for this, particularly if there are many ceilings and corners. Ceilings in particular are very hard for beginners, as they are large, flat areas which catch light and really require a professional touch for a good job.

Simple walls with horizontal joints are relatively

The corner trowel is necessary when tackling inside corners.

easy and can be done by the beginner. There are lots of simple tricks which you should know. First, you need proper equipment. THIS IS VITAL. You have undoubtedly seen illustrations of someone applying Sheetrock compound with a tiny putty knife. This just doesn't work. You need a good, professional, wide taping knife. These are usually 9 inches to 13 inches wide and have a slight built-in taper so that they feather the compound over the Sheetrock joints.

Inside corners are a nightmare for the beginner, particularly if done without a corner trowel. This is a 90°, double-faced, tapered trowel which will save many hours of frustration. You will also need a plasterer's hawk to hold your compound so that you can apply it easily. This is a square metal plate with a vertical handle on the bottom. A piece of smooth plywood with a handle screwed to the bottom makes a good, inexpensive substitute. Finally, you need a 5-inch-wide Sheetrock trowel which is similar to a putty knife, but bigger. This is used for covering the heads of the Sheetrock screws with compound. Use pre-mixed compound in a large container. One 5-gallon can will do.

Lay out your Sheetrock installation with the absolute minimum of joints. Longitudinal joints are tapered to receive Sheetrock tape. Use standard paper tape. Before applying tape, wet it slightly. This will cause the taping compound to adhere more tightly. Now apply a very thin coat of compound along the tapered edges with the 5-inch trowel. Then apply the dampened tape, setting it into the compound with the same trowel. Now apply a very thin coat of compound *over* the tape with your wide knife. The compound should just cover the tape. Make sure all edges are embedded in compound, and remove all bubbles.

The trick to finishing Sheetrock is to go over it quickly with a number of very thin coats. Move the trowel briskly. Don't worry about voids; they will be filled by later coats. Most beginners make the mistake of applying too much compound leaving lumps and ridges which require a long drying time and much sanding. A true professional has to do little or no sanding. A quick once-over between coats with the edge of your trowel will remove any slight ridges or grains of compound. A damp sponge is good for a final touch-up.

Make sure that your tools are spotlessly clean at all times and use fresh compound. *Do not put compound back in the bucket.* Buy your compound from a reputable dealer who stores it in a heated warehouse and keeps it from freezing. If it freezes either in the can or on the wall, it is ruined and must be discarded or removed.

For a really fine Sheetrock installation, use two layers of ⅜-inch Sheetrock. Install the first layer with Sheetrock screws and the second primarily with mastic with just enough screws to hold the sheet in place. Using this system, you get plenty of opportunity to practice cutting and fitting on your first layer. If you use the surface electrical system or the perfectly rectangular outlet boxes which I recommend in Chapter 9, your job will be much easier. Brookstone Co.† stocks a jig which slips into the outlet boxes and marks their position for cutting when a sheet is pressed in place against the wall.

The two layers of this Sheetrock system have the joints staggered so that all seams are completely concealed by taping. Also, any irregularities in the framing system are concealed much better. With conventional one-layer Sheetrock systems, after several years, seams may begin to show slightly. The major suppliers of gypsum board are National Gypsum Co.,† makers of Gold Bond, and United States Gypsum.† Either of them can supply very detailed instructions for installing Sheetrock. Check in *Sweets Architectural Catalog Files* for installation directions, or order them from one of the manufacturers.

Wood Paneling

Walls and ceilings can be economically and attractively finished in roughsawn paneling. Any of the patterns which I described in the last chapter will conceal shrinkage at the joints nicely. Cedar shingles also make a nice interior finish. Hand-split shakes could also be used, but are too rough for my taste.

Roughsawn siding and shingles can be very difficult to fit because of the unevenness of the material. These problems can be solved by leaving a slot at the floor and ceiling. Just paint the framing members to which they will be nailed a dark color such as black or brown before installing the paneling. Square-cut all of the paneling to the same length and nail it to the wall, leaving about ¾ inch of the dark framing showing at the top and bottom. Using the workbench and saw guide, a stop can be applied to the bench and everything cut to exact length. Not only does this system give very professional-looking results, it can be done

with ease. A similar technique can be used for standard V-jointed cedar or hardwood paneling. The V-jointed planks are much easier to fit, but much more expensive. Since they are of uniform thickness, you can apply any trim you choose.

Interior Trim

Cutting and fitting trim around windows, doors, baseboards, and other places where materials meet take lots of time and can cost a great deal for the materials themselves. Thinking ahead and using advanced design details can eliminate much of this cost. If materials are designed and cut so that they go together properly, they won't need trim. In cases where trim is necessary, it can be much simpler and easier to apply than typical lumberyard patterns.

Metal Trim

Commercial installations use low-cost metal trim pieces called L-channels around windows and doors in both plaster and Sheetrock construction. This is galvanized metal trim which allows plaster or spackling to be applied to the surface of the wall and to be terminated in a neat square edge with no additional work. I use the L-channel as a standard trim, because I feel that houses with full wood ceilings and a post and beam frame have enough wood without adding wood around doors and windows. When installing your L-channels, apply masking tape to the wood surface before putting the channels in place. In this way, you can paint the channels without getting paint on the wood frames. If you wish, you can paint the channels before installing them. In any case, a neat paint line is required for a professional job.

Narrow Wood Trim

The idea of metal trim may not appeal to you but you may still want an easy way to trim Sheetrock. (Plaster can be run up against wood members with no additional trim; Sheetrock spackling compound will shrink and crack at the wood members.) A very narrow wood molding which is shaped like an angle is made in a variety of sizes and is a stock item for most lumberyards. It is usually used to trim corners of plywood paneling so that the edges don't show. It also makes a

---

†The address of this and other manufacturers and associations so indicated will be found under "Addresses of Manufacturers and Associations" in Part IV.

dandy means of finishing off my window and door jambs. The Sheetrock is lapped about half-way over the framing member, and the wooden angle trim is surface-applied. In this case, the Sheetrock should be painted and the trim finished before it is nailed in place. This will give it a crisp, professional appearance. The wooden angle is available in different sizes so that you can trim either ½- or ¾-inch (double layer of ⅜-inch) Sheetrock jobs with this material.

Traditional Wood Trim

Maybe you want some authentic trim to go with multipaned windows, post and beam frame, and antique furniture. A visit to most lumberyards will prove discouraging. All of the stock patterns are ugly, complex moldings. None of them are authentic, and they all have to be mitered or coped to fit together at the corners. Mitering is very difficult for the beginner and the cheap wood from which they make the moldings will shrink and cause the mitered joints to open up.

As an alternate to this, make your own trim. You will need a router, but the cost of the router is considerably lower than the cost of Colonial trim for a typical house. There are many other uses for the router in finishing your house. The trim pattern I have in mind was a very common one in the late 1700s and early 1800s. It consists of a simple 1X3-inch or 1X4-inch board with an easy-to-cut rounded bead on one or both edges. In Colonial America, this was accomplished with a hand plane. I use a router. If you want to be completely authentic, Woodcraft Supply Corp.† has molding planes which will make the pattern by hand. Since this is not an ornate molding, it doesn't have to be mitered around corners. If you want it to turn a corner, you can make a lap joint and then run the bead down one side and across the end of the board.

Baseboards

Whether or not you use Colonial trim around windows and doors, the above trim will serve nicely as a baseboard. I have also used 1X3-inch pieces of roughsawn pine. Paint the wall and stain the baseboard before putting it in place. Plane or sand the top of the baseboard smooth, or it will collect dirt and be very difficult to clean without making a mess of the wall finish.

This beautiful door was designed and built for Bill Caddell by Konrod Jubstel of Valparaiso, Indiana.

Sliding, bypassing doors are simple and use space efficiently.

Doors, Stairs, Cabinets, and Counter Tops

These complex millwork items usually strike terror into the heart of the beginner. If you approach them the right way, they can be easy and fun to build. The prime rule is to keep it simple. Instead of using tricky cabinetmaker's joinery, use butted or lapped joints pinned with dowels to hold the corners together. The workbench and miter arm will enable you to make perfect 90° flush cuts every time. Set a block on your bench and make all cuts for parallel sides at the same time. Use Aerobond, a high-quality epoxy adhesive, available from Adhesive Engineering Co.,† to fasten the parts together.

Doors

Nothing is more sickening than the prices, designs, and quality of the doors at your local lumberyard. Basically, all of the doors I use are constructed of two layers of wood, one ¾ inch

Open riser-type stairs are easy to build using stair gauges and a framing square for the layout.

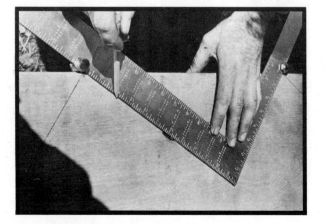

The gauges hold the square at a uniform angle.

thick, the other 1¼ inches thick (commonly called ⁵⁄₄ or five-quarter). If the doors are glazed or paneled, the framing members overlap at the corners. For flush doors, the boards are tongue and grooved or shiplapped and appear flush on one face. The opposite face either has a simple frame for the modern door or a crossbuck for the traditional style. For a more refined detail, the edges of the boards can be finished with a rounded bead as described under "Traditional Wood Trim" above.

The doors should be hung in the openings with surface-type hinges and latches as described in Chapter 13. The frame-type doors are particularly suited for closets. Sliding, bypassing doors make for easy access to a closet. Do not buy the usual Stanley-type sliding-door hardware. It is not durable and does not slide well. Buy Grant sliding-door hardware. It has four-wheel trolleys which are exceptionally smooth rolling and easy to adjust. In many cases, a door which slides along the wall works well. These are particularly handy for winter vestibules, greenhouses, and the like where the door can be left open in the summer without being in the way.

Stairs

Traditional closed-riser staircases are expensive and quite difficult to build. Use an open-riser stair. It is very simply made of roughsawn 2X12-inch stringers (side supports for the stairs) with planed 2X10-inch treads of oak or pine. The two stringers are cut to fit the opening, and equally spaced base lines for the treads are drawn on both stringers. This is done by means of two small brass gadgets known as stair gauges (also called rafter gauges), which are simply fastened to the edge of a standard carpenter's framing square, enabling it to be held at a uniform angle at all times. The edge of the stringer is then di-

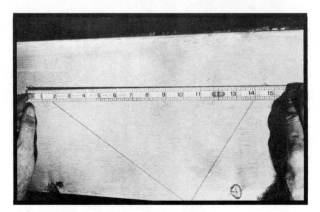

Divide the stringers into equal parts.

vided into equal parts and the square slid along, marking a line for the top of each tread. Transfer this mark to both faces of the stringers.

Now cut the treads to length to fit exactly between the stringers. This is where your miter arm really shines, as you can cut them all perfectly in just a few minutes. Apply epoxy glue to the ends of each tread and assemble the staircase, tacking the treads in place with finish nails from the outside of the stringer. Leave these nails projecting; they will be removed later. Now, lay the assembled stairs carefully on one side, placing blocks between the nails. Drill three ¾-inch-diameter holes through the stringers and 2 inches into the end of each tread. Dip 5-inch lengths of hardwood dowel into glue and pound them into the holes. After the glue dries, cut the dowels off flush with the stringer. Continue this operation for all the treads; then turn the stairs over and repeat on the opposite side.

Set the stairs in place while the glue is drying, checking to make sure that they are square and level. You may want to push them just a bit out of square to make them fit the house better. A simple railing can be constructed of a piece of 2X6 turned on edge with its edges and ends rounded off. The rail is attached to 4X4 newel posts by means of 1-inch-diameter dowels.

Cabinets

Kitchen cabinets are likely to be one of the most complicated items in the house for the first-time builder. Standard commercial cabinets are extremely wasteful of both labor and materials. You have already built a room which has a floor and walls. Then you buy a bunch of factory- or shop-built boxes, each of which has sides, a bottom, and a back. The result is a mass of multiple layers

of unnecessary, expensive materials which serve no useful purpose. If you build your own cabinets, you can eliminate all these wasteful duplicate pieces. Directions for building very simple cabinets can be found in USDA Handbook #364 by L. O. Anderson, *Low-Cost Homes for Rural America.* It is available from your local extension agent, or from the U.S. Government Printing Office, for $2. It also shows you how to make easy open shelving units. These, I have found, are much more useful for storing kitchen items and are much cheaper than closed cabinets.

By the time you get to the kitchen, you may be just too tired or rushed to build your own cabinets. You will quickly discover that your lovable local cabinet dealer wants several thousand dollars for some "Cathedral Oak, Genuine Formica, Mediterranean-Style" kitchen cabinets topped off with pale green, imitation marble counters with gold flecks embedded in them. Somehow, the proprietors of cabinet shops never seem to have heard of good taste.

Sears makes a line of crisp, contemporary cabinets of exceptional quality at a very low price (cat. no. 65 KY 6346–6350). They have steel frames with Formica-surfaced particle board fronts and shelves, come knocked down, and are

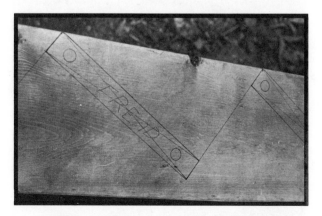

Mark the stringer for position of the tread and dowel.

Finished open riser-type stairs.

easy to assemble. The prices are so low that you couldn't even purchase the materials for that amount. The base cabinets come in only four different sizes, not including a sink front. The individual cabinets do not have wasteful ends, though these are sold separately and match the fronts. It is easy to construct a sink cabinet using a pair of the end panels for the doors. Five different sizes of matching wall cabinets are also available. For slightly more money, Sears sells unfinished pine, knocked-down cabinets in a wide variety of sizes (you have to apply your own finish). Sears also stocks very expensive, fully assembled wood cabinets with every possible accessory.

Sears kitchen cabinets — inexpensive, easy to assemble, and available throughout the United States and Canada (here and on facing page).

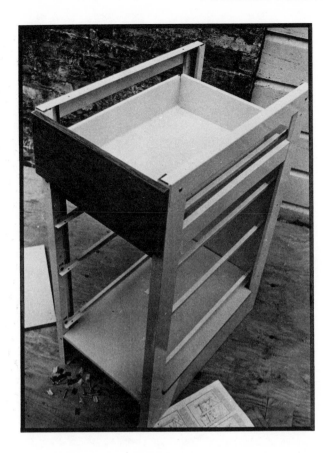

A hardwood edge prevents chipping and cracking of Formica or quarry tile.

Counter Tops

You can really get taken buying counter tops at your local cabinet shop. Most places want $1.00 to $1.50 *per inch* for their formed counter tops (the ones with the lumpy raised edge which chips easily and the integral, coved backsplash). Invariably, these monstrosities are encrusted with all sorts of glitter and colored flakes. Most shops never stock plain white or tasteful colors and always want a steep premium for plain, good-looking solid colors.

If you want Formica or a similar plastic laminate for its easy cleanability, buy the laminate in sheet form, which for some reason is readily available in plain colors, and install it yourself. Backsplashes add a lot to the cost and are hard to clean. I prefer to make the whole back wall cleanable. I either laminate a sheet of Formica directly to the wall or cover the wall with tile or another impervious covering. A full piece of Formica for the wall between base and wall cabinets costs about the same as that 4-inch-high, lumpy, dirt-catching backsplash.

Rather than having a fragile strip of Formica on the front edge of the cabinets, trim the front edge with a piece of hardwood. Formica is brittle and chips easily along the edge. If you use the hardwood edge strip, this possibility is eliminated. For a really easy-to-clean, totally heatproof counter top (ever see what a cigarette does to Formica?), use ceramic or quarry tile installed over ¾-inch plywood. Again, I use a hardwood edge strip. For

instructions for working with masonry materials, see Chapter 12.

Laminated maple tops — known as butcher block — make exceptionally nice counter tops. I always like to have one large section of maple block counter top in my kitchens. A wide section can also be used as an eating area. Local lumberyards can order these tops; they are also available from Sears. These tops can easily be homemade using scrap maple flooring and Aerobond epoxy glue.

Painting and Finishing

Some general rules: Buy only major brand-name paints and finishes, not Sears, Truvalu, or other chain brands of undetermined origin. Major name brands are Pittsburgh, Glidden, Devoe, Dutch Boy, and Sherwin-Williams. Minwax and Olympic make fine stains and varnishes. Modern paints are complex chemical combinations which can be defective. You are in much better shape to complain if you bought from a major manufacturer. If you buy good paint, chances are that it will be durable. Always buy in 5-gallon lots if possible, and buy from a commercial paint dealer, not a hardware store. A 5-gallon can can be bought for less than the combined cost of four 1-gallon cans.

Finish both sides of all wooden pieces wherever possible. Sealing just one side of wood is a sure invitation to warpage. Paint or stain all adjoining materials with different finishes before assembly. Prepare all surfaces thoroughly. Make sure that they are clean, dry, and dust-free. Prime all surfaces, except those with a stain finish, with an appropriate primer. Bin, made by Zinsser and Co.,† is an excellent alcohol-based primer which acts as a sealer and doesn't raise grain. It should be used as a first coat for all painted woodwork. It can also be used on any surface where there is a problem with bleeding or staining. Almost all reputable paint stores stock Bin. For high-quality finish work, all surfaces should be buffed with fine sandpaper or steel wool between coats.

Weather is very critical to painting and finishing. Many painting materials, particularly latex paints and stains, are instantly ruined by freezing. The weather should be dry, and the temperature should be over 55°F. Your house should have a heat source if nighttime temperatures are likely to drop below 40°F. before the paint is dry. All adjacent materials with different finishes should be protected.

Colors

One frequently suspects that the paint companies hire the same tasteless decorators who select colors for GM cars to formulate their paint colors. Most clerks in paint stores don't have the foggiest notion of how to mix a color. I usually mix my own.

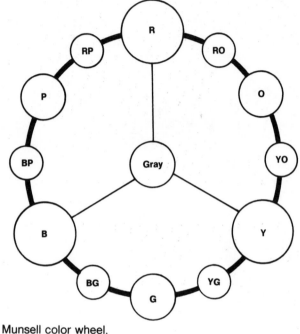

Munsell color wheel.

Color mixing is easy once you understand the basic principles. The drawing shows a Munsell color wheel which graphically demonstrates the relationship of primary and secondary colors to each other. Red, blue, and yellow are the primaries. Equal mixtures of two of the three primaries create the secondaries, orange, purple, and green. The center of the diagram is occupied by gray. Equal mixtures of any of the colors opposite each other will produce gray. In practical application, I use this chart to modify commercial colors, which are usually too bright. By adding a bit of green to a red paint I mute it and take it toward gray. Similarly, a bit of orange added to blue will tone it down or vice versa.

The Munsell system can completely define any visible color with a reference number. If you will imagine the color wheel as a circle of colors surrounding the equator of a globe with white at the North Pole and black at the South Pole, you will have a Munsell solid. Munsell publishes a book of precisely accurate color plates which can be represented as slices taken out of this solid somewhat similar to sections of an orange. This system is an international standard for color reference. Any major paint company can mix a color to one of the numbers. If you ever have to match a color exactly, check the Munsell hue book in a large technical library. (The books are for sale, but cost several hundred dollars due to the high costs involved in manufacturing color chips to precise, accurate colors.)

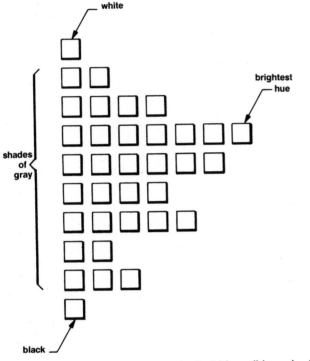

Typical Munsell hue chart.

Munsell also provides a color-matching service. You send the color to be matched to them, and they will furnish you with the proper color number. Their address is: Munsell Color System, 2442 N. Calvert St., Baltimore, MD 21218. Be sure to write first for a price quotation.

For most interiors, I use a plain white with accent colors. Avoid so-called "off-whites," bone white, and the like. They show dirt very quickly. They are carefully formulated to do so. Pittsburgh #630 is a pure white which stays nice looking. When I want a neutral background shade, I mix my own. I add quantities of yellow ochre, burnt umber, and lampblack to a white tinting base until I get the shade I want. Depending upon the proportion of the colors, you get a warm gray or a light yellow brown. I find that this range of color goes nicely with natural woods.

Natural Wood Finishes

If stained finishes are desired on pine, I find the Minwax Fruitwood or Colonial Pine shades do a good job. Surfaces must be sanded thoroughly in order for stain to penetrate uniformly. Minwax antique oil also makes a fine finish that can be applied over the stain or directly to the wood. It produces a soft, mellow finish. Linseed oil makes a good sealer for exposed beams and decking. Use boiled, not raw, linseed oil for a fast-drying finish. It is particularly good if the surface finish is uneven. For areas of heavy wear such as floors, stairs, and cabinets, polyurethane varnish is the best bet. The gloss finish is much harder than the satin, but not very attractive.

To get a nice-looking floor finish, I apply two coats of gloss, buffing well between coats, and then finish-coat with a light application of satin. This gives a hard finish without the high gloss. Gloss finishes show every imperfection; avoid them unless you are a real pro.

Chapter 15

Roofing, Flashings, Skylights, and Greenhouses

Early houses on this continent were roofed with readily available natural materials such as thatch, bark, and handsplit shakes. Such materials have become largely obsolete due to the high costs of hand labor. Indeed, I know of only one person in all of North America who knows how to weave a thatched roof.

Later houses had roofs of tile, slate, and metal. Copper and a lead-coated steel known as terne were very popular. Terne is so durable that one still sees it on the roofs of many old houses throughout the country.

Early in this century, industry started copying these traditional materials with mass-produced, low-cost substitutes. Standing-seam terne and copper were replaced by corrugated aluminum or galvanized steel sheets. Wood and slate shingles were replaced by imitations made of asphalt sheet impregnated with mineral granules. Even though they were applied in long strips, they were notched to look as though they were real, individual shingles.

Older roofs had widely spaced roof boards or lath to support the shingles or standing-seam roofs. These boards were replaced by labor-saving plywood sheets. "Modern" design dictated increas-ingly lower roof slopes, allowing moisture condensation and snow build-up, causing rapid deterioration. Finally, the day of reckoning came. Oil supplies became tight, and the price of asphalt doubled and then tripled. Increasingly expensive plywood became a major cost in building a house. Housing prices rose dramatically as builders simply passed on the increased material cost without once considering alternatives.

In this chapter, I detail several alternatives to the plywood and asphalt shingle "tract roof." These roofs are made from ecologically sound, economical materials which can be used to collect rainfall.

Standing-Seam Terne Roofs

This roof is my favorite, and three of the houses in this book use terne roofs. Hundreds of people have written to me asking how they are installed — no other single material I have advocated seems to have created so much interest. Back in the days of cheap oil, terne was a luxury material. Now the material cost is about the same as for heavy-duty asphalt shingles. Unfortunately, buying the metal is just the beginning. These roofs require much hand work. They are not all that

Terne roofing — light in weight, yet very durable and attractive.

Sheet-metal brake — for making accurate bends in sheet metals, such as terne roofs.

difficult if you know exactly how to approach them and have lots of patience.

First, make a layout of your roof to determine exactly how much material to order. Terne is available through distributors of Follansbee Steel Corp. or at many roofer's supply houses. (See "Terne Roofing Distributors" in Part IV.) It comes in a wide variety of rolls and also in cut sheets in varying widths, weights, and with different coating thicknesses. Since cut sheets are more expensive and have to be special-ordered, I have always used the rolls.

The rolls which you should order are 28 inches wide by 50 feet long. You should also specify 40-pound IC terne. (This designates the weight of the lead coating per 100 square feet and the thickness of the metal itself.) The 28-inch-wide roll, when made into finished sections (called pans), covers almost exactly 25 inches. From experience, I have found that this is a very economical width. Roofers who are trying to make a lot of money will try to talk you into using narrower pans; 16-inch-wide pans will require 50 percent more work to fabricate and install than 25-inch ones, since all of the work is in bending the seams.

For purposes of the layout, divide your roof into 2-foot segments and count up the number of rows required. Check the exact dimensions of the roof to see if an even number of pans will fit. Our standard 36-foot-long house requires eighteen rows of pans. The two end rows will have to be trimmed about 3½ inches in width. The exact dimension will be determined by the amount of roof overhang, thickness of siding, and the dimensions of your drip edge. I use a standard galvanized drip edge as is used with asphalt shingles at all of the exposed edges of my terne roofs. These project ¾ inch, and the material is folded over them. Therefore, each edge adds 1½ inches to the dimension of the roof.

The device which bends the material is known as a brake. It is usually 8 or 10 feet long; 8 feet is the most common length and about the maximum-length roof pan which can be handled easily. With this in mind, divide your roof into 8-foot panels. Cross joints should be staggered, as the roof is weakened if they are in line from row to row. Also, it is very difficult to bend the seam with too many thicknesses of metal. See the sample layout of Frank Gilbert's roof here.

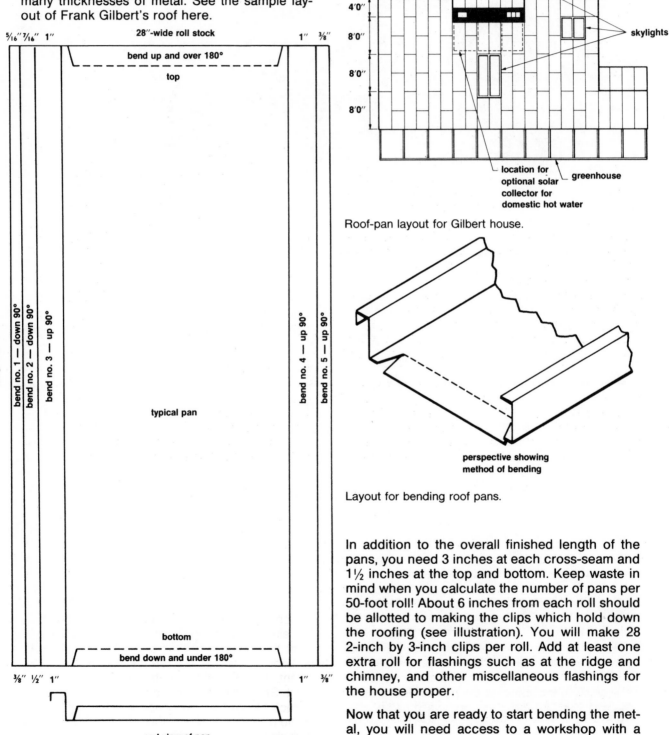

Roof-pan layout for Gilbert house.

Layout for bending roof pans.

In addition to the overall finished length of the pans, you need 3 inches at each cross-seam and 1½ inches at the top and bottom. Keep waste in mind when you calculate the number of pans per 50-foot roll! About 6 inches from each roll should be allotted to making the clips which hold down the roofing (see illustration). You will make 28 2-inch by 3-inch clips per roll. Add at least one extra roll for flashings such as at the ridge and chimney, and other miscellaneous flashings for the house proper.

Now that you are ready to start bending the metal, you will need access to a workshop with a

Mark each sheet with a pointed instrument as you go.

Bend number 2.

Bend number 1.

Bend number 3.

sheet metal brake. Most roofing shops and heating and air-conditioning firms of any size will have one of these tools. If you are lucky, you may be able to rent the shop for a weekend and hire one of the workmen to assist you in bending the sheets. It is definitely a two-person project. The sheets are long and cumbersome and must be aligned at both ends of the brake. You have to use a heavy-duty, cast-iron brake, not one of the portable aluminum ones used by the aluminum siding contractors.

First, cut a 2-inch strip of metal from the end of one of the rolls. This will be your pattern. Following the dimensions shown on the drawing, punch tiny holes in the metal at the points where bends are required. An awl or a very sharp nail is good for this. Punch the top and bottom clearly and mark each sheet as you go. Regardless of the

length of sheet, the top and bottom dimensions are the same. The dimensions shown on the pattern allow for a slight taper so that the sheets will nest together accurately.

First, cut each sheet to length, remembering to add 3 inches to each sheet for lateral joints. Now place the sheet on a workbench with one person on either side of the sheet. Place the pattern over first the top and then the bottom of the sheet, making a mark on the terne with a sharp instrument. Just dimple the metal, do not punch a hole in it. Start with short pans so that you can easily check for fit. The sequence of bends is tricky. I have numbered them 1 through 5, starting at the left side.

Begin bending with bend number 2; slide the right edge of the sheet into the brake and line up the second mark with the edge of the bending dog. It is very difficult for two people to line up and clamp both ends simultaneously. You should lightly clamp one end first and then align the other end. Now, pull the clamps tight. Grasp the rail on the bending arm and briskly swing it up so that you form a 90° bend at point number 2. Leave the sheet standing on edge and loosen the clamps slightly.

Now, slide the sheet toward you so that the marks for bend number 1 line up with the edge of the dog. Again clamp the sheet tightly, fastening one end lightly at first and then aligning the other end. Check carefully; on a long sheet this bend may not be uniform at the center of the sheet, and it *is* critical. Clamp tightly and bend. Fully loosen the brake. Slide sheet through the brake away from you so that the dog lines up with bend number 3. Clamp the sheet in place and bend the left side up at 90°. Loosen the brake fully and pull the sheet completely out of the brake. Drop the large portion of the sheet toward the floor so that the flange which you just bent is resting on the table of the brake.

Line up bend number 4 with the edge of the brake. You are now working from the reverse side of the sheet from that which you originally marked. Make another 90° bend. Loosen the brake slightly and move the sheet toward you to make the final bend, number 5. Push the brake as far as you can without creasing the metal. It will make installation on the roof easier if this bend is just a bit over 90°. Loosen clamps; remove from the brake. Examine the sheet carefully to see if your bends are exactly centered on the marks from the pattern. Remember to mark the top of the sheet. Check to see that all the bends are uniform and parallel. Bends 1, 4, and 5 are the most difficult and require extra care.

Repeat the entire process with a second sheet. Check to see that the left side of one sheet slips smoothly over the right side of the other sheet. Switch the sheets side to side to make sure you made both of them uniform. Place the sheets end to end; they should slip together easily, with the bottom of one sheet sliding over the top of the next. Again transpose the sheets to make sure that they are the same. If something doesn't fit, go back and check your pattern. Make absolutely sure that you didn't mix up tops and bottoms of the sheets and that they are clearly marked. Make any necessary adjustments to your pattern and continue making the sheets until all have been completed.

Bend number 4.

Bend number 5.

The sheets which start and finish the roof only have one edge bent; the other edge will be anchored to the roof by folding over the edge, not made into a standing seam.

At this stage, paint all of the roof pans, including scrap pieces. Only two companies in this country still make red iron oxide primer for metals. Follansbee requires this for their 40-year guarantee. Red primer as well as finish coats in several colors (the red primer is a fine finish coat if you want a red roof) are available under the trade name

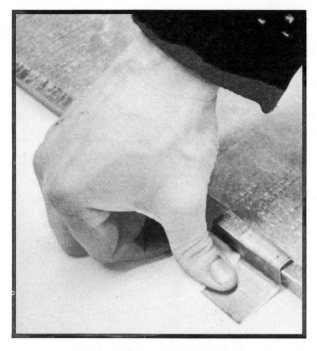

The clips should be bent into the figure Z.

Set up a make-shift brake by cutting a slot in a board before you start so that you can make final trimmings and adjustments and use it to bend small areas of metal.

Tin-O-Lin from Calbar, Inc.† Don't use anything else. This is an oil-base paint and takes several days to dry thoroughly.

After the paint has dried, the end seams still have to be bent. Make a ¾-inch-long cut about ⅜ inch away from the standing seam at the top and bottom of all sheets except those at the peak of the roof. The latter sheets only get cut at the bottom. Cut a piece of 2X4 to the length of the center section of the pan between the cuts. Now make a ¾-inch-deep saw cut the length of one edge of the 2X4. Slip the 2X4 over the center section of metal and bend it to 90°. The bottom of each sheet is bent down, the top is bent up. Now place the sheets on a hard surface and press down on the flap of metal until it is loosely folded over, parallel with the surface of the pan. This completes fabrication of the panels themselves.

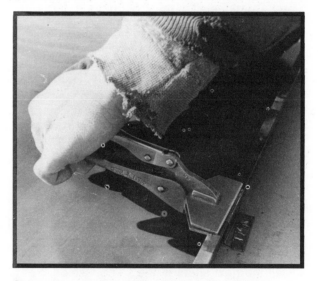

Secure the right-hand side of the pan by crimping the free end of the anchor clip over the seam edge.

From the painted scrap, cut a quantity of 2-inch by 3-inch clips, enough to install one about every 20 to 24 inches of standing seam. Bend into a Z-shape of the dimensions shown. Paint enough galvanized roof-edging strips to completely cover all edges of the roof. Nail these strips securely every 8 inches around the entire perimeter of the roof. Take a final measurement across the length of the roof. Double-check at the midpoint and ridge to see that the roof doesn't taper.

Calculate your 25-inch pans from the center of the roof, and allow ¾ inch extra to fold over the drip edge. Trim the excess width from one of the sheets which has only one edge of the sheet bent up. Start at the lower left edge of the roof, using the sheets with two bends at the right side. Hook the bottom fold over the drip edge, and slide the

†The address of this and other manufacturers and associations so indicated will be found under "Addresses of Manufacturers and Associations" in Part IV.

sheet so that ¾ inch of metal hangs over the roof at the left edge. With a small block of wood, fold the metal over the side drip edge. Use Vise-Grip crimpers to crimp the seam tightly. Also crimp the sheet across the bottom edge.

Install anchor clips at approximately 2-foot intervals along the right edge of the sheet. Fasten the clips down with two 1-inch roofing nails, and fold the tail of the clips back over the nailheads. The overhanging end of the clip should then be bent over the edge of the metal, thereby holding the right side of the sheet in place.

Install the second sheet of roofing at the left edge of the roof above the first sheet. Hook the two folded ends of the sheet together, and slide the top sheet up the roof until the seam is tightly locked. Holding the sheet firmly in place, flatten the seam with a block of wood and a hammer. Use light blows of the hammer, and move the wood quickly to avoid dimpling the metal. Before hammering the joint tight, check your edge overhang to insure that it is ¾ inch at the top of the sheet. Adjust if necessary. Now fold the edge of the sheet over the drip edge, and install the cleats on the right edge as you did on the first sheet. Continue all of the way up the roof in similar fashion until the first row of panels is in place.

Set the first sheet of the second row in place. Hook the triple bend over the double bend, and slide the sheet up the roof until the bottom cross-seam hooks over the drip edge. Crimp the bottom edge with your Vise-Grips, and install anchor clips at the right edge as on the first row. Now you are ready to start crimping your first standing seam. Using the Vise-Grips, crimp the small flange over the top of the double bend. Stop about 4 inches from the top of the sheet. Now, working from the bottom, take a hammer and a block of wood and fold the seam part way down so that it can easily be gripped by the Vise-Grips. Finally, crimp the seam tight with your Vise-Grips.

Install the next sheet in the same fashion. Keep moving up the roof. Stagger the cross-seams on adjacent rows, and check occasionally to see that you are holding a uniform panel width. (The panels can sometimes creep slightly.) Note that you have to start the two sides of the roof from opposite corners, both starting at the left as you view the roof and moving to the right. If you are left-handed, as I am, you may want to make the panels reversed, with the triple bend on the right and the double bend on the left. The procedure is exactly the same, just reversed.

To finish the ridge, flatten the seams about 3

Be sure to check all your alignments before closing the seams. Tap the seam lightly and then use your crimpers.

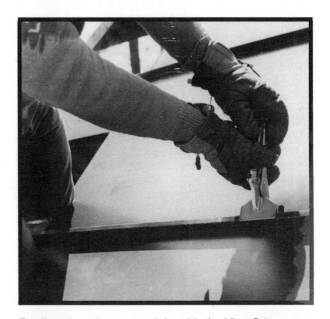

Finally, crimp the seams tight with the Vise-Grips.

inches from the top of the sheet and fold as shown in the working drawings. Install a 2-inch by 1-inch block of treated wood and then a C-shaped cap piece. Surface-nail the cap at 2-foot intervals and seal the nails with Mono caulking.

Now you have a handcrafted, fire-resistive roof which will last several lifetimes. In case it sounds like a lot of work, it is. Depending upon their native skill, it took the owner-builders in this book anywhere from five days to five weeks to fabricate and install the roof. The Stoners had it done by professionals who required less than two days. Good professionals, who know what they are doing, can put one of these roofs on for a very reasonable price. Unfortunately, they are just about as scarce as the aforementioned thatcher. A price of $150 per square (100 sq. ft.)

should be top price for a simple roof, less if they are really good. Materials cost $60 to $70 per square depending upon where you buy them.

Metal Roof Tiles

I uncovered this roofing technique while doing research on terne roofs and an unhappy accident on Frank Gilbert's roof resulted in my being able to try out the system. It works well.

Some clumsy workmen on Frank's house walked on some of the prefabricated pans for the roof, ruining them. The standing seams were crimped beyond repair. I salvaged the sheets, cut them into square roof tiles, and installed them in diamond fashion on a small roof. This particular

The tool in the left foreground is a set of roof crimpers. They are used by professionals, are expensive, and can't be rented. Don't worry, your Vise-Grips will do just as well.

technique is used with a variety of metals such as copper, zinc, and lead for flat roofs. In the case of flat roofs, the seams are laboriously soldered. If they are used on slopes of over 6/12 and laid on the diagonal, they can be very simply crimped in place. The result is a singularly striking roof.

Unlike the standing-seam roofs, these can be easily fabricated at home with no more than a pair of tin snips and a board to use for bending the pans. You do waste a bit more material in the overlapping joints, but it's such an easy roof that the waste is probably acceptable. While I recommend terne, almost any metal will work. For a very inexpensive roof, 28-gauge galvanized iron can be substituted for the terne. Pans should be fabricated from 28-inch-square pieces of metal. These can be cut from a 50-foot roll or ordered

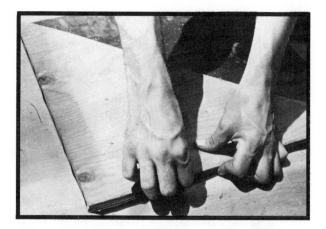

Make a half-pan-size template; it speeds up the cuts and makes bending the metal easier. Alternatively fold the metal over the edge of a table or workbench.

Measure ½ inch back from each corner and make a 45° cut.

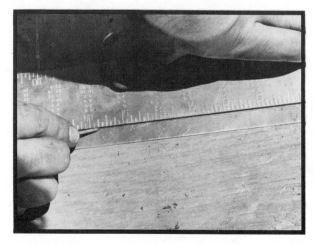

Score along the bend with a nail; it makes folding the metal much easier.

With a piece of scrap wood, bend the tabs nearly flat. You can use the same technique for making flashings, but you may find it easier to clamp the sheet between two pieces of wood along the seam, and then bend it.

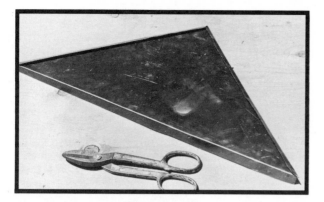

A row of half-pans is necessary for starting the roof. Cut them as shown.

Start the first course with half-pans.

Take particular care with the alignment; a small error at the bottom becomes impossible two rows up.

cut, boxed, and flattened. This latter method of ordering greatly simplifies your job. Make a mark ½ inch from each corner and cut off a 45° slice of metal. Now, bend two of the resulting tabs up and the opposite pair down as shown in the photos.

Cut six 2-inch by 3-inch anchor straps for each sheet, paint your shingles, and you are ready to install the roof. Your finished pans will cover an area 26 inches square.

The roof is installed in much the same fashion as the standing-seam roof. Standard galvanized roof edging is installed at all edges of the roof. Find the exact center of the roof and start there with half-pans, folding the edge over the edging just as we did with the standing-seam roof. Install three anchor clips on each of the top edges of the shingles. Trim the end shingles as necessary and fold the ends over the galvanized edging. Now, set the second row (full shingles) in place, hooking the bottom edge of the full shingles over the top edges of each pair of half-shingles. Using a block of wood, gently flatten the seams. Again, install three anchor clips per edge and proceed to the next row. The ridge should be finished exactly as in the standing-seam roof. Be careful to line up the pans exactly. It may help to run a chalk line up the roof to keep the pans in line.

Factory-Made Galvanized Roofing Panels

A galvanized roof, if painted with Tin-O-Lin, is good for forty to fifty years in most climates, and should be considered as an alternative if the terne roof sounds like too much work. The two standard patterns which are available are V-ribbed and corrugated. Do not be tempted to buy aluminum or prepainted steel sheets. The prepainted sheets cost much more than the standard galvanized finish and the Tin-O-Lin paint provides a more durable finish. Be sure to paint both sides of the sheets.

If the roof members are applied laterally as shown on the alternate framing plans for the Volkswagen and basic saltbox houses, these metal roofs can be applied directly over the framing members without additional sheathing. The sheets are applied in the same order as the pans for the terne roof. Installation is very simple and fast, provided that your roof is accurately framed. Roof sheets are held in place with special gasketed nails which have a neoprene washer under the head. Care is required when driving the nails to just compress the washer against the metal. Otherwise the system is almost foolproof.

The sheets are overlapped at the edges and ends to provide a weathertight roof. To protect against leakage in high winds, I recommend sealing all lap joints with Mono caulking. Matching translucent plastic panels are available for instant, easily installed skylights.

This roof system is normally used on commercial and industrial buildings, but is very well suited for houses. In the days before oil prices began to rise, these roofs were more expensive than standard asphalt shingle roofs. Now, all but the cheapest grade asphalt roofs are more expensive than galvanized metal.

Neoprene Roofs

The third roofing system combines the elegant vertical lines of the standing-seam roof with modern chemistry. This roof is a sheet of neoprene applied in liquid form. The system was developed about thirty years ago and is an excellent way of permanently weatherproofing wood or concrete roofs and decks. I have used it many times over the past twenty years with good success. These roofs are rarely seen on houses. They are usually found on large commercial buildings with complicated roof shapes such as the TWA terminal at Kennedy Airport or Dulles International Airport. Since the material is applied with a roller like paint, conventional roofers tend to be uninterested in the installation. This is an ideal material for owner-builders, provided you are careful and thorough in your installation.

One factor which has limited the use of the neoprene roof on houses is aesthetics. It is perfectly smooth and flat and lacks the texture and interest of conventional roofing materials. I solve this problem by applying half-round moldings to the surface of the roof at 2-foot intervals.

While the material also works very well on concrete, the application I describe is over exterior plywood. When conventional asphalt shingles are used as roofing, CDX-grade sheathing plywood is normally used under the shingles with a layer of tar paper to protect the plywood. For the neoprene roof, upgrade the plywood to ½-inch AC exterior-grade sanded plywood. (This costs about $15 per square more than the CDX-grade.) The neoprene is applied directly to the plywood before installation on the roof, making the job much easier and insuring that the plywood is always protected from the weather.

Use an 11-inch-wide roller with a heavy nap. First, prime the plywood with one coat of neoprene diluted in half with Gates or xylene thinner (one part neoprene to one part thinner). After the primer dries, apply another coat of neoprene, full strength. After this coat dries (usually within one

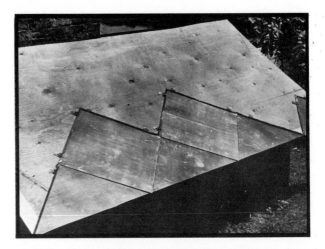

Hook the bottom fold of the full pans over the top edge of the half-pans.

The half-round moldings are set in place to break up the flat neoprene roof.

hour), install the precoated plywood over the roof-framing members with the long dimension of the plywood perpendicular to the direction of the framing members. Caulk all cross-seams with the neoprene caulking supplied with the system. Then apply a 3-inch-wide coat of neoprene along the cross-seams, and embed fiberglass tape in the joint as you go. Do not cut the tape before applying; leave it on the roll and apply directly to the seam from the roll. In this way, the tape goes on smoothly, and you can apply it evenly to the plywood joint. Apply a heavy coat of neoprene to the top of the tape, working it in well with a brush as you go. Pay careful attention to the tape to insure that there are no air bubbles and that the edges seal tightly to the plywood.

Have ready a sufficient quantity of ¾-inch-diameter half-round molding to provide strips at 2 feet on center, placed vertically up the roof. They should be primed and first-coated as was the plywood. Snap chalk lines on the plywood at 2-foot intervals. (If the plywood is applied vertically, there will be a continuous seam every 4 feet.) Now apply a bead of neoprene caulking along each chalk line, making sure that the seams are filled. Embed the molding in the caulking and attach with 8d finish nails.

Now recoat the entire roof surface, paying very careful attention to all seams and nailheads so that they are thoroughly sealed. The roof is finished off with two coats of Hypalon in the desired color. Fine sand can be mixed with the final coat if a textured surface is desired. This Hypalon top coating is a synthetic coating of very high density. It is extremely resistant to fire, abrasion, and most chemicals. This roof, like the terne roof, will last a lifetime. The original test roof, applied over thirty years ago, is still in excellent condition.

If you don't want to use neoprene for a roof, keep the process in mind, as the material is versatile and easy to use on anything requiring a smooth, waterproof surface. Over the years, I have used it for a hot tub, a kitchen sink, a kid's pool with a sliding board, and a number of roof decks and complicated flashing situations. If you are using it for an area of heavy wear, apply it to a smooth base such as overlaid plywood. The materials for this waterproofing system can be ordered from Gates Engineering Co.[†]

Other Possible Materials

While these three roofing systems are my favorites, there are other possibilities, most of them too costly for the homebuilder on a budget. Slate and tile are two roof materials which are long-lasting, fireproof, and of very high quality. Our framing system will readily accept those heavy materials. They are so expensive new that you will probably have to find them used in order to consider them. The Laskin house has a very fine tile roof.

Cedar shakes or shingles are available in a bewildering variety of types and sizes. I describe them under "Siding" in Chapter 13. They make a beautiful, natural, very durable roof, but unfortunately they are a fire hazard, and if you use them, you may have to pay a higher insurance rate. Using them on homes that have wood stoves, with the possibilities of chimney fires and sparks, causes me considerable concern. If you live in a warm climate or plan some other heat source, cedar shakes make an excellent, if expensive, choice for a roof. The Red Cedar Shingle and Handsplit Shake Bureau[†] provides absolutely explicit directions for the complicated procedure of installing shingles and shakes.

Lightning Rods

Houses in exposed locations or with steep roofs, particularly if made with metal, should have an approved lightning-rod system installed. Insurance companies usually require that these rods be installed by a specialist, as they can be very dangerous if they are incorrectly grounded. See your insurance agent for an installer in your area.

Flashings

Flashings are usually required where different materials or different planes meet, allowing possible water leakage. If a material projects horizontally from the surface of a building, as at window and door trims, or at the insulation around a foundation, metal flashing is required. Tract houses use flimsy aluminum flashings. Aluminum expands and contracts excessively under changing temperature conditions and eventually develops cracks. It is also very soft and gets bent out of shape easily. Contractors almost always use it, because it is cheap and readily available. Use terne, if possible. In an emergency, use a heavy-gauge galvanized metal. For a very small flashing or one in a prominent position, you might want to use copper, but it will be very, very expensive.

To look good and work well, flashings should be bent to shape on a brake (see "Standing-Seam Terne Roofs" in this chapter for a description of the use of a brake). If a brake is not readily available, clamp the flashing material between two boards and bend gently with another board placed against the edge of the metal. Metal flashings are expensive and should be avoided wherever possible. Mono caulking and neoprene/Hypalon are effective substitutes, if you are using them on the job anyway.

Skylights

My houses are designed to take advantage of the heat gain and natural daylight generated by south-facing skylights. These same skylights lose lots of heat at night and let in unwanted heat in summer. Commercially available skylights make no provisions for insulating the skylight and are absurdly expensive. They are considered a luxury item and are priced accordingly. I use stock

Skylights, like this one in the Volkswagen house, can be built inexpensively to add light and space.

sheets of Plexiglas for my skylights and can build them for a small fraction of the cost of factory-built models. The working drawings show how these are constructioned.

Plexiglas requires some special installation techniques but is very easy to work with once you understand the techniques. I frequently use it for greenhouses as well as skylights. For exact installation techniques, see "Greenhouses" below.

Greenhouses

Greenhouses have become increasingly popular with my correspondents. They can substantially increase the heat retention of a house and provide a useful indoor growing space. Even if you don't want to use the greenhouse all year, it is great for starting plants and saving a few plants to have tomatoes and peppers for Christmas.

I show two different types of greenhouses, both attached to the south face of the basic saltbox house. The choice between the two depends upon whether you want maximum heat gain and minimum construction cost, or slightly less heat gain and slightly higher cost with much more space for growing plants. The basic greenhouse plan has a 60° sloping wall attached to the edge of the roof overhang. Since the glass goes down to the ground, it has to be either tempered glass or other breakage-resistant glazing. The standard sloping greenhouse is designed to be glazed with 46-inch by 76-inch tempered glass. It can be double- or single-glazed. Single glazing is

much cheaper, but requires an insulating cover at night. Sometimes used sheets of insulating glass with a leaky seal resulting in moisture condensed inside the panes can be bought very inexpensively from a glass company. If you don't mind the moisture, you can just reuse them. Alternatively, you can separate the panes of glass and use them separately.

The small doors on each end of the greenhouse are designed to use standard-size insulating glass panels. The triangular panes should be glazed with a single layer of Plexiglas.

The other greenhouse style has a "broken" front. The roof line is continued out from the house at the same angle and then the front is constructed with a vertical wall to the ground. We used this greenhouse on the Gilberts' house, as they grow all their own food and need as much space as possible. This version of the greenhouse is designed to be glazed with standard 4-foot by 8-foot sheets of Plexiglas, ¼ inch thick. My glazing techniques save a lot of money because I design the system very simply. It takes advantage of the excellent adhesive qualities of Mono caulking compound. The frame is made up of standard framing members with the glazing material literally glued to the outside face of the members. In this way, the wood framing is completely protected from the weather, and the glazing material presents a flush surface to the elements.

Plexiglas is a unique material and is very easily worked with hand or power tools. If a few simple precautions are observed, you will have a perfect

Simple, 60°-sloped greenhouse is attached directly to the south roof overhang.

job. First, leave the masking paper in place while working on the material to avoid scratching it. Sawing should be done with a fine-toothed handsaw or a medium-toothed crosscut blade. Contrary to most recommendations, a plywood blade does not work. It revolves too fast, melting the material instead of cutting it. Edges can be planed, filed, sanded, or polished like wood. A Stanley Surform tool is excellent for working edges. All exposed, freshly cut edges will need some additional finishing to look professional. Where possible, use full sheets or plan your cuts so that the factory edges are the exposed ones.

This greenhouse is designed to use part of a sheet for the roof panel and the remainder for the top portion of the vertical front wall. If you turn the pieces so that the factory-cut edges meet at the eave line, you won't have to do any finishing. One of the reasons that I use Plexiglas for this greenhouse is that it has great structural strength and can be used to brace the framing members, allowing us to eliminate the lateral framing member which would normally be used at the eave line. If this member were used, it would shut out too much sunlight. Notice that many commercial greenhouses use a curved panel at this point to accomplish the same thing.

The Plexiglas is attached to the framing members with a bead of Mono caulking and wood screws. Before applying Mono to the framing members, stain them the same color as the caulking so the bead of Mono won't look messy. Plexiglas expands and contracts more than wood, and you must be careful when using screws on a large panel of it. Carefully space the screw holes *uniformly* about 2 feet apart. Drill the holes 1/16 oversize, and use round-headed screws with washers for attachment. Put a small bead of Mono on top of the screw heads and washers to make the assembly completely watertight.

The masking should be stripped from the inside of the sheets before installing them. Leave the exterior paper in place until you are through working over the top of the material. Remove it immediately; exposure to rain or sunlight makes the masking extremely difficult to remove. Remember this when storing the sheets of Plexiglas prior to use.

Costs

This 300-square-foot greenhouse was amazingly inexpensive. It took two men one morning to frame it. The Plexiglas cost about $1,000, framing lumber another $60. Total cost was about $1,600.

Standard-size glass being installed in a sloping front greenhouse. (Courtesy of Heartwood Owner/ Builder School, Washington, Massachusetts.)

Roof framing in place for traditional breakfront-type greenhouse. See the Gilbert house for the finished product.

Installing Plexiglas Skylights

Plexiglas skylights are installed in a very similar fashion to the greenhouse glazing. The major difference is that the skylight overlaps onto the roof surface at the sides and bottom about 3 inches.

Care of Plexiglas

Many people say, "You can't use Plexiglas, it scratches and gets cloudy." Plexiglas does require some special techniques, but is just as easy to care for as glass. In the first place, it *can* be scratched, so don't use it in a full-length door in a house with jumping dogs or small children. (Notice that there is a cross-member and operating vents with glass near the ground in the greenhouse.) Second, never use abrasives or ammonia-base glass cleaners on Plexiglas. There are wax-base cleaner-polishes designed especially for plastics which work very well. Silverbrite is

Proper sealing is necessary in Plexiglas installation.

one trade name. The wax-type cleaners put a film on the material, making it harder to scratch. If it does get scratched, however, it can be buffed with Simoniz paste wax to remove the scratches.

Part III

Examples of Energy-Saving Houses

Introduction

The following houses have been very carefully selected to give the builder the most value for the money and to be easy and quick to build. I have developed a very basic saltbox based upon my low-cost and energy-saving methods. To date, five variations of this basic house have been built here in the Northeast, and this design is versatile enough to have application in most parts of the country with moderate to cold climates. The plans in the back of the book represent a composite of all of the best ideas from the five designs. Note that it is planned so that it can be built in stages as your family grows and when you can afford more house.

With three exceptions, all of the houses in this book are new designs. The three exceptions are houses from *30 Energy-Efficient Houses* which were designed but not built at time of publication. Despite the lack of finished photographs, these three designs were the most popular in that book. The plans included herein represent considerable refinement of the designs shown in the earlier book, and I am also able to discuss construction methods, problems, and performance of these houses.

Most of the photos in this part of the book have letters below them that correspond to letters on the floor plans. By matching up letters you will be able to see which exterior view or interior space is shown in each photo.

173

House 1: **Jones**

A

B

C

This house has a curious history. Many years ago, as an architectural student, I designed a very similar house. The design had slipped my mind completely. Since the faculty was interested in flat-roofed boxes, it wasn't received too enthusiastically, and I received a low grade. More recently, I received many requests for my 24-foot-square Volkswagen house, featured in *30 Energy-Efficient Houses.* Many people ordered plans and then returned them, because the house was too small for their needs or not acceptable to building or zoning authorities due to smaller-than-legal floor area. Several people asked about making it one bay longer. It was then that I remembered my old saltbox from school days — it seemed the perfect solution. I resurrected it and made a considerable number of refinements to incorporate passive solar heating techniques.

D

F

E

About this time, a women's magazine reviewed my book and included a rather nice saltbox design as an illustration. They gave no credit to the designer of the saltbox, and readers assumed it was mine. The result was another large pile of letters all wanting plans for the saltbox. Realizing how popular this type of house was with the general public, I was spurred on to more refinements. Finally, I was approached by a young carpenter, Vince Jones, who wanted to build one of the saltbox houses as a speculative venture. His objective was to build a passive solar, ecologically sound house which could compete with the conventional ranches being built in his area. Since the house was still in the developmental stages, this was a tall order. Another problem was that the carpenter was inexperienced and had never even seen post and beam construction. The project looked very difficult until I met Vince's father.

Mr. Jones had been disabled by a lung disease about ten years earlier and told that he had six months or less to live. As a talented research scientist, Mr. Jones was not ready to accept this verdict. He began researching the causes and possible treatments of his disease. As a lifetime reader of *Prevention* magazine, he felt that vitamin and mineral deficiencies might play a part. While he has not completely conquered his disease, his health has improved dramatically, and he is now regarded as an expert in this field. His contributions include design and construction of sophisticated portable lung machines which free the victims from the hospital and a carefully controlled diet which counteracts disabling effects of the disease as well as toxic effects of medications used to control its progress.

This same mind was put to work researching every possible component of our basic house to see that we were getting the most for our money without sacrificing ecology or the aesthetics of the building. Detailed models were constructed, and drawings were made of every aspect of the house. Heat loss and gain, placement of windows, doors, greenhouse, and skylights all received thorough attention. Each construction operation was analyzed on paper before actual work began. If Mr. Jones had not had all of this free time, we would have been unable to build the house, at least not nearly as well as it was done. During the course of construction, Mr. Jones' medical condition improved so dramatically that he was able to do very heavy construction work with no evidence of strain.

A concrete foundation was selected on my recommendations and was the big failure of the job. The major culprits were inexperience and an unskilled excavator. To preserve as much of the natural vegetation as possible, Vince had the original excavator make a very small clearing for the house with access only from the driveway side of the house, giving us a nice, level clearing for building. Unfortunately, the site was in a remote location in a county where I knew no excavators, and finding someone with a narrow bucket on their machine was a problem. Vince had a solution — the local tool rental company had a Ditch-Witch for rent. Since I had used one of these in the past this sounded ideal.

Vince made an appointment for 7:30 A.M. to pick up the machine. The people at the rental place finally got it running at 11:00 A.M. The normal Ditch-Witch is a medium-size riding tractor with a small standard bucket on one end and a device similar to a chain saw with digger teeth on the other. But the creature we got resembled a walking garden tractor with a chain digger attached. Its teeth were hopelessly dull and all its drive belts loose and worn. As the last straw, our site was heavily wooded and laced with large tree roots and small boulders. The machine had no weight and could not cope with the roots and rocks as well as a heavier riding machine with sharp teeth might have done.

A masonry contractor for one of the other houses, hearing of our plight, volunteered his small backhoe; we accepted. The difficulty was that he was a mason, not an excavator, and his machine was in terrible shape. A very ragged, crooked trench was the result. This meant that both sides of the foundation had to be formed, a tedious and expensive process. For the outside, we used the 2-inch urethane insulation board reinforced with a 2X6 at grade. This worked well. The inside had to be formed with plywood, later reused for roof sheathing.

The actual pour was another headache. Since there was access to one side of the house only, I cautioned Vince to order extension chutes on the concrete truck so that the concrete would reach the other side of the foundation. We would still have had to use a wheelbarrow for the far-

G

thest part of the greenhouse, though. Vince bought a brand-new, large-capacity wheelbarrow for this purpose. The concrete truck arrived — without the extension chutes. Someone else, a regular customer, needed them. You learn by experience to bribe the counterman on something like this, or send the concrete back and pour another day. As we were already behind schedule, we chose to pour anyway — a serious mistake. For a while things went smoothly, until the tire blew on the brand-new wheelbarrow. We were left with one old wheelbarrow of small capacity.

In several spots, the forms gave way a bit, and we wasted concrete (fortunately this was at the bottom where no damage was done). The second truck was ordered with enough concrete to finish the job. Unevenness at the bottom of the trench, spillage, and bulging of formwork can add 5 to 10 percent to the amount required. Another problem is that concrete plants have minimum orders, and you may have to pay a premium for a small quantity. We ordered extra and used it to pour an apron at the highway end of the driveway as required by zoning. The empty concrete truck got stuck going out of the driveway and had to be towed by the full truck. Then the first driver stuck around for the rest of the pour and towed the second truck out for us. Concrete plants allow a minimum time for delivery, usually just the time required for a simple basement slab; after that there is an overtime charge. We paid almost $100 in overtime. It would have been much worse except that the first driver didn't charge for his time waiting to tow the second truck — imagine the expenses if we had had to summon a tow truck!

This experience points up the folly of beginners trying to pour concrete, so here are a few pointers. If you possibly can, hire a professional concrete contractor. He will insist upon excavating on both sides of the foundation wall to full depth, but he has reusable forms and professional form ties which make this quick and easy (see Chapter 7 for more discussion on this point). If you can get a neat trench dug, formwork is much, much easier. Make sure that the truck has access to all parts of the house. Also, make sure that the truck has adequate access to the site on a *solid* road. Extension chutes make pouring concrete walls much faster — get them and avoid overtime charges. Some advanced companies have pumping systems in which the concrete is pumped through high-pressure hoses. This can solve access, road, and time problems all in one. These companies usually charge more for their concrete, though.

The next problem was framing the house. We were in such a big rush for the foundation because I had arranged a "house raising" for the next weekend, and many people were scheduled to be there. Since eight houses were in the planning stages for the summer, it was necessary to train someone to cut and erect post and beam frames pronto. I brought along two good carpenters, and Vince and his father furnished two workmen. Various other clients also showed up to help with the heavy lifting.

I had instructed Vince to remove the plywood, backfill the trenches, and get sawhorses and work stations ready. I also asked him to install the pressure-treated sill plate. Almost none of this was done. The concrete had oozed up around the plywood forms making them very difficult and time-consuming to remove. As it turned out, the preliminary cutting and notching of the beams took quite a bit of time, and by the time we were ready to start erecting the frame, the site was ready to go.

The actual framing went well and made up for our difficulties with the foundation. The house proper consists of six structural bays. The house is 3 12-foot-long bays, for a total length of 36 feet. The width is 26 feet — one 12- and one 14-foot bay. The three rear bays extend up to form a second-floor balcony. The roof is framed in 2X12s at 24 inches on center. One of the unique aspects of this design is the way it takes advantage of larger-than-normal framing members. If you redesign a conventional house to take advantage of 6-inch wall insulation and 12-inch roof insulation, you will normally waste a great deal of material, because you are making your supports much heavier than they need to be for structural reasons to accommodate the thicker insulation. In this house, the main supports are spaced farther apart than usual to make efficient use of the framing members.

All plumbing is located back-to-back in the center rear bay for efficiency. The optional forced air furnace is also located in this area. If you don't want or need the furnace, this is a dandy place for a sauna. The carport is optional and can be enclosed to form a garage. If another bedroom is desired, a dormer can be added over the garage/carport. Vince's house had a very small greenhouse on the south wall, but the greenhouse can be any size, as some of the later variations show.

All of the insulating glass was purchased direct from a manufacturer at very considerable savings. Windows and glass doors were all built at the site. The windows are very simple, consisting of Andersen basement vents below with fixed glass set directly between the framing members, thus avoiding the expense and potential air leakage of separate frames.

The masonry chimney wall in this house is constructed of concrete block which is scored to resemble brick. Concrete block is the cheapest material you can use. In this case the results are surprisingly good, due to the efforts of a first-class mason. In the hands of amateurs, this material can be a disaster. If the hand-laid joints don't match the scored ones it looks tacky. I recommend that you score it into thirds which is much more pleasing than fake brick. Unscored block has a very unpleasant scale to it, as well as undesirable connotations.

The roof rafters were a major problem on this house. Despite detailed instructions on layout, the inexperienced carpenters launched out on their own with unfortunate results. They required a lot of time-consuming shimming and planing to get them even. Rafters of the required length were unobtainable from the mill where we got our roughcut lumber and only at a very premium price with a long wait at the lumberyard. Consequently we spliced them with plywood gussets. This would have worked well if they had been laid out accurately, but they weren't. On later versions of the house, we spliced the rafters at the overhang and used kiln-dried 2X12s which solved the problem.

Construction moved slowly, and work was difficult during the severe winter weather. Much of the bad weather was spent fabricating such items as stairs, cabinets, and doors for installation in better weather. The finish woodwork was kept plain and simple in keeping with the overall design of the house. The Sheetrock is finished off with metal L-channels as described under "Metal Trim" in Chapter 14.

Kitchen cabinets are made of inexpensive, V-grooved, tongue-and-groove pine. This works well for cabinets *provided* you get a coat of finish on both surfaces of the wood immediately. I even apply it before fabricating the cabinets. Thin pieces of pine warp quickly, and this finish usually prevents it. The cabinets were time-consuming, but inexpensive and very satisfying. They also provided an opportunity for productive work during an otherwise miserable winter. We have already shown many of the construction steps for this house in Part II. In particular, see Chapter 8 for step-by-step illustrations of how to build the frame. Even though the house took much longer than we anticipated, the final product is handsome and has been enthusiastically received by prospective buyers.

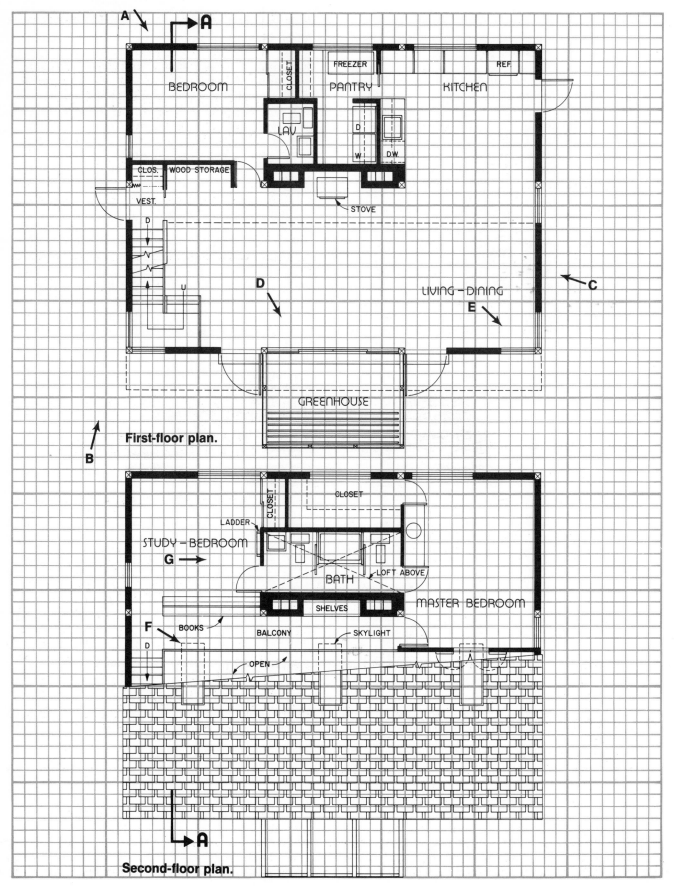

First-floor plan.

Second-floor plan.

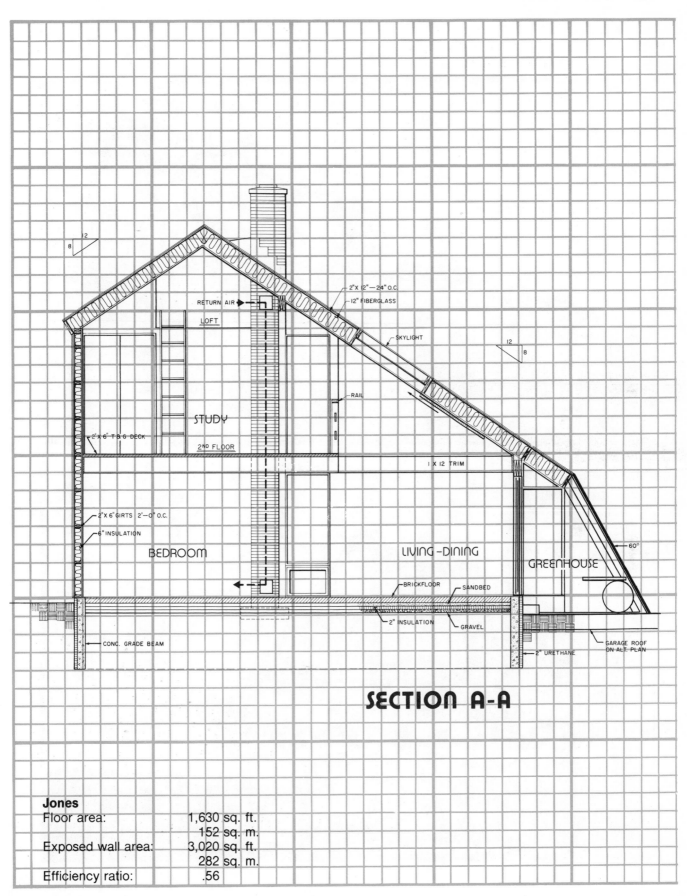

12
8

RETURN AIR

LOFT

2"X 12"—24" O.C.
12" FIBERGLASS

SKYLIGHT

12
8

RAIL

STUDY

2"X 6" T & G DECK

2ND FLOOR

1 X 12 TRIM

2"X 6" GIRTS 2'-0" O.C.

6" INSULATION

BEDROOM

LIVING –DINING

60°

GREENHOUSE

BRICKFLOOR   SANDBED

2" INSULATION

GRAVEL

CONC. GRADE BEAM

2" URETHANE

GARAGE ROOF
ON ALT. PLAN

SECTION A-A

Jones

Floor area:	1,630 sq. ft.
	152 sq. m.
Exposed wall area:	3,020 sq. ft.
	282 sq. m.
Efficiency ratio:	.56

House 2: **Lillio**

A

B

Some people feel that they must have a basement and an attached garage. Pete and Rosemary Lillio took my basic saltbox plan, enlarged it slightly, and added a basement and two-car garage. Since they had selected an extremely steep, south-facing hillside, an attached garage was quite a feat. There was just no reasonable way to get a driveway up to the level of the house and maintain a reasonable grade which would be navigable in winter. I finally decided to put the garage right on the front of the house and bury it well into the ground, thereby decreasing the length of the climb necessary to get to it. Entry is from the side of the garage, and the earth is bermed up around the front so that the garage is less obtrusive. The garage roof provides a large, south-facing deck adjacent to the living room.

In addition to the garage, Pete wanted an exercise room and pushed hard to have a full basement. Since the thermal efficiency of my houses is greatly dependent upon a masonry floor and the tempering effect of the ground, I was very reluctant to give in. The steeply sloping grade and the garage location did make a basement easy, though, especially for the front half of the house. We compromised and put in the basement with a slate floor set in a bed of concrete in the living room above. This is a very expensive solution, but the Lillios had been saving for a house for years and were not too concerned about costs. In fact, they usually wanted the most expensive finishes possible and generally decided to pay the price rather than compromise. The slate floor also required a special floor structure; I specified steel joists, a trusslike structural member made of light steel angles at the top and bottom with steel rods crisscrossing between them. These are very common in commercial construction, but rarely used in houses.

Since the Lillios entertain a lot, they wanted a huge living room. Over my strenuous objections, the front part of the basic saltbox was increased by 4 feet, making an 18-foot by 36-foot living room with a very high ceiling. The resulting room is magnificent, and, despite the extra cubage, the house is very easy to heat.

Building the house was something of a problem. Pete fancies himself as quite handy with tools and had dreams of building the entire house himself. Unfortunately, he also has a full-time job which made this impossible. Since my usual crews were doing so many houses, I couldn't recommend anyone. We particularly needed someone who was knowledgeable on post and beam construction. Fortunately for us all, Pete had heard of a young contractor named Kevin Berry who specialized in post and beam houses. I made an immediate appointment to meet Kevin, and enlisted a major source for help for this book. Not only did Kevin know post and beam construction, he had also taken courses in the design of passive solar heating systems. Finally, a contractor who understands the need for tight, well-insulated construction!

C

E

H

I   F

Kevin feels, as I do, that big houses are wasteful. The extremely long spans necessary for the roof joists and the steel joists supporting the suspended floor structure were sore points. Last-ditch efforts to get Pete and Rosemary to cut down the size of the living room to make it 2 feet narrower, were futile. After considerable negotiation, numerous small compromises were made.

The final quotation for the shell of the 1,700-square-foot structure was $15,500. This quote just included the rough shell (no doors, windows, or finish materials), the suspended floor over the entire basement, and the 2X6 tongue-and-groove decking which forms the first-floor ceiling and the finish second floor. The roof for the garage was omitted as Pete and Rosemary wanted to try their hands at some of the actual building.

Total construction time for the frame was less than two weeks, and it would have been even faster had the house not been so tall (making the house wider also makes it taller if the same roof slope is used). Since backfilling around the foundation wasn't done, very tall ladders and scaffolding had to be used around the perimeter. Pete

G

also wanted an underground electrical service; this was not completed in time to use it in building the frame.

Both of these items point up the necessity of proper planning and preparation before starting construction of your house. Sometimes the delays are impossible to avoid, but in this case, Pete just didn't get around to some of the work he was planning to do himself, and since the contract was signed and materials bought, Kevin went right ahead. While these inconveniences did slow him down and cost a bit more money, the efficiencies of my framing method more than offset the difference.

After Kevin finished the frame, Pete took an extensive vacation to work on the house himself. Rosemary teaches school, so she had the entire summer free, too. The garage roof turned out to be more of a task than Pete had expected. To make it easier, I suggested that he use a tongue-and-grooved plywood roof deck system. This plywood is thicker and heavier to allow room for the tongue and groove. As a result, the supporting members can be spaced further apart, and no blocking is required at edges of panels. Lumberyards charge a premium for this type of plywood, but it can save money in the long run, especially if you have to cover a surface that has irregularly spaced supporting members or which is laid out in such a manner that plywood has to be cut and wasted in order to make the sheets fit the framing spacing.

When the plywood arrived, I helped Pete carry it inside, cautioning him to keep it dry so that the joints would fit together easily. Pete and Rosemary worked very hard and erected the frame which supports the plywood deck. A few calls to me and some help from their electrician helped this phase along without difficulty. Some friends volunteered to help lay the plywood — "It's easy, anyone can do it," they said. But well-meaning friends can cause trouble, as the Lillios found out; sometimes they can actually cost you money. Their first maneuver was to drag all of the plywood out on the deck to provide a dangerous walking surface. (*Never* place boards or sheets of material for walkways unless they are fastened down.) Then they started laying the sheets of plywood, setting two rows in place, carefully lining up the plywood joints in both directions. (Plywood joints should always be staggered.) At this point, it started to rain and they went home, leaving all of the plywood in the rain. Of course, the edge joints swelled up and the sheets warped.

After drying out the plywood for a week, Pete and Rosemary were able to install the rest of the deck with great difficulty. A roofer friend had previously offered to put a hot asphalt roof deck on the garage and did a very nice job on the deck itself, but used handmade aluminum flashings around the edge. These are wiggly and unsightly. Pete is building some wooden deck boards for a walking surface and the edge pieces will eventually cover the ugly flashing. If you install a hot asphalt roof that is to be used as a walking surface, make sure that you provide a second wearing surface. The asphalt is brittle or sticky depending upon the weather and will deteriorate rapidly if walked upon. A much better solution is to use the neoprene/Hypalon system described in Chapter 15.

Pete was extraordinarily lucky in his choice of subcontractors. Almost without exception, they were first-rate craftsmen who worked for very reasonable prices. Pete or Rosemary worked as assistants to many of them, and the care which went into their house shows at every turn. Pete and Rosemary bought the roughsawn siding which had been nicely air-dried. They and their parents laboriously prefinished both sides before it was installed, using a brown Cuprinol stain which is particularly handsome. Bob Dakin meticulously applied the siding, and the result is an extraordinary finish job.

The mason was a fine craftsman who turned sour. We took three bids on the foundations: large nonunion masonry contractor, $6,800; unemployed union mason, $7,900; small nonunion contractor, $4,500. Not only was the latter price much lower, but the quality was excellent. He did the entire foundation and poured the floor slabs before we started. Pete was so pleased that he decided to build a massive stone chimney from the native stone on his property and hired the same mason to put in a stone floor in his living room. Pete and Rosemary carefully selected stones and hauled them into the living room and the mason started work (slowly). We discovered that he was building his own house — and of course, you know whose house came first.

The situation was complicated by the fact that Pete was moving very slowly with his own work, primarily on weekends, so the mason could easily see that he was not holding up anything. Since the price was reasonable, the workmanship exquisite, and the weather bad, it was very difficult for any of us to get tough with the mason. He made repeated promises to finish the job, but always seemed to be working on his own house. Finally, after his house was completed, he finished the chimney, but not until everyone's temper had worn a bit thin.

Sometimes there is no other way out than to have patience. In this case, we considered having someone else finish the chimney, but the work wouldn't have matched. All contractors have a tendency to feel slighted when called in to complete someone else's work — "Why didn't you call me in the first place instead of waiting until

D

you got in trouble?" they say. Usually, as in this case, it's better to analyze the problem and try to work with the difficult contractor rather than dismiss him outright.

Pete's careful shopping paid off handsomely on the installation of the heating system. I advocate a small, centrally located duct system which distributes the heat from the center of the house, rather than the common perimeter duct systems which wash the outside walls with warm air, thereby wasting a great deal of energy. Since the perimeter system has been thoroughly ingrained into all heating system installers, it is very, very

difficult to overcome their prejudice for this system. For resale purposes, Pete wanted a conventional furnace. His job with a large corporation exposes him to constant dangers of abrupt transfer. The efficient duct system was quickly installed for about $1,000 less than competitors wanted for a conventional perimeter duct system. The furnace is much bigger than really required, but the best we could find with an efficient burner design. Final cost of the system was less than $1,800. It was thoroughly tested in some extremely nasty winter weather and works fine. For a similar layout for the standard saltbox house, see the working drawings bound at the back of the book.

Pete installed the final finish roof and the greenhouse himself the next summer. In the meantime, the roof was covered with 30-pound roofing felt which was fastened extra securely to allow for a delay in the final roofing installation.

The house is the largest and most conventional in the book. It has all of the features found in a standard commercially available house, but also makes use of ecological materials and passive solar heating. Because of the hard work done by the owners and a good selection of contractors, it was also built for substantially less than the conventional house.

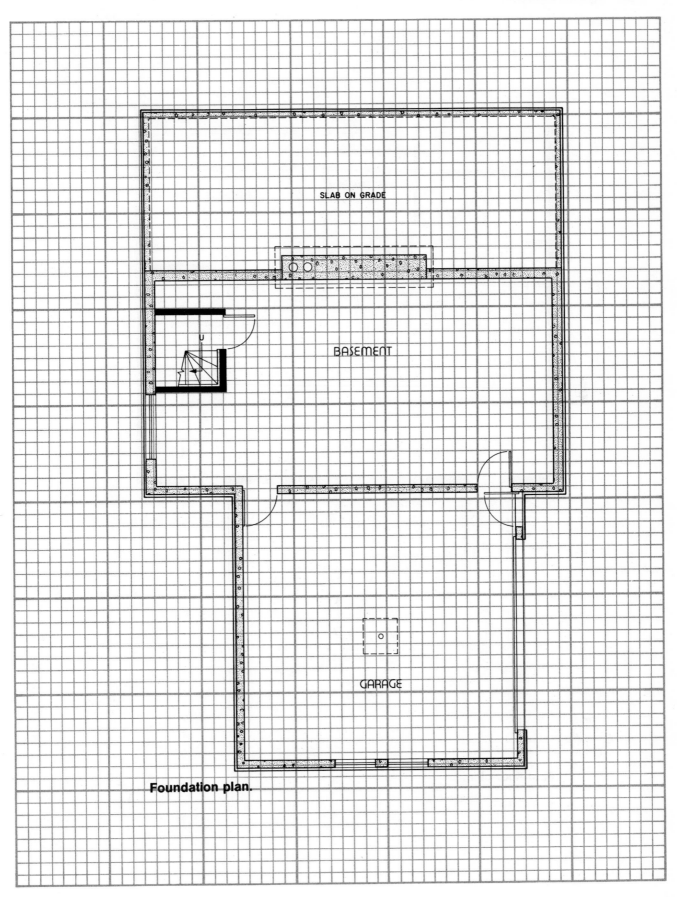

SLAB ON GRADE

BASEMENT

GARAGE

Foundation plan.

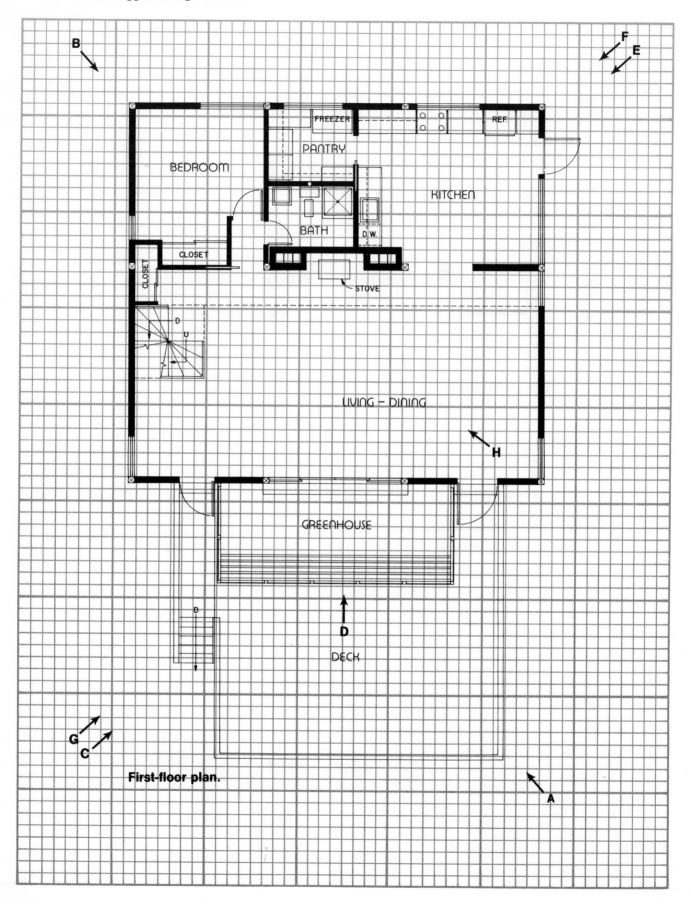

First-floor plan.

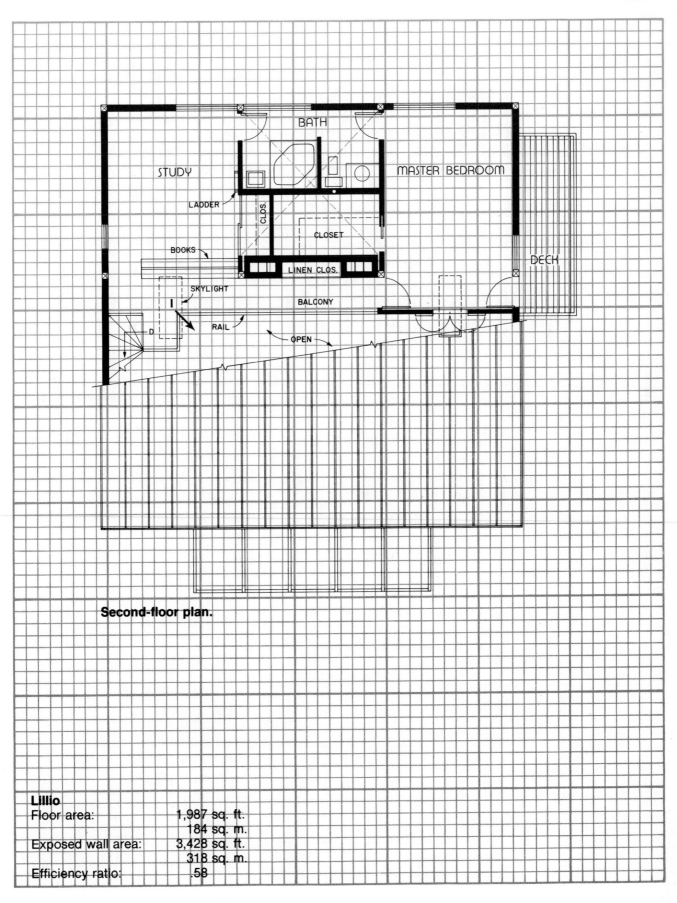

BATH

STUDY

MASTER BEDROOM

LADDER

CLOS.

CLOSET

DECK

BOOKS

LINEN CLOS.

SKYLIGHT

BALCONY

D

RAIL

OPEN

Second-floor plan.

Lillio
Floor area: 1,987 sq. ft.
                     184 sq. m.
Exposed wall area: 3,428 sq. ft.
                     318 sq. m.
Efficiency ratio: .58

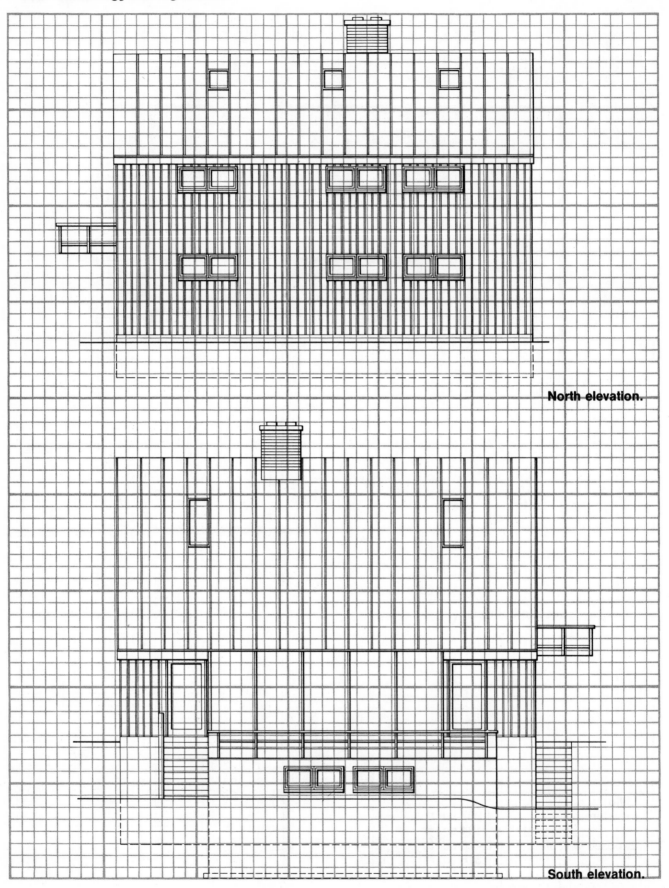

North elevation.

South elevation.

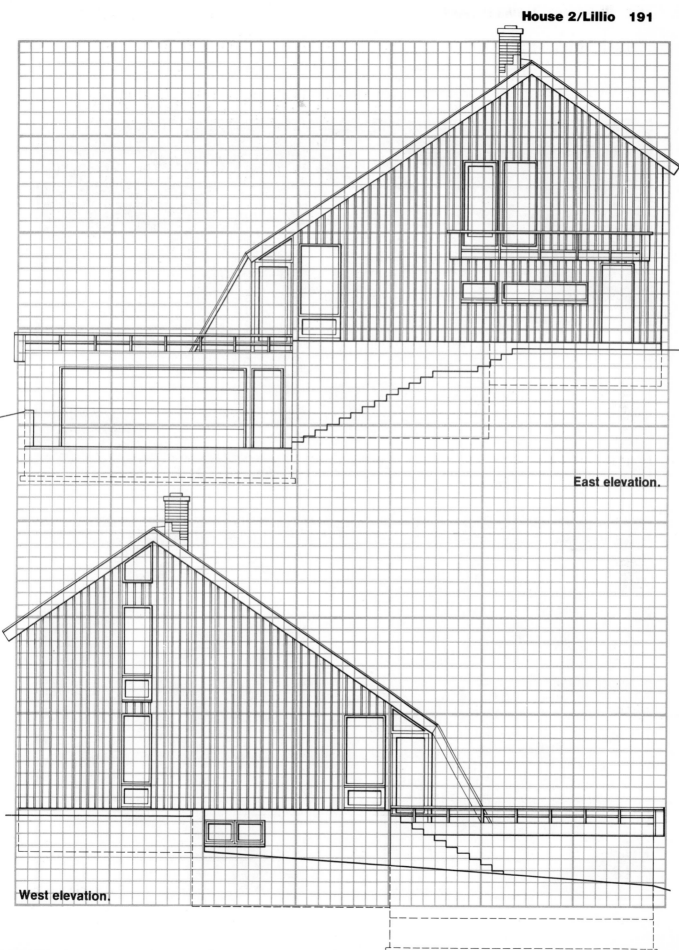

East elevation.

West elevation.

House 3: **Gilbert**

Frank Gilbert's house represents the ultimate extension of the basic saltbox. Hard as it may be to believe, it is the same basic house. Underneath the full-length greenhouse and the north-facing workshop/garage is exactly the same frame as used on the basic Jones house. Frank is the illustrator for this book and much of the credit for the revisions belongs to him.

Frank's requirements are somewhat different than those of the average family, but with continued energy shortages and economic instability many people should become interested in this house. Two major factors influenced its design. First, Frank works at home as an illustrator, thereby saving the energy costs involved in traveling to a job each day. This does mean that he needs to have a larger house with conveniently located work space. He not only does graphic artwork, but also occasionally needs a workshop for building mock-ups, models, etc.

Since I had already planned for expansion of the basic house to include a possible garage, it was a simple matter to run this addition full length along the north side of the house, thereby providing a garage at one end and a workshop at the other. What wasn't so easy was finding a location for Frank's studio. Frank wanted north light in the studio; north light is neutral and provides better natural color rendition. We considered putting some steps between the garage/shop and the main part of the house so that we could widen the addition and combine the shop and studio. By stepping the floor down, we could get more width and still use the same roof slope. This turned out to be an expensive solution, and besides, Frank really needed two separate spaces.

Frank took the plans home. After much study, he came up with the idea of adding a dormer to the second floor right behind the chimney, thereby creating an extra room. North-facing skylights are provided for good daylighting right over Frank's work table. The windows are fitted with light-tight shades because Frank also uses the space as a darkroom. They are also a very good heat barrier. The storage loft was left open to Frank's studio so that he can use it for extra file space. It also houses the storage tank for the solar water heater.

This dormer is a very economical way of adding an extra room to the house. It can be built as a part of the original house or easily added later. The roof of the dormer was extended forward at the same slope to intersect the north face of the chimney. The small triangles created at either end are used for summer ventilation.

I

The greenhouse is the other significant addition. Frank and his wife Louise grow most of their own food and were very anxious to have a greenhouse which would be big enough for growing lots of food and would provide a solar heat gain to the house. The siting of the house caused a problem with the airlock entry usually located under the stairs. On the Gilbert's site it was on the west face of the house exposed to severe winter winds and in such a location that it wouldn't have been used. Again, Frank went to work on the problem. The result was a greenhouse and a generous-size entry vestibule conveniently located next to the driveway.

Now that the basic design was resolved to Frank's satisfaction, he proceeded to make a quick model of the house and found a couple of problems. First, the greenhouse needed outside access and the sloping glass wall would make that very difficult. A second problem which became evident about this time is that the sloping glass front severely limited the utility of the greenhouse. It was very lucky for us that the Joneses were just framing their greenhouse and we had an actual sample to view. The Joneses decided to lower the floor of their greenhouse to solve the problem. Frank didn't like this solution; he wanted to be able to get in and out of the greenhouse at grade with a wheelbarrow.

One of the major reasons why I used the sloping front design on the prototype house was because it is very inexpensive to construct by simply adding sloping members to the edge of the roof overhang and glazing the exterior face of the framing members with standard sheets of tempered insulating glass. While the broken-front-type greenhouse is more difficult to build, Frank felt that the change was imperative to provide proper access and to gain extra space. A de-

A

scription of greenhouse types is in Chapter 15, and construction details for both are in the working drawings at the back of the book.

Frank was very lucky to have a contractor for a next-door neighbor. While the contractor was too busy to construct the actual shell of the house, he was able to make excellent recommendations for local subcontractors. The concrete foundation for this house is particularly critical in that there is a rock storage bin for storing excess heat from the large greenhouse under the front half of the house. The foundation contractor was one of the best I have ever seen and did the job quickly at a very reasonable cost ($2,200).

Frank was on a tight timetable and got a quote from Kevin Berry to build the shell of the house. The experience Kevin gained at Lillio's house

B

paid off. Frank's house was constructed in less time and for less money, even though the northern extension makes the ground area bigger.

Frank took advantage of the economies of the house and his skill as a craftsman to install a luxury roof. At least, it would have been a luxury if he had subcontracted it to someone in our area. This is the terne roof described in detail in Chapter 15. I did the basic layout of the roof for Frank and he cut and bent the necessary pans, then took them home and painted them. I went to the job with Frank and we showed the carpenters how the pans should be installed. Three carpenters started at noon one day and put five rows of roofing on the south side of the roof. The next day they finished almost three-quarters of the roof. Then trouble set in — three solid weeks of snow, rain, and bitter cold weather. Absolutely no way to work on the roof. And then, the last straw. Some careless workmen walked on the pile of remaining roof pans on which Frank had worked so hard and ruined about $100 worth of material — not counting all of the time spent bending and painting. Frank bought extra materials and went back to the shop and made replacement pans. The resulting job is beautifully done and well worth the trouble.

The primary heat source for this house is the oversize greenhouse. A serious problem with this type of greenhouse is overheating. Either the greenhouse has to be vented to the outside, or some means must be devised for storing the excess heat from daytime sun so it can supply heat at night. Fifty-five-gallon steel drums filled with water are a favorite storage medium of passive solar enthusiasts. They are effective, and I find them useful for fine-tuning the heat storage capabilities of a sun-heated space. In this case, however, we were faced with huge quantities of excess heat that required a more sophisticated storage method. We used a rock storage bin under the floor at the south wall of the living room.

Heat is transferred from the top of the greenhouse to the rock storage bin by means of small fans and ductwork located near either end of the greenhouse. Heat from the rock storage bin can be recirculated either to the house or to the greenhouse as necessary. Simple manual dampers are set to provide full heat either to the house or to the greenhouse or at any desired proportional split. In the summertime, ducts are rearranged to allow heat from the greenhouse to be exhausted directly outside. Cool night air is circulated through the rock storage bin to provide natural daytime cooling. The controls for this system are all simple manual devices rather than an engineer's delight of complex thermostats, relays, and motorized dampers. While this does save a considerable amount of money, it also requires work and daily attention by the homeowner and a manual reconnection twice a year to convert from summer to winter use. This system would not be suitable for people who are away from home for long periods of time or those who want everything to happen automatically.

In order to make the greenhouse affordable, it was single-glazed with Plexiglas for the roof and the upper portion of the front wall, glass for the vents, and fixed glass near the ground. In the winter, nighttime insulation must be provided. I devised a system of sliding white Styrofoam panels for the greenhouse roof which can be slid back into the solid part of the roof overhang. These panels have several other functions as well. In hot summer weather, they are left closed

D

F

to prevent excessive heat buildup. Since they are translucent rather than opaque, they provide diffuse natural lighting without excessive heat for the plants. The vertical portions of the greenhouse are insulated with similar, removable Styrofoam panels. When I use this design again, I will provide a slot under the windows so that the vertical insulating panels can drop down into the ground rather than having to be removed and stored, which is a nuisance.

Total cost of this greenhouse was less than $5 per square foot. This was accomplished by using standard-size sheets of Plexiglas bought wholesale in quantity, and by integrating the structure of the house with the greenhouse to avoid extra expense. One of the major costs was in the concrete foundation, but since we had an expert foundation contractor who worked at very reasonable rates, the cost wasn't too bad. The exterior walls of the greenhouse support very little load, as most of the weight is carried by the roof structure of the main house. This means that you could easily use a direct-buried, pressure-treated wood foundation similar to the one used on the Volkswagen house. This foundation is shown on the working drawings at the back of the book.

Since Frank and Louise will be getting most of their heat from the greenhouse, they have very minimal provisions for backup. Louise has a combination electric-wood cooking stove which is located so that it can provide heat to the entire house. In addition, there is a small Lange stove in the living room which is set in a recess in the masonry chimney in the center of the house. The chimney is located so that sunlight from the large skylight on the south side of the house hits it for much of the day and stores additional heat. A sliding insulating cover over the skylight provides insulation on winter nights and summer protection. At the west end of the chimney, a heat-return duct recycles hot air from near the ceiling to

E

H

the first floor to prevent stratification. The hot air can also be diverted from this duct to the shop area when needed.

All in all, a most successful house. I am a bit sad that Frank, the most skilled of all my clients, got to do the least amount of work on his own house. I think his efforts on this book were worth the sacrifice. I hope he does too.

G   C

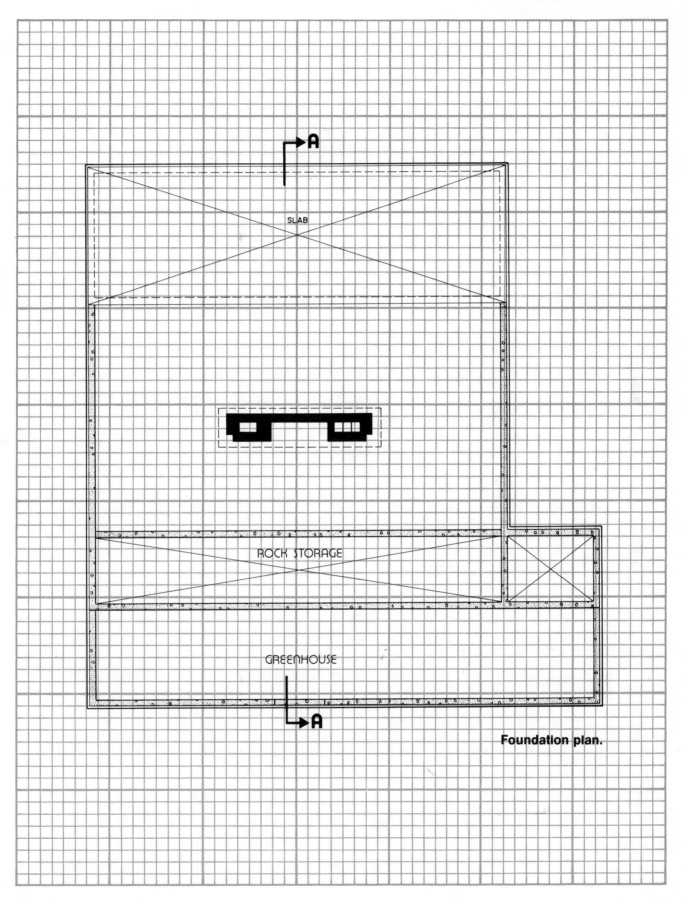

A

SLAB

ROCK STORAGE

GREENHOUSE

A

Foundation plan.

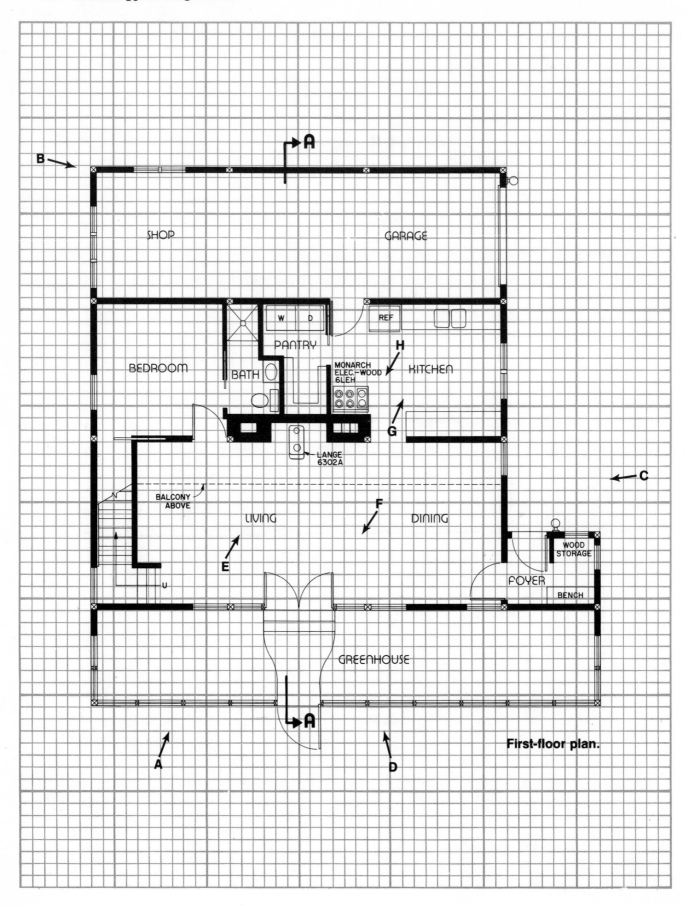

A

B

SHOP

GARAGE

W D

REF

PANTRY

BEDROOM

BATH

MONARCH
ELEC.-WOOD
6LEH

H

KITCHEN

G

LANGE
6302A

C

BALCONY
ABOVE

N

LIVING

F

DINING

E

WOOD
STORAGE

FOYER

BENCH

U

GREENHOUSE

A

A

D

First-floor plan.

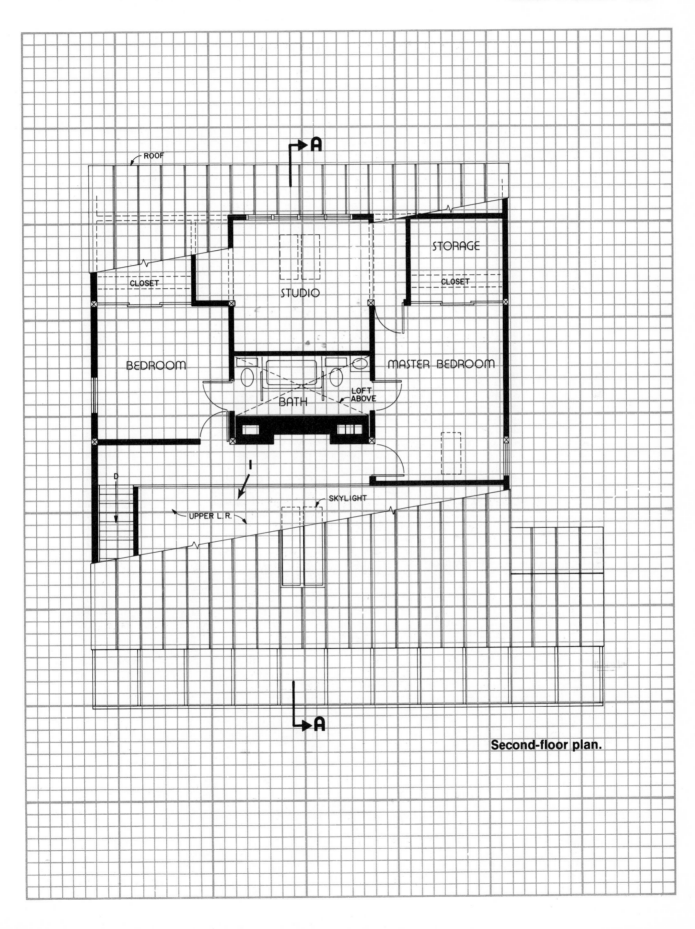

ROOF

A

CLOSET

STUDIO

STORAGE

CLOSET

BEDROOM

MASTER BEDROOM

BATH

LOFT ABOVE

D

I

UPPER L.R.

SKYLIGHT

A

Second-floor plan.

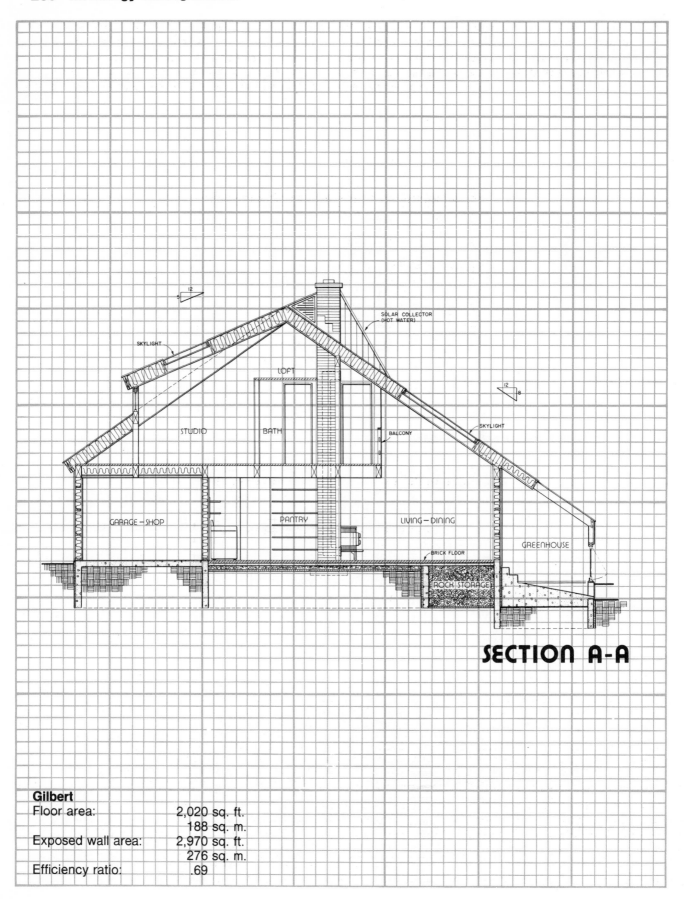

SKYLIGHT

SOLAR COLLECTOR
(HOT WATER)

LOFT

12
8

SKYLIGHT

STUDIO   BATH

BALCONY

GARAGE – SHOP

PANTRY

LIVING – DINING

GREENHOUSE

BRICK FLOOR

ROCK STORAGE

SECTION A-A

Gilbert
Floor area:	2,020 sq. ft.
	188 sq. m.
Exposed wall area:	2,970 sq. ft.
	276 sq. m.
Efficiency ratio:	.69

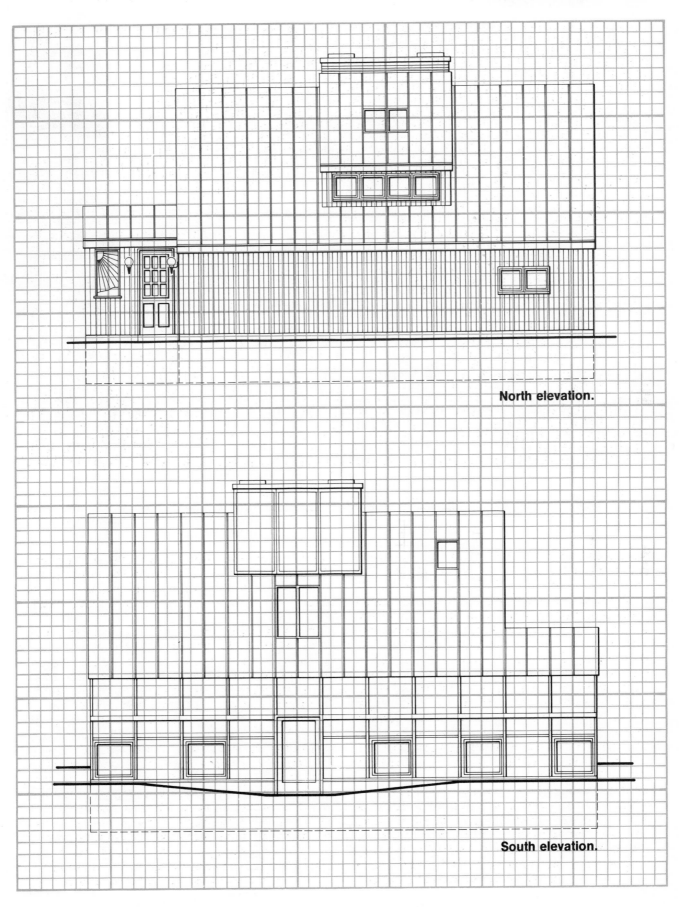

North elevation.

South elevation.

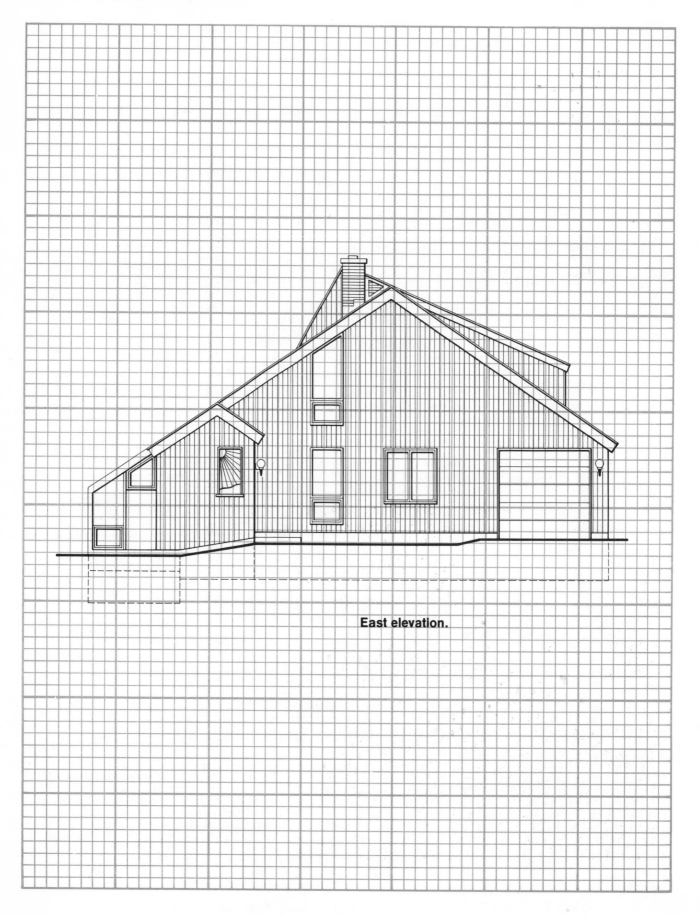

East elevation.

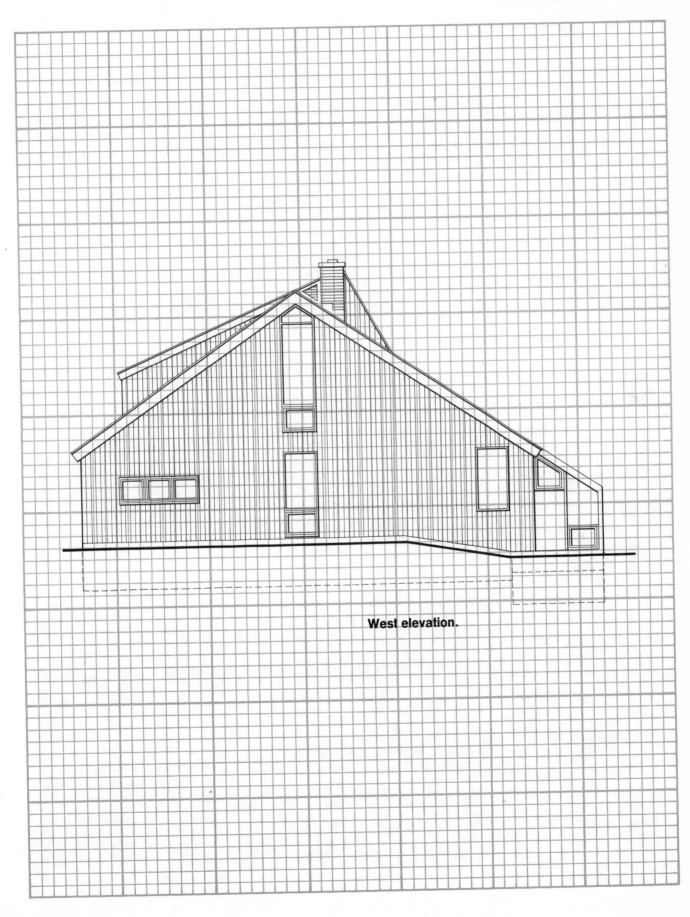

West elevation.

House 4: **Volkswagen**

The Volkswagen house started off as a sketch by a client who wanted a 24-foot-square vacation house. He took my ideas and worked them up into a nice plan. I made some minor revisions and got prices for the various components of the house. Since many people had asked for a very low cost house, I offered to sell plans for this house in *30 Energy-Efficient Houses*. When I drew the final working drawings, I made many refinements on the original, including a version with a steep roof which provided a third level for a sleeping loft.

As the economy got tighter, many people asked about this house, even though most people wanted bigger houses with garages and more space. Several have been built to date. The going price for the 900-square-foot house is about $22,000 if built by a commercial contractor. But even this may be out of reach for some budgets. I was approached by a client with a maximum of $8,000 to spend for everything including land. This seemed to be the ultimate challenge. Of course, if you have unlimited time to scout up used or salvaged materials, it is still possible to build a very low cost house, but my client was a schoolteacher with just a summer in which to build. This meant that all the low-priced materials must be readily available; a double challenge.

The first break came when we located a remote, but still handy, piece of property which could be leased for $40/month. There were a few strings, though. The leaseholder stipulated that there could be no electric lines brought onto the site and no excessive disturbance of soil or heavy road building. Since the terrain was quite rocky the only way to "improve" the property was by blasting, with likely damage to fragile rock cliffs. Buried water lines and embedded power poles, which meant extensive blasting, were not allowed. The low-cost lease helped the finances considerably, but we still had to arrange for a water supply, waste disposal, and some alternative source of power.

C

Direct embedded post and beam frame under construction (from left top to right bottom).

As it was obvious that we were going to have an extreme budget crunch, I took another look at the house design. Two items stood out as areas of major costs: the foundations and roof framing. The foundation system which I devised uses no masonry and is permanent and economical. It is fully described in Chapter 7.

The roof system I designed is described in Chapter 8. At the very last minute, we went with a conventional roof surface instead of the ribbed, galvanized roof. There were two reasons for the change. First, the galvanized roofing needed to span the framing members had to be special-ordered. Although it had supposedly arrived at the dealer's yard, no one could find the order. Also, we found that the roof was slightly out of square, and the sheets would have run at a strange angle. With considerable reluctance, we substituted double-coverage roll roofing. This is the same type of material from which standard asphalt roofing shingles are made. It is applied across the roof in continuous rolls and each layer is overlapped halfway over the preceding layer; hence, a double-coverage roof. I recommended these roofs in the past, but with the oil shortage, I no longer recommend them. They are still a relatively low-cost option, though.

All of the materials were ordered from a wholesale lumber dealer. We combined the order with that of Gene Tompkins. Both orders were delivered on a Friday, and everyone chipped in to unload the truck. Since it was 98°F., this wasn't much fun. A further complication was that the truck couldn't make it around the first bend in the road, and we had to unload into a smaller truck, working in relay fashion. We finished well after

dark. The dealer was furious because his driver was so late and refused to supply any of my other clients; he later relented for David Laskin.

We had scheduled a "house raising" for the weekend, since we expected to finish staking out the house Friday afternoon. Of course, we couldn't get this done because of the unloading problem. The weatherman helpfully promised 103°F. temperatures for Saturday and Sunday.

A

"Oh well," we said, "no one will show up in that heat anyway." The next morning there were fifteen people ready to work. We had many volunteers show up uninvited. Word of my unique construction systems had spread. But there were even a couple of trees in the way. So far, we had no clearing, no stakeout, no foundation, and excess people.

Somehow, it all got organized. Frank Gilbert jumped in and started digging the hole for the first foundation post. The rest of us set up a work area to cut timbers, and a "survey crew" laid out the rest of the foundation so we could dig the other holes. Despite the hot weather, lack of preparation, and too many people, we did get the basic shell of the house up by the end of the weekend. One of the volunteers, a carpenter for a nasty-tempered union contractor, was fired when his boss heard about it. Generosity sometimes gets repaid in strange ways.

The heat and the rush to get the house up resulted in a roof which was 3 inches out of square. Pushing and pulling on the structure eliminated about half of the error, but this was as far as it would go. On later houses, we revised the framing system so that the posts only go up one floor at a time. Straightening out a warped post 16 feet in the air is no easy feat.

All of the materials for the shell of the house cost about $3,000, ordered new. Some windows and doors were obtained from a salvage yard. New Andersen basement vents were bought on sale. One "splurge" item was a fancy, wood-framed, sliding glass door. This door alone cost over $400. Beware of such temptation if you are on a limited budget! We bought tempered glass for the greenhouse in standard 46-inch by 76-inch sheets for only $5 per sheet from a local glass company. They sold off all their reserve stock of damaged insulating glass from standard sliding doors. If the glass had clouded or one of the panes was broken, they replaced it, but kept the damaged unit in storage. Damaged double panes can be cut apart with a knife; the result is at least one panel of tempered glass.

Water supply for this house is fairly easy. In the summer, it comes from a spring-fed pond. A 5,000-gallon tank bought at salvage was connected to the roof gutter to store water and act as a heat sink for the greenhouse. The tank is placed against the south wall of the house at the rear of the greenhouse. A 12-volt pump provides

B

D

F

E

pressurized water to the house. Wastewater from the sinks and shower is discharged into a gravel bed in the greenhouse. A composting toilet handles human wastes.

Four skylights face south and supplement the heat from the greenhouse. A dark gray slate floor set in a sand-cement bed stores heat. A Cawley-LeMay woodstove with an insulated stainless steel stovepipe provides backup heating. Bottled gas provides fuel for summertime cooking, a refrigerator, and hot water.

For the time being, a gasoline-powered generator is being used to recharge a 12-volt battery pack for very limited electrical use. Eventually, my client plans to erect a wind generator. Erecting the tower for a windmill is a problem, however, as it must be pinned to the rock, which requires blasting. The secret, in the meantime, is to use as little electrical energy as possible. See Chapter 1 for means of reducing or eliminating the need for outside electrical connections.

When building the frame for the Volkswagen house note that, while it is very similar to the basic saltbox framing, there are some differences. Basically, I took the same framing system and rotated it 90°. This was done to accommodate the stairway which is contained within the second-floor structure, rather than being located in front of it as in the saltbox plan. My original plans showed conventional framing for this house, but virtually everyone who wrote had been sold on the advantages of post and beam framing. For this reason, I revised the final plans for this type of construction. We took very careful step-by-step photographs of the procedure for erecting the frame. Study them carefully before building.

If you build the version of this house with the steep 6/12 roof pitch, you will have room to add a sleeping loft on the top floor. This sleeping loft provides considerably more space in the bedrooms, and I recommend this version highly for a typical family. For one or two people, the version shown in the photographs is ample.

For those who require a maximum house for minimum money, this is about the best I can do. Judging by the popularity of these plans, many people like this design. If you are desperate for low-cost housing and feel that you don't have the time or skill to build this house, take a look at the Shelter-Kit houses described in Part IV. They are very low-cost and come completely cut out, ready to assemble with hand tools. Even the tools are included.

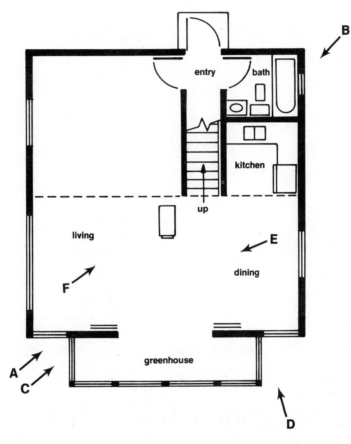

Volkswagen house as built.

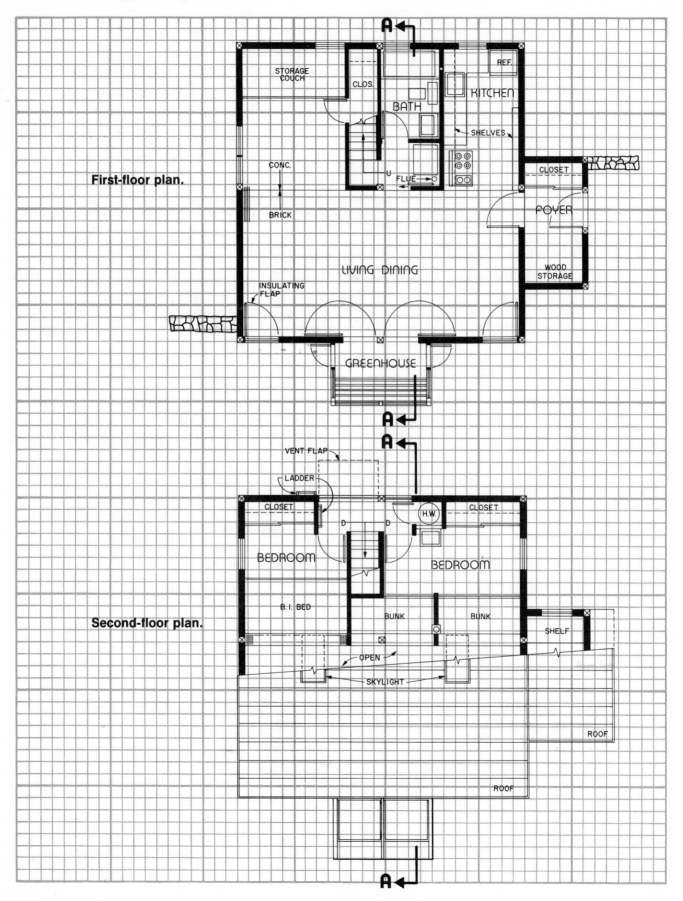

First-floor plan.

Second-floor plan.

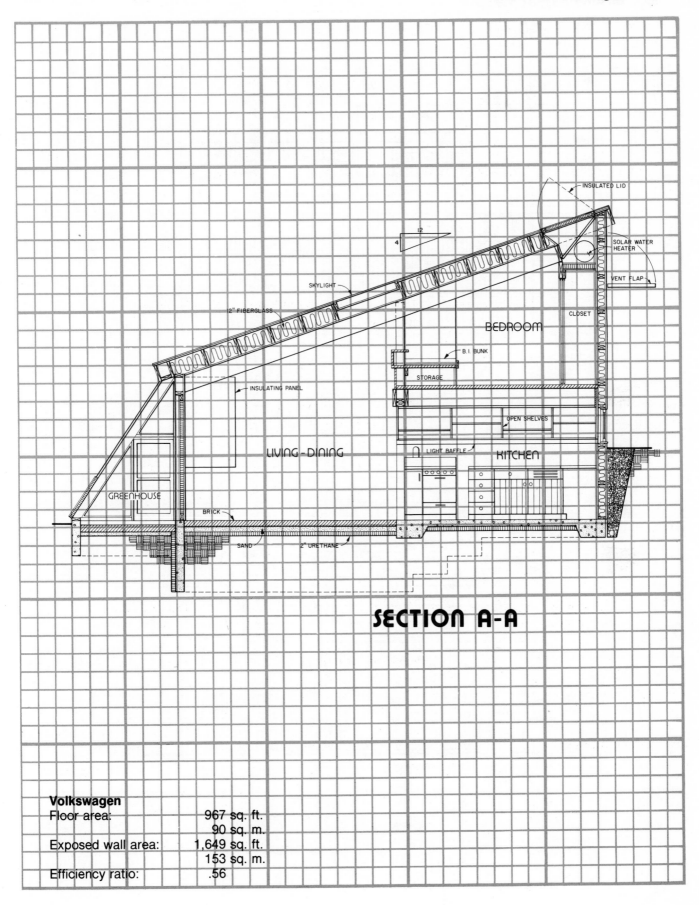

INSULATED LID

SOLAR WATER
HEATER

VENT FLAP

12
4

SKYLIGHT

12" FIBERGLASS

CLOSET

BEDROOM

B.I. BUNK

STORAGE

INSULATING PANEL

OPEN SHELVES

LIVING - DINING

LIGHT BAFFLE

KITCHEN

GREENHOUSE

BRICK

SAND   2" URETHANE

SECTION A-A

Volkswagen

Floor area:	967 sq. ft.
	90 sq. m.
Exposed wall area:	1,649 sq. ft.
	153 sq. m.
Efficiency ratio:	.56

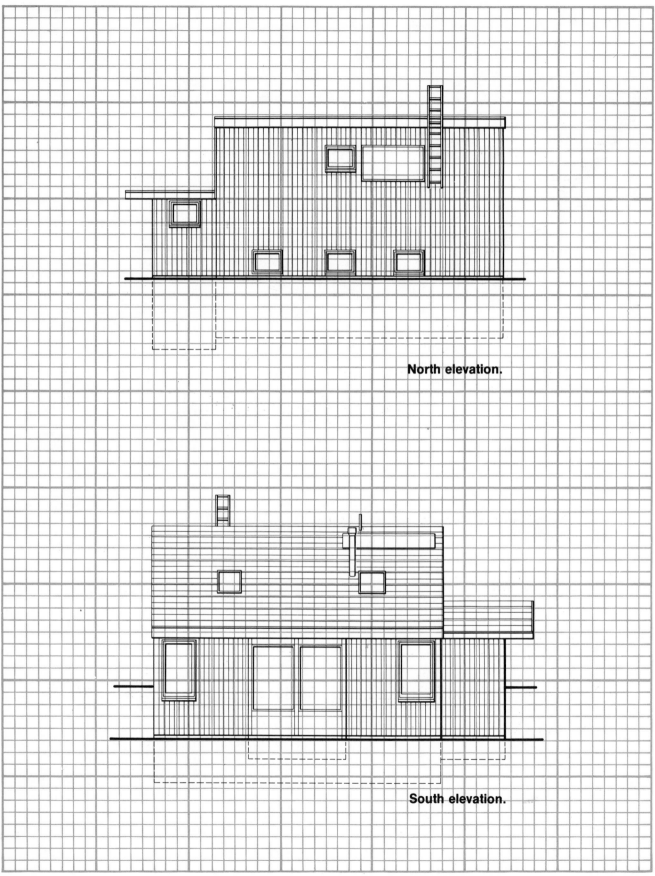

North elevation.

South elevation.

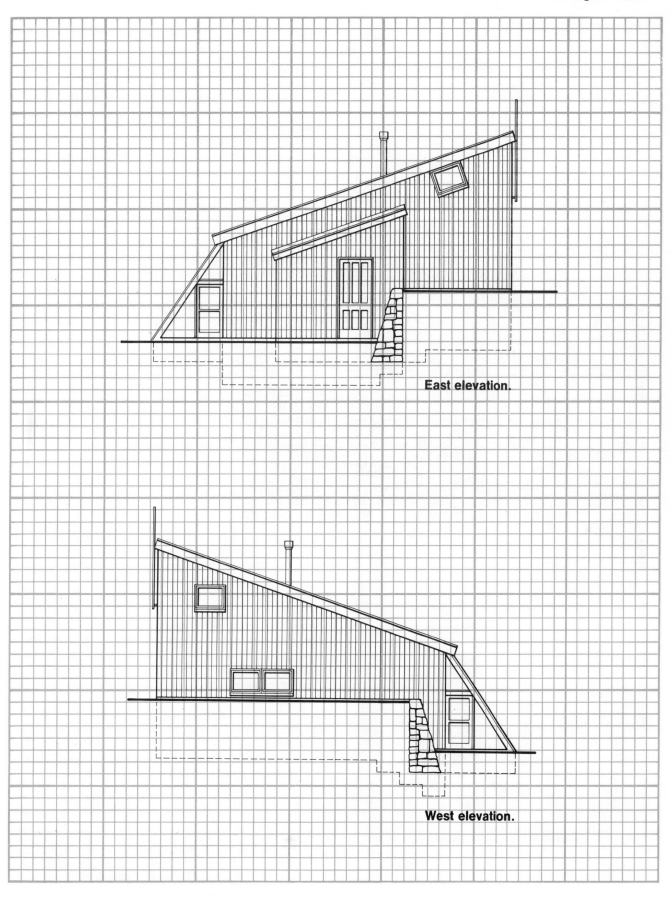

East elevation.

West elevation.

House 5: **Tompkins**

This house is the most efficient house I have ever designed. The floor plan contains almost exactly the same amount of area as the basic saltbox, yet there is nearly 30 percent less exposed exterior surface than on the saltbox.

First member in place.

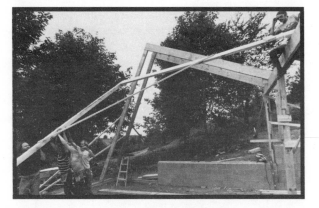

The framing members need to be well braced.

The house frame is simple to erect, requiring just a bit of muscle.

The thermal efficiency of the house reflects the efficiencies of the envelope which has a very large floor area compared to exposed exterior surface. Late last winter we had a period of two weeks of weather in which the daily high temperatures only reached the teens. Nighttime temperatures were 0°F. or below. At 10:30 on a cold, sunny morning, a friend visited the uncompleted house. The exterior temperature was -8°F.; the inside temperature 55°F. No supplemental heating was installed, so only the heating effect of the sun through the sloping south wall plus the storage capacity of the dark brick floor were capable of maintaining this temperature in cold, sunny weather. At the time this reading was taken, the exterior shell was thoroughly caulked and weatherstripped, the roof was insulated with 12 inches of fiberglass, but no insulation had been installed in the sidewalls. The foundation and buried portions of the exterior walls were insulated with 2 inches of urethane insulation board.

The design for this house evolved from a set of plans which I offered in *30 Energy-Efficient Houses.* As presented in the book, the house was only 30 feet square and had four posts supporting the second floor and roof. When I drew the working drawings for sale, I made a few modifications. The roof at the front of the second floor was self-supporting and really didn't need the posts and beam. I also discovered that the house could be extended 4 feet to the rear very economically, creating added floor area and making the room arrangement more flexible. The final plans showed a 30-foot-wide by 34-foot-deep house with a greenhouse across the front and a second floor over the front half of the house.

About the time I was completing these plans, I was approached by Gene Tompkins, a schoolteacher and passive solar enthusiast. He purchased a set of my plans and spent many months drawing possible modifications. Since his site offered spectacular views to the south, he decided to eliminate the separate greenhouse for an unobstructed view. This did leave two posts and a staircase very much in the way. We solved this problem by beefing up the roof and hanging the second floor from it. This resulted in a wide-open space on both floors with only two posts near the rear of the first floor to limit any possible interior arrangement.

We thought we had solved all of our problems with the plan, but didn't realize that we had made possible an almost infinite number of solutions and thereby made our task very difficult. We went ahead with the construction of the shell, confident that the final interior arrangement would be very easy. Gene, my assistant Gregg, and I all drew floor plans, only to discover some element which could be changed for the better. The plans which we show with this house design are not the ones which Gene used, but rather a design Gregg devised which I feel would have the widest application for most people. Gene's final plan was governed by his desire to partake of the view at all times. Since the view is to the south and east, the kitchen-bath complex was moved to the southeast corner of the house and combined with the entryway.

If this is the most efficient plan which I have ever done, why isn't it the featured house of this book instead of the saltbox? The same features which make this house efficient also limit its appeal. In selecting the saltbox, I am trying to present a house which can be built in a wide variety of locations for families with differing needs. I also hope to influence the commercial housing market with the saltbox. The Tompkins solar shed is best suited for a sloping site and by its very geometry is inflexible. It cannot readily be expanded or have an attached garage. If the specific design and the various layouts of this house appeal to you, build it! I feel that more people will prefer the saltbox and that builders and bank will like it better, too.

A second major reason for not featuring this house more prominently is that it is more difficult to build than the saltbox. The sloping front wall, when installed without vertical posts, exerts considerable horizontal pressure toward the rear of the house. Since I emphasize construction methods which will be easy for the beginning builder, I feel that this particular structure poses some significant problems. During framing, the roof beams *must* be braced to prevent them from sliding to the rear of the house. The sidewalls *must* have diagonal bracing members built into them to counteract this thrust. Finally, the roof deck *must* have plywood sheathing nailed very thoroughly to transmit the pressures from the center of the roof to the sidewalls.

As an added precaution to remove some of the roof load, we installed the 2X6 decking for the second floor at a 45° angle starting from the center of the floor. By doing this we converted the rearward thrust of the sloping south wall into sideways pressure on the east and west sidewalls.

The construction isn't really that difficult, it just

A

B

requires special precautions and doesn't take advantage of the efficiencies of my post and beam system. If you have an experienced carpenter working with you and alert him to the fact that the sloping wall exerts a strong rearward thrust, you should have no trouble constructing this house. Actual construction of the house went very smoothly for us, despite considerable differences of opinion over siding application and finishes.

In my opinion, Gene did the best job of any of my clients in managing his house. I think this is attributable to several factors. Most important, Gene was there at all times to oversee the work. Although he never took a major part in the construction, he was always available as a helping hand to run errands, or to handle emergencies, such as arranging for an emergency generator when the old one was obviously dying. Gene's role was a bit frustrating for him because he has had some construction experience and would have liked to have done more of the actual construction, but I feel that he got a better job this way. The workmen related well to the job with the client right there and helping all of the time. Second, Gene allowed plenty of lead time to study just what he wanted, to acquire materials, and to make all of the arrangements necessary for the construction of this house.

Intricate notching is required where several beams meet at the rear post.

Even with all of Gene's hard work and forethought, some problems did occur. The worst one involved the septic system. The county health department required that Gene hire an engineer to lay out the septic system and provide them with a topographic layout of the exact site. The engineer agreed to a price of $350 for doing the work and then dragged his feet for several months. The health department finally issued a temporary permit subject to final approval of the

system after preliminary tests indicated that the soil was suitable for a septic system. Finally, many months later, after constant pressure from Gene, the engineers presented their septic system layout to the health department and handed Gene a bill for $750. The health department rejected the septic system design because the engineers had surveyed the wrong site. Gene rejected the bill and hired new engineers to start all over again.

I include this story to illustrate just one of the factors which tend to push up the cost of houses. Even a knowledgeable person can get into trouble because the system is so disorganized and the so-called "professionals" are incompetent. Engineers are to be avoided wherever possible. They are slow, expensive, and rarely do their job properly. Sadly, they are not alone. Both my clients and I have learned from bitter experiences that the same can be said of architects and lawyers who handle housing matters. The private house just doesn't provide a juicy enough fee to attract competent professionals.

Gene's other problem actually worked well to his advantage. The house is located a good distance from the main road, both for privacy and to take advantage of a sheltered, south-facing slope. He had intended to have a buried electric service put in at the same time as his road, but the very high cost of direct-burial cable stopped him. He started trying to locate someone to set poles and a line. He found some workmen for the local power company who moonlight and work very reasonably. The only problem was timing — they were booked up, and a long wait was involved. The alternative was to use someone who wanted almost $1,000 more for the line. This meant that we had to build the house using noisy, balky, portable generators which cost time and money. Finally, Gene borrowed a high-quality diesel generator from a friend and we finished the shell without incident.

I think he probably came out a bit ahead; no temporary service was really required. By the time the power line was brought to the house, the siding was installed and the permanent service was run to the main electric panel, completely saving the cost of a temporary service.

Costs for the house have been quite reasonable considering the steep costs of road and electric service. All labor was hired except for Gene's labor in supervising construction and ordering materials. Gene and Bob Dakin worked together on a materials takeoff with some of my suggestions. The cost of the framing materials and siding was

E

about $3,500. The materials were not up to previous quality, but we used them anyway. The buried block wall and concrete footings were subcontracted for about $2,500.

The only real construction problems came with the windows. The sloping south wall is glazed with standard tempered insulating glass units. Andersen basement vents are used for venting at the top of the wall. Installing these on a sloping wall was a serious mistake. They are made to open inward and hence are not very weatherproof. We solved the problem with tricky metal flashings, but it would be easier to use windows which are hinged to swing outward.

I strongly disapprove of Gene's selections for the other windows for the house. These are very expensive Andersen casements and sliders which have a layer of white plastic glop encasing the wood frames. They are a reaction to years of living in old houses with peeling, rotting, wooden windows. If wooden windows are naturally finished with a thorough coating of wood preservative and a stain, they will last the lifetime of the house — without the expensive plastic coating. The integral flange also posed a problem as the siding had already been installed, and the flange was designed to fit underneath the siding for a weathertight seal. We solved this problem by removing framing members and installing the windows from the inside. This is an advantage of my framing system since the nonloadbearing girts can be easily changed.

Gregg Torchio built the south wall of glass and handsplit cedar shakes. These are very tricky to install and are not a job for the beginner. I would recommend sawn cedar shingles which are uniform and much easier to install. The windows are simply glued to the sloping framing members, using Mono caulking compound. Surface battens are screwed in place over the seams to lock the glass in place; a second bead of Mono provides a double seal. I made up special flashings for the head and sills using a metal brake. The installation was not easy but the results were worth all the hard work. The east and west sides of the house and the tiny portion of the north wall which projects above grade were sided with rough-sawn, shiplapped pine. The siding had air-dried for several months and has performed very well with little shrinking or cupping.

Gene used new, medium brown brick pavers for his floor. They were expensive, but make a very tight, neat installation. This is one of the few jobs which Gene did entirely by himself.

D

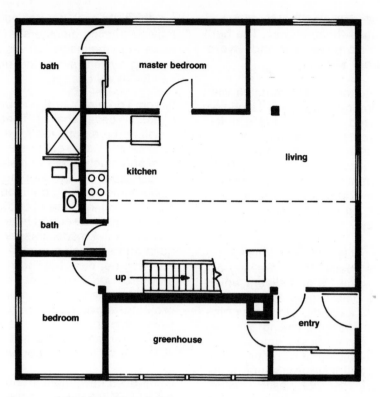

First-floor plan — original Tompkins design.

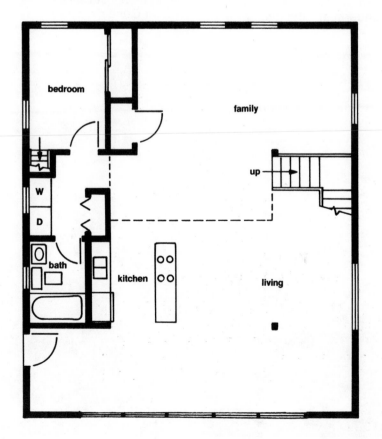

First-floor plan — Tompkins house as built.

C

F

H

G

Total project cost for the shell, including driveway and electric service and all hired labor, was about $19,000. Gene is finishing off the interior himself. Since the floor is brick and the second-floor structure forms a finish ceiling and finish second floor at the same time, there is very little interior finish to be done. Costs to finish the project will range between $5,000 and $10,000. Figuring the maximum, the house will cost less than $20 per square foot.

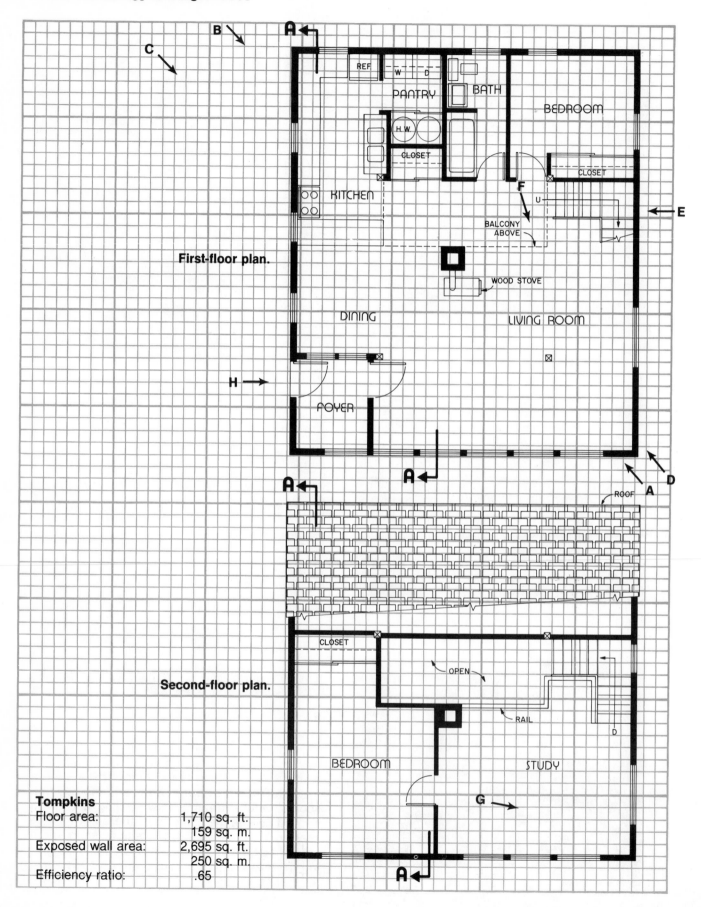

B

C

A

REF
W   D

PANTRY   BATH

BEDROOM

H.W.

CLOSET

CLOSET

KITCHEN

F

U

E

First-floor plan.

BALCONY
ABOVE

WOOD STOVE

DINING

LIVING ROOM

H

FOYER

A

A

A   D

A

A   ROOF

Second-floor plan.

CLOSET

OPEN

RAIL

D

BEDROOM

STUDY

G

A

Tompkins

Floor area:	1,710 sq. ft.
	159 sq. m.
Exposed wall area:	2,695 sq. ft.
	250 sq. m.
Efficiency ratio:	.65

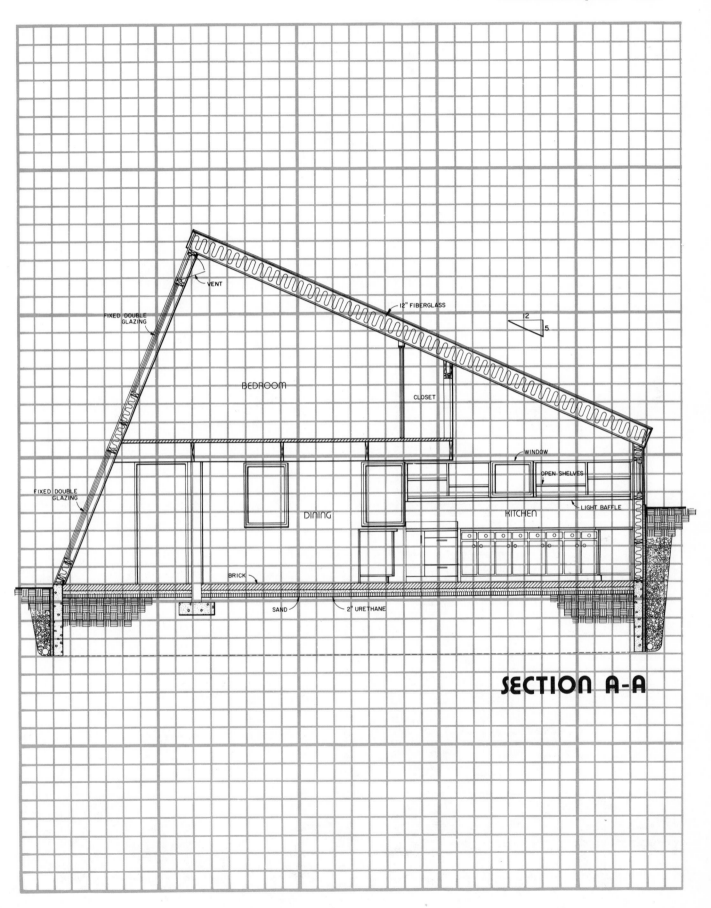

VENT

FIXED DOUBLE
GLAZING

12" FIBERGLASS

12
5

BEDROOM

CLOSET

WINDOW

OPEN SHELVES

FIXED DOUBLE
GLAZING

DINING

KITCHEN

LIGHT BAFFLE

BRICK

SAND   2" URETHANE

SECTION A-A

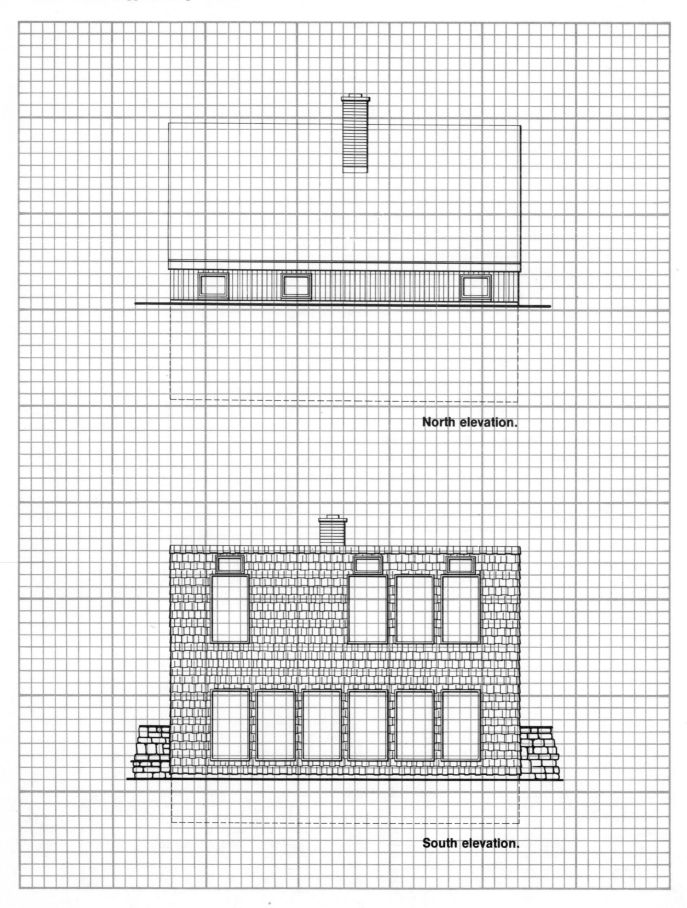

North elevation.

South elevation.

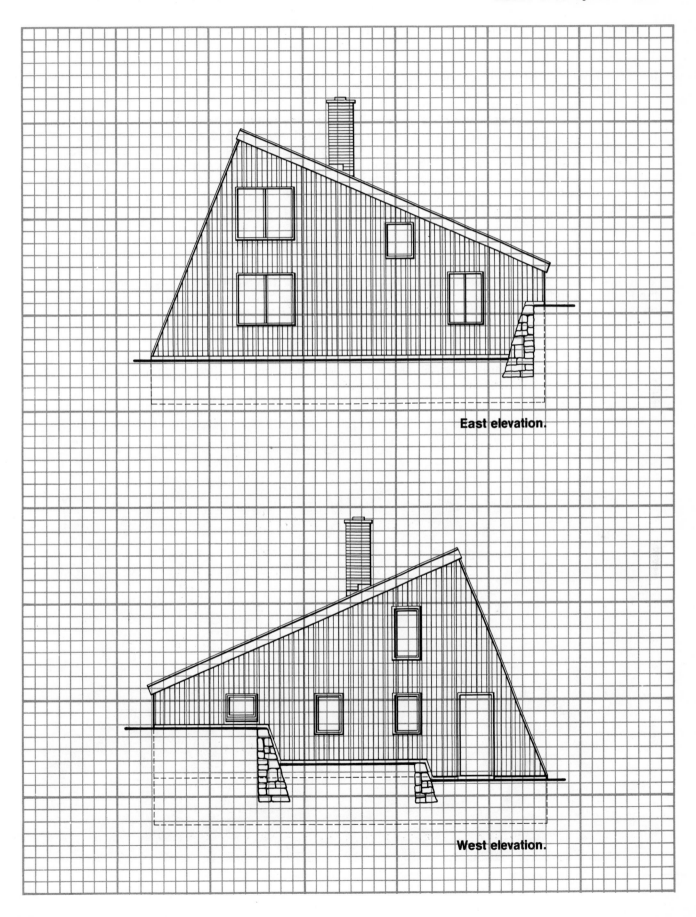

East elevation.

West elevation.

House 6: **Perlberg/Price**

In *30 Energy-Efficient Houses,* I included plans and a photograph of a model for a house being built by the Perlbergs in upstate New York. I also included an outline specification and a contractor's estimate for the house and described various difficulties we had with the local health department, banks, and so forth. At that point, however, construction was just beginning, and I had little idea of the problems that lay ahead. So you can see some of the pitfalls *you* may encounter, I will relate the remainder of the saga.

Since my book was published under an extremely tight schedule, I had to spend much time at Rodale Press to expedite production. This left the Perlbergs and the contractor, Ben Bromiley, on their own. Bromiley started off very well, albeit quite late. He was so late, in fact, that we tried very hard to find a replacement, but the only interested people were luxury custom homebuilders who wanted two to three times Bromiley's

price of $32,500. With considerable reluctance, we let Bromiley go ahead.

Bromiley built the formwork for the foundation using inexperienced workmen. The forms were constructed of very thin plywood, poorly braced, and when the concrete was poured, the forms bowed out like a surrealist sculpture. The foundation took several extra yards of concrete and we were left with terribly irregular faces on the concrete. Since none of the concrete was going to be exposed when the job was completed, we didn't worry too much about it at the time.

The post and beam frame was a shining example of efficiency at its best. Using details from *The Timber Framing Book,* by a group called the Housesmiths, Bromiley and the crew precut and erected the frame in about two weeks. Carpenters are used to concealed framing members, allowing them to do fast, often sloppy, work. The

A

B

exposed post and beam frame was a great challenge to them.

The shell itself was completed quite speedily with only one mistake. A young, inexperienced worker made a mistake in the roof framing for the construction of the third-floor penthouse. It was drawn with a raised roof permitting a strip of clerestory windows on both sides. Somehow, the kid misread the drawings and raised the penthouse only slightly above the main roof with no space for windows. Since we were already so far behind schedule, I allowed Bromiley to add a skylight rather than remove and reframe the roof correctly.

At this point, everyone was excited about the job and it was going smoothly. From here on in, however, everything went downhill. The first major blow came from the bank. Even though the shell was completed and the finished floors in place in the second and third stories, the bank only released a fraction of the money due. This caused serious financial problems for everyone. The Perlbergs had obligated themselves to Bromiley, who, in turn, had obligated himself to suppliers. Furthermore, clients on another of Bromiley's projects had spent money like drunken sailors

and now had no money to pay him the balance due on that contract. The Perlbergs partially solved the problem by taking out a small personal loan that just enabled the job to proceed; there was not enough money to order materials ahead or to conduct business properly, however.

After the shell is up, one wants rough wiring and plumbing and insulation to proceed as rapidly as possible. We lucked out and got three of the worst subcontractors I have ever worked with. The plumber was from Puerto Rico and had never seen freezing weather. The insulation contractor didn't show up for weeks and then bungled the job. But the electrician took the prize as the worst subcontractor I have ever had on a job. Strangely, all came with good recommendations, and all were pleasant people who started off well and made an initial good impression.

The plumber followed instructions for the waste lines accurately and installed them quickly, then disappeared for a couple of weeks. When he did return, he couldn't find his plans and had forgotten my instructions for installing the supply pipes. He strung piping all over the house, wasting lots of pipe and burying much of it in the outside walls, where it later froze. He refused to correct his mistakes unless he was fully paid and then given extra money for changes. We gave him partial payment on the condition that he correct the piping. He took his money and ran; another plumber had to be engaged to straighten out the mess. All of these mistakes were correctable, and very little money was directly lost since the original plumber hadn't been fully paid.

The electrical work was another story. Bromiley engaged a very competent professional electrician who was very busy and kept postponing the job. We didn't even have a quote from him. When he finally showed up, tempers were short. He insisted that we had to put an ugly pipe mast on the front of the house for the electric service despite the fact that the power company said the mast was unnecessary, and his price was considerably over budget. A well-meaning neighbor recommended a "super," low-priced electrician who had a sizable firm and did lots of work. I made a serious blunder and gave my second and only other copy of the electrical drawings to this electrician. His quote was almost as steep as the first one, but he said that he could start immediately. That's all he did immediately — start.

We soon learned that we were being used as "filler" for his commercial work. Never, in the entire course of the project, did he send the same workmen, so they never knew what they were doing. He claimed that I had never given him any plans, so his workmen never had any guidance other than time-consuming verbal instructions on the job. A new set of directions were necessary for each batch of workmen. Many feed wires were omitted, and others were so confusing that no one could figure them out. Despite the sloppy work, the rough wiring passed inspection, even though it was far from finished, because the inspector was the contractor's good buddy. The local power company contributed to the mess by omitting one of the poles along the main road and then telling us that installation of the pole could take months — "that has to be approved by engineering" — when we had applied for service nine months before. Back to the noisy, undependable generator.

The insulation contractor provided the final nightmare of the piece. At the time I designed this house, urea-formaldehyde foam was being widely recommended by most authorities as the "best" insulation material. In fact, I had used it on several remodeling jobs with superb results. The houses were warm and cosy, and the clients were happy. We did not even consider using any other material on the Perlberg house. Unfortunately, all of the New York State apple growers had also discovered the foam and were all having it put in their storage barns, tying up all of the established contractors. We finally located a young contractor who agreed to do the job and said he would also spray urethane foam on the lumpy concrete foundation which was so rough that air whistled under the sill plate. Bromiley, who had omitted a sill seal, was counting on the foam to close the gaps. By now, the job was months behind, and Perlberg's house had been sold out from under them, and Bromiley and the suppliers were desperate for money which the bank wasn't giving out.

On a cold, rainy day the insulation was finally pumped in from the outside after the Sheetrock had been installed. No vapor barrier was used, as the contractor said we didn't need one (one of the selling points for the foam when installed in existing houses is that it doesn't need a vapor barrier). The contractor had constant trouble with his foam mixture. It bulged out the Sheetrock; excess water ran down the walls. Finally he gave up, to return the following day. We all breathed a sigh of relief when he was finished, and we could get on with finishing the house. I went away on a publicity tour. When I returned two weeks later, everyone was grim. The fumes were so bad no one could work in the house. The foam mixture was incorrect — there was excess formaldehyde, causing the odor problem.

Since there was no vapor barrier and the exterior of the house was sheathed in plywood, vapor migrated into the Sheetrock and gradually into the house. On Indian summer days the house was unbearable; on cold days, barely tolerable. The insulation contractor blamed the manufacturer; the manufacturer blamed the contractor; Bromiley blamed me for specifying the stuff. All of the "experts" assured us that the problem was only temporary and would go away in about three weeks. We pointed out rather icily that *five* weeks had already elapsed.

I wasted $400 having a testing lab run an analysis to try to find out what was wrong and whether the fault lay with the manufacturer or the installer. The lab didn't want to be on the hook and sent us an unexplained spectrograph, a special type of photograph which can determine chemical composition. A lawyer was contacted. It turned out that it would be much cheaper to tear out the Sheetrock and remove the insulation than to pay court costs and fees for the lab to testify in a slim chance of collecting money many years hence. So much for our legal system. We opened up some of the walls and discovered that many of the cavities were only partly filled with foam; others had huge gaps where the foam had shrunk.

Cold gradually penetrated the as-yet-uninsulated foundation walls, and drafts penetrated the badly insulated walls. The workmen struggled with the cold, fumes, and lack of electricity to get the house finished for a Christmas moving date. A shyster salesman sold the Perlbergs an off-brand "Scandinavian" woodstove which refused to supply any heat. After several weeks a suitable replacement was found, but not until the house had cooled off drastically.

The electrician sent some other new workmen who connected what few wires had been installed in the right places, and the power company finally got the main power line connected. We told the electrician to get lost; we'd manage the best we could. Some hasty insulation around the foundation and a quick siding installation permitted the Perlbergs to move into the disaster.

Everyone began to crack under the strain. Bromiley drove his car up onto a snow bank and started to bash on it with a 2X4. A rich college kid took over his firm and assumed the debts. New faces appeared on the job. Somehow it creaked along to a sloppy state of semicompletion. The college kid demanded extra money for his sloppy work. Certainly the delays had been beyond the contractor's control, but no one was about to pay him extra money for them so he was let go.

Two treatments of the same window. Above in the
Perlberg house and below in the Price house.

The Perlbergs and I each hired a carpenter and the two of them worked together to finish the house and correct the mistakes. One room at a time was stripped of Sheetrock and foam, reinsulated with fiberglass, and refinished. Fortunately, the ceilings were already insulated with 12-inch fiberglass and didn't have to be redone. As soon as the weather began to warm up, we moved to the exterior, where mistakes in the siding could be corrected along with the insulation. The workmen had hastily mashed a piece of aluminum over the top edge of the badly fitted insulation board. All of the material was removed and properly reset, with a new heavy-gauge flashing all around the base of the house.

The Perlbergs spent their summer vacation reworking details to their satisfaction. "You know, I thought this stuff was really hard until I tried it," said Eric after his first effort. He built a set of closet doors to replace the cheap plywood ones which were installed hastily to get final bank approval. Now that he is no longer intimidated by construction, Eric has made many changes large and small. As they live in the house, the Perlbergs find things to change and don't hesitate to jump in and change them. For instance, he decided that the sauna was too big and their closet too small, so he tore out the wall between them and moved it.

In case I have made it all sound hopelessly gloomy, there were aspects which went well. The mason did a fine job on the chimney. Generally, we were very lucky on materials. The floor and chimney are made of handsome brick. The wood was generally nice except for a distressing tendency for the floor decking to shrink (never use over 6-inch-wide decking). The roof worked well, as the frame of the house was built quite accurately to the dimensions on the plans. And finally, the house is strikingly beautiful. Even with just a set of plans and a poor-quality photograph of a model, many, many people have written for more information. Everyone who has seen it has been spellbound. To date, it has been the most popular of my houses.

C

D

E

F

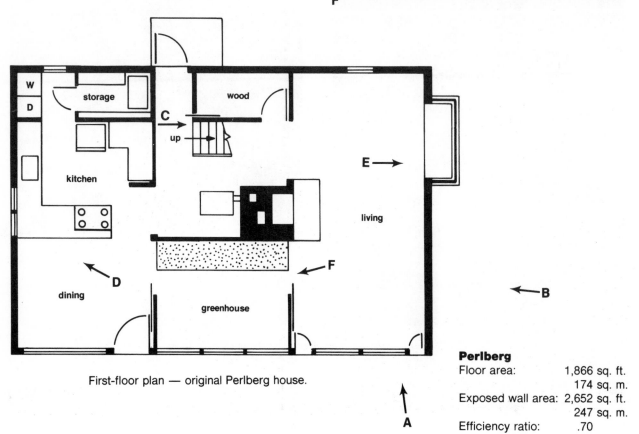

First-floor plan — original Perlberg house.

Perlberg

Floor area:	1,866 sq. ft.
	174 sq. m.
Exposed wall area:	2,652 sq. ft.
	247 sq. m.
Efficiency ratio:	.70

One of the first to inquire about the house was Don Price of Ann Arbor, Michigan. Then I received a call from his contractor, Fritz Dodge. He asked many questions about post and beam framing and finally went up to study with David Howard, the top expert in this country. "Perlberg West," as Don calls it, went up without a hitch. Several significant changes were made which improve the plan. Most noticeably, a garage was added to the north side of the house. The garage ties into the lines of the house handsomely and permits an expansion of the upstairs to allow more bedroom space. I have further refined the design in the plans which are shown here to permit a very economical plumbing layout, with the bath and kitchen aligned on one plumbing stack.

Don took a year's leave of absence from his job to help Fritz build the house. They carefully researched every detail of the house to make all possible improvements. Since they were borrowing money for the house, they went first-class all the way. Instead of roughsawn pine, they used planed red oak for the frame. All connections were mortised and tenoned and doweled together. Cross-braces at 45° were installed at all frame intersections. (On the original Perlberg house, plywood sheathing was used for structural bracing.)

Exterior wall insulation is 4-inch Styrofoam applied completely over the exterior of the frame of the house, a technique advocated by David Howard. In this case, it increases the size of the house slightly (the walls have been moved out so that the frame is exposed inside them). The fireplace was eliminated and the brick floor extended to cover the living room. For more even heat distribution, the Defiant stove was moved to the living room side of the stone chimney.

A

B

Hardwood paneling is used as an interior surface on the walls. It's too much for my taste. I feel that it detracts from the beautiful frame which is striking if set off with plaster; it's a very minor quibble, though.

Both houses performed well thermally this past winter. Perlberg West did the better of the two, probably because it is sited so that it is sheltered from wind and gets more hours of sunlight. There is a nice stand of pine trees to the west of the original house which cuts off the low winter sun about 2:00 P.M. Remember, when siting your house, that the sun angle is much lower in winter and trees which don't block the sun in warm weather may completely block it in winter.

C

G

H

J

E

K

D

F

"Oak generates doubts in carpenters like Lake Superior does in sailors. Some common oak tales: A hammer just bounces off it; it twists while drying; you can't work oak; it is extremely heavy. . . . We found only the last tale to be true.

"We employed the help of Fritz Dodge, a carpenter/builder from Charlevoix, Michigan, and an acquaintance of some ten years. We cut the frame in five working days. Fritz did the layout; my father and I cleaned the cuts with chisels and mallets. The wet oak worked easily, if a cut did not fall on a knot. We made more than 300 pegs by driving 1-inch cuttings through successively smaller holes in a steel plate. These pegs hold the joints in place.

"Raising day: August 3, 1978. Since we were new at this procedure, we hired a crane for the day. In 5½ hours the frame was up and pegged in place. It was a beautiful, rich gold in the afternoon sun. We went to town to celebrate."

Don Price,
Michigan Solar Energy Association Bulletin

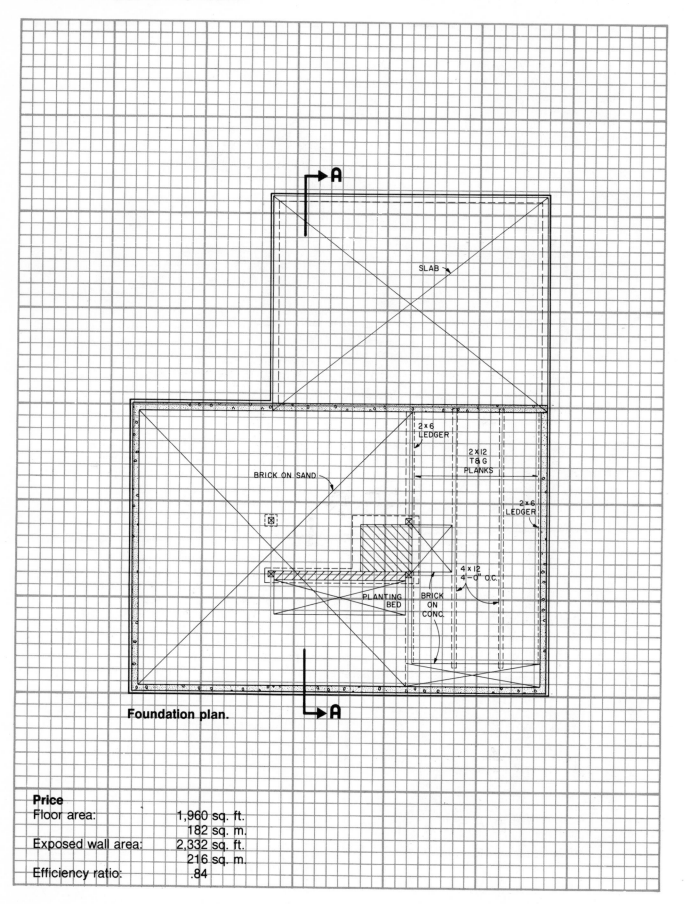

A

SLAB

2 x 6
LEDGER

2 X 12
T & G
PLANKS

BRICK ON SAND

2 x 6
LEDGER

4 x 12
4'-0" O.C.

PLANTING
BED

BRICK
ON
CONC.

Foundation plan.

A

Price

Floor area:	1,960	sq. ft.
	182	sq. m.
Exposed wall area:	2,332	sq. ft.
	216	sq. m.
Efficiency ratio:	.84	

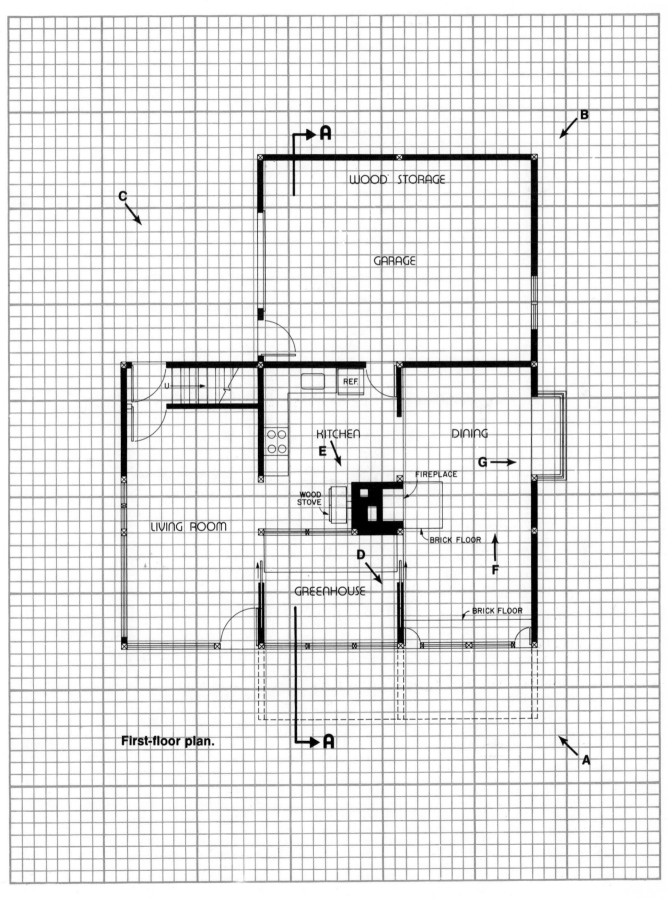

A

B

C

WOOD STORAGE

GARAGE

A

U

REF.

KITCHEN

E

DINING

G

WOOD STOVE

FIREPLACE

BRICK FLOOR

F

LIVING ROOM

D

GREENHOUSE

BRICK FLOOR

First-floor plan.

A

A

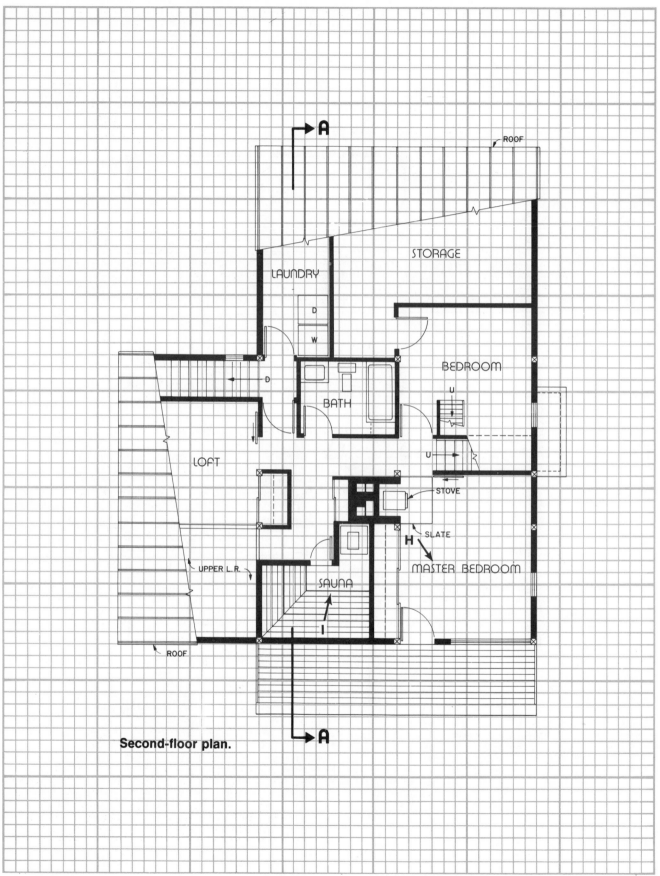

Second-floor plan.

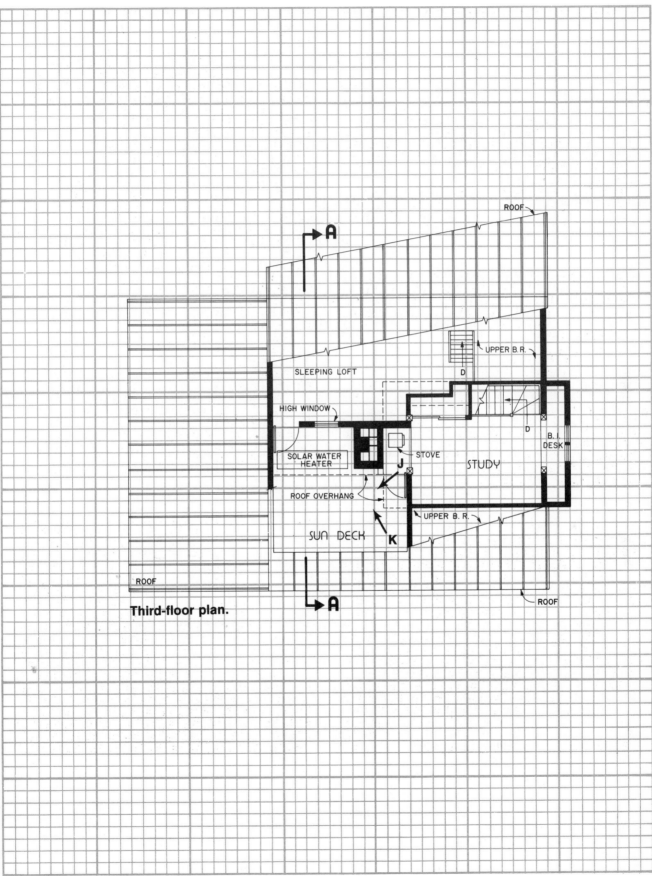

ROOF

A

SLEEPING LOFT

UPPER B.R.

D

HIGH WINDOW

SOLAR WATER
HEATER

STOVE

J

B.I.
DESK

D

STUDY

ROOF OVERHANG

UPPER B. R.

SUN DECK

K

ROOF

ROOF

Third-floor plan.

A

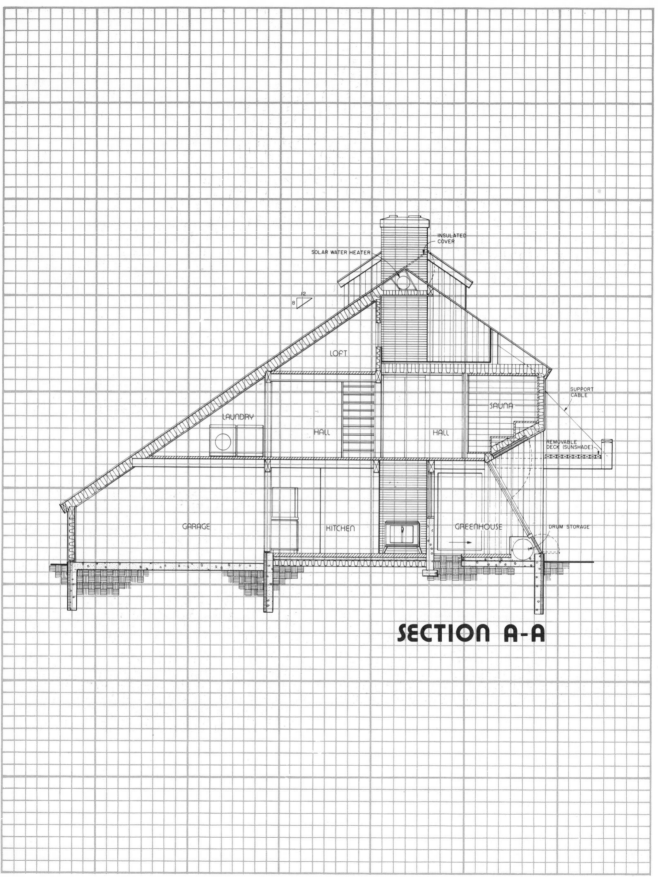

SECTION A-A

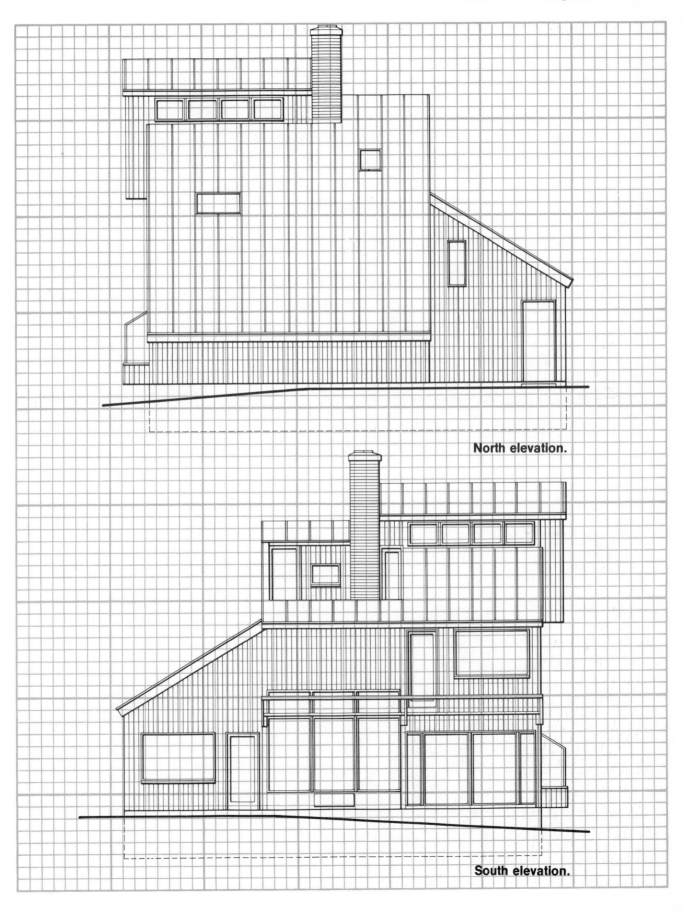

North elevation.

South elevation.

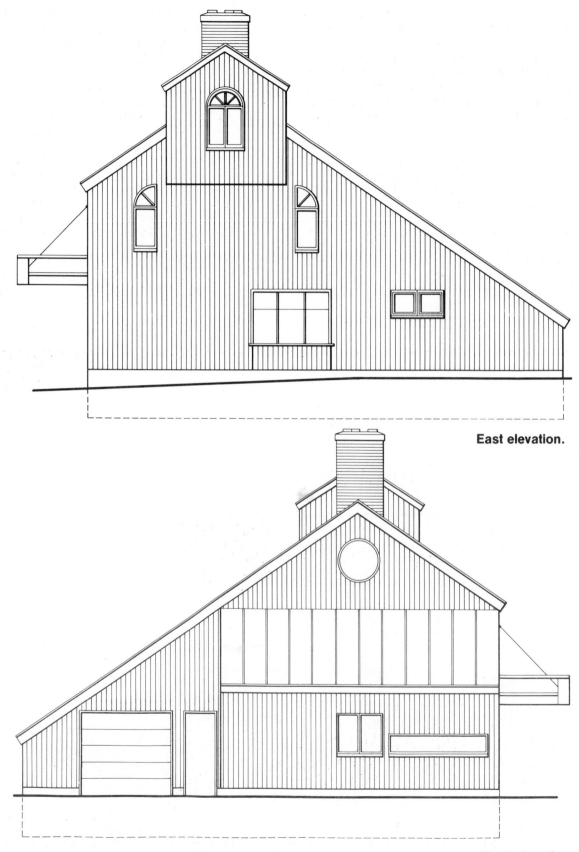

East elevation.

West elevation.

House 7: **Pole**

Pole houses have always especially fascinated me. I define a pole house as a house raised entirely above ground level, including the first-floor structure, using pressure-treated poles as a foundation. Pole houses were probably derived from tree houses. In hot or wet climates, they protect the house structure and occupants from ground dampness while promoting good air circulation for natural cooling. They are frequently used in low-lying areas where occasional flooding can be a problem. Ecologically, they delight me, as they cause little disturbance to the natural terrain and don't block the flow of groundwater. Finally, they are very economical to build.

If they are so good, why don't I recommend them for all areas? My houses, primarily designed for cool climates, depend a great deal upon use of a masonry floor for heat storage. The traditional pole house with its raised floor not only doesn't store heat, but requires an insulated floor to conserve heat. One exception should be noted, however. In extreme northern areas of the United States and Canada where snowfall is early, heavy, and stays on the ground all winter, a pole house is well worth considering. This is because the snow piles up underneath the house and insulates the floor structure. If you have under 3,000 degree-days and lots of rain with hot summers or over 6,000 degree-days with constant snow, read ahead; this could be a good housing solution for you.

I have designed two pole houses. One, a 24-foot-square house supported on four posts, was included in Eugene Eccli's book, *Low-Cost, En-*

A

B

C

ergy-Efficient Shelter. Many people built it as a small primary house or as a vacation cottage. The second pole house was the Pergola house featured in *30 Energy-Efficient Houses.* Many people from the South have asked me for this much larger plan. Unfortunately, one of these pole houses is too big and one too small for the average-size, energy-conscious family. Last year, Pat Morris, who lives in the North Carolina mountain country, asked me to develop a set of working drawings for an intermediate-size pole house. He sent along some sketches which I refined into the house shown here.

This house has great potential as a conventionally built house. It could easily be built on-grade on a flat site, or adapted to a steeply sloping site with a basement on the south side. The plans include a generous deck, sauna, and a direct passive solar water heater. More about this later.

Pole house construction allows the builder to eliminate conventional foundations with attendant disruption of the earth and expensive, time-consuming concrete and masonry work. In most cases, the poles on which the house rests can be directly embedded into the soil without an additional footing under the posts. At most, a small concrete pad is poured at the bottom of the hole for extra bearing. In soft soils, the earth immediately around the post is replaced with a soil-cement mixture.

Most people don't understand how pole foundations work and are quite skeptical. Much of the load-carrying capacity of the post is derived from soil friction between the sides of the post and the surrounding soil. In fact, wooden pilings are driven into unstable ground underneath skyscrapers to hold up concrete foundations which, in turn, support the loads of the structure.

In addition to the pictures of Pat's house under construction, I show here how we constructed the four-post house which was built locally. The post spacing and construction techniques are exactly the same on Pat's house; the difference is the number of posts. The house in the photographs has only four poles, Pat's house has nine.

Holes for the posts were dug with a rented, gasoline-powered posthole digger. Since the soil is soft clay, 6-inch-thick concrete pads were poured at the bottom of each hole. Soil-cement (four parts soil to one part cement) was mixed dry and tamped into place around the posts. Setting

the poles is somewhat difficult and can be critical in some designs. When I do a pole building, I try to locate the poles so that the exterior walls don't have to be framed around them. Long poles are not noted for being perfectly straight; one that is perfectly located at the first-floor line may be 2 or 3 inches out at the roof, causing serious problems for the framers. Divorcing the poles from the exterior walls has another advantage; it allows the builder to use recycled utility poles which are free for the asking in many parts of the country.

Framing around a round pole in an exterior wall is almost impossible. Placing it freestanding in an interior location is relatively easy. Do not try to use new poles for this purpose. They are heavily creosoted, causing an odor and sometimes toxic reactions. After the pole has weathered for many years, the creosote leaves the surface of the wood. If you are working with old poles, inspect the bottoms and trim as necessary before resetting them. Then, recoat with several coats of creosote to about 18 inches above grade line.

One secret of assembling pole-type structures is to use the unique fittings marketed by TECO (Timber Engineering Co.†). These metal devices transmit loads from a beam to a round or square pole when the beam is bolted to the side of the pole. A "spike grid" is a heavy casting with projecting teeth on both sides which is inserted between the beam and pole and wedged into place by tightening a high-strength bolt. These grids are manufactured in a variety of sizes and shapes to accommodate almost any combination of poles and beams. Another device from the same company is called a "split-ring connector." It is much cheaper, as it only requires a steel ring much like a 2-inch-long section of pipe which is bolted into the pole-to-beam connection with a standard-weight bolt.

The only catch is that the process requires an expensive drill bit. One is available from Smallplan, Box 43, Barrytown, NY 12507, for $100 refundable deposit plus postage. The bit is used to cut a circular groove in each of the pieces to be assembled. The metal ring is inserted between the two pieces of wood and a bolt or threaded rod tightened to hold them in place. If two or more sets of rings are inserted into a joint, a completely rigid, permanent connection is effected. These rings are widely used for assembling large timber structures such as bridges and trusses and can be used for quick post and beam. They have many applications where a

---

†The address of this and other manufacturers and associations so indicated will be found under "Addresses of Manufacturers and Associations" in Part IV.

The Morris house under construction (here and on facing page.

high-strength, economical, easy-to-fabricate timber joint is required. Their use need not be limited to pole houses.

I have combined round and square poles in the Morris house design. All of the poles are round where they are embedded in the ground. The four which had to have walls intersecting them were cut off at the first-floor deck and changed to square posts from there up. Since the majority of the posts are continuous, this doesn't affect the strength of the building, but does make building the exterior walls easier. TECO makes a steel fitting for post bases which simplifies attachment of the post to a flat deck. Pease Co.[†] handles a full line of TECO products which can be mail-ordered; check with very large lumberyards in your area to see if the fittings are available locally.

The Morris house is basically a shed with just enough elements added to the front to break up the lines. The greenhouse has a south-facing sloping roof, and the first-floor glass is shaded by removable deck boards (see the Perlberg house for details). Obviously, the greenhouse section could be run along the full length of the south wall if one needed more living space or wanted a more extensive greenhouse.

This house contains a unique, easy-to-build passive solar water heater. Most passive solar water heaters use horizontal tanks with reflective lids that are opened along a horizontal axis to reflect sunlight on the tanks (see the Perlberg house for an example). These work well, but are sometimes difficult to incorporate into the house structure because they are too wide. In this case we had plenty of height, but not enough width for the horizontal tanks. Since I wanted to keep the tanks close to the plumbing, we used a vertical design. The two insulated doors open just like window shutters and can be reached from the second-floor deck. The curved parabolic reflectors catch the maximum amount of sunlight at any time of day to create maximum efficiency. The vertical tanks do cause stratification and are not quite as efficient as they would be if placed horizontally. We compensate for this by adding a third tank.

The overall efficiency of this system is better than the two-tank horizontal system, because a greater area of the tanks is exposed to the sun. By using otherwise wasted space in the building and recycled water tanks with used plate glass covers, the cost was kept to less than the cost of a cheap conventional water heater (somewhat less than the $2,400 figure widely bandied about as the price of domestic solar hot water). One final advantage of this particular setup is that it is

Construction shots of the basic 4-post house from which the Morris house was derived.

much more forgiving of orientation than the horizontal tank arrangement. In this case, the south wall points about 15° west of due south. If it pointed due south, the greenhouse would shade the heaters for much of the afternoon. Remember this heater design if you can't face your heater exactly south. The parabolic reflectors combined with the flexible angle of the hinged shutters will make the heater work well even if it is as much as 30° off due south in direction.

Recycled electric water heater tanks were used to construct the heater. The lower heating element in these tanks frequently "freezes" in place so that it can't be removed, causing the tank to be discarded. Bear in mind that the tanks are old and be prepared to have to replace them in a relatively short time.

One of the ways in which this house works well is in its use of space. Except for the master bedroom, all sleeping spaces are in lofts in otherwise wasted spaces. The downstairs bedroom has the child's bunk located over a hallway, and the sewing room/bedroom on the second floor uses the top of its roof space as well as some upper area of an adjoining room for a loft. In this way, the guest bed isn't using valuable floor-level space, but is still readily available. Other roof-level space is taken up with the aforementioned solar water heater and a large overhead storage cabinet in the master bedroom.

Like the Saviches, Pat built his house by "remote control," with frequent phone calls to me for clarification when needed. Since I was very busy at the time, he had to make do with some very hasty sketches and just the basic four-pole house details. If you take a careful look at the plan, you will see that this house is really just the four-pole house with the greenhouse added to the front and 6 extra feet of living room on the left side of the plan. It is amazing how much more space these two rather small additions create.

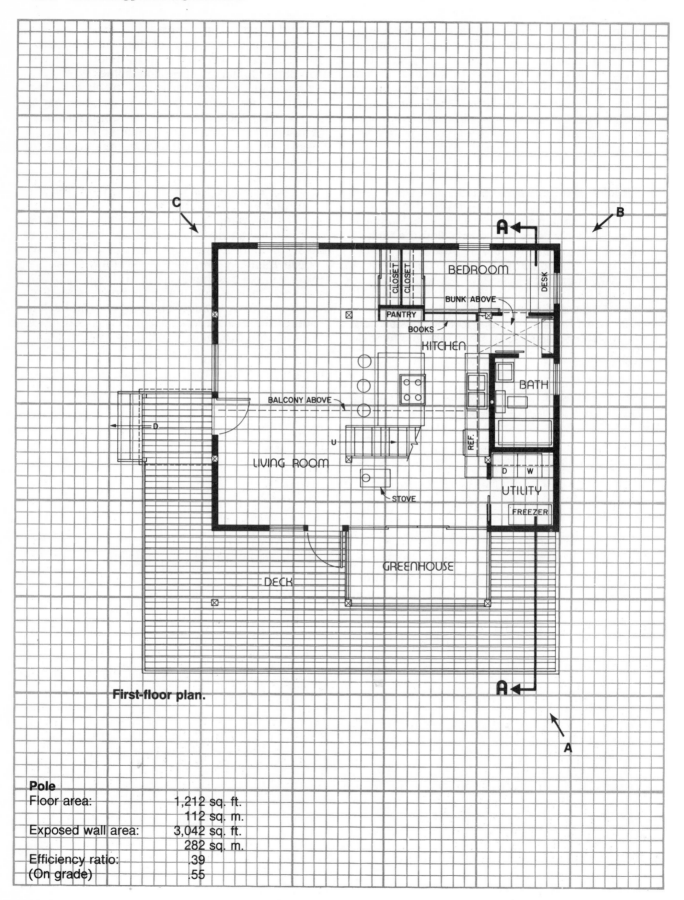

First-floor plan.

BEDROOM

CLOSET · CLOSET

DESK

BUNK ABOVE

PANTRY

BOOKS

KITCHEN

BATH

BALCONY ABOVE

D

REF.

U

LIVING ROOM

D   W

STOVE

UTILITY

FREEZER

GREENHOUSE

DECK

A

B

C

Pole
Floor area: 1,212 sq. ft.
                         112 sq. m.
Exposed wall area: 3,042 sq. ft.
                         282 sq. m.
Efficiency ratio: .39
(On grade)   .55

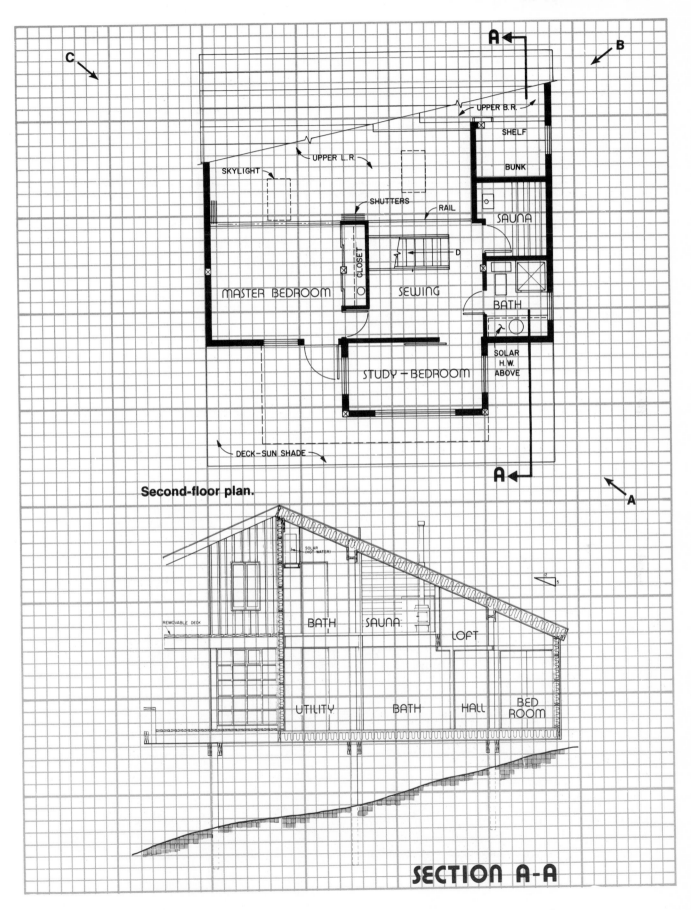

C

B

A ←

UPPER B.R.

SHELF

BUNK

SKYLIGHT

UPPER L.R.

SHUTTERS   RAIL

SAUNA

CLOSET

D

MASTER BEDROOM   SEWING

BATH

STUDY – BEDROOM

SOLAR
H.W.
ABOVE

DECK–SUN SHADE

A ←

A

Second-floor plan.

SOLAR
(HOT WATER)

REMOVABLE DECK

BATH   SAUNA   LOFT

UTILITY   BATH   HALL   BED
ROOM

SECTION A-A

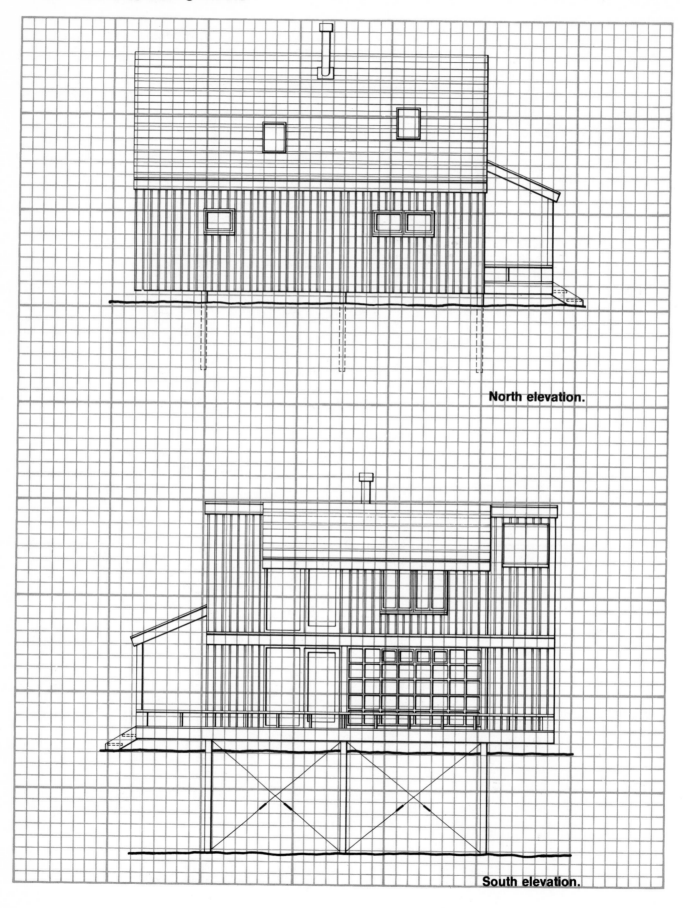

North elevation.

South elevation.

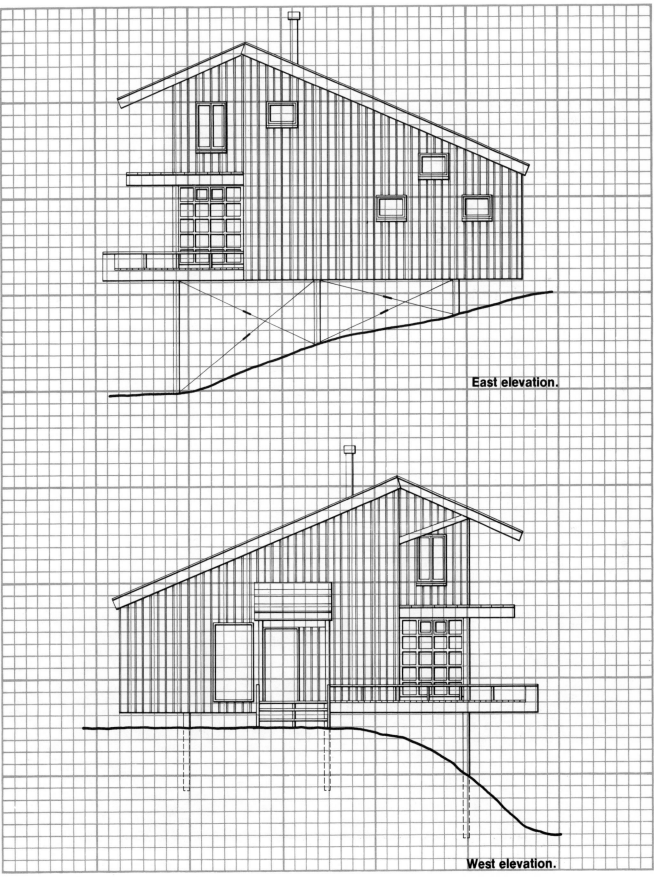

East elevation.

West elevation.

House 8: **Stoner**

Mike and Carol Stoner have been personally involved in all of my recent writing efforts. Carol edited my work with Eugene Eccli, and both worked on *30 Energy-Efficient Houses* and this book. During the year in which *30 Energy-Efficient Houses* was being written and produced, they were in the process of planning and building their own home. The plans for their house were drawn up by Michael Ondra and Mic Curd, local architects who specialize in solar-tempered houses. Michael Ondra also distributes Clivis Multrum composting toilets. Their experiences in designing and constructing their own house are excellent background for the beginning owner-builder.

They presented their requirements in some detail: a basic house, suitable for two people, with an open living-dining-kitchen space, two bedrooms, and a large study. The house was to use ecological materials, passive solar heating with woodstove backup, and have a Clivus Multrum. They wanted an exposed post and beam frame, a natural cedar exterior finish, and a simple traditional design.

If you will notice, the plans which are included are different in interior arrangement from the final house design. No matter how carefully you plan, there will always be a few changes. Keep your eyes open during all phases of construction for simple changes which will make your house work better for you. In this case, Mike and Carol made a couple of major changes. On the second floor, they discovered that their study wasn't going to be big enough for both of them to spread out their work. While searching for ways to enlarge the study, they discovered that there was plenty of room for a stand-up-height sleeping loft over the front entrance. (This is shown on the plans as a closet.) A small winding stair provides access to this loft. This enabled the south portion of the bedroom, originally designated to receive the bed, to be reduced in size, thereby enlarging the study space. Changes of this nature are not always obvious from looking at a set of plans.

A second, slightly less successful change involved the greenhouse. After framing up the house, Mike and Carol decided that the kitchen-dining space was too small and omitted the wall

A   B

between the greenhouse and the main living area. The planting bench for the greenhouse is now right in the living area, and there is much more room for a dining table. Too much, it seems to me. Now there is more space than is really required for a dining table but not enough extra to be useful for other purposes. Eventually, the Stoners plan to correct the situation by adding to the east side of the house to provide a real

greenhouse and rearranging the living area so that they have a greater kitchen counter space and dining area.

One other problem which resulted from this change involves the trickle filter for the greywater. It was supposed to be located under a brick floor in the greenhouse. When the greenhouse was eliminated, the wooden floor of the main house was extended out to the planting bench and a trapdoor added to provide access to the filter. The moisture from under the floor has warped the wooden door, causing its corners to project above the surrounding finish floor. These changes demonstrate the importance of actually laying out your living areas to exact size within an existing building, if possible, so that you can see exactly how much space is available. This is important if you find floor plans incomprehensible. Understanding a two-dimensional representation of a three-dimensional space at a greatly reduced scale is often difficult for the layman. Many of my clients don't begin to understand what their house is like until the shell is up and the rooms framed out. By this time it may be too late to make changes. Almost everyone will have second thoughts and find some detail that they would

C

D

E

have built otherwise, but lots of good hard research will help to avoid any major mistakes.

Mike and Carol feel that they would build a somewhat more modern, decidedly passive solar house were they to build again. The extension they plan will undoubtedly have some of those large panes of glass which they rejected on the first design. "I guess you can say that our tastes changed as we learned more about building and passive solar houses," Carol remarked recently.

The construction of their house is quite a bit different from the others in this book. A unique building system was used for the foundation and the partially buried first floor of the house. The foundation rests on pressure-treated wood plates; the framing members are covered with exterior plywood thoroughly smeared with foundation coating and then covered with plastic. There are concrete pads for two reinforcing piers and the chimney, but otherwise the house sits on a bed of gravel. The gravel bed foundation has been used all over the world for centuries, but has never become a major foundation type even though it works very well. The late Frank Lloyd Wright made frequent use of this economical solution for carrying the weight of a building. The pressure-treated foundation system is being promoted by the United States Plywood Association and the American Wood Preservers Institute. With imminent concrete shortage and rapidly rising prices, much more may be seen of this foundation type. I am very fond of burying the north wall as was done in this case, but I prefer to use a masonry wall so that heat can be stored within the structure. More on this later.

The foundation walls in the front of the house were framed with pressure-treated 2X6s set on top of 2X12 plates and surrounded by gravel. The system works well for a small house in stable soils. If you do use this system, it is very important to have it properly engineered by a qualified professional. I doubt that it would be satisfactory for a large house or for heavy, wet clay soil. A small concrete pad carries the weight of the masonry column; two other pads have a piece of strap iron bolted to deeply embedded anchor bolts. The strap iron is bolted through double floor joists, providing additional stability.

Backfilling around the foundation on wood-framed foundations is especially critical. Many, many standard block foundation walls have been caved in by careless excavators who got their machine too close to the building. The several-ton weight of an excavating machine can squeeze the soil against a foundation much like squeezing toothpaste out of a tube. For any foundation, and particularly wooden ones, a uniform porous gravel is vital to keep groundwater away from the foundation. A properly pitched, perforated drain tile which has its joints covered with strips of tar paper to prevent clogging is important. It is also vital to keep sharp stones away from the waterproofing on the outside of the foundation wall. None of this work requires any special skills, but can cause serious problems if not done properly. This is one area where doing it yourself can really pay off. Typical construction workmen do not take care, and when the foundation starts to leak, they are long gone!

Mike says that the worst problems which he encountered in building were in obtaining the proper quantities of materials at the right time. Upon my advice, the Stoners ordered materials well in advance; everything was supposedly stockpiled at the lumberyard for delivery. But never believe any construction supplier. The only way you can be sure that the materials are stockpiled for your job is if they are in your possession. In this case, Mike was constantly requesting deliveries, only to discover that the materials had been sold or were not ready. When they were delivered, he was often sent the wrong materials. Instead of the 2-inch oak floor decking for the second floor which was supposedly stockpiled, he was sent 1-inch and told that there would be a long wait for the 2-inch stock. This explains why Mike and Carol have a double-layer floor deck comprised of two layers of 1-inch oak. Of course, it's more material (and more money) than a single layer, and it took longer to install.

Mike said that he had a particularly hard time calculating waste for tongue and groove over and above the normal amount of construction waste. The materials list for our basic saltbox has been used several times, so I'm sure that the quantities are accurate. In Chapter 3, I suggest extra percentages which should be added for edge matching and waste for various types of wood siding and decking which I have used in building these houses.

The framing system for the Stoner house is more conventional than that which I commonly use. The exterior walls were framed with 2X6 vertical studs spaced 24 inches on center, except in the buried north wall where they are 12 inches on center. Posts and beams carry the interior loads of the house, and the upstairs ceiling is sloped and follows the rafters to make maximum use of interior space.

Extensive use is made of wood as an interior finish. The wood paneling set on a diagonal is particularly handsome. Diagonal paneling is easy to install, makes good use of material, and actually braces the wall. It can be readily installed on either horizontal or vertical studs. It has become very popular as both an interior and exterior finish, but I don't recommend it as an exterior siding unless you use a kiln-dried, tongue-and-groove siding. You may have water leakage problems if you use the roughcut siding shown on most of the houses in this book.

More than any of the other houses in this book, the Stoner's house abounds in special touches like the paneling just mentioned. This is one of the great luxuries of building your own house with your own hands. You can take the extra time to have specialty items made to your specifications. For instance, the Stoners had a large custom tub fabricated of steel and coated with an epoxy finish. This cost but a small fraction of the price of similar commercially available tubs. The wash basin in the bathroom is ceramic, thrown by a potter friend. The kitchen sink is surrounded by hand-painted tiles. Carol's father made a stained glass window for the bathroom. The kitchen cabinets are solid walnut. Of course, if you were on an extremely limited budget, you would forgo all of these specialty items, but building the house yourself permits you to have luxury touches on a moderate budget.

There have been some minor problems with the house. The north side of the terne roof has had a tendency to sweat and drip water inside in cer-

tain changing weather conditions. This was corrected by the subcontractor — an excellent local craftsman who installed a turbine to circulate air under the terne and dry it out. The roof also tends to make booming noises in windy weather. I feel that this is because there is a continuous eaves-vent which lets air get under the roofing. The terne on this house is applied over spaced roofing boards, permitting air to get at the underside of the roofing and causing the noise problem. I prefer to seal the edge of the roof tightly,

G

F H

just providing a vent to allow any accumulated moisture to evaporate into the atmosphere. I hasten to add that you shouldn't do this on a very low slope roof, such as is used on ranch houses, as the moisture will not tend to rise to the peak. Both

the Perlberg and Gilbert houses have the terne applied over a solid roof deck without vents. Gilbert's house does have a venting ridge cap (see Chapter 15), but the Perlberg house doesn't need one, as all major roof areas butt against a vertical surface instead of an actual ridgeline. Any accumulated moisture can escape where the metal turns up against the wall.

Thermally, the house doesn't perform as well as hoped. I feel that this is a combination of lack of masonry volume for storage and a somewhat too small area of south-facing glass. The house has neither a masonry floor nor interior masonry walls to store heat. I don't think it has to have both, but it needs one or the other. The south glass areas are a bit too small, and some temporary windows are single glazed. No insulating covers are used on the glass areas at night. I feel that this would help considerably. Mike says that some of the problem is due to poorly sealed openings that he will seal properly.

The house is not uncomfortable, but does require a good fire in the Morso stove to keep it warm in cold, cloudy weather. An extra flue is provided in the chimney with a fan to return hot air to the first floor. It has not been used yet due to an improperly sized fan. It will be replaced for next winter, but it is somewhat doubtful if it will help much, as thermometers indicate very little heat stratification in the house. If there was a bigger wood stove or more south glass, I think the system would work well. Michael Ondra has used it in several other houses with success, and I have had excellent results with the same system.

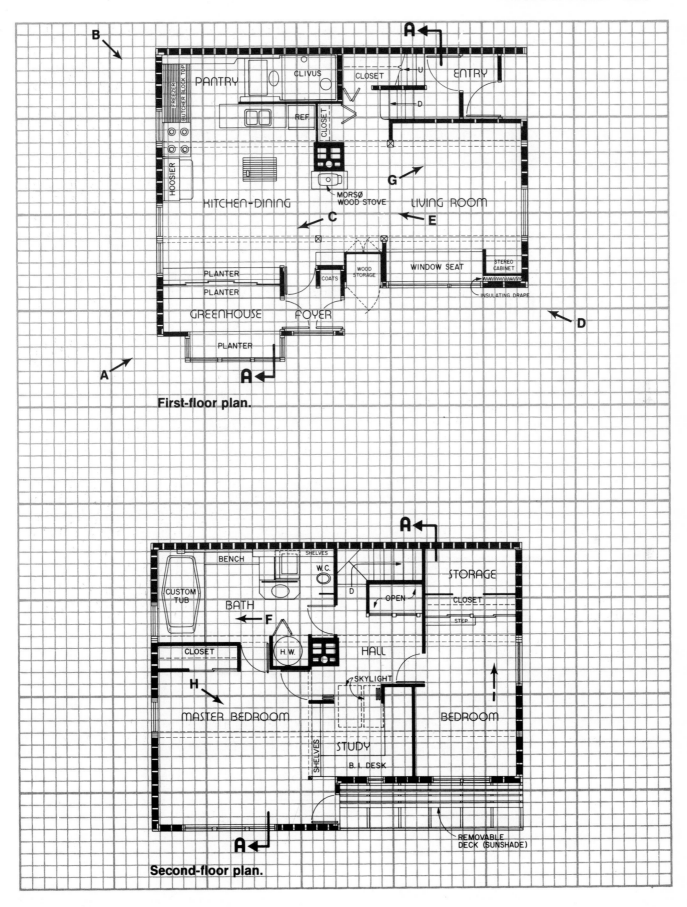

B

A ← ←

ENTRY

PANTRY

CLIVUS

CLOSET

FREEZER
BUTCHER BLOCK TOP

REF

G

HOOSIER

KITCHEN·DINING

MORSØ
WOOD STOVE

LIVING ROOM

C

E

PLANTER

PLANTER

COATS

WOOD
STORAGE

WINDOW SEAT

STEREO
CABINET

INSULATING DRAPE

D

GREENHOUSE

FOYER

PLANTER

A

A

First-floor plan.

A ← ←

BENCH

SHELVES

W.C.

STORAGE

CUSTOM
TUB

OPEN

CLOSET

BATH

D

STEP

F ←

CLOSET

H.W.

HALL

H

SKYLIGHT

MASTER BEDROOM

BEDROOM

SHELVES

STUDY

B.I. DESK

REMOVABLE
DECK (SUNSHADE)

A ←

Second-floor plan.

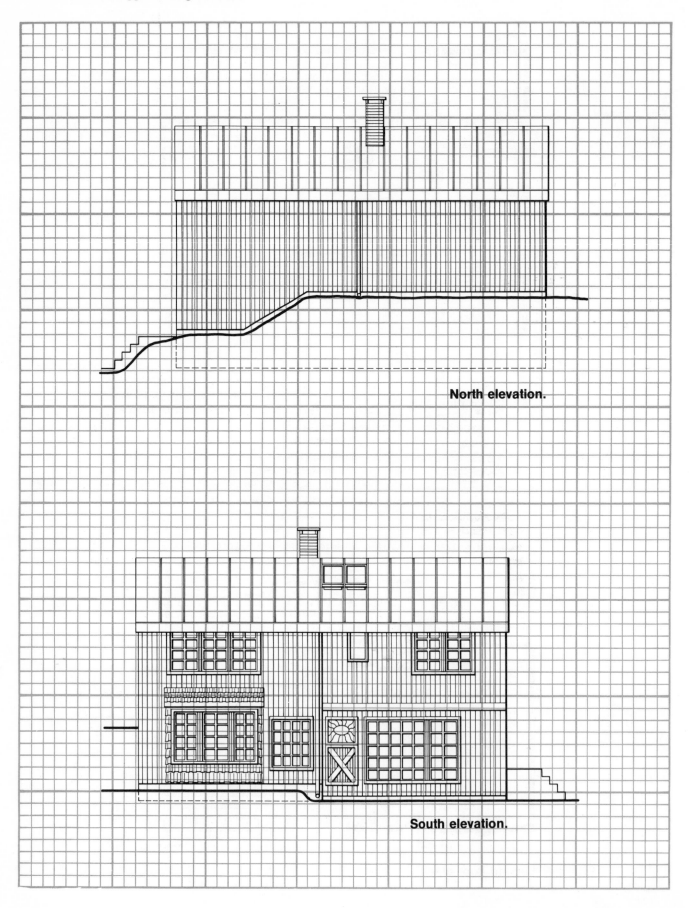

North elevation.

South elevation.

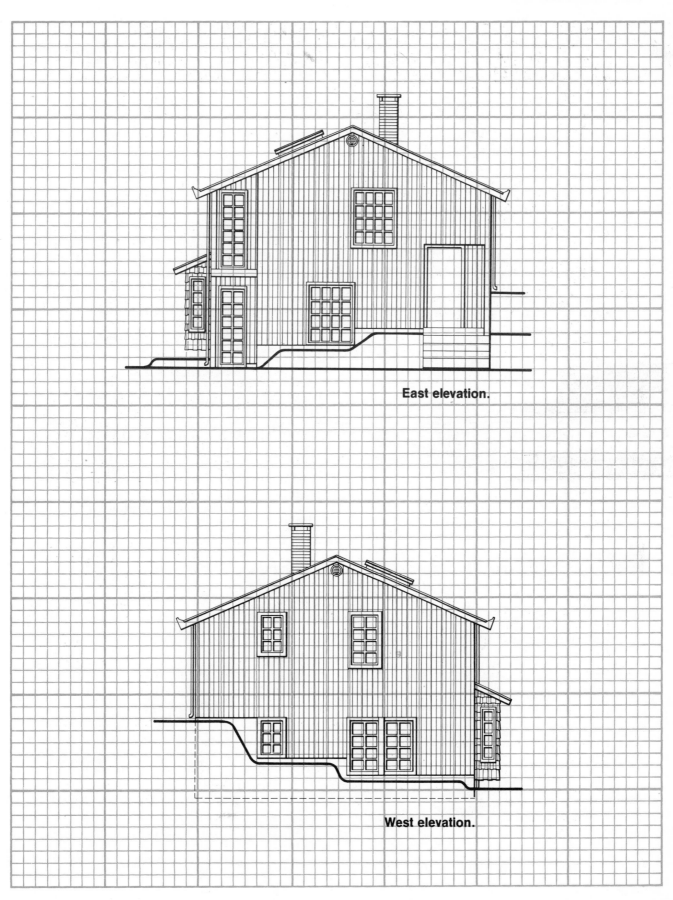

East elevation.

West elevation.

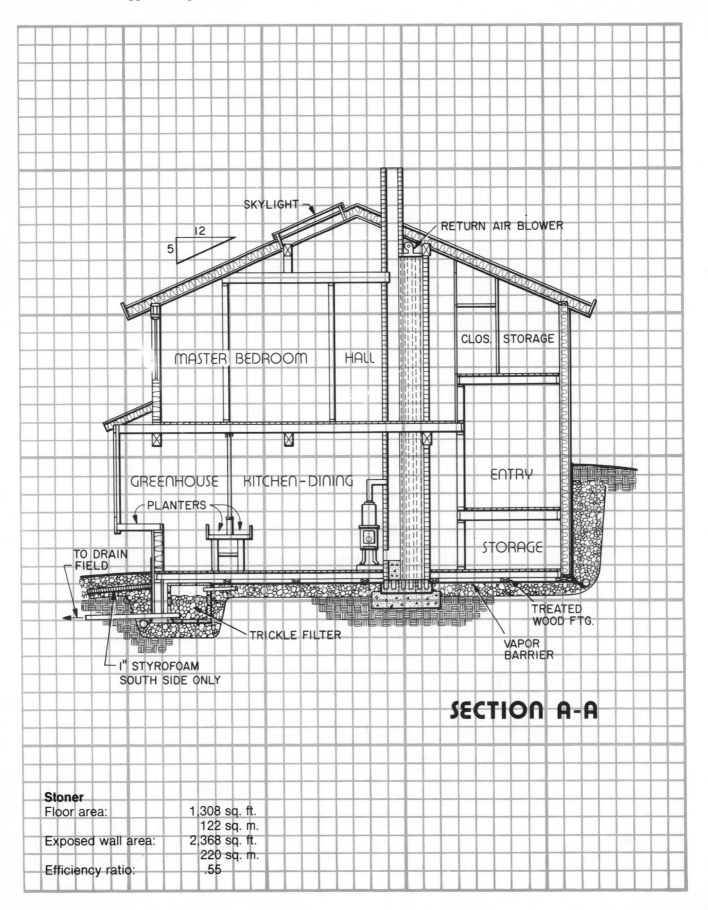

SKYLIGHT

12
5

RETURN AIR BLOWER

MASTER BEDROOM   HALL

CLOS.   STORAGE

GREENHOUSE   KITCHEN-DINING

ENTRY

PLANTERS

TO DRAIN
FIELD

STORAGE

TRICKLE FILTER

TREATED
WOOD FTG.

I" STYROFOAM
SOUTH SIDE ONLY

VAPOR
BARRIER

SECTION A-A

Stoner
Floor area:	1,308 sq. ft.
	122 sq. m.
Exposed wall area:	2,368 sq. ft.
	220 sq. m.
Efficiency ratio:	.55

House 9: **Caddell**

Bill Caddell is an extraordinary person. He is a librarian in a small town in central Indiana and a dedicated ecologist who feels strongly about protecting our environment and fighting against excessive power consumption. Two years ago, he proposed an alternate energy conference for his town. Everyone was highly skeptical. "You'll never get any name speakers to come to Frankfort. And if you do entice some speakers, no one in the Midwest is interested in alternate forms of energy." Well, the critics were dead wrong. Bill got his name speakers and a full house with about twelve hundred people. In fact, he had almost as many participants as the prestigious Second Annual Passive Solar Conference held at the University of Pennsylvania in Philadelphia a few months earlier.

When I visited Bill at his conference, he had started building his own energy-saving house. Bill's house is the most energy-efficient of all the houses in this book and makes the greatest use of recycled materials. It is a showcase of ecological techniques.

Bill bartered some artwork to a local architect in return for the plans. They had quite a time with the plan development because of the nonstandard sizes of the recycled materials. Bill had been busy acquiring materials for several years, and the plans had to accommodate the glass and main support beams that Bill had on hand. Most architects resent restrictions and want to be free to determine the sizes, shapes, and spans of materials in their houses, so this was a unique experience for both Bill and the architect.

The architect insisted upon beveling the corners of the house to "add interest." I find that this is a fatal flaw in today's architects. They are too busy "adding interest" when they should be adding efficiency and reducing costs. But the architect did cooperate fully, and the results are quite handsome.

Next to Frank Gilbert, Bill is the most skilled craftsman represented in this book. Unfortunately, his job and ecological interests keep him very busy. He worked on his house during two

A

B

C

was replaced inside the house. A large section of the foundation caved in. Fortunately, the house was self-supporting by this time, and no really serious damage was done, but the front wall had to be rebuilt. Then the contractor generously allowed Bill to use an excavating machine. The first time he backed it up, one of the drive wheels fell off, causing $800 damage. As a result, Bill couldn't collect anything from the contractor for damages to his foundation wall.

Similar troubles plagued the carpentry on the house. The carpenters refused to use the horizontal framing system and even set vertical studs at 16 inches on center just for spite. They made similar "mistakes" with the siding and roofing, all of which they found objectionable because they were "different."

The house is located on the edge of a lovely north-facing ravine. The ground slopes steeply toward the ravine. A greenhouse drops down a half-level from the first floor; the partial basement drops another half-level from the greenhouse.

The 1½-story-high greenhouse runs across the entire front of the house. In fact, the length of the

vacations but hired others to work the rest of the time. Sad to say, many of his workmen were semicompetent, and Bill had great difficulties getting his house built. Many times, as Bill's experience illustrates, it will pay to take your time and do all of the work yourself rather than trust tradesmen.

Bill's biggest troubles occurred during excavation and backfilling. His contractor insisted upon backfilling the foundation wall before the earth house was determined by the greenhouse. Bill bought the tempered insulating glass from a glass company that made a dimensional error and was stuck with twelve panes of non-stock-size glass. The long, sloping roof design permits venting the greenhouse over the main living space on the north side.

Supplemental heating for the house is provided by a Russian-type fireplace located in the partial basement. Bill is building the fireplace himself. With his luck with hired workmen, I don't blame him at all.

Water is supplied by a wind-powered pump mounted on a drilled well. These are still readily available; see Chapter 6. Bill uses a Servel refrigerator and a kerosene-fired freezer to cut down on electrical needs. The electrical system is 12-volt DC supplied by a small generator. The local power company gave Bill considerable right-of-way difficulties, so the alternate energy solutions are not entirely prompted by ecological considerations alone.

The interior of this house is extraordinary. The main supporting structure is made from timbers salvaged from an old barn. The interior is finished in used lumber from various sources and is much more rustic than the rather formal-looking plan would suggest. Everything possible was salvaged or handmade from old lumber. The exterior doors in particular are magnificent.

This house shows beautifully how one can site a house to take advantage of sunlight *and* a north view at the same time. While the major glass areas are oriented to the greenhouse to receive heat, there are still substantial windows to the north. The main living areas of the house open directly onto the deck.

The really dramatic element of this house is its roof. From the southern approach one sees just the soaring roof. There is a wide overhang shielding the south-facing glass from the treeless field. The house nestles low on the edge of the ravine, giving little hint of the sawtooth, offset roof. Clerestory windows facing to the north promote good summer air circulation and excellent balanced natural daylighting. The northern light softly illuminates the south-sloping roof with just the right amount of light. This magical house defies the ability of photographs or drawings to show its beauty adequately. It just has to be experienced to be understood.

The roof itself is unusual in construction and finish. It is made of heavy decking placed over main

D

E

beams spaced 10 feet apart. Four-inch Styrofoam insulation is placed over the decking with 2X4s nailed vertically between the insulation boards at 2-foot centers. A brown, factory-finished, ribbed metal roof provides the finish surface. There is no plywood decking involved in this roof system and no need to apply a separate ceiling finish underneath. The only flaw is the finish of the roof

F

itself. It is baked enamel, factory applied. The sheets were stacked outside for a few days before installation, and the moisture condensation which occurred between the sheets was enough to cause the expensive finish to deteriorate. The manufacturers charge almost double for this finish. Buy the same material in galvanized metal and paint it yourself with Calbar's† good, oil-based roof paint.

Even though he had to subcontract most of the work, and much work had to be redone, Bill was still able to build a large, self-sufficient house for under $25,000. Better not tell the realtor with the $75,000 house. He won't believe it.

†The address of this and other manufacturers and associations so indicated will be found under "Addresses of Manufacturers and Associations" in Part IV.

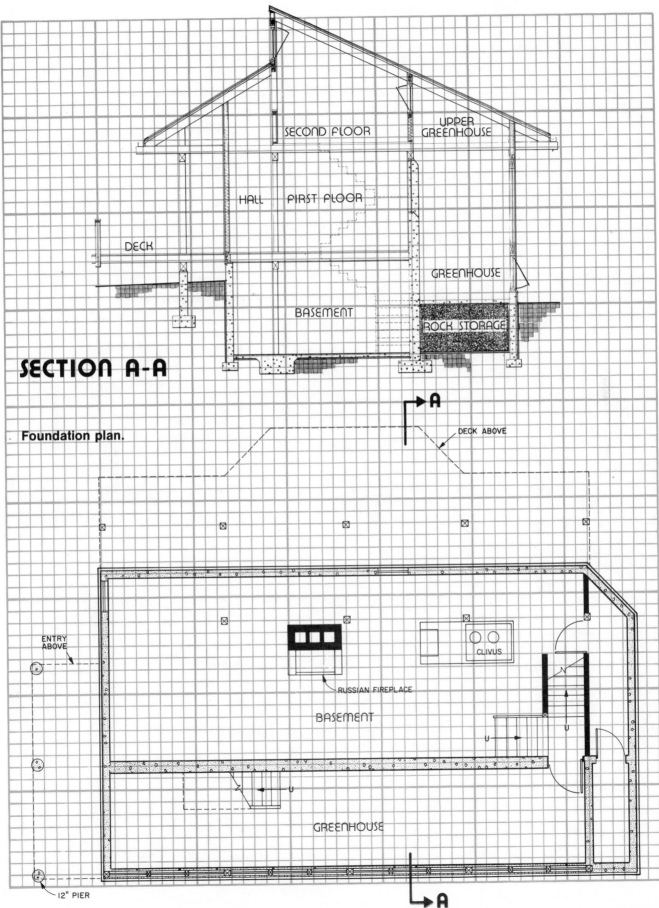

SECTION A-A

SECOND FLOOR

UPPER GREENHOUSE

HALL   FIRST FLOOR

DECK

GREENHOUSE

BASEMENT

ROCK STORAGE

A

Foundation plan.

DECK ABOVE

ENTRY ABOVE

RUSSIAN FIREPLACE

CLIVUS

BASEMENT

U

U

GREENHOUSE

12" PIER

A

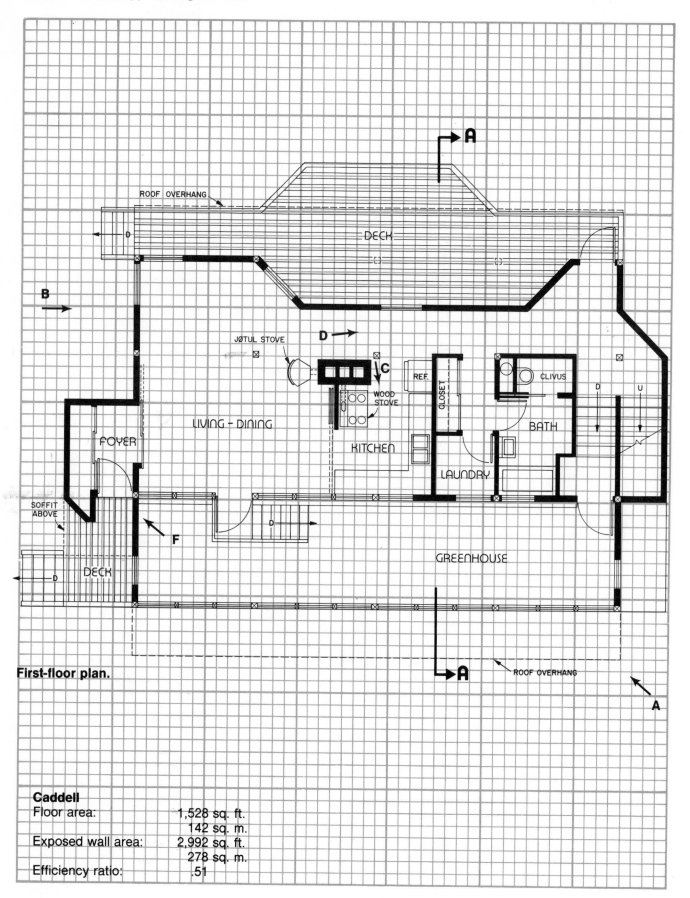

ROOF OVERHANG

A

DECK

B

JØTUL STOVE

D

C

REF.

CLIVUS

CLOSET

WOOD
STOVE

LIVING – DINING

BATH

D   U

FOYER

KITCHEN

LAUNDRY

SOFFIT
ABOVE

F

D

DECK

GREENHOUSE

First-floor plan.

A

ROOF OVERHANG

A

Caddell
Floor area: 1,528 sq. ft.
                      142 sq. m.
Exposed wall area: 2,992 sq. ft.
                      278 sq. m.
Efficiency ratio: .51

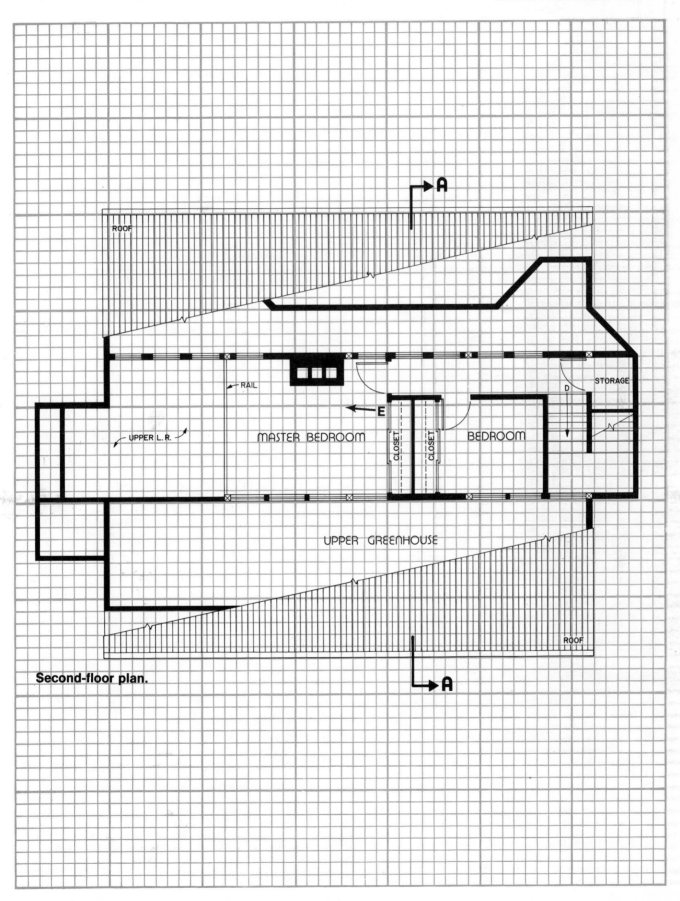

Second-floor plan.

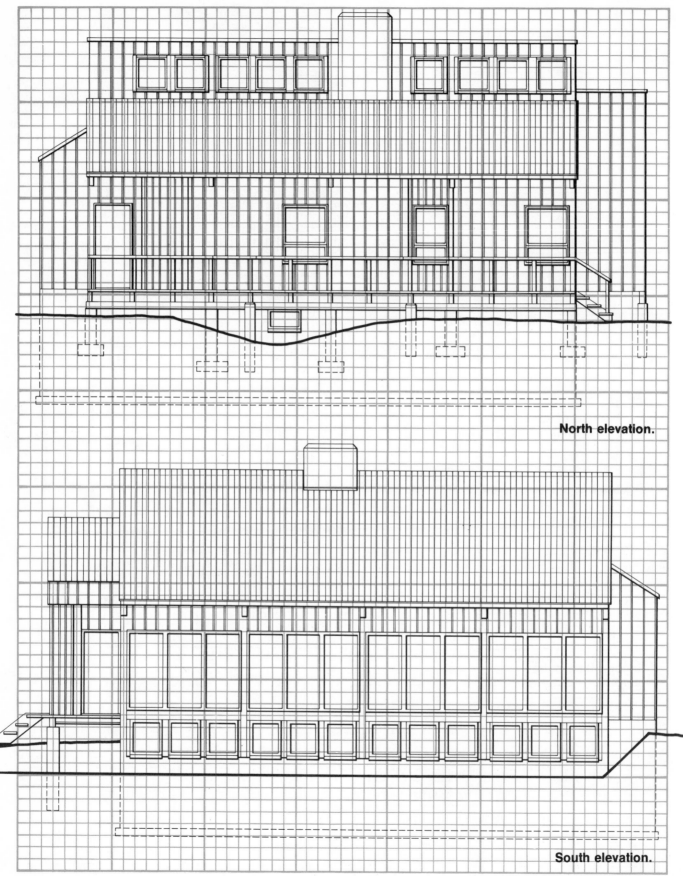

North elevation.

South elevation.

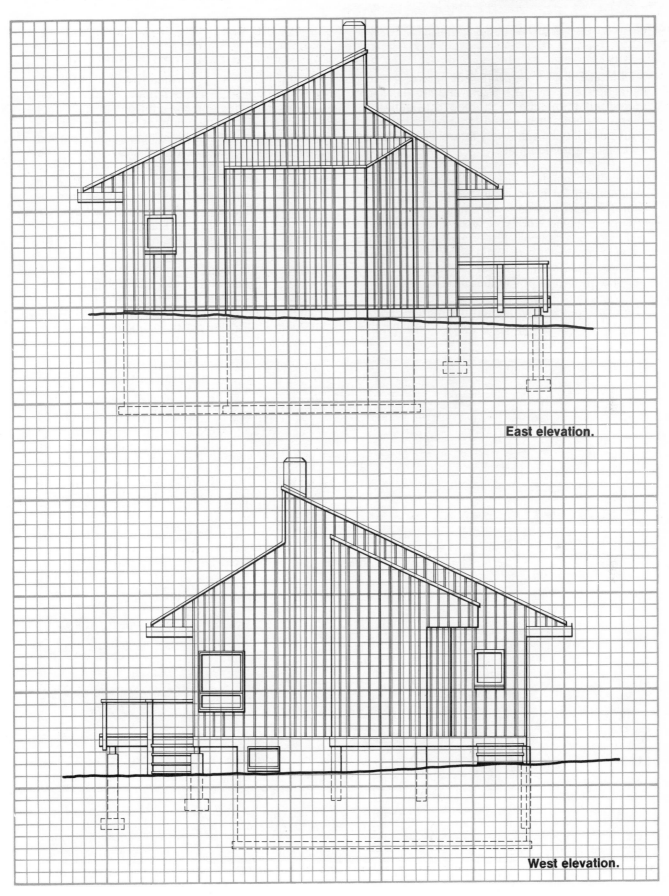

East elevation.

West elevation.

House 10: **Laskin**

This house is of a very different nature than my usual houses. It is much larger and more lavishly appointed than most. I include it because its shape is particularly suited for a partially buried house and it uses some very interesting materials and building techniques.

The house, which is three stories tall, is located near the top of a mountain range, and from its roof deck one can see five states. The same basic house would work very well without the third story which is basically just one large, extra living room. Even though it is quite large, with fancy finishes, this house has one of the lowest costs per square foot of any in the book.

The Laskins first approached me wanting an octagonal house. People are fascinated by this

shape (I have also gotten many requests for designs for domes). While octagonal houses are efficient in that they enclose a maximum amount of floor space with a minimum of wall area, the resulting angular spaces are difficult to put to good use. Octagons have a long history here in the Hudson Valley. Back in 1853 a whole book, *A Home for All, or the Gravel Wall, an Octagon Mode of Building* by Orson S. Fowler (republished in 1973 as *The Octagon House: a Home for All*), was devoted to this shape, claiming many strange advantages including better health for the occupants. In this case, I used three sides of the octagon to form the greenhouse and filled in the back corner with a specially designed staircase. This enables us to use the same basic framing system of three 12-foot bays for the center section. Framing for the back was laid out at

A

45° and took a long time. On the second floor, we changed to a straight framing system which was faster and easier, but not as pretty. See the pictures for a comparison.

The odd angles of this house caused many difficulties in laying a foundation. Most would-be foundation contractors were terrified of the angles. Finally, a masonry contractor agreed to work on an hourly basis. Except for his being sloppy and wasting a fair amount of concrete, the foundation work went very well. The mason then went ahead and laid up concrete block walls for the back of the house — badly. They were neither level nor plumb. Since the walls were to be buried on the outside and covered with other finishes on the inside, it didn't seem to matter. What did matter, though, was that the 90° angle at the north corner was now 87°. This meant that all cuts for the back framing section had to be custom-measured rather than simple 45° angle cuts.

Additional problems occurred because of the Laskins' taste for expensive materials. They came to me after reading *30 Energy-Efficient Houses* and said that they liked my houses and the things I talked about. But the first problems came to light when we were about to order lumber for the frame. "I want planed hardwood," said David. Since I had never done a frame in hardwood before, I was skeptical, but David prevailed. We finally located the hardwood, but couldn't get anyone to plane it. Machines large enough to plane 6X12 timbers are not readily available. Fortunately, one member of the framing crew had just purchased a large (6-inch cut) Makita planer. We hastily ordered another and started planing. Our local cabinetmaker figured all of us had taken leave of our senses, but after the men got used to the new tools, the planing went quite speedily. The major problems were the weather and the difficulties in lifting and turning the very heavy timbers. If we originally had

B

C

planned to hand-plane the timbers, we would have rented shop space, and certainly will do so if this is ever done again.

The hardwood frame is made of beech, a very colorful wood with a handsome grain frequently used for handles of expensive hand tools. It is not usually used in construction, because it has a tendency to split and check, and is so dense that it is virtually impossible to nail into after it has dried. Our material was green and still workable. Our wood came from Canada and was of very high quality. (Many of the beech trees in the United States are diseased and have rotted from the center of the tree out.) Even though our results are spectacular, I would urge extreme caution for any others attempting to use this wood.

The three-sided greenhouse presents a very large glass area to the sun. The 45° walls on the southeast and southwest enable it to absorb greater amounts of heat for a longer period of time than a conventional greenhouse with only south-facing glass. For optimum heat retention, insulating panels have to be placed on the southwest in the morning and the southeast in the afternoon, but only in very extreme weather. The height of the greenhouse permits three levels of planting, which makes up for the somewhat small floor area. Heat is transferred to the first floor by means of a duct under the built-in beds and with

D

E

F

H

K

a thermostatically controlled fan. The three second-floor bedrooms have direct solar gain from a south-facing window wall set at 58° to vertical. Four active solar collectors are set into this wall and provide domestic hot water. IS shades from IS Insulating Shade Co., Inc.† provide nighttime cover for these windows.

Backup heating for the house is provided by a Defiant stove on the first floor and a Rumsford fireplace on the top floor. Bedrooms, baths, and other remote spaces have Aztec† radiant heaters as a supplemental heating source.

The main roof is surfaced with recycled clay tiles which were bought used for $50. The roof deck is surfaced with liquid neoprene carefully applied by Jeanne Laskin. Money saved on the roof was put into cypress siding. Although it was expensive, the installation of the precisely milled tongue-and-groove material was quick and easy,

at least compared to the roughsawn pine which I normally use.

One of the unique features of this house is the "square spiral" staircase. While it looks complicated, the use of repetitive parts makes it very easy. There are three different treads, a rail, and a newel post. By inserting steel ties at the corners, we were able to make the stair self-supporting like the grand spiral staircases in old southern mansions. This is the second time I have used this type of staircase, and my first experience resulted in a considerable number of design improvements. The open shaft down the center allows light from the skylight to penetrate all the way down the stairs. The door to the roof deck provides a chimney effect for excellent natural ventilation in summertime.

Long hours of discussion took place concerning the design and manufacturer of the windows. The high-pressure Andersen sales pitch had thoroughly sold the Laskins. Finally, we compromised and used the Andersen basement sash with custom-made fixed glass for other windows. Careful use of standard sizes enabled us to hold

†The address of this and other manufacturers and associations so indicated will be found under "Address of Manufacturers and Associations" in Part IV.

the costs well below the usual per-square-foot prices for this particular type of glazing.

The unusual shape works very well for a solar-tempered house. The two diagonal walls face northwest and northeast and are virtually windowless. They also have extra-heavy insulation (R 38) to provide extra protection from the cold winter winds. The first floor of this house is completely buried on the north. The pointed prow does an excellent job of deflecting groundwater around the structure, as well as giving the north winds an elusive target. By placing all the circulation and utility areas along this wall, heat-wasting windows aren't required, and a considerable amount of heat loss is prevented.

David does not like roughsawn woods, so, unlike the rest of my houses, all trim and paneling are planed hardwood except of a few areas of cypress which were used indoors. Cypress is very desirable because its natural oils prevent decay, and it weathers to a beautiful, light silver gray color. Cedar and redwood have the same properties, but redwood is an endangered species.

Therefore, for those wanting a maintenance-free siding, I would strongly recommend cedar.

Mechanical trades worked very well on this house, partly because of superior mechanics and partly because of the house layout. By building in the winter, we were able to get top-quality commercial electricians and plumbers who otherwise would not have taken on residential work. The electrical system was carefully thought out, and all holes and chases were provided for the electrician by the owner to save on his time. The horizontal girts and spaced perimeter beams helped considerably. The plumbing system is much more spread out than I recommend. I would eliminate the second bathroom on the bedroom level for economy of plumbing.

This house shows that many cost benefits can be achieved by building in winter, even though it may be quite unpleasant at times. There were days that it was too cold to work, however. But the exotic shape of the house appealed to many of the carpenters and speeded up the work in spite of the bad weather.

J

G   I

David Laskin signs in.

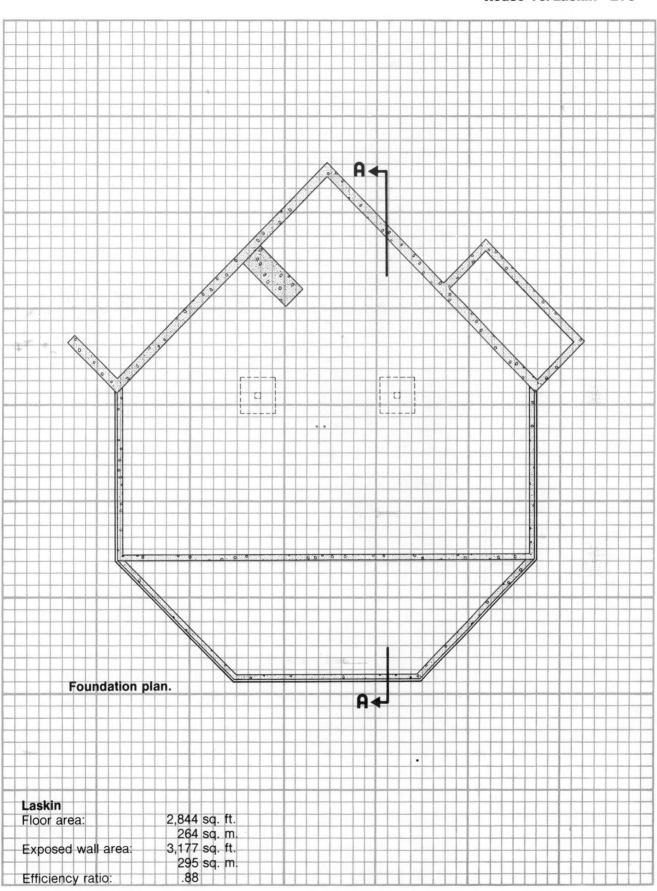

Foundation plan.

Laskin
Floor area:	2,844 sq. ft.
	264 sq. m.
Exposed wall area:	3,177 sq. ft.
	295 sq. m.
Efficiency ratio:	.88

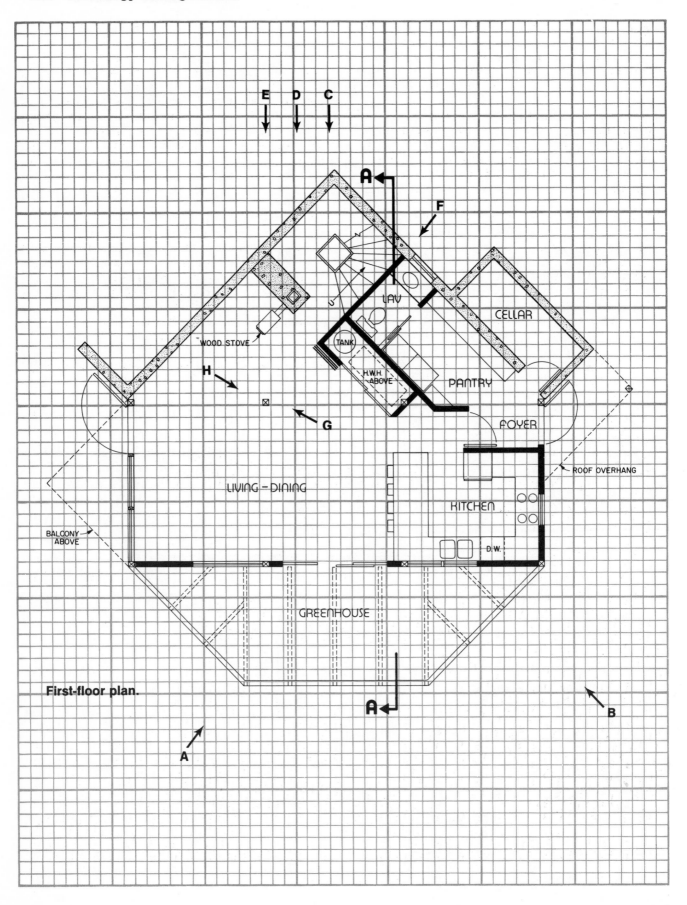

E D C

A

F

WOOD STOVE

LAV

CELLAR

TANK

H.W.H.
ABOVE

PANTRY

H

G

FOYER

ROOF OVERHANG

LIVING – DINING

KITCHEN

BALCONY
ABOVE

D. W.

GREENHOUSE

First-floor plan.

A

A

B

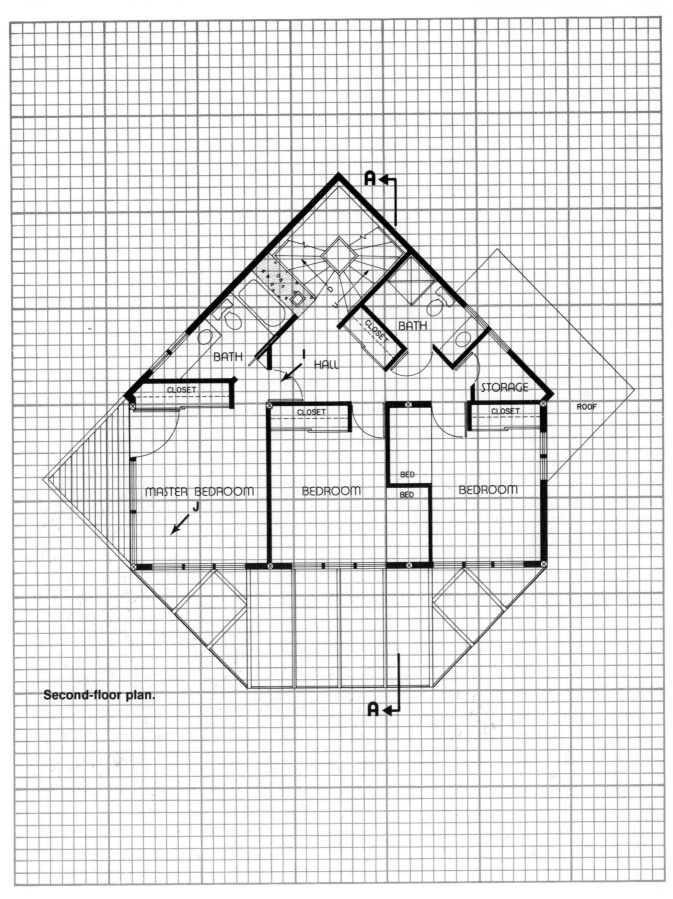

Second-floor plan.

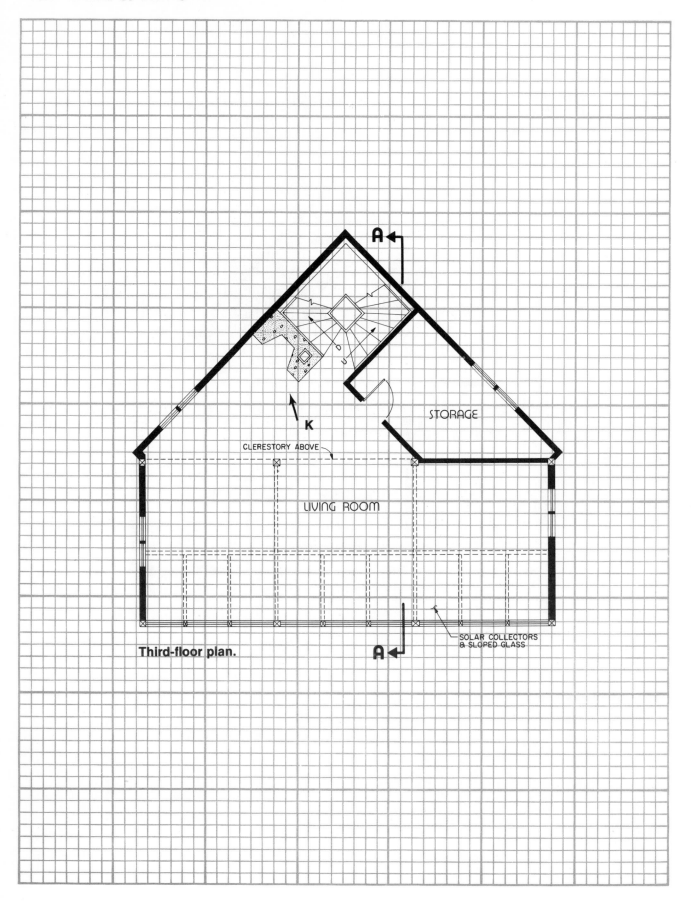

Third-floor plan.

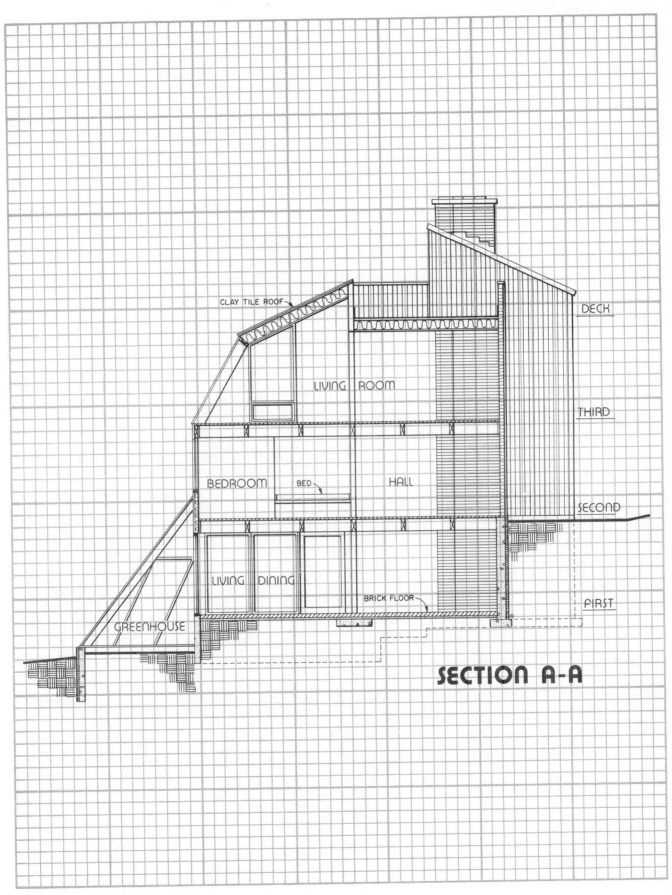

CLAY TILE ROOF

LIVING ROOM

DECK

THIRD

BEDROOM   BED

HALL

SECOND

LIVING   DINING

BRICK FLOOR

FIRST

GREENHOUSE

SECTION A-A

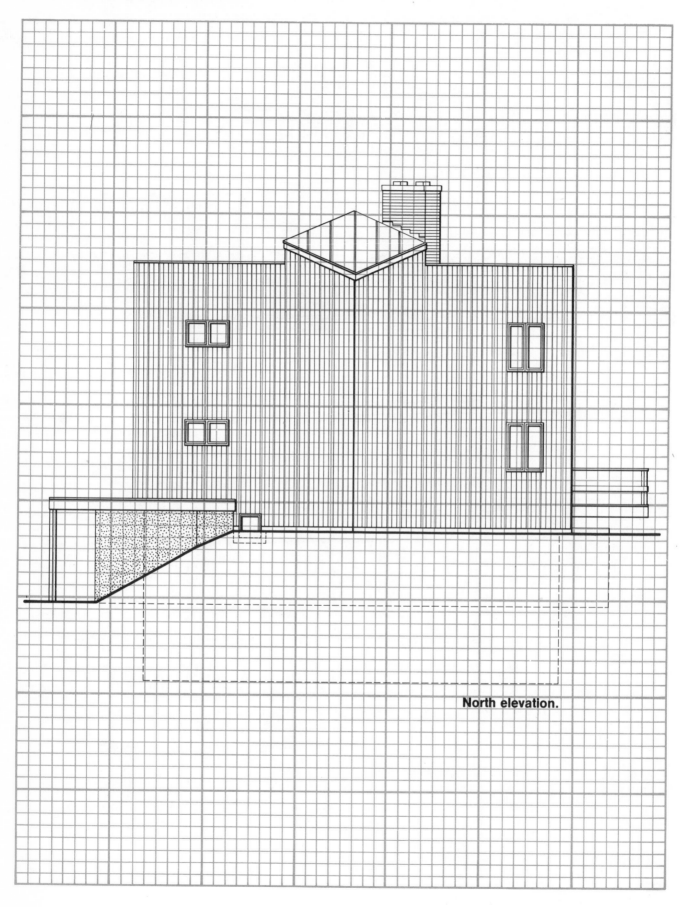

North elevation.

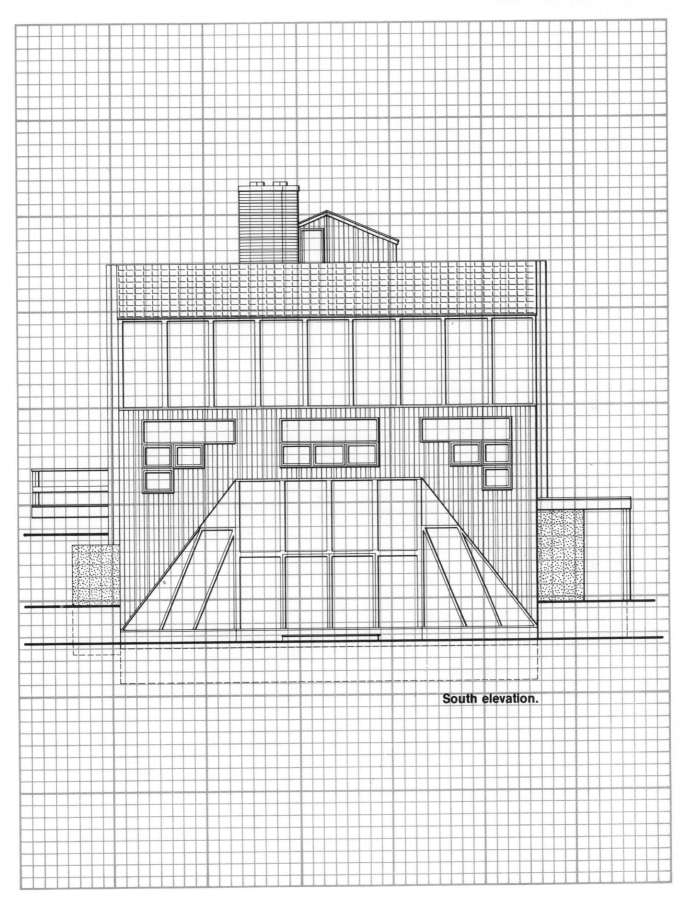

South elevation.

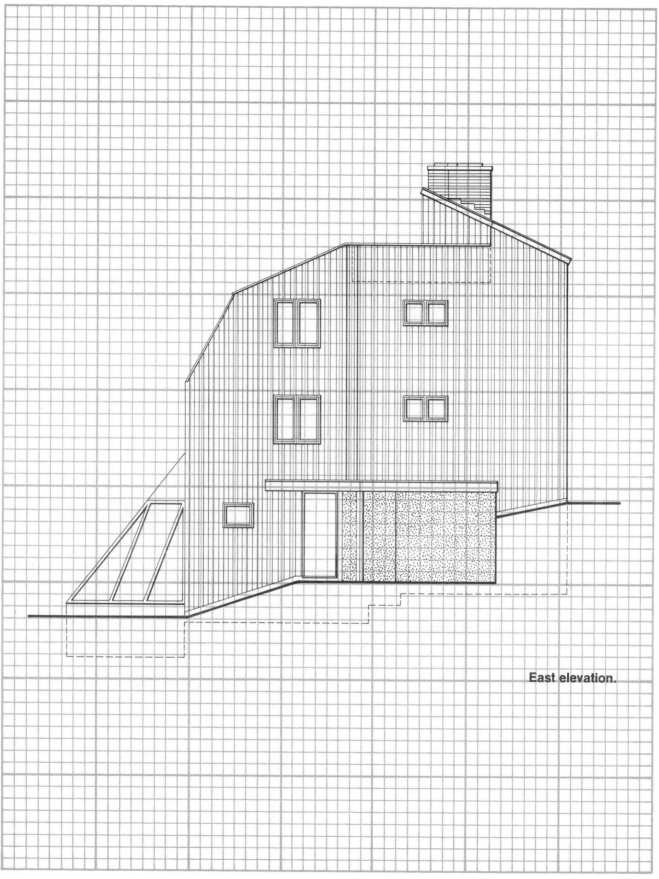

East elevation.

West elevation.

House 11: **Savich**

This house was designed as an alternative to the Volkswagen house. Specifically, I reduced the spans so that the structural members would be small enough for one person to handle. I also changed the roofline. Even though the shed roof is easier to construct, most people like the aesthetics of the saltbox shape. The final major change is that the bathroom is located in a separate wing, permitting a larger kitchen.

The Saviches contacted me from upstate Michigan and wanted to know if I could design a house for their budget of $20,000, provided that they did most of the work themselves. They sent along sketches of several houses they liked, particularly one with a second-floor bay window. The house with the bay window turned out to be very similar in size to the Volkswagen house, so I sent the plans for the Volkswagen house to them. They wrote back and said that they didn't want a shed roof, and they also felt that the plan was just too cramped, particularly the kitchen. They also wanted a separate dining space which might later be converted into a bedroom. I sent them the plans for my saltbox which is featured in this book. We finally arrived at a compromise and I drew up plans for a small saltbox with the bathroom and entry vestibule in a separate wing.

One of the purposes of the broken roofline at the bathroom-kitchen wall was to make the addition easy. It's very hard to extend the lower edge of a roof after the upper portion has been roofed without tearing everything off and starting over. By stepping a roof, though, the extension is quickly done. Also, when planning to add to a house at a later date, use vertical siding, not the traditional clapboards, to make the job easier.

The Saviches planned to build the 24-foot-square section the first summer, adding the bathroom wing with the well and septic system the second year. By doing this, they could build without getting a mortgage. Since there was already a small excavation on the site, we put a basement containing a small furnace under one corner of the house. The Saviches plan to travel after retirement and wanted an automatic heating system (other than electricity) which could keep plants and pipes from freezing.

A

The heating system is particularly unique in that the return air duct for the furnace is connected to a flue in the chimney up near the second-floor ceiling. By making the connection at this point, the prewarmed air that collects at ceiling level can be circulated through the house using the ductwork installed for the furnace. The furnace works less, and heat is evenly distributed. If you are using a wood stove, the furnace blower can be activated to circulate the warm air. By doing this, you can avoid turning on the burner for the furnace and save fuel.

This furnace setup also reduces heat stratification. Conventional furnaces pull colder air from floor level, heat it, and return it to the room via wall registers placed at a higher level. As a result, air tends to stratify from colder air at floor level to warmer air at ceiling height. Newly introduced commercial warm-air heating systems claim to prevent heat stratification and use 40 percent less fuel. I think they are overstating the savings,

particularly for a well-insulated house, but there will be some savings and the house will be uniformly heated, an important consideration for older people who are much more sensitive to temperature fluctuations.

The bay windows in this house (one on each end) are very flexible and make the small bedrooms seem quite large. One is used as a desk and has drawers on both sides and a kneehole in the center. The other is used as a chest; a slide-out top makes it a 4-foot by 5-foot work table.

An insulating shade is recessed into the wall on a line with the main house wall. It slides out to cover the entire bay window opening so that hot summer sun or winter cold can be effectively shut out. Each side of the bay has a single casement window which opens flat against the side of the house. The bay windows provide excellent ventilation, as they actually create a suction effect, pulling air out of the room, using the air cir-

B

C

D

culating in the bay. You could use similar windows if you need more space or cross ventilation in a bedroom and don't want to add any expensive space.

Vic and Carolyn did all of the work themselves. Right after they bought the materials and just before they planned to start, the recession cost Vic his job. They decided to go right ahead with construction, but there was no money to hire a carpenter to help with the building. Vic asked if I could help in any way. I decided to use the Saviches as guinea pigs for this book — seeing if they, as relatively inexperienced carpenters, could follow drawings for the framing system. I drew sketches for all of the different framing members, similar to the ones in Chapter 8, and then wrote instructions to accompany the drawings. Vic called frequently, and I refined the instructions in response to his questions.

Vic and Carolyn took a weekend course at a local community college and learned how to lay their own masonry. They asked several contractors for bids for the foundation and basement. These were so out of line that they knew they would have to do the work themselves if they were going to stay within their budget. While they were working on the foundation, I continued to refine

the house design to make it easy for one or two people to build without scaffolding, heavy machinery, or lots of help

The horizontal trim board that covers the joint between the siding of the first and second floors is an example of a refinement. Long boards are very hard for one person to handle. This detail shortens the length of the board and provides a way of tying the windows together visually. This design also permits the use of easy-to-install plywood sidings. The trim board conceals the butt joint in the plywood which usually looks awkward and gives away the fact that the grooves cut into the plywood sheets don't represent real boards.

By doing all of their own work, Vic and Carolyn were able to bring the cost of the house well below their budget. Since Vic was able to work on the job full-time, they completed the whole house at once instead of in stages as originally planned.

This house is ideal as a vacation cabin (with or without the bathroom wing), but this version was designed with retirement living in mind. By adding a first-floor bedroom where the dining room

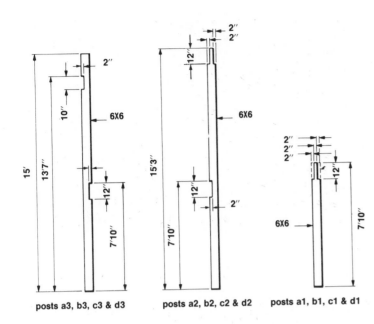

posts a3, b3, c3 & d3

posts a2, b2, c2 & d2

posts a1, b1, c1 & d1

6X6

6X6

6X6

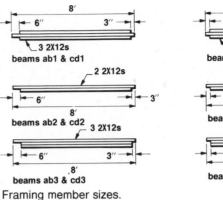

3 2X12s

beams ab1 & cd1

2 2X12s

beams ab2 & cd2

3 2X12s

beams ab3 & cd3

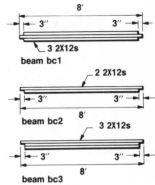

3 2X12s

beam bc1

2 2X12s

beam bc2

3 2X12s

beam bc3

Framing member sizes.

Roof beams at row 3 are identical to
row 1; roof beams at row 2 are similar
to row 1 except for 2X10 as center piece
of beam.

beams a2-3 & d2-3

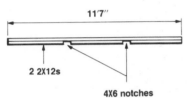

2 2X12s

4X6 notches

3 2X12s

beams b2-3 & c2-3

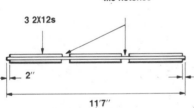

E

Formwork for combined concrete slab and foundation. Heating duct is buried in the slab.

is now located, it is perfectly suited for a couple
with a small upstairs space for guests or an attendant. Complete with well and septic system, and
using all new materials, it cost just under $19,000.
The Saviches did everything except drill the well
and dig the foundation and septic system. A
greenhouse will be added to the south wall later.

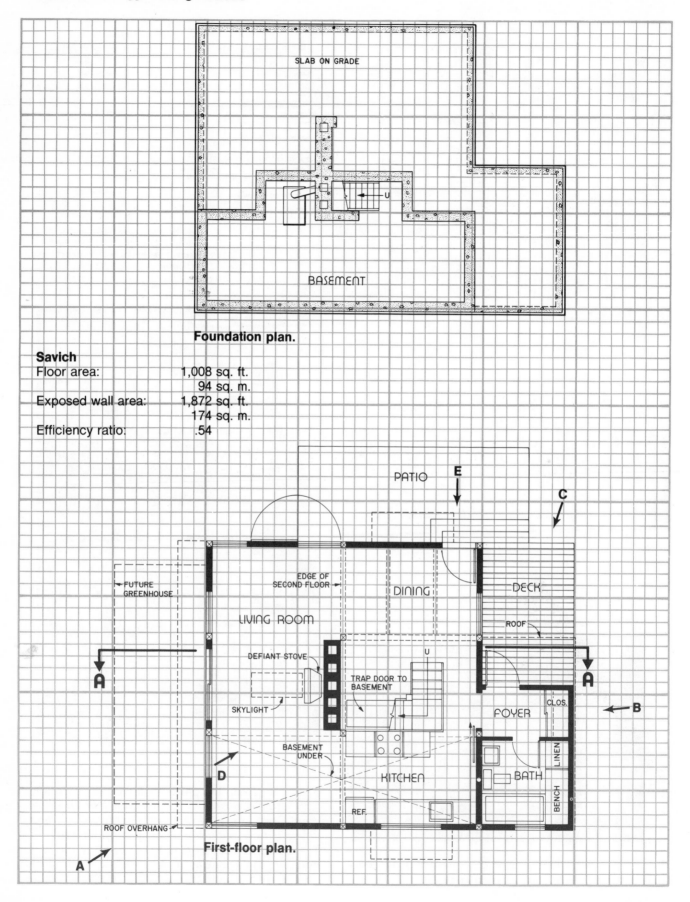

SLAB ON GRADE

U

BASEMENT

Foundation plan.

Savich
Floor area: 1,008 sq. ft.
                     94 sq. m.
Exposed wall area: 1,872 sq. ft.
                     174 sq. m.
Efficiency ratio: .54

PATIO

E

C

FUTURE
GREENHOUSE

EDGE OF
SECOND FLOOR

DINING

DECK

LIVING ROOM

ROOF

A

DEFIANT STOVE

U

TRAP DOOR TO
BASEMENT

SKYLIGHT

CLOS.

FOYER

A

B

BASEMENT
UNDER

LINEN

D

BATH

KITCHEN

BENCH

REF.

ROOF OVERHANG

First-floor plan.

A

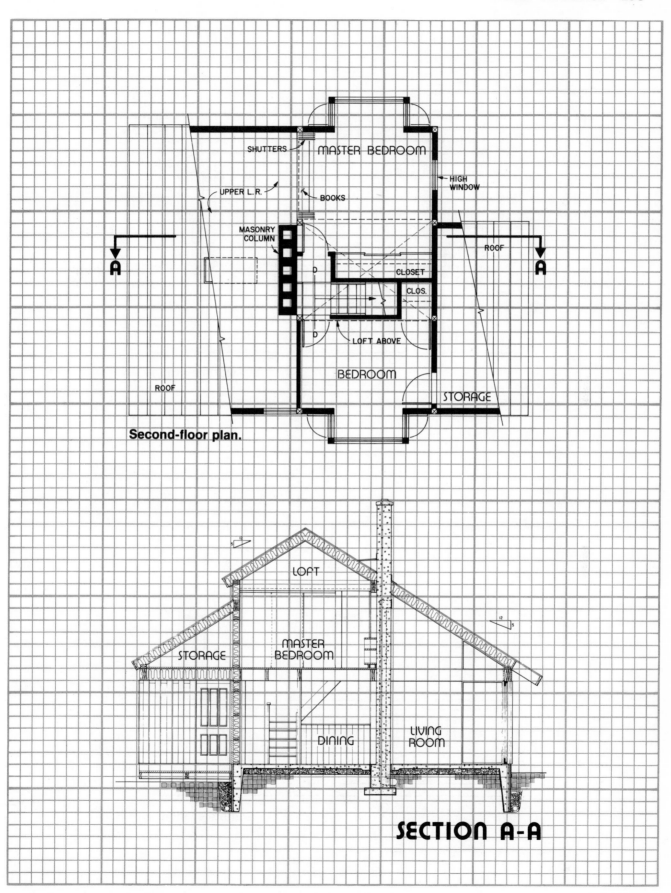

Second-floor plan.

SECTION A-A

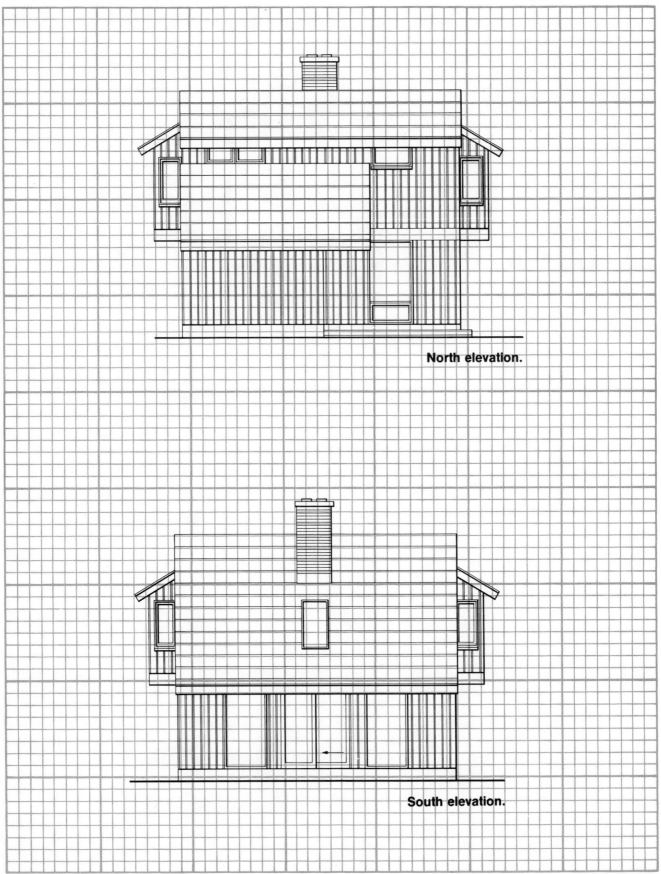

North elevation.

South elevation.

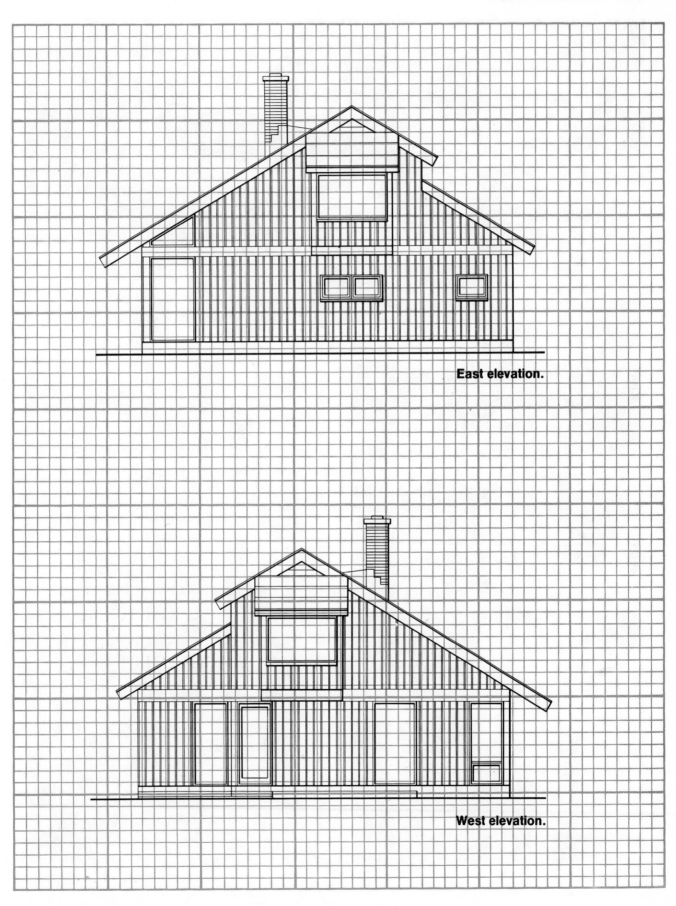

East elevation.

West elevation.

Part IV

Sources and Materials

Introduction

Now that you have found out what goes into building an energy-saving house and have seen examples of what can be done, you are ready to find a house design which suits you and start building. At this point, many people get cold feet and sit down and write Alex a letter. "Do you know any architects in the San Francisco area who build . . . ?" "Has anyone built any of your houses in Missouri?" "Could you help us find a contractor in . . . ?" "Do you have any other plans available for something a bit larger with four bathrooms and . . . ?" "Could you send a detailed list of materials and a cost estimate to . . . ?" The great majority of the people who write to me want help with the design for a house which is to be located in some part of the country which is quite distant from me. Since there are thousands of you and only one of me, the amount of help which I can provide is limited. With this in mind, I have compiled several lists of different people to help with design and construction.

As I know all too well from personal experience,

this type of listing can generate a lot of mail. A few pointers on writing for help are in order.

1. Always include a stamped, self-addressed envelope; mailing costs can get astronomical when there are several thousand letters.

2. Keep your initial request simple, and limit it to one or two clearly stated points. The 9X12 manila envelopes with four pages of plans and twelve handwritten pages of questions tend to get relegated to the bottom of the pile. If you do wish to send such a letter, send a preliminary inquiry first to make sure that the person has time to review something extensive in detail. A consulting fee may be in order.

3. If you have something to discuss in detail, give your phone number and suggest a collect call giving preferred times for the call.

4. Much better than a long letter is a cassette tape which can be returned with an answer easily and quickly.

Architects and Designers

Most architects only build expensive commercial buildings or white cubistic palaces for the very rich. Almost none of them ever venture actually to build anything themselves. Those who have jumped onto the solar bandwagon tend to get even more impractical and costly. From the many thousands of architects and designers on this continent, I have culled a very short list of those who have designed and built houses which are low-cost and ecologically sound and which I feel are attractive. They are the antithesis of the typical architect described in the book review here:

This is really a book for people like architects who don't want to get their hands dirty, but who want to talk reasonably knowledgeably to the engineers who will do any necessary nuts and bolts designing. It may help with the planning of a collector installation, but don't expect it to tell you how to do anything in the real world.

Robert Vale
Part of a very negative review of a solar energy book in Undercurrents *magazine.*

Gregg Allen
344 King St. E., Studio 505
Toronto, ON M5A 1K7, Canada

Gregory Archer
17017 SW Westview Dr.
Lake Oswego, OR 97034

Jim Bier
Rt. 2, Box 35
Ferrum, VA 24088

Dick Crowther
310 Steele St.
Denver, CO 80206

Alfredo DeVido
679 Madison Ave.
New York, NY 10021

Mike Jantzen
Box 172
Carlyle, IL 62231

David Kruschke
Rt. 2
Wild Rose, WI 54984

Nick Nicholson
Box 344
Ayer's Cliff, PQ JOB 1CO, Canada

Lewis Roberts
P.O. Box 143
Roxbury, CT 06783

Gregg Torchio
Jessie Bridge Rd.
Elmer, NJ 08318

Alex Wade
Mt. Marion, NY 12456

Most of these architects are noted for their solar design work; their designs are all of a very simple nature and use either direct passive systems or low-cost, air-type collectors. The extremely inexpensive designs of Bier and Crowther are great favorites of mine.

Plans (Working Drawings)

The set of plans bound at the end of this book covers details for the three basic saltbox designs of the Jones, Lillio, and Gilbert houses and can be modified for any of these designs. I offer five other sets of plans for the house examples presented in this book. They are:

Volkswagen house
Tompkins house
Perlberg/Price house
Pole house
Savich house

Plans for these houses are available at $30 for the first set and $10 for any additional sets ordered at the same time. In case you don't want to go to the work of assembling the basic saltbox house set from this book, they are also available for $15 per set, maximum six sets per customer. All of my plans are available from Smallplan, Box 43, Barrytown, NY 12507.

Several other very excellent plans are available from various sources. Plans of the widely published USDA solar attic house (Plan 7220) are available free of charge or for a nominal printing fee from your local U.S. Department of Agriculture extension office. The house is a very standard, one-story house with a double-level attic which serves both heating and cooling functions admirably. For hot climates which still require some winter heat, it's well worth considering. The USDA solar attic house is also known as the helio-thermics house in various press articles. The designer, Harold Zorig, may be reached at the U.S. Department of Agriculture, Rural Housing Research Unit, Box 792, Clemson, SC 29631.

In Canada, plans for economical, energy-efficient

homes are available from the Institute of Experimental Housing, Box 4134, Vancouver, BC V6B 3E6, Canada. These houses are specifically designed for the Pacific Northwest.

Finally, even Sears has some good plans available. Some of the smaller houses in their assortment of energy-saving designs are excellent. Order *Home Design Booklet* 64 KY 5207.

Factory-Built Houses

Many companies make precut and prefabricated houses. Most of them are ugly, inefficient, and vastly overpriced. The prefab concept is very attractive for the owner-builder, as it eliminates much of the difficult work of figuring out the basics of framing the shell of the house and gives the owner a good headstart as well as a great psychological boost. Of the extensive list of available factory-built houses, I have selected four companies whose products are of interest to energy-conscious homebuilders. They are presented in order of rising costs. Not coincidentally, the amount of owner participation varies inversely to the costs.

Shelter-Kit one-bedroom house.

Shelter-Kit, Inc., Dept. WN, Franklin Mills, Franklin, NH 03235, produces small post and beam structures which are very much in tune with the types of designs I advocate. The kits are available for the post and beam frame only or as an entire module complete with siding, roofing, and doors and windows.

Two different sets of construction modules are provided. They can be used either as a small basic living unit or combined in multiples. The different types of modules cannot be combined with each other, however. The smaller module is 12 feet square with a shed roof. The larger module

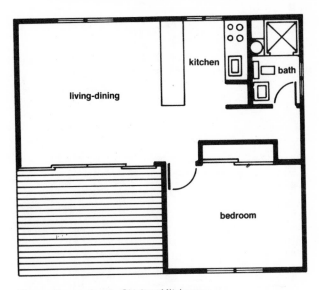

Floor plan — basic Shelter-Kit house — two 12'X12' modules and one 8'X12' shed.

is 16 feet square with a steeply pitched gable roof which provides a story-and-a-half height for a sleeping loft. A 10-foot by 16-foot lean-to is provided as a part of the 16-foot module system.

Costs are quite modest. The complete kit for the 12-foot module is less than $3,000; for the 16-foot, about $5,000. Framing kits only are about $1,200 for the 12-foot module and $2,400 for the 16-foot module. The framing can be readily shipped by common carrier. For complete houses, the company offers a unique service. They rent an appropriate-size U-Haul truck for you. Then you journey to their factory, view a film on the erection of your house, ask questions, and drive home with your U-Haul filled with precut house. For those with little time or money to spare, these houses are well worth considering.

The second company is run by my old friend David Howard of Alstead, New Hampshire. Many of his houses were featured in *30 Energy-Efficient Houses*. My book created so much demand for David that he has had to increase the size of his operation considerably. He no longer provides custom architectural services for each house as he originally did. He now has several stock plans. These are available at fixed prices for the handmade oak post and beam frame delivered and erected. Prices vary from about $10 to $15 per square foot, in place, depending upon size and complexity. David also furnishes one frame for do-it-yourself builders which is engineered to be erected by the owner.

The houses are extremely well insulated and of heirloom-type construction. David makes no effort at solar designs. His houses all have provi-

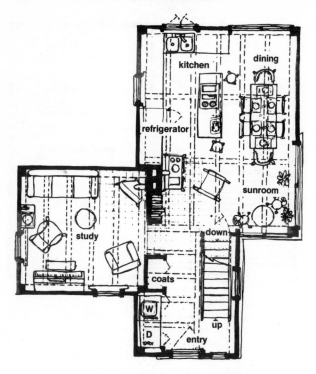

First-floor plan — David Howard house.

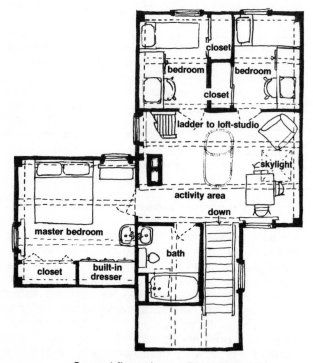

Second-floor plan — David Howard house.

sions for wood heat as a primary heat source. A brochure of 35 different designs is $5 from David Howard, Box 38, Alstead, NH 03602.

The third company is Barn Homes, Box 579, Woodstock, NY 12498. Barn Homes ships an al-

most complete kit of parts for your house. Virtually everything except roofing materials, paint, and plumbing and heating materials is provided. A prefabricated post and beam frame is enclosed with factory-built wall and roof panels. The panels are wired, insulated, and have doors and Pella windows in place.

Nine different models are provided with several variations. One of the houses is called a "solar barn" and is quite similar to the very efficient Tompkins house. Quality is high and so is cost—about $25 to $30 per square foot.

First-floor plan — Acorn house.

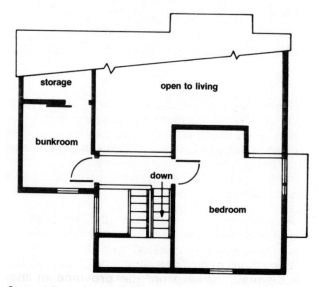

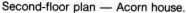

Second-floor plan — Acorn house.

Acorn Saltbox house.

Acorn Nutshell house.

The fourth company, Acorn Structures, Inc., Box 250, Concord, MA 01742, has a national reputation as a solar innovator. For several years, they have offered active solar collectors as a part of their houses. The houses are factory-built components which are assembled at the site with a crane. Except for providing the foundation and some finishing work, there is little for the owner-builder to do. The house designs are of high quality, and the active solar system (space or hot-water) qualifies for a full $2,200 tax credit to somewhat offset the higher costs. Depending upon location, size, and complexity, the houses range from $32 to $42 per square foot. A domestic solar-heated, hot-water system adds about $2,000 to this base cost; a solar space-heating system for the house itself adds another $8,000. Even though the costs are higher than those of most other houses in this book, one of the compact houses with active solar heating will still cost less than the average tract house with an oil or gas furnace.

Other Types of Houses

Many people have written requesting sources of information for structures other than the types I advocate. Certain other structures *are* worth considering, but are beyond the scope of this book. For those who want to investigate further, some suggestions follow.

Underground Houses

Underground houses are a valid, attractive way to save energy. They usually require expensive poured concrete construction and should have professionally applied waterproofing. This tends to disqualify them from the province of the owner-builder, unless he is uncommonly quali-

fied. Malcom Wells, P.O. Box 1149, Brewster, MA 02631, is the primary advocate of underground houses and has several publications on the subject. Another architect who specializes in this type of structure is Don Metz of Earthtech, Box 52, Lyme, NH 03768.

Several universities have also researched underground structures. The two best known are the University of Minnesota and the University of Texas. Both have books and pamphlets on the subject. Write to the Underground Space Center, 112 Civil and Mineral Engineering Dept., University of Minnesota, Minneapolis, MN 55455, or to the Clearinghouse for Earth-Covered Settlements, University of Texas, Arlington, TX 76019.

Stackwall Construction

A very unique construction method has been researched and developed by the University of Manitoba in Winnipeg, Canada. These buildings are useful as very low cost structures in remote, heavily forested areas. The exterior walls of the houses are built of 2-foot-long sections of logs stacked up with the ends facing out. Mortar is placed between the logs, much as in a brick wall. The structures are designed to sit on a gravel-bed-type foundation, so no expensive foundation work is required. Since the log walls are 2 feet thick, they exceed the most rigorous insulating standards. There are very few areas where this technique is applicable, but it does lower the cost of a house drastically.

The University of Manitoba has a book on the subject, *Stackwall: How to Build It,* available from the University of Manitoba Bookstore, Fort Garry Campus, Winnipeg, MB R3T 2N2, Canada.

Dome Structures

Domes and other round structures have a great fascination for many people. They are quite useful as studios and work spaces but have limited application as a full-time house. As homebuilt structures, they tend to have leakage problems. The techniques of mass production are very well suited to domes, however, and many are available commercially. A complete listing is available from the National Association of Dome Home Manufacturers, 1701 Lake Ave., Suite 470, Glenview, IL 60025. A related structure is the round building which has also been popular with my correspondents. Components for silos are available from Unadilla Silo Co., Unadilla, NY 13849.

Contractors

Of all the requests for help, the most prevalent one is: "Please recommend a contractor in . . ." These contractors have all used my plans to build houses and may be available as consultants if they are near your geographical area. Some will travel if the project is interesting enough.

Kevin Berry
63 Grandview Ave.
Catskill, NY 12414

Kevin built several of the houses in this book. Practice limited to upstate New York and western Massachusetts and Connecticut.

Umpqua Builders Guild
Kevin O'Fay, Russell Radcliffe
Box 52
Umpqua, OR 97486

Consultants for owner-builders, they provide trained craftsmen to build energy-saving houses.

Virginia Thigpen
232 Elendil Lane
Davis, CA 95616

Contractor for passive solar homes.

Fritz Dodge
120 E. Hurlburt St.
Charlevoix, MI 49720

Fritz visited David Howard and studied his authentic braced post and beam frames and returned to Michigan to build the Price house in Ann Arbor. It is a variation of the Perlberg house. Fritz is single and can be induced to travel if the project is interesting.

Bob Dakin
Box 229
Tivoli, NY 12583

Bob helped with the great majority of the houses in this book. He is very good at materials takeoffs and layout for timber frames. I would recommend him as a consultant for erecting the frame of your house. He plans to return to school to study architecture. If you are lucky, you might nab him in the summers.

Frank Kotajarvi
Rt. 1, Box 139B
Thayer, MO 65791

Frank and his wife Jeanne built their own house from my plans and became so enthused with post and beam construction that they went into the business.

Charles Simms
343 Duane St.
New York, NY 10013

John Farrell
RFD #1
Exeter, NH 03833

Chet Gilmore
P.O. Box 2283
Peace River, AB TOH 2XO, Canada

John Nelson
RR #3, ON KOK 3EO, Canada

Building Schools

If you can't find someone to help, learn to do it yourself. These groups offer courses in how to build energy-saving houses with post and beam frames.

Cornerstones
54 Cumberland St.
Brunswick, ME 04011

Just down the street from the Shelter Institute; a result of a parting of the ways of some of the originators of the Shelter Institute. Charlie Wing, coauthor (with John N. Cole) of *From the Ground Up,* runs the school.

Heartwood Owner-Builder School
Johnson Rd.
Washington, MA 01223

Protégés of Charlie Wing have set up a new school using his principles.

The Shelter Institute
Bath, ME 04530

The original school—very popular; classes fill quickly so plan well ahead.

Umpqua Builders Guild
Box 52
Umpqua, OR 97486

In addition to providing direct help, Umpqua gives classes for all of you who find Bath, Maine, a bit of a jaunt.

Basic Tools

These are the basic tools which you will need to build your own house. Those listed first are essential. Many of the less-common tools are described throughout the text. I have tried to list catalog numbers for both Sears and Stanley where possible, and my personal preferences are listed first. These two companies are widely distributed throughout the country, and the numbers are primarily for reference.

Tools for Basic House

Nail bag and hammer holster
Stanley HH-2. Leather hammer holster with U-shaped steel loop. Worn on belt. Use with standard cloth nail apron distributed free by most lumberyards.

Sears 9 HT 45143. Leather nail and tool bag. Large and medium nail pockets, four small tool pockets, two hammer loops.

Hammer
Estwing E3-20S. Straight-claw, 20-oz. head, nylon handle.

Sears 9 HT 38273. Like above, with neoprene handle.

Carpenter's pencils
Standard lumberyard/hardware store item.

Locking tape
Sears 9 HT 39217. 20′ long by 3/4″ wide, spring-return tape. Metal case, belt clip.

Stanley PL-320. Like above, except locking button less convenient to use.

Manual tape
Stanley "Extender." Rigid, 8′ tape which coils into a case. Very useful.

Winding reel tape
Stanley 34-450. 3/8″ wide by 50′ long. Plastic case.

Sears 9 HT 39001. Like Stanley but with more expensive steel case.

Framing square
Stanley 900. Black with white numerals; 24″. Easy to read with useful tables on square.

Sears 9 HT 39641 C. Similar to Stanley, but bright steel with no tables.

Sears 9 HT 3956. Stair or rafter gauges. Inexpensive accessory for framing squares.

Combination square
Stanley 1222 1/2. Built-in scriber and level.

Sears 9 HT 39543. Identical to Stanley.

Sliding bevel square
Sears 9 HT 39485. Adjustable blade for transferring angles.

Meter stick
Sears 9 HT 3762 C. 1-meter-long metal rule for metric measurement.

Chalk line and chalk
Stanley 47-671. Plastic chalk reel with chalk. Inexpensive, but adequate for the job.

Sears 9 HT 3773. Combination plumb bob/chalk line. Aluminum case.

Level
Stanley 2513-HB. 4′-long wooden level. Edges are bound with brass. Metal levels can bend and should be avoided. Sears makes only metal.

Nylon twine
Sears 9 HT 76551. 300′, #21 nylon twine for layout and levels.

Line level
Stanley 187. Can be useful for layout if used carefully. Inexpensive.

Utility knife
Stanley 199. The old standby. Do not use the retractable blade type, as they are not durable.

Hand saw
Stanley 39-108. Chrome-nickel-molybdenum steel. Taper-ground teeth, 8 points to the inch. Top-of-the-line saw for use only if power is not available or for professionals.

Sears 9 HT 36153 C. Chrome-nickel steel, taper-ground teeth, 8 points to the inch. Medium quality for general use.

Rip saw
Bushman boardsaw, Leichtung. Much faster than conventional rip saw. Excellent quality.

Trim saw

Sandvik cabinetmakers saw. 15 teeth per inch; curved, toothed end for plunge cuts. (Also available from Leichtung.)

Block plane

Stanley H 1247. 6⅝″-long block plane for general use. Inexpensive. Professional planes are very expensive and not much used.

Sears 9 HT 37051. 7″-long block plane. Similar to above, but longer.

Rasp-type plane

Stanley 285. "Surform." Adjustable for use either as a plane or file. Blades are similar to a cheese grater. Finish is somewhat rough. Extra-heavy model (no. 1485) works better. Surform tools are made in a variety of configurations.

Sears 9 HT 67722. Surform plane. Identical to Stanley, but not adjustable.

Chisels

Stanley H-1252-R. Set of four chisels; ¼″, ½″, ¾″, and 1″ wide.

Sears 9 HT 36826. Identical to Stanley.

Screwdrivers

Sears 9 HT 41099. Nine-piece screwdriver set. Good assortment of regular and Phillips-head.

Nail sets

Stanley H-1211-S. Package of three commonly used sizes of nail sets.

Adjustable wrench

Crescent wrench. The original adjustable wrench; imitations are inferior. Buy the 8″ size.

Sears Craftsman 9 HT 44603. Similar to above.

Hatchet

Sears 9 HT 4812. 3¼″-cut, all steel hatchet with neoprene grip.

Stanley SH 1½. Similar to above.

Sledge hammer

Stanley 58-810. 10-lb. head, hickory handle.

Sears 9 HT 50752 C. Identical to Stanley.

Safety goggles

Sears 9 HT 1859. Polycarbonate lenses, ventilated side panels.

Stanley 54-060. Similar to above.

Ladder

Sears 30 B 42278 N. Four-way commercial ladder. Functions as stepladder, extension ladder, offset stair ladder, and two separate straight ladders. 8′ high used as a stepladder; 15′ high used as an extension ladder.

Pry bar

Stanley H-515. "Wonder Bar." Double-ended bar for prying and nail pulling.

Sears 9 HT 6591. Similar to above.

Saw horse legs

Sears 9 HT 28884 C. Portable folding steel legs. Use these instead of the commonly sold brackets which don't work well, or build your own from wood.

Extension cords

Sears 34 HT 5834. 14-gauge, 25′ cord. Two required. For longer distances, use 12/2 Romex cable. For outdoor use or in wet areas, make sure that cords are attached to a GFI circuit breaker.

Hacksaw

Sears 9 HT 3559. Designed for flush cutting with adjustable tension and tubular frame with blade-storage compartment.

Stanley 15-150. Similar to above without adjustable tension.

Caulking gun

Sears 30 B 38306. High-quality gun with built-in spout trimmer to cut spout to correct angle. Also has built-in punch for cartridge seal.

Circular saw (skillsaw)

Sears 9 HT 1096. 2⅛ h.p., 7½″ saw. Ball, needle, and roller bearings, helical gearing. Replaces top-of-the-line with electronic brake.

Makita 5801B. Similar to above, 7¼″ blade.

Milwaukee contractor's saw. Similar to Makita.

(The above saws are all of excellent quality. Listed in ascending order of price.)

Miter arm

Sears 9 HT 1715 IN. Accurate saw guide which clamps work in place and permits precise repetitive cuts, angles, and miters. Fits all above saws.

Saw guide

Swanson Speed Square (see Chapter 4). Hand-held guide for accurate cuts with circular saw.

Sears 9 HT 1719. Similar to above, but cumbersome.

Saw blades

Framing blades. Sears 9 HT 32464. 7¼″ carbide tipped. One needed for average job. Or, Sears 9 HT 32712. 7¼″ disposable blade. Three needed for average job.

Combination blades. Sears 9 HT 32495. 7½″ blade with 60 teeth for smooth cuts. Order 9 HT 32494 for 7¼″ saws. Three blades needed for average job. Sears 9 HT 32489 is carbide-tipped combination blade. One blade should last the job and costs about the same as three steel blades.

Nicholson saw blades. Nicholson makes the top-quality blades, but must be special-ordered. Available in sizes and types as described for Sears. Order from Silvo Hardware Co.

Electric drill
Sears 9 HT 1148. ⅜″ chuck, variable-speed, reversible, medium-quality, general-purpose drill. Variable speed makes tool useful for setting screws. For a little extra money, the same drill is available with a rotary hammer feature for drilling in masonry (Sears 9 HT 1181).

Drill bits
Stanley 105-A. Power bore bits. Patented, well-designed bits. Use instead of common flat "spade-type" bits. Set includes popular sizes; they are also available singly.

Drill guides
Sears 9 HT 25926. Drill stand. Allows precise use of portable drill as a bench tool. Fits Sears and Makita drills.

Router
Sears 9 HT 1747. 1 h.p., 25,000 rpm router. Useful for cabinetmaking and complex joinery. Built-in worklight is excellent feature not found elsewhere. Use with table below for homemade moldings and joinery.

Router table
Sears 9 HT 25444. Portable table. Accepts either router or sabre saw for bench use. Safety guard covers blades.

Backsaw guide
Jointmaster SS-80. Leichtung. A versatile guide for use with hand backsaws where electric power is not used. Comes complete with Spear and Jackson backsaw. Makes complex cabinetmaker joinery and miter cuts.

Power sanders
Sears 9 HT 1157. 1 h.p. rotary disk sander. Good for removing large amounts of wood in a hurry or straightening uneven wood or metal surfaces (such as auto bodies). Order fiber-backed sanding disks with sander. Sears stores don't carry them, and local hardware stores charge two to three times the price.

Sears 9 HT 1176 C. 4″ belt-type sander. Excellent for fine finishing.

Addresses
Stanley, 600 Myrtle St., New Britain, CT 06053. The Stanley Works of Canada, Ltd., P.O. Box 3001, Station B, Hamilton, ON L8H 7J3, Canada. Stanley tools are available at most hardware and lumber yards; for tools not available locally, see their *Tool Catalog* #34. Leichtung, 5187 Mayfield Rd.,

Cleveland, OH 44124. Silvo Hardware Co., 107–109 Walnut St., Philadelphia, PA 19106.

Addresses for specialty tool companies are listed in Chapter 4 and in "Addresses of Manufacturers and Associations" below.

Commercial Sawmills

Wood is the basic resource needed to construct these houses. The Mobile Dimension saw is portable and can come directly to your stand of trees. The following owners are using their mills commercially in the United States and Canada.

Dan Sharp
P.O. Box 50
Craig, AK 99921

John Peterson
Box 206
Seldovia, AK 99663

Kowboy Kountry
John Avery
P.O. Box Y
East Flagstaff, AZ 86001

J. T. Beene
RFD 2, Box 422
Greenbrier, AR 72058

Michael Smith
Star Rt., Osage
Green Forest, AR 72638

Les Liebenberg
P.O. Box 756
Ben Lomond, CA 95005

Dr. John P. Miller
P.O. Box 9274
South Lake Tahoe, CA 95731

Mark Frasier
Rist Canyon Rt.
Bellvue, CO 80512

Bear Creek Basin Milling
Tom Hayden
P.O. Box 280
Evergreen, CO 80439

Craig C. Barton
Rt. 1, Box 213
Bunnell, FL 32010

Haw Creek Loggers
Raymond Heaton
Rt. 1, Box 240
Bunnell, FL 32010

Clay R. Steffee
112 S. Clyde Ave.
Kissimmee, FL 32741

W. E. Mixon
Rt. 4, Box 300
Milledgeville, GA 31061

Robert Smith
RR 1, Box 186
Captain Cook, HI 96704

Dean Puzey
Fairmount, IL 61841

R. T. Rehtmeyer
Timber Creek Farm
McLean, IL 61754

Charles Jones
Rt. 4, Box 101
Rockville, IN 47872

Hopson Karr
Rt. 2, Box 117
Salem, KY 42078

Rivers Brown
Rt. 1, Box 168
Ethel, LA 70730

David W. Emond
Snow Rd., Box 93
Bridgewater, ME 04735

Richard Mead
Box 45
Freedom, ME 04941

John Luczak
10390 Rawsonville Rd.
Belleville, MI 48111

Brink Forest Products
Lawrence Brink
1202 Bass Lake Rd.
Traverse City, MI 49684

Larris Freyholtz
Blackduck, MN 56630

B. L. Cooper
Box C
Boulder, MT 59632

D. C. Enterprises
Richard Converse
22 Sharon Dr.
Great Falls, MT 59405

Frederick C. Nielsen
Box 176, RD 1
Titusville, NJ 08560

Dan Rauscher
P.O. Box 81
Eaton, NY 13334

Robert Sessions
Box 97
Greig, NY 13345

Turtle Mountain Forest Industries
Richard Gilmore, Robert Indvik
RR 1
Bottineau, ND 58318

George M. Wilson
Rt. 2
Rockford, OH 45882

Ronald E. Albers
2033 Russia-Houston Rd.
Russia, OH 45363

Hogdance Hollow, Inc.
Steve Randall
P.O. Box 655
Clayton, OK 74536

Jerry Creasy
P.O. Box 385
Garibaldi, OR 97118

Roundy Brothers
Box 22
Alton, UT 84710

William "Red" Reese
P.O. Box 870
Newport, WA 99156

John Pieper
RR 1
Chaseburg, WI 54621

David Schnell
Rt. 3, Box 202
Dairyland, WI 54830

Dennis R. Fredrickson
General Delivery
Donald Station 1, BC V0A 1C0, Canada

North Mabel Lake Lumber Co.
Duane Bemister
RR 2
Enderby, BC V0E 1V0, Canada

Frank Beban Logging Ltd.
G. Gunnell
3249 Ross Rd.
Nanaimo, BC V9T 2S3, Canada

Hart-Mar Industries
J. A. Hart
27195 116th Ave.
Whonnock, BC V0M 1S0, Canada

Douglas McIntosh
Bay 42-3001 Glendale
Williams Lake, BC V2G 3N9, Canada

Insulating Glass Manufacturers*

The following manufacturers make insulating glass units in standard and special sizes up to 70 square feet. Buying direct in quantity can provide substantial savings.

Western Insulated Glass Co.
Phoenix, Ariz.

Southern Wholesale Glass
Marietta, Calif.

Blomberg Window
Sacramento, Calif.

Havlin Witkin-Sacramento
Sacramento, Calif.

Armour Worldwide Glass
Santa Fe Springs, Calif.

General Glass Corp.
Denver, Colo.

Independent Insulating Glass Co.
Chicago, Ill.

Illinois Valley Glass & Mirror Co.
Peoria, Ill.

Glastek, Inc.
Indianapolis, Ind.

Soule Glass Ind.
Portland, Maine

Economy Glass Corp.
Boston, Mass.

North American Mfg., Inc.
Holliston, Mass.

Solar Seal Corp.
Stoughton, Mass.

Multipane of New England, Inc.
Waltham, Mass.

Acorn Building Components, Inc.
Detroit, Mich.

Twin Pane Div/Philips Ind.
Livonia, Mich.

Ohio Plate Glass Co.
Monroe, Mich.

Cardinal Insulated Glass Co.
Minneapolis, Minn.

Viracon, Inc.
Owatonna, Minn.

Delaware Valley Insulating Glass Co., Inc.
Beverly, N.J.

C-E Glass
Pennsauken, N.J.

Burton Enterprises, Inc.
Cobleskill, N.Y.

F.G.M. Glass Dist. Inc.
Hauppauge, N.Y.

Vega Ind., Inc.
Syracuse, N.Y.

Utica Glass Co. Chromalloy
Utica, N.Y.

Louisiana Pacific Corp.
Barberton, Ohio

A.B.S. Enterprises
Oklahoma City, Okla.

Thermoglas, Inc.
Oklahoma City, Okla.

Mercer Ind., Inc.
Portland, Oreg.

Viking Ind., Inc.
Portland, Oreg.

Salem Aluminum Window Co.
Salem, Oreg.

Dorco Mfg. Co., Inc.
Gallatin, Tenn.

General Aluminum Corp.
Carrollton, Tex.

Ideal Co.
Waco, Tex.

AMSCO
Salt Lake City, Utah

Bennett's
Salt Lake City, Utah

*This list was provided by the Sealed Insulating Glass Manufacturers Assoc., 3310 Harrison St., Topeka, KS 66611.

Linford Bros. Utah Glass Co.
Salt Lake City, Utah

Ketter Aluminum Prod. of Virginia
Milford, Va.

Belknap Glass Co.
Seattle, Wash.

Elstrom Mfg. Co.
Seattle, Wash.

Fentron Ind.
Seattle, Wash.

Milgard Mfg., Inc.
Tacoma, Wash.

Weather Shield Glass Div.
Medford, Wis.

Semling-Menke Co., Inc.
Merrill, Wis.

Terne Roofing Distributors

Follansbee Steel Corp: District Offices

P.O. Box 60363
Terminal Annex
Los Angeles, CA 90060

P.O. Box 378
Millbrae, CA 94030

5438 N. Milwaukee Ave.
Chicago, IL 60630

6229 N. Charles St.
Baltimore, MD 21212

1414 Fisher Bldg.
Detroit, MI 48202

11004 E. 40 Hwy.
Independence, MO 64055

527 Madison Ave.
New York, NY 10022

1133 Terminal Tower
Cleveland, OH 44113

947 Old York Rd.
Abington, PA 19001

1412 Frick Bldg.
Pittsburgh, PA 15219

Melrose Center West Bldg.
Nashville, TN 37204

7746 Menomonee River Parkway, N.
Wauwatosa, WI 53225

A. C. Leslie Co.
P.O. Box 1160, Montreal, PQ H3C 2Y6, Canada

Addresses of Manufacturers and Associations

This is a list of important manufacturers and associations which are referred to throughout the text.

Adhesive Engineering Co.
1411 Industrial Rd.
San Carlos, CA 94070

AGA Corp.
550 Country Ave.
Secaucus, NJ 07094

American Plywood Assoc.
P.O. Box 2277
Tacoma, WA 98401

AquaBug International
100 Merrick Rd.
Rockville Center, NY 11570

Barnes Engineering
30 Commerce Rd.
Stamford, CT 06902

Benco Industrial Supply
Washington and Ludwick Sts.
Greensburg, PA 15601

Brookstone Co.
127 Vose Farm Rd.
Peterborough, NH 03458

Calbar, Inc.
2626 N. Martha St.
Philadelphia, PA 19125

Ceramic Radiant Heat
Pleasant Dr.
Lochmere, NH 03252

Construction Products
P.O. Box 368
Hooksett, NH 03106

Craftsman Wood Service Co.
2727 S. Mary St.
Chicago, IL 60608

Cumberland General Store
Rt. 3, Box 479
Crossville, TN 38555

Dryvit Systems, Inc.
420 Lincoln Ave.
Warwick, RI 02888

Duro-Lite Lamps, Inc.
17-10 Willow St.
Fair Lawn, NJ 07410

Duro-Test Corp.
2321 Kennedy Blvd.
North Bergen, NJ 07047

Duro-Test Electric Ltd.
315 Flint Rd.
Downsview, ON M3J 2J, Canada

Dynamote Corp.
1200 W. Nickerson St.
Seattle, WA 98119

Enertron Corp.
241 Crescent St.
Waltham, MA 02154

Estwing Mfg. Co.
2647 Eighth St., Dept. C4
Rockford, IL 61101

Farallones Institute
15290 Coleman Valley Rd.
Occidental, CA 95465

Fingerle Lumber Co.
108 E. Madison St.
Ann Arbor, MI 48104

Gates Engineering Co.
P.O. Box 1711
Wilmington, DE 19899

Hydrolevel
P.O. Box G
Ocean Springs, MS 39564

Industrial Gasket and Shim Co.
P.O. Box 368
Meadow Lands, PA 15347

Insulating Shade Co., Inc.
P.O. Box 406
Guilford, CT 06437

Kero-Sun
Main St.
Kent, CT 06757

Lehman Hardware and Appliance
Box 41
Kidron, OH 44636

Lightolier, Inc.
346 Claremont Ave.
Jersey City, NJ 07305

Marvin Window Co.
Warroad, MN 56763

National Gypsum Co.
325 Delaware Ave.
Buffalo, NY 14202

Norcold Co.
1501 Michigan Ave.
Sidney, OH 45365

Pease Lumber Co.
900-T Laurel Ave.
Hamilton, OH 45015

The Prestolite Co.
511 Hamilton Ave.
Toledo, OH 43602

Quaker City Mfg. Co.
705 Center Pike
Sharon Hill, PA 19079

Rapco Foam, Inc.
122 E. 42nd St.
New York, NY 10017

Raven Industries, Inc.
Box 1007
Sioux Falls, SD 57101

Red Cedar Shingle and Handsplit Shake Bureau
Suite 275, 515 116th Ave., NE
Bellevue, WA 98004

Rife Hydraulic Engine Mfg. Co.
132 Main St.
Andover, NJ 07821

Rollscreen Co.
Pella, IA 50219

Romar Alarm Systems
85 76th St.
Brooklyn, NY 11209

The Rothenberger System
7317 Cahill Rd.
Minneapolis, MN 55435

Sterling Faucet Co.
Morgantown, WV 26505

Sturgis Heat Recovery, Inc.
Stone Ridge, NY 12484

Swanson Tool Co.
P.O. Box 434
Oak Lawn, IL 60454

Timber Engineering Co.
5530 Wisconsin Ave.
Washington, DC 20015

Tremco Mfg. Co.
10701 Shaker Blvd.
Cleveland, OH 44104

United States Gypsum Co.
325 Delaware Ave.
Buffalo, NY 14202

Whirlpool Corp.
1900 Whirlpool Dr.
LaPorte, IN 46350

Woodcraft Supply Corp.
313 Montvale Ave.
Woburn, MA 01801

Zinsser and Co.
39 Belmont Dr.
Somerset, NJ 08873

Zomeworks
P.O. Box 712
Albuquerque, NM 87103

Recommended Efficient Appliances and Equipment for Energy-Saving Houses

Once you have constructed an energy-saving house, how do you equip it? Many purists will shun modern appliances altogether. For those who want to equip their house in normal fashion, I have researched the best available appliances at this writing. Bear in mind that energy shortages are producing rapid changes, particularly in solar-related equipment. I have frequently used Sears products for comparison purposes. Examine the features and energy consumption of these specific models, and use them as a basis for selecting competitive equipment.

Kitchen Appliances

Kitchen appliances represent almost 40 percent of the energy used in the home, heating excluded. Electricity in resistance heating elements should be avoided wherever possible. Microwave ovens present possible health hazards, but save a lot of energy if you can't obtain other fuels for cooking. Specific recommendations:

Wood-gas combination range
Monarch Model HF 36HW. About $1,000. (Malleable Iron Range Co., Beaver Dam, WI 53916.)

30″ gas ranges
Sears 22 K 73881 N. Deluxe model. About $600.

Waist-high broiler, electric ignition, and heavy oven insulation for self-cleaning oven. A fine piece of equipment. Roper and Magic Chef make similar models.

Sears 22 K 71591 N. Budget model. About $280. With electronic ignition, bottom broiler. No automatic controls or gadgets.

Microwave oven
Sears 22 K 99471 N. About $280. 1.3-cu.-ft. capacity, 600W, 110V.

Bottom-freezer refrigerator
Sears 46 K 69821 N. About $680. 13-cu.-ft., automatic defrost refrigerator with 6-cu.-ft. freezer drawer on bottom (very desirable). Or use separate refrigerator and freezer. Amana and Whirlpool make models of similar design.

Budget-priced refrigerator
Sears 46 K 69121 N. About $280. Manual defrost. 11.5-cu.-ft. refrigerator section with small top freezer. Plain and simple.

Chest-type freezer
Sears 46 K 19151 N. About $220. 15-cu.-ft., no-frills freezer. Indispensable for home food storage.

Bottled or natural gas-type refrigerator
6-cu.-ft. refrigerator, triple-powered: 110V AC, 12V DC, or gas. About $600. (Norcold, 1501 Michigan Ave., Sidney, OH 45365. Or, J. C. Whitney, Box 8410, Chicago, IL 60680.)

Laundry Equipment

If practical and convenient, a centrally located Laundromat is more efficient than appliances in the home, particularly if you use an extractor and then air-dry the clothes. Also look for the large Swedish multiload washers marketed under the Wascomat trade name. They do a far superior washing job to the common household-type washer. If you need equipment at home I recommend:

Automatic washer
Sears 26 K 39851 N. About $360. Adjustable water level and water-saver which allows reuse of wash water. Heavy-duty machine.

Gas dryer
Sears 26 K 79301 N. About $230. Electric ignition, includes air-dry cycle.

Nonautomatic agitator-type washer
Maytag Manual wringer-type washer. About $220. Comes with 110V belt-driven electric motor, but can be converted to other voltages or gasoline engine. Unchanged for thirty years; an old standby. Maytag also makes excellent but very expensive automatic washers and dryers.

Hot-Water Heaters

The "average" family uses about 15 percent of its household energy supply to heat water. "Average" is very misleading here; it lumps together gas, oil, and electric hot-water heaters. If you use an electric hot-water heater, you may consume two to three times the average figure. Most solar hot-water heaters use an electric backup; be sure your solar system operates efficiently. If you must use electricity for heating water, add extra insulation to the standard package, and use a timer for most efficient operation. Recommendations for hot-water heaters follow:

Electric water heater
Sears 42 K 3981 N. About $200. 52-gal., low-density, high-efficiency dual elements. Capacity, 25 gal./hour at 90°F. temperature rise. Use an extra, insulated, 30-gal. tank for tempering water. Also use timer listed below.

Water heater timer
Intermatic Water Heater Time Switch. About $25. Sets time at which heating elements turn on and off to correspond with actual usage. (Intermatic Inc., Spring Grove, IL 60081.)

Gas water heaters
Sears 42 K 33731 N (natural gas). About $170. Sears 42 K 33738 N (bottled gas). About $170. Very highly insulated with extra flue baffling for improved heat transfer.

Solar water heaters
Rheem Sun Director 120 Automatic. About $800 (heater package only; collectors extra). Drain-down-type heater, no heat exchanger or undesirable antifreeze required. Sun Director II is a direct circulating system for southern climates. Rheem is at or near the top in quality water heaters. (Rheem Water Heater Division, City Investing Co., Chicago, IL 60652.)

Rom-Aire Domestic Hot-Water System. About $1,400. An air-collector system which passes heated air over a heat exchanger to produce hot water. No freeze protection or antifreeze is needed. Larger versions can also supply general heating to the house. (Solar Energy Products Co., Avon Lake, OH 44012.)

Solar water heater collector
Solar King DG-15. About $250/collector. Excellent-quality, factory-built solar collectors of top efficiency. (American Solar King Corp., 6801 New McGregor Hwy., Waco, TX 76710.)

Components for home-built collectors
SolaRoll Absorber Mat. About $6.00 per sq. ft. Can vary considerably with layout of system. A high-quality, durable, freeze-tolerant collector which comes shipped in a roll for easy transportation. A low-cost collector which is easy to use. (Bio-Energy Systems, Inc., SolaRoll Div., Box 489A, Spring Glenn, NY 12483.)

Solar Glazing Panels. About $3.00 per sq. ft. for minimum order of 460 sq. ft. Double-insulating glass panels. Special high-transmission glass with high-temperature sealants used to laminate two layers for insulating glass panels. (ASG Industries, Inc., P.O. Box 929, Kingsport, TN 37662.)

Demand-type hot-water heaters
Direct-fired heaters using various fuels which only operate when the hot-water faucet is turned on. About $200 to $300. Gas heaters are Paloma (distributed by John Condon Co., 1103 N. 36th Ave., Seattle, WA 98103) and Junkers (distributed by Pressure Cleaning Systems, Inc., 612 N. 16th Ave., Yakima, WA 98901).

An American competitor (naturally, electrically powered) is available in a wide variety of sizes at much lower cost—less than $100. (Manufacturers: Chronomite Labs, 21011 S. Figueroa St., Carson, CA 90745; or, Solar Usage Now, 450 E. Tiffin St., Bascom, OH 44809. Solar Usage Now distributes a full line of solar equipment. Write for catalog.)

Heating Equipment

Oil and gas furnaces and boilers can be made to operate much more efficiently than those currently installed. Outside combustion air and fine-tuning of the combustion process can increase furnace efficiency by several percent. Fine-tuning should be done by a furnace expert equipped with devices for measuring stack temperature, carbon monoxide, and fuel-air mixture. The efficiency of oil burners in particular can be greatly improved. Fuel shortages may make such adjustments tempting to the novice. This can be dangerous. Even if you do hire an expert, I recommend installing an alarm for carbon monoxide, just to be safe (see Safety Equipment in this section).

Electricity should be avoided as a heat source wherever possible. If absolutely necessary, use efficient sources of electric heat such as radiant heat panels or heat pumps.

Oil-fired boiler
Hot-water heat is prized because of its uniformity. Oil is the common fuel for boilers. The Meenan Oil Co. of Syosset, L.I., has developed an efficient burner which is marketed under the trade name "Blueray" (about $1,500). The burner can cut fuel usage by 40% under ideal conditions. It is marketed by the following licensees: Blueray (22 Jericho

Turnpike, Mineola, NY 11501) and Imperial Oil Co. (111 St. Clair Ave. W., Toronto, ON M5W IK3 Canada).

Gas-fired furnaces

The common gas-fired, forced-air furnace is used by a majority of Americans for home heating. Typical furnaces are much too large for an efficient house, and unlike a boiler, the capacity can't be easily adjusted. My compact houses can make good use of ductless wall-mounted furnaces. Sears 42 AC 73628 N2 has a counterflow fan (30,000 Btu., about $230). For a nonelectric unit, try Sears 42 AC 73499 N (20,000 Btu., about $180).

Radiant electric heat panels

Available in 2'X2' and 2'X4' panels for mounting at or on the ceiling, these draw 1,000 to 1,500W, 230V. (Aztech International Ltd., 3434 Girard Blvd. NE, Albuquerque, NM 87107; Continental Radiant Glass Heat Co., 215-B Central Ave., E. Farmingdale, NY 11735.) Heaters similar to Aztech's in 120V only from Sears; 34 K 7115 C or 34 K 7116 N. Sizing and installation directions, 39 K 7100.

Energy-Cote radiant panels are slightly more efficient than above. Available from TVI Corp. (4267 Howard Ave., Kensington, MD 20795).

All makes about $60 to $100.

Single unit heat pump

Single unit designed for through-the-wall installation. Approximately 18,000 to 34,000 Btu., heating and cooling. Heating supplemented by undesirable resistance heating units. Sears 48 K 81201 N, EER 7.3, about $1,500.

Solar heating equipment

This material is beyond the scope of this book. Equipment is changing rapidly. The American Society of Heating, Refrigerating, and Airconditioning Engineers (ASHRAE) keeps an updated listing of solar equipment manufacturers. (ASHRAE, Research and Technical Services, 345 E. 47 St., New York, NY 10017.)

Cooling

Use natural siting and window placement for cooling where possible. The heat pump described above will provide heating and cooling for moderate climates. Do not use it for very hot climates where cooling only is required. Our open-plan, basic saltbox is well suited to either a natural or fan-forced circulation system. It will also accommodate a through-the-wall, package-type air conditioner. When choosing an air conditioner, check its Energy Efficiency Rating (EER), the ratio of Btu. of cooling obtained per watt of electricity used. The rating should be 7 or higher.

Package-type air conditioners

Sears 47 K 79219 N. About $540. 21,000 Btu., 230V. EER 7.7.

Sears 47 K 79099 N. About $400. 9,000 Btu., 110V. EER 9.6.

Safety Equipment

Safety is often ignored when equipping a house. The National Electric Code will force you to install a smoke detector on each level, but otherwise you are pretty much on your own. For the ultimate in fire protection, install a sprinkler system. One is detailed on the working drawings.

Smoke detectors

Sears 9 LY 57311. About $30. Battery-operated, photo-ionization-type combination heat/smoke detector. Two test switches, one for each mode. Can be wall- or ceiling-mounted. Adaptable for remote signaling. Use one for each level of house.

Sears 9 LY 57084. Automatic telephone dialer. About $150. Used with above detector and/or burglar alarm for transmitting emergency recording to four different phone numbers.

Gas detector

Sears 9 K 57044. About $30. 115V. detector for natural or bottled gas and carbon monoxide.

Fire extinguishers

Sears 9 K 5805. About $23. Medium-size unit for kitchen.

Sears 9 K 5808 C. About $50. Large, general-purpose unit. Locate where indicated on first-floor plan.

Ground fault detectors

Sears 34 K 5337. About $30. 20A. Commonly known as GFIs, these are special circuit breakers which detect dangerous grounding conditions in electric wiring and automatically disconnect the circuit. Use for all wet areas and exterior outlets. As an added safety precaution, use them for the entire first floor of slab-on-grade houses.

Emergency Electrical Power

Those who have a windmill, waterwheel, or all propane appliances don't have to worry about blackouts and power shortages. A large backup generator is an obvious choice, but they are noisy, hard to start, and expensive to buy and maintain. There are other ways to get emergency power.

Vehicle-powered inverter

Dynamote President B5KKK. About $550. Industrial-quality inverter attaches to vehicle and provides 120V AC power from batteries with or without engine running. Low-voltage disconnect prevents battery drain. (Dynamote Corp., 1200 W. Nickerson St., Seattle, WA 98177. This firm makes a wide line of inverters and accessories for emergency power equipment.)

Lightweight generator

AquaBug: 300W at 110V AC; 12A at 12V DC. Cost: $300. Lightweight and rugged. Can be used either to charge batteries for emergency use or for small amounts of 110V power. (AquaBug International, 100 Merrick Rd., Rockville Center, NY 11570.)

Household generator

Honda E-2500 (described in Chapter 4). About $850. 2,500W AC. Can power major appliances if care is used.

Specifications

Specifications comprise a complex legalistic document which usually accompanies the working drawings for a house. An owner-builder who performs all of his own work will have little direct use for them. However, banks, building inspectors, and the like are highly impressed by excess bulk of paper and may even demand a full set of specifications.

The specifications are divided into three parts. General Conditions, Special Conditions and Contract Forms, and Technical Specifications. The General Conditions are a desperate attempt to cover all possible conditions and to provide for any possible contingencies. They are usually slanted heavily in favor of the owner and the architect (not surprisingly since the architect prepares them). Contractors may even be offended by some of the phrases contained in the forms. The General Conditions are usually written with the aid of a lawyer and in theory can be used to collect damages from a contractor for violations of the contract. In actual practice, they are useful as leverage and a means of settling disputes and almost completely worthless as a means of compelling the contractor to do anything. I once saw the mighty state of New York reduced to impotence by a large Mafia contractor with an expensive contingent of lawyers. They found loopholes, real or imagined, in every section of the specifications.

Study the General Conditions carefully if you hire a contractor to do any major portion of your work. If you sign a contract with a contractor, you may wish to use these General Conditions as a part of the contract documents. If you want an almost airtight legal document preprinted to insert into your specifications, your local chapter of the American Institute of Architects has copies for sale listed under AIA Document A201, "General Conditions of the Contract for Construction." They are available for $2.50 each from AIA chapters in most major cities. Otherwise, xerox the enclosed General Conditions along with the other portions of the specifications.

Special Conditions enumerate all of the component parts of the contract documents including a detailed listing of plans (always number everything and enumerate *all* plans and parts of specifications to be included in the contract). Special Conditions also list the requirements for insurance by both the owner and contractor and list any items which are to be excluded or for which a stated allowance is to be provided in the contract. The Special Conditions are filled with blank spaces to be completed for each individual contract. Pay careful attention to their completion.

Along with the Special Conditions, I include a Release of Liens form. This is normally used by a general contractor to protect himself from claims from workmen or suppliers at a later date. If you are doing your own contracting, the bank may require that you submit them for all suppliers and subcontractors. Sometimes banks will supply their own forms. Check with your bank before executing these forms. In any case, you should have these forms completed for your own financial protection, even if you are not borrowing money or your bank doesn't require them.

The Technical Specifications will probably be of much more use to you. They divide the work into standardized sections referred to as "divisions" by professional specifications writers. The divisions describe the materials and methods of workmanship required for each trade. These Technical Specifications are written to describe my special techniques which are employed in the construction of the saltbox house as well as most of the other houses illustrated in this book. Note that several sections are duplicated to describe alternative forms of construction such as several different types of foundation construction. The numbers of these divisions correspond generally to the division numbers used in the standard builder's reference, *Sweet's Architectural Catalog File*. If you need more information about a product, just look in the *Sweet's* file division with the corresponding number.

SPECIFICATIONS
Contents

This list of contents is included for convenience and is not a legal part of this contract.

GENERAL CONDITIONS

1. Contract and Contract Documents

The Plans, Specifications, and Addenda, hereinafter enumerated in the Supplemental General Conditions, shall form part of this contract, and the provisions thereof shall be as binding upon the parties hereto as if they were herein fully set forth. The table of contents, titles, headings, and marginal notes contained herein and in said documents are solely to facilitate reference to various provisions of the Contract Documents and in no way affect, limit, or cast light on the interpretation of the provisions to which they refer.

2. Definitions

The following terms as used in this contract are respectively defined as follows:
(a) "Contractor": A person, firm, or corporation with whom the contract is made by the Owner.
(b) "Subcontractor": A person, firm, or corporation supplying labor and materials or only labor for work at the site of the project for, and under separate contract or agreement with, the Contractor.
(c) "Work on (at) the project": Work to be performed at the location of the project, including the transportation of materials and supplies to or from the location of the project by employees of the Contractor and any subcontractor.

3. Shop or Setting Drawings

The Contractor shall submit promptly to the Architect/Owner two copies of each shop or setting drawing prepared in accordance with the schedule predetermined as aforesaid. After the return thereof, the Contractor shall make such corrections to the drawings as have been indicated and shall furnish the Architect/Owner with two corrected copies.

4. Materials, Services, and Facilities

(a) It is understood that except as otherwise specifically stated in the Contract Documents, the Contractor shall provide and pay for all materials, labor, tools, equipment, water, light, power, transportation, superintendence, temporary construction of every nature, and all other services and facilities of every nature whatsoever necessary to execute, complete, and deliver the work within the specified time.
(b) Any work necessary to be performed after regular working hours, on Sundays or Legal Holidays, shall be performed without additional expense to the Owner.

5. Contractor's Title to Materials

No materials or supplies for the work shall be purchased by the Contractor or by any subcontractor subject to any chattel mortgage or under a conditional sale contract or other agreement by which an interest is retained by the seller. The Contractor warrants that he has good title to all materials and supplies used by him in the work, free from all liens, claims, or encumbrances.

6. "Or Equal" Clause

Whenever a material, article, or piece of equipment is identified on the plans or in the specifications by reference to manufacturers' or vendors' names, trade names, catalogue numbers, etc., it is intended merely to establish a standard;

and any material, article, or equipment of other manufacturers and vendors which will perform adequately the duties imposed by the general design will be considered equally acceptable provided the material, article, or equipment so proposed is, in the opinion of the Architect/Owner, of equal substance and function. It shall not be purchased or installed by the Contractor without the Architect/Owner's written approval.

7. Patents

(a) The Contractor shall hold and save the Owner and its officers, agents, servants, and employees harmless from liability of any nature or kind, including cost and expenses for, or on account of, any patented or unpatented invention, process, article, or appliance manufactured or used in the performance of the contract, including its use by the Owner, unless otherwise specifically stipulated in the Contract Documents.

(b) License or Royalty Fees: License and/or Royalty Fees for the use of a process which is authorized by the Owner of the project must be reasonable, and paid to the holder of the patent, or his authorized licensee, direct by the Owner and not by or through the Contractor.

(c) If the Contractor uses any design, device, or materials covered by letters, patent, or copyright, he shall provide for such use by suitable agreement with the Owner of such patented or copyrighted design, device, or material. It is mutually agreed and understood, that, without exception, the contract prices shall include all royalties or costs arising from the use of such design, device, or materials, in any way involved in the work. The Contractor and/or his Sureties shall indemnify and save harmless the Owner of the project from any and all claims for infringement by reason of the use of such patented or copyrighted design, device, or materials or any trademark or copyright in connection with work agreed to be performed under this contract, and shall indemnify the Owner for any cost, expense, or damage which it may be obliged to pay by reason of such infringement at any time during the prosecution of the work or after completion of the work.

8. Surveys, Permits, and Regulations

Unless otherwise expressly provided for in the Specifications, the Owner will furnish to the Contractor all surveys necessary for the execution of the work.

The Contractor shall procure and pay for all permits, licenses, and approvals necessary for the execution of his contract.

The Contractor shall comply with all laws, ordinances, rules, orders, and regulations relating to the performance of the work, the protection of adjacent property, and the maintenance of passageways, guard fences, or other protective facilities.

9. Contractor's Obligations

The Contractor shall and will, in good workmanlike manner, do and perform all work and furnish all supplies and materials, machinery, equipment, facilities, and means, except as herein otherwise expressly specified, necessary or proper to perform and complete all the work required by this contract, within the time herein specified, in accordance with the provisions of this contract and said specifications and in accordance with the plans and drawings covered by this contract, any and all supplemental plans and drawings, and in accordance with the directions of the Architect/Owner as given from time to time during the progress of the work. He shall furnish, erect, maintain, and remove such construction plant and such temporary works as may be required. The Contractor shall observe, comply with, and be subject to all terms, conditions, requirements, and limitations of the contract and specifications, and shall do, carry on, and complete the entire work to the satisfaction of the Architect/Owner.

10. Weather Conditions

In the event of temporary suspension of work, or during inclement weather, or whenever the Architect/Owner shall direct, the Contractor will, and will cause his subcontractors to protect carefully his and their work and materials against damage or injury from the weather. If, in the opinion of the Architect/Owner, any work or materials shall have been damaged or injured by reason of failure on the part of the Contractor or any of his subcontractors so to protect his work, such materials shall be removed and replaced at the expense of the Contractor.

11. Protection of Work and Property—Emergency

The Contractor shall at all times safely guard the Owner's property from injury or loss in connection with this contract. He shall at all times safely guard and protect his own work, and that of adjacent property, from damage. The Contractor shall replace or make good any such damage, loss, or injury, unless such be caused directly by errors contained in the contract or by the Owner, or his duly authorized representatives.

In case of an emergency which threatens loss or injury of property and/or safety of life, the Contractor will be allowed to act, without previous instructions from the Architect/Owner, in a diligent manner. He shall notify the Architect/Owner immediately thereafter. Any claim for compensation by the Contractor due to such extra work shall be promptly submitted to the Architect/Owner for approval.

Where the Contractor has not taken action but has notified the Architect/Owner of an emergency threatening injury to persons or damage to the work or any adjoining property, he shall act as instructed or authorized by the Architect/Owner.

The amount of reimbursement claimed by the Contractor on account of any emergency action shall be determined in the manner provided in Paragraph 14 of the General Conditions.

12. Reports, Records, and Data

The Contractor shall submit to the Owner such schedules of quantities and costs, progress schedules, payrolls, reports, estimates, records, and other data as the Owner may request concerning work performed or to be performed under this contract.

13. Superintendence by Contractor

At the site of the work the Contractor shall employ a construction superintendent or foreman who shall have full authority to act for the Contractor. It is understood that such representative shall be acceptable to the Architect/Owner and shall be one who can be continued in that capacity for the particular job involved unless he ceases to be on the Contractor's payroll.

14. Changes in Work

No changes in the work covered by the approved Contract Documents shall be made without having prior written approval of the Owner. Charges or credits for the work covered by the approved change shall be determined by one or more, or a combination, of the following methods:

(a) Unit bid prices previously approved.
(b) An agreed lump sum.
(c) The actual cost of:
    1. Labor, including foremen;
    2. Materials entering permanently into the work;
    3. The ownership or rental cost of construction plant and equipment during the time of use on the extra work;
    4. Power and consumable supplies for the operation of power equipment;
    5. Insurance;
    6. Social Security and old age and unemployment contributions.

To the cost under (c) there shall be added a fixed fee to be agreed upon but not to exceed fifteen percent (15%) of the actual cost of the work. The fee shall be compensation to cover the cost of supervision, overhead, bond, profit, and any other general expenses.

15. Extras

Without invalidating the contract, the Owner may order extra work or make changes by altering, adding to, or deducting from the work, the contract sum being adjusted accordingly, and the consent of the Surety being first obtained where necessary or desirable. All the work of the kind bid upon shall be paid for at the price stipulated in the proposal, and no claims for any extra work or materials shall be allowed unless the work is ordered in writing by the Owner or its Architect, acting officially for the Owner, and the price is stated in such order.

16. Time for Completion and Liquidated Damages

It is hereby understood and mutually agreed, by and between the Contractor and the Owner, that the date of beginning and the time for completion as specified in the contract of the work to be done hereunder are ESSENTIAL CONDITIONS of this contract; and it is further mutually understood and agreed that the work embraced in this contract shall be commenced on a date to be specified in the "Notice to Proceed."

The Contractor agrees that said work shall be prosecuted regularly, diligently, and uninterruptedly at such rate of progress as will insure full completion thereof within the time specified. It is expressly understood and agreed, by and between the Contractor and the Owner, that the time for the completion of the work described herein is a reasonable time for the completion of the same, taking into consideration the average climatic range and usual industrial conditions prevailing in this locality.

If the Contractor shall neglect, fail, or refuse to complete the work within the time herein specified, or any proper extension thereof granted by the Owner, then the Contractor does hereby agree, as a part consideration for the awarding of this contract, to pay to the Owner the amount specified in the contract, not as a penalty but as liquidated damages for such breach of contract as hereinafter set forth, for each and every calendar day that the Contractor shall be in default after the time stipulated in the contract for completing the work.

The said amount is fixed and agreed upon by and between the Contractor and the Owner because of the impracticability and extreme difficulty of fixing and ascertaining the actual damages the Owner would in such event sustain, and said amount is agreed to be the amount of damages which the Owner would sustain and said amount shall be retained from time to time by the Owner from current periodical estimates.

It is further agreed that time is of the essence of each and every portion of this contract and of the specifications wherein a definite and certain length of time is fixed for the performance of any act whatsoever; and where under the contract an additional time is allowed for the completion of any work, the new time limit fixed by such extension shall be of the essence of this contract. PROVIDED, That the Contractor shall not be charged with liquidated damages or any excess cost when the Owner determines that the Contractor is without fault and the Contractor's reasons for the time extension are acceptable to the Owner; Provided further, that the Contractor shall not be charged with liquidated damages or any excess cost when the delay in completion of the work is due:
(a) To unforeseeable cause beyond the control and without the fault or negligence of the Contractor, including, but not restricted to, acts of God, or of the public enemy, acts of the Owner, acts of another Contractor in the performance of a contract with the Owner, fires, floods, epidemics, quarantine restrictions, strikes, freight embargoes, and severe weather; and
(b) To any delays of subcontractors or suppliers occasioned by any of the causes specified in subsection (a) of this article:

Provided, further, that the Contractor shall, within ten (10) days from the beginning of such delay, unless the Owner shall grant a further period of time prior to the date of final settlement of the contract, notify the Owner, in writing, of the causes of the delay, who shall ascertain the facts and extent of the delay and notify the Contractor within a reasonable time of its decision in the matter.

17. Correction of Work

All work, all materials, whether incorporated in the work or not, all processes of manufacture, and all methods of construction shall be at all times and places subject to the inspection of the Architect/Owner who shall be the final judge of the quality and suitability of the work, materials, processes of manufacture, and methods of construction for the purposes for which they are used. Should they fail to meet his approval they shall be forthwith reconstructed, made good, replaced, and/or corrected, as the case may be, by the Contractor at his own expense. Rejected material shall immediately be removed from the site. If, in the opinion of the Architect/Owner, it is undesirable to replace any defective or damaged materials or to reconstruct or correct any portion of the work injured or not performed in accordance with the Contract Documents, the compensation to be paid to the Contractor hereunder shall be reduced by such amount as in the judgment of the Architect/Owner shall be equitable.

18. Subsurface Conditions Found Different

Should the Contractor encounter subsurface and/or latent conditions at the site materially differing from those shown on the plans or indicated in the specifications, he shall immediately give notice to the Architect/Owner of such conditions before they are disturbed. The Architect/Owner will thereupon promptly investigate the conditions, and if he finds that they materially differ from those shown on the plans or indicated in the specifications, he will at once make such changes in the plans and/or specifications as he may find necessary, any increase or decrease of cost resulting from such changes to be adjusted in the manner provided in Paragraph 14 of the General Conditions.

19. Claims for Extra Costs

No claim for extra work or cost shall be allowed unless the same was done in pursuance of a written order of the Architect/Owner approved by the Owner, as aforesaid, and the claim presented with the first estimate after the changed or extra work is done. When work is performed under the terms of subparagraph 14(c) of the General Conditions, the Contractor shall furnish satisfactory bills, payrolls, and vouchers covering all items of cost and when requested by the Owner, give the Owner access to accounts relating thereto.

20. Right of the Owner to Terminate Contract

In the event that any of the provisions of this contract are violated by the Contractor, or by any of his subcontractors, the Owner may serve written notice upon the Contractor and the Surety of its intention to terminate the contract, such notices to contain the reasons for such intention to terminate the contract, and unless within ten (10) days after the serving of such notice upon the Contractor, such violation or delay shall cease and satisfactory arrangement of correction be made, the contract shall, upon the expiration of said ten (10) days, cease and terminate. In the event of any such termination, the Owner shall immediately serve notice thereof upon the Surety and the Contractor, and the Surety shall have the right to take over and perform the contract; Provided, however, that if the Surety does not commence performance thereof within ten (10) days from the date of the mailing to such Surety of notice of termination, the Owner may take over the work and prosecute the same to completion by contract or by force account for the contract and at the expense of the Contractor, and the Contractor and his Surety shall be liable to the Owner for any excess cost occasioned the Owner thereby, and in such event the Owner may take possession of and utilize in completing the work, such materials, appliances, and plant as may be on the site of the work and necessary therefor.

21. Construction Schedule and Periodic Estimates

Immediately after execution and delivery of the contract, and before the first partial payment is made, the Contractor shall deliver to the Owner an estimated construction progress schedule in form satisfactory to the Owner, showing the proposed dates of commencement and completion of each of the various subdivisions of work required under the Contract Documents and the anticipated amount of each monthly payment that will become due the Contractor in accordance with the progress schedule. The Contractor shall also furnish on forms to be supplied by the Owner (a) a detailed estimate giving a complete breakdown of the contract price and (b) periodic itemized estimates of work done for the purpose of making partial payments thereon. The costs employed in making up any of these schedules will be used only for determining the basis of partial payments and will not be considered as fixing a basis for additions to or deductions from the contract price.

22. Payments to Contractor

(a) Not later than the 15th day of each calendar month the Owner shall make a progress payment to the Contractor on the basis of a duly certified and approved estimate of the work performed during the preceding calendar month under this contract, but to insure the proper performance of this contract, the Owner shall retain ten percent (10%) of the amount of each estimate until final completion and acceptance of all work covered by this contract; Provided, that the Contractor shall submit his estimate not later than the first day of the month; Provided, further, that the Owner at any time after fifty percent (50%) of the work has been completed, if it is found that satisfactory progress is being made, may make any of the remaining progress payments in full; Provided, further, that on completion and acceptance of each division of the contract, on which the price is stated separately in the contract, payment may be made in full, including retained percentages thereon, less authorized deductions.

(b) In preparing estimates, the material delivered on the site and preparatory work done may be taken into consideration.

(c) All material and work covered by partial payments made shall thereupon become the sole property of the Owner, but this provision shall not be construed as relieving the Contractor from the sole responsibility for the care and protection of materials and work upon which payments have been made or the restoration of any damaged work, or as a waiver of the right of the Owner to require the fulfillment of all of the terms of the contract.

(d) Owner's Right to Withhold Certain Amounts and Make Application Thereof: The Contractor agrees that he will indemnify and save the Owner harmless from all claims growing out of the lawful demands of subcontractors, laborers, workmen, mechanics, materialmen, and furnishers of machinery and parts thereof, equipment, power tools, and all supplies, including commissary, incurred in the furtherance of the performance of this contract. The Contractor shall, at the Owner's request, furnish satisfactory evidence that all obligations of the nature hereinabove designated have been paid, discharged, or waived. If the Contractor fails so to do, then the Owner may, after having served written notice on the said Contractor, either pay unpaid bills, of which the Owner has written notice, direct, or withhold from the Contractor's unpaid compensation a sum of money deemed reasonably sufficient to pay any and all such lawful claims until satisfactory evidence is furnished that all liabilities have been fully discharged, whereupon payment to the Contractor shall be resumed, in accordance with the terms of this contract, but in no event shall the provisions of this sentence be construed to impose any obligations upon the Owner to either the Contractor or his Surety. In paying any unpaid bills of the Contractor, the Owner shall be deemed the agent of the Contractor, and any payment so made by the Owner, shall be considered as a payment made under the contract by the Owner to the Contractor and the Owner shall not be liable to the Contractor for any such payment made in good faith.

23. Acceptance of Final Payment Constitutes Release

The acceptance by the Contractor of final payment shall be and shall operate as a release to the Owner of all claims and all liability to the Contractor for all things done or furnished in connection with this work and for every act and neglect of the Owner and others relating to or arising out of this work. No payment, however, final or otherwise, shall operate to release the Contractor or his Sureties from any obligations under this contract or the Performance and Payment Bond.

24. Payments by Contractor

The Contractor shall pay (a) for all transportation and utility services not later than the 20th day of the calendar month following that in which services are rendered, (b) for all materials, tools, and other expendable equipment to the extent of ninety percent (90%) of the cost thereof, not later than the 20th day of the calendar month following that in which such materials, tools, and equipment are delivered at the site of the project, and the balance of the cost thereof not later than the 30th day of the month following the completion of that part of the work in or on which such materials, tools, and equipment are incorporated or used, and (c) to each of his subcontractors, not later than the 5th day following each payment to the Contractor, the respective amounts allowed the Contractor on account of the work performed by his subcontractors to the extent of each subcontractor's interest therein.

25. Insurance

The Contractor shall not commence work under this contract until he has obtained all the insurance required under this paragraph and such insurance has been approved by the Owner, nor shall the Contractor allow any subcontractor to commence work on his subcontract until the insurance required of the subcontractor has been so obtained and approved.

(a) Compensation Insurance: The Contractor shall procure and shall maintain during the life of this contract Workmen's Compensation Insurance as required by applicable State or territorial law for all of his employees to be engaged in work at the site of the project under this contract and, in case of any such work sublet, the Contractor shall require the subcontractor similarly to provide Workmen's Compensation Insurance for all of the latter's employees to be engaged in such work unless such employees are covered by the protection afforded by the Contractor's Workmen's Compensation Insurance. In case any class of employees engaged in hazardous work on the project under this contract is not protected under the Workmen's Compensation Statute, the Contractor shall provide and shall cause each subcontractor to provide adequate employer's liability insurance for the protection of such of his employees as are not otherwise protected.

(b) Contractor's Public Liability and Property Damage Insurance and Vehicle Liability Insurance: The Contractor shall procure and shall maintain during the life of this contract Contractor's Public Liability Insurance, Contractor's Property Damage Insurance, and Vehicle Liability Insurance.

(c) Subcontractor's Public Liability and Property Damage Insurance and Vehicle Liability Insurance: The Contractor shall either (1) require each of his subcontractors to procure and to maintain during the life of his subcontract, Subcontractor's Public Liability and Property Damage Insurance and Vehicle Liability Insurance, or (2) insure the activities of his subcontractors in his policy, specified in subparagraph (b) hereof.

(d) Scope of Insurance and Special Hazards: The insurance required under subparagraphs (b) and (c) hereof shall provide adequate protection for the Contractor and his subcontractors, respectively, against damage claims which may arise from operations under this contract, whether such operations be by the insured or by anyone directly or indirectly employed by him and, also, against any of the special hazards which may be encountered in the performance of this contract.

(e) Builder's Risk Insurance (Fire and Extended Coverage): Until the project is completed and accepted by the Owner, the Owner, or Contractor is required to maintain Builder's Risk Insurance (fire and extended coverage) on a one hundred percent (100%) completed value basis on the insurable portion of the project for the benefit of the Owner, the Contractor, and subcontractors as their interest may appear. The Contractor shall not include any costs for Builder's Risk Insurance (fire and extended coverage) premiums during construction unless the Contractor is required to provide such insurance; however, this provision shall not release the Contractor from his obligation to complete, according to plans and specifications, the project covered by the contract, and the Contractor and his surety shall be obligated to full performance of the Contractor's undertaking.

(f) Proof of Carriage of Insurance: The Contractor shall furnish the Owner with certificates showing the type, amount, class of operations covered, effective dates, and dates of expiration of policies. Such certificates shall also contain substantially the following statement: "The insurance covered by this certificate will not be cancelled or materially altered, except after ten (10) days written notice has been received by the Owner."

26. Contract Security

The Contractor shall furnish a performance bond in an amount at least equal to one hundred percent (100%) of the contract prices as security for the faithful performance of this contract and also a payment bond in an amount not less than fifty percent (50%) of the contract price or in a penal sum not less than that prescribed by State, territorial or local law, as security for the payment of all persons performing labor on the project under this contract and furnishing materials in connection with this contract. The performance bond and the payment bond may be in one or in separate instruments in accordance with local law.

27. Additional or Substitute Bond

If at any time the Owner for justifiable cause shall be or become dissatisfied with any surety or sureties then upon the Performance or Payment Bonds, the Contractor shall within five (5) days after notice from the Owner so to do, substitute an acceptable bond (or bonds) in such form and sum and signed by such other surety or sureties as may be satisfactory to the Owner. The premiums on such bond shall be paid by the Contractor. No further payments shall be deemed due nor shall be made until the new surety or sureties shall have furnished such as acceptable bond to the Owner.

28. Assignments

The Contractor shall not assign the whole or any part of this contract or any moneys due or to become due hereunder without written consent of the Owner. In case the Contractor assigns all or any part of any moneys due or to become due under this contract, the instrument of assignment shall contain a clause substantially to the effect that it is agreed that the right of the assignee in and to any moneys due or to become due to the Contractor shall be subject to prior claims of all persons, firms, and corporations for services rendered or materials supplied for the performance of the work called for in this contract.

29. Mutual Responsibility of Contractors

If, through acts of neglect on the part of the Contractor, any other Contractor or any subcontractor shall suffer loss of damage on the work, the Contractor agrees to settle with such other Contractor or subcontractor by agreement or arbitration if such other Contractor or subcontractors will so settle. If such other Contractor or subcontractor shall assert any claim against the Owner on account of any damage alleged to have been sustained, the Owner shall notify the Contractor, who shall indemnify and save harmless the Owner against any such claim.

30. Separate Contracts

The Contractor shall coordinate his operations with those of other Contractors. Cooperation will be required in the arrangement for the storage of materials and in the detailed execution of the work. The Contractor, including his subcontractors, shall keep informed of the progress and the detail work of other work of other Contractors and shall notify the Architect/Owner immediately of lack of progress or defective workmanship on the part of other Contractors. Failure of a Contractor to keep informed of the work progressing on the site and failure to give notice of lack of progress or defective workmanship by others shall be construed as acceptance by him of the status of the work as being satisfactory for proper coordination with his own work.

31. Subcontracting

(a) The Contractor may utilize the services of specialty subcontractors on those parts of the work which, under normal contracting practices, are performed by specialty subcontractors.

(b) The Contractor shall not award any work to any subcontractor without prior written approval of the Owner, which approval will not be given until the Contractor submits to the Owner a written statement concerning the proposed award to the subcontractor, which statement shall contain such information as the Owner may require.

(c) The Contractor shall be as fully responsible to the Owner for the acts and omissions of his subcontractors, and of persons either directly or indirectly employed by them, as he is for the acts and omissions of persons directly employed by him.

(d) The Contractor shall cause appropriate provisions to be inserted in all subcontracts relative to the work to bind subcontractors to the Contractor by the terms of the General Conditions and other contract documents insofar as applicable to the work of subcontractors and to give the Contractor the same power as regards terminating any subcontract that the Owner may exercise over the Contractor under any provisions of the Contract Documents.

(e) Nothing contained in this contract shall create any contractual relation between any subcontractor and the Owner.

32. Architect/Owner's Authority

The Architect/Owner shall give all orders and directions contemplated under this contract and specifications relative to the execution of the work. The Architect/Owner shall determine the amount, quality, acceptability, and fitness of the several kinds of work and materials which are to be paid for under this contract and shall decide all questions which may arise in relation to said work and the construction thereof. The Architect/Owner's estimates and decisions shall be final and conclusive, except as herein otherwise expressly provided. In case any question shall arise between the parties hereto relative to said contract or specifications, the determination or decision of the Architect/Owner shall be a condition precedent to the right of the Contractor to receive any money or payment for work under this contract affected in any manner or to any extent by such question.

The Architect/Owner shall decide the meaning and intent of any portion of the specifications and of any plans or drawings where the same may be found obscure or be in dispute. Any differences or conflicts in regard to their work which may arise between the Contractor under this contract and other Contractors performing work for the Owner shall be adjusted and determined by the Architect/Owner.

33. Stated Allowances

The Contractor shall include in his proposal the cash allowances stated in the Supplemental General Conditions. The Contractor shall purchase the "Allowed Materials" as directed by the Owner on the basis of the lowest and best bid of at least three competitive bids. If the actual price for purchasing the "Allowed Materials" is more or less than the "Cash Allowance," the contract price shall be adjusted accordingly. The adjustment in contract price shall be made on the basis of the purchase price without additional charges for overhead, profit, insurance, or any other incidental expenses. The cost of installation of the "Allowed Materials" shall be included in the applicable sections of the Contract Specifications covering this work.

34. Use of Premises and Removal of Debris

The Contractor expressly undertakes at his own expense:
(a) to take every precaution against injuries to persons or damage to property;
(b) to store his apparatus, materials, supplies, and equipment in such orderly fashion at the site of the work as will not unduly interfere with the progress of his work or the work of any other Contractors;
(c) to place upon the work or any part thereof only such loads as are consistent with the safety of that portion of the work;
(d) to clean up frequently all refuse, rubbish, scrap materials, and debris caused by his operations, to the end that at all times the site of the work shall present a neat, orderly, and workmanlike appearance;
(e) before final payment to remove all surplus material, false-work, temporary structures, including foundations thereof, plant of any description and debris of every nature resulting from his operations, and to put the site in a neat, orderly condition;
(f) to effect all cutting, fitting or patching of his work required to make the same to conform to the plans and specifications and, except with the consent of the Architect/Owner, not to cut or otherwise alter the work of any other Contractor.

35. Quantities of Estimate

Wherever the estimated quantities of work to be done and materials to be furnished under this contract are shown in any of the documents including the proposal, they are given for use in comparing bids and the right is especially reserved except as herein otherwise specifically limited, to increase or diminish them as may be deemed reasonably necessary or desirable by the Owner to complete the work contemplated by this contract, and such increase or diminution shall in no way vitiate this contract, nor shall any such increase or diminution give cause for claims or liability for damages.

36. Lands and Rights-of-Way

Prior to the start of construction, the Owner shall obtain all lands and rights-of-way necessary for the carrying out and completion of work to be performed under this contract.

37. General Guaranty

Neither the final certificate of payment nor any provision in the Contract Documents nor partial or entire occupancy of the premises by the Owner shall constitute an acceptance of work not done in accordance with the Contract Documents or relieve the Contractor of liability in respect to any express warranties or responsibility for faulty materials or workmanship. The Contractor shall remedy any defects in the work and pay for any damage to other work resulting therefrom, which shall appear within a period of one year from the date of final acceptance of the work unless a longer period is specified. The Owner will give notice of observed defects with reasonable promptness.

38. Conflicting Conditions

Any provisions in any of the Contract Documents which may be in conflict or inconsistent with any of the paragraphs in these General Conditions shall be void to the extent of such conflict or inconsistency.

39. Notice and Service Thereof

Any notice to any Contractor from the Owner relative to any part of this contract shall be in writing and considered delivered and the service thereof completed, when said notice is posted, by certified or registered mail, to the said Contractor at his last given address, or delivered in person to said Contractor or his authorized representative on the work.

40. Protection of Lives and Health

In order to protect the lives and health of his employees under the contract, the Contractor shall comply with all pertinent provisions of the "Manual of Accident Prevention in Construction" issued by the Associated General Contractors of America, Inc., and shall maintain an accurate record of all cases of death, occupational disease, and injury requiring medical attention or causing loss of time from work, arising out of and in the course of employment on work under the contract. He alone shall be responsible for the safety, efficiency, and adequacy of his plant, appliances, and methods, and for any damage which may result from their failure or their improper construction, maintenance, or operation.

41. Suspension of Work

Should the owner be prevented or enjoined from proceeding with work either before or after the start of construction by reason of any litigation or other reason beyond the control of the Owner, the Contractor shall not be entitled to make or assert claim for damage by reason of said delay.

SPECIAL CONDITIONS
AND CONTRACT FORMS

1. ENUMERATION OF PLANS, SPECIFICATIONS, AND ADDENDA

Following are the Plans, Specifications, and Addenda which form a part of this contract, as set forth in Paragraph 1 of the General Conditions, "Contract and Contract Documents":

DRAWINGS

General Construction: Nos. _____

Heating and Ventilating: " _____

Plumbing: " _____

Electrical: " _____

_____   " _____

_____   " _____

SPECIFICATIONS:

General Construction: Page ____ to ____, incl.

Heating and Ventilating: " ____ to ____, incl.

Plumbing: " ____ to ____, incl.

Electrical: " ____ to ____, incl.

_____   " ____ to ____, incl.

_____   " ____ to ____, incl.

ADDENDA:

No. _____ Date _____   No. _____ Date _____

No. _____ Date _____   No. _____ Date _____

2. STATED ALLOWANCES

Pursuant to Paragraph 36 of the General Conditions, the contractor shall include the following cash allowances in his proposal:

(a) For _____ (Page _____ of Specifications) $ _____

(b) For _____ (Page _____ of Specifications) $ _____

(c) For _____ (Page _____ of Specifications) $ _____

(d) For _____ (Page _____ of Specifications) $ _____

(e) For _____ (Page _____ of Specifications) $ _____

(f) For _____ (Page _____ of Specifications) $ _____

3. SPECIAL HAZARDS

The Contractor's and his Subcontractor's Public Liability and Property Damage Insurance shall provide adequate protection against the following special hazards:

4. CONTRACTOR'S AND SUBCONTRACTOR'S PUBLIC LIABILITY, VEHICLE LIABILITY, AND PROPERTY DAMAGE INSURANCE

As required under Paragraph 28 of the General Conditions, the Contractor's Public Liability Insurance and Vehicle Liability Insurance shall be in an amount not less than $_____ for injuries, including accidental death, to any one person, and subject to the same limit for each person, in an amount not less than $_____ on account of one accident, and Contractor's Property Damage Insurance in an amount not less than $_____ .

The Contractor shall either (1) require each of his subcontractors to procure and to maintain during the life of his subcontract, Subcontractor's Public Liability and Property Damage of the type and in the same amounts as specified in the preceding paragraph, or (2) insure the activities of his subcontractors in his own policy.

5. BUILDER'S RISK INSURANCE

As provided in the General Conditions, Paragraph 28(e), the Contractor will/will not* maintain Builder's Risk Insurance (fire and extended coverage) on a 100 percent completed value basis on the insurable portions of the project for the benefit of the Owner, the Contractor, and all subcontractors, as their interests may appear.

*Strike out one.

CONTRACT

THIS AGREEMENT, made this _____ day of _____, 19_____, by and between

_____, herein called "Owner."

STRIKE OUT   (a corporation) (a partnership)
INAPPLICABLE   (an individual doing business as) _____
TERMS

of _____, County of _____, and State of _____,
hereinafter called "Contractor."

WITNESSETH: That for and in consideration of the payments and agreements hereinafter mentioned, to be made and performed by the OWNER, the CONTRACTOR hereby agrees with the OWNER to commence and complete the construction described as follows:

Hereinafter called the project, for the sum of _____ Dollars ($_____) and all extra work in connection therewith, under the terms as stated in the General and Special Conditions of the Contract; and at his (its or their) own proper cost and expense to furnish all the materials, supplies, machinery, equipment, tools, superintendence, labor, insurance, and other accessories and services necessary to complete the said project in accordance with the conditions and prices stated in the Proposal, the General Conditions, Supplemental General Conditions and Special Conditions of the Contract, the plans, which include all maps, plans, blueprints, and other drawings and printed or written explanatory matter thereof, the specifications and contract documents therefor as prepared by _____, herein entitled the Architect and as enumerated in Paragraph 1 of the Supplemental General Conditions, all of which are made a part hereof and collectively evidence and constitute the contract.

The Contractor hereby agrees to commence work under this contract on or before a date to be specified in a written "Notice to Proceed" of the Owner and to fully complete the project within _____ consecutive calendar days thereafter.

The OWNER agrees to pay the CONTRACTOR in current funds for the performance of the contract, subject to additions and deductions, as provided in the General Conditions of the Contract, and to make payments on account thereof as provided in Paragraph 22 "Payments to Contractor," of the General Conditions.

IN WITNESS WHEREOF, the parties to these presents have executed this contract in three (3) counterparts, each of which shall be deemed an original, in the year and day first above mentioned.

_____
(Owner)

by _____

_____
(Title)

_____
(Contractor)

by _____

_____
(Title)

_____
(Address)

RELEASE OF LIENS

To:

Contract for:

Contract Date:

Project Address:

State of:

County of:

The undersigned hereby certifies that to the best of his knowledge, information, and belief, except as listed below, the Releases or Waivers of Lien attached hereto include the Contractor, all Subcontractors, all suppliers of materials and equipment, and all performers of work, labor, or services who have or may have liens against any property of the Owner arising in any manner whatsoever out of the performance of the contract referenced above.

Exceptions:

_____

CONTRACTOR

Business Address:

Attachments:

1.   Contractors Release or Waiver of Liens.

2.   Releases or Waivers of Liens from major subcontractors and materials suppliers, if requested by owner.

Subscribed and sworn to before me this_____day of _____, 19___.

Notary Public

My Commission Expires:

TECHNICAL SPECIFICATIONS

Division 1
General Requirements

SECTION 1A—DESCRIPTION OF WORK

1A—1 WORK TO BE DONE

The work to be done under the Contract and in accordance with the Contract Documents consists of performing, installing, furnishing, and supplying all materials, equipment, labor, insurance, incidentals, and everything else necessary for a single family dwelling unit as shown on the working drawings and specified herein, and the carrying out of all duties and obligations imposed upon the contractors by the Contract documents.

Nothing herein shall prohibit the owner from subcontracting specified trades to other contractors. In this case, however, the owner, or his authorized representative, is responsible for coordination of the work of the various trades.

1A—2 ARBITRATION

All contracts with contractors or subcontractors for this project are bound to compulsory arbitration as follows:

> Any controversy or claim arising out of or relating to this contract, or the breach thereof, shall be settled by arbitration in accordance with the Construction Industry Arbitration Rules of the American Arbitration Association, and judgement upon the award rendered by the Arbitrator(s) may be entered in any court having jurisdiction thereof.

Details on arbitration proceedings may be obtained from:

American Arbitration Assoc.
140 W. 51st. St.
New York, NY 10020

1A—3 WORK NOT INCLUDED

The following items are not included in the work covered by this contract.

(a) All items marked N.I.C. (Not in Contract)
(b) All landscaping and movable equipment.

Division 2
Site Work

SECTION 2A—EXCAVATING, BACKFILLING,
AND GRADING

2A—1   GENERAL REQUIREMENTS

Applicable provisions of the Agreement and of Division 1, General Requirements of the specifications govern the work of this section.

Definition: The term *building area* as used throughout this section of the
specifications shall mean and refer to the area within a line *5 feet* outside of
and parallel to the exterior periphery of the building.

2A—2   WORK INCLUDED

The work of this section includes all excavating, backfilling, filling, and grading work and all related work, complete, as indicated on the drawings or
specified herein, or both, in general including but not limited to the items
listed below:

1. Clearing of all trees, shrubs, and other plant material not
    indicated to remain from within the Contract Limit Lines.
2. Excavating for all footings, trenches, and all other parts of
    the building and building appurtenances below grade.
3. Shoring and bracing as necessary for the safe and proper
    execution of the work of this section.
4. Excavating for trenches and pits and for all services and
    utilities within the building area.
5. Providing and installing perimeter drains where and as indi-
    cated on the drawings and to extent hereinafter specified.
6. Filling and backfilling against footings, pipe trenches, and
    the like.
7. Rough grading for all areas within the Contract Limit Lines.

2A—3   MATERIALS

"Backfill": Any approved material removed from excavations that is free from
wood, rocks, roots, rubbish, decaying matter, and other objectionable matter;
which contains not more than five percent (5%) by volume of stones larger
than 5 inches in diameter. Obtain all additional fill material from one source of
own choice but approved by the Architect.

2A—4   PERMITS

Obtain all permits and licenses required and/or necessary for the proper and
legal execution of the work of this section.

2A—5   DEFINITIONS

"Earth": All material, including hard pan, loose rocks, and boulders that can be broken up or removed by a 2-cubic-yard power shovel and similar materials that can be loosened and removed by hand pick and shovel.

"Soft rock": Rock of such formations that it can be loosened by hand pick and shovel without the use of drilling and explosives. For the purposes of the contract, "soft rock" shall be classed with and synonymous with "earth".

"Rock": Solid ledge rock, loose rocks, and boulders of a size that precludes their being broken up and removed with a 2-cubic-yard power shovel without drilling and blasting.

"Trench" excavation means: Excavations for pipe tunnels and trenches, sewer trenches, and similar excavations below grade.

"Pit" excavation means: Excavations for columns of pier footings.

"Open cut," "mass," or "general excavating" means: All excavations other than trench or pit excavations.

2A—6   COOPERATION

Cooperate with all other trades supplying materials or performing work in contact with the work of this trade and with all other trades whose work is affected by or dependent upon the work of this section.

2A—7   CLEARING AND STRIPPING TOPSOIL

Remove all trees, shrubs, and other plant material not indicated to remain from the area within the Contract Limit Lines including from the building area and from all portions of the site indicated on the drawings. Fell trees to be removed in a manner to prevent injury to trees, shrubs, and other property, if any, which is to remain in the finished work. Remove all stumps, roots, and the like completely. Remove all debris, plant materials, including trees and stumps, which result from clearing operations.

2A—8   STAKING OUT THE WORK

Prior to starting the work of this section, stake out the proposed locations of the buildings as indicated on the drawings. Mark off the boundaries and configurations of such items with stakes and tapes to clearly indicate their locations in the finished work. Stake out the perimeter of the new building in the same way. Engage and pay for the services of a licensed surveyor to lay out the major column locations and to establish all lines, grades, datums, and levels required in connection with the work. Require the Architect to inspect all layouts and do not start work until layouts have been inspected and approved by him.

2A—9   EXCAVATING

Remove all materials of every kind, nature, and description encountered on excavating to the dimensions, depth, lines, and levels indicated on the drawings plus sufficient space as necessary for the installation and/or erection of forms, shoring, bracing, sheet piling, porous fill, underpinning, and the inspection of work. Trim all excavations as closely as possible to the indicated lines and trim all excavation bottoms to the required lines and grades. No payment will be made for excavations carried beyond or below the indicated lines and grades unless such additional excavating is ordered in writing by the Architect.

Excavate to make all footings bear on level undisturbed soil. Excavate for pipe trenches as indicated on drawings.

When mass or unauthorized excavating is performed beyond indicated levels, lines, and/or grades, fill in without extra cost to Owner using a concrete fill of the same strength and proportions as specified for concrete foundations. Do not place any concrete until all bearing surfaces have been inspected.

2A—10   ROCK EXCAVATING

When and if rock is encountered in excavating operations, completely uncover it and notify the Architect.

Do not remove rock until record and certification of its extent have been approved by the Architect; rock removed without such record and certification will not be paid for.

Include in bid proposal the cost to excavate rock. Payments will be made for quantities of rock actually excavated at the additive unit price included in the bid, provided that it is made a part of the Contract, and irrespective of the means used to excavate the rock, whether by drilling, blasting, or other approved means.

Channel rock as necessary to form trenches and chases for pipe lines. Allow 6 inches in depth below bottom of pipes for bells of piping. Do all necessary boring of rock for the passage of piping.

If rock is encountered and if blasting is required, employ only persons skilled in such work. Do all drilling and handle, store, and use all explosives and detonators in accordance with the rules and regulations of the authorities having jurisdiction. Cover all blasts and take precautions to protect and insure the safety of persons and property. Assume full and sole responsibility for any and all damage or injury, or both, to all persons and property. Replace, repair, and/or restore all damaged property, pay all costs in connection therewith, and do so with no extra cost to the Owner. Examine bottoms of foundations, and remove all loose and shaken rock; avoid shattering and removal of rock beyond authorized lines and grades; roughly level or shelf bottoms as necessary; remove all materials until solid bearing is reached.

2A—11 BACKFILLING, FILLING, AND GRADING

Backfill all excavated areas promptly as possible and as fast as the work permits but not before the concrete work has attained its full strength. Material excavated from the site may be used as fill material provided that it meets the requirements specified. Do not use materials containing wood, rocks, rubbish, debris for fill. Begin filling in the lower sections of the areas first. Fill in layers as hereinafter specified. Make the surface of each layer approximately horizontal but provide with sufficient longitudinal or transverse slopes to provide for run-off of surface water from every point. In the event that excavated materials are unsuitable or insufficient to provide all of the backfill and grading required, provide and place additional backfill from approved source without extra cost to the Owner.

Do not place backfill which will cover or otherwise conceal other work until all such other work has been inspected and approved by the Architect.

Do all filling, backfilling, and grading as necessary to obtain the rough grades indicated on and/or required by the drawings. Do all rough grading within the Contract Limit Lines as required and/or necessary to produce the indicated rough grades. Do not complete grading and/or filling operations until all service and utility lines required to be installed below grade have been installed, completed, tested, inspected, and approved.

2A—12 DISPOSALS

Remove all excavated materials which are unsuitable for fill and which are in excess of that which is required for grading and filling operations and all debris from clearing operations from building site and store where directed for disposal by Owner.

Division 3
Foundations

SECTION 3A—PRESSURE-TREATED POST FOUNDATIONS

3A—1 GENERAL REQUIREMENTS

Applicable provisions of the Agreement and of Division 1—General Requirements of the specifications govern the work of this section.

3A—2 WORK INCLUDED

Furnish and install a direct-embedment, post-type foundation constructed of pressure-treated members conforming to specifications of the American Wood Preservers Institute (AWPA), 1651 Old Meadow Rd., McLean, VA 22101.

3A—3 MATERIALS

Poles for direct embedment shall be #2 pine, 1,400 psi minimum allowable compressive strength conforming to AWPA C23 and shall be pressure-treated with Penta-type B or D, conforming to AWPA LP4. Field cuts and holes shall be treated in accordance with AWPA M4.

Members for horizontal girts between poles at grade level shall conform to AWPA LP2 or LP4.

Foundation insulation shall be foil-faced rigid urethane insulation board of thickness as shown on working drawings.

Insulation board to be protected by ¼″ cement-asbestos board, Johns-Manville "Transite" or approved equal.

3A—4 INSTALLATION

Poles to be installed in strict accordance with AWPA printed directions. In areas of poor soil bearing, concrete bearing pads are required. Posts may be spliced to nontreated posts if desired. Follow splice detail on drawings. Splice to be a minimum of 18″ above grade.

Division 3
Foundations

SECTION 3B—POURED CONCRETE FOUNDATIONS

3B—1 GENERAL REQUIREMENTS

Applicable provisions of the Agreement and of Division 1—General Requirements of the specifications govern the work of this section.

3B—2 WORK INCLUDED

Furnish all labor, material, formwork, reinforcement steel, and related inserts for concrete foundations and slabs as shown on the drawings and specified herein.

3B—3 MATERIALS

All materials to be clean; free from oils, greases, and foreign matter, and stored to prevent damage or moisture penetration.

Cement to be a standard brand of Portland cement meeting latest ASTM standards.

Water to be clean and potable.

Fine aggregate shall be sand.

Reinforcing steel to be as indicated on drawings.

3B—4 CONCRETE

All concrete to be 3,000 psi, Class C at 28 days. Slump 2 to 4 inches.

3B—5 PROTECTION

All concrete to be protected from freezing or rapid drying. Auxiliary heat to be provided in subfreezing weather. Concrete to be covered and kept wet for three days in hot, dry weather.

3B—6 FINISHES

Exposed wall surfaces to be steel-troweled smooth. Finished concrete floor slabs to be finished by power trowel.

Division 3
Foundations

SECTION 3C—CONCRETE BLOCK FOUNDATIONS

3C—1 GENERAL REQUIREMENTS

Applicable provisions of the Agreement and of Division 1—General Requirements of the specifications govern the work of this section.

3C—2 WORK INCLUDED

Furnish and install all concrete footings, concrete block foundation walls, and related reinforcements and anchorages as shown on the drawings and specified herein.

3C—3 MATERIALS

Concrete for footings to be 2,500 psi, Class C at 28 days. Slump 1 to 3 inches.

Block to be standard lightweight aggregate, 3-core-type, of standard modular dimensions.

Horizontal reinforcement to be trussed-type wire reinforcement, inserted in mortar joints every other course.

Vertical reinforcement to be #4 bars inserted into cores of block at 12-foot centers. Vertical reinforcement is only required if basement is constructed.

3C—4 ENGINEERING

In areas of seismic activity, unstable soils, or other unusual conditions, a licensed professional engineer shall be engaged to review foundation design.

3C—5 LAYING BLOCK

Block to be laid to lines set accurately to foundations. Top of foundation wall to be level within $\frac{1}{2}''$ $\mp$. Install anchor bolts as shown on foundation plan. TECO Able Anchors are acceptable in lieu of anchor bolts if installed at the same spacing.

Division 4
Framing

SECTION 4A—POST AND BEAM FRAMING

4A—1 GENERAL REQUIREMENTS

Applicable provisions of the Agreement and of Division 1—General Requirements of the specifications govern the work of this section.

4A—2 MATERIALS

Exposed structural members to be No. 1 and better pine. Material to be selected for exposed finish. No blueing, no mud or exposure to sunlight is allowed. Care shall be used in handling to prevent damage. Materials to be stored so that they are protected from the weather; sticking to be placed between boards while they are stored.

Where standard framing lumber is used, it shall be Standard Grade Douglas fir, spruce, or hemlock with a minimum fiber stress of 1,400 psi, well seasoned, square, sound, and free from damaging knots and shakes. If the material is to be used in an exposed position, members shall be selected for appearance.

Exposed decking to be select spruce, 2X6 tongue and groove with V-jointed edges on bottom face. Decking to be freshly milled and used immediately.

Plywood sheathing to be Standard grade with intermediate glue.

4A—3 INSTALLATION

Exterior beams shall be framed so as to permit continuous installation of insulation. Solid beams not permitted for perimeter except in temperate climates. Plywood sheathing or steel corner braces to be used at all corners. All beam connections to be mortised, overlapped, or strapped together, as shown on drawings.

Exposed beams for floor structure can be either solid roughsawn timbers or laminated from standard framing members as shown on details. Blind nail decking with 16d cement-coated sinkers.

4A—4 PROTECTION

All exposed finish materials to be protected with one coat of boiled linseed oil before installation and exposure to weather. All ferrous metals to be kept away from wood to prevent staining. Where decking is to be painted or stained a contrasting color, masking shall be installed on bearing edge of beams before decking is installed.

Division 5
Metals

SECTION 5A—FLASHINGS

5A—1 GENERAL REQUIREMENTS

Applicable provisions of the Agreement and of Division 1—General Requirements of the specifications govern the work of this section.

5A—2 QUALIFICATIONS

Lead-coated steel flashing material to be as manufactured by Follansbee Steel Corp., Follansbee, WV 26037. Material to be IC (30-gauge) steel with 40-lb. lead coating. Material to be supplied in 6″-wide rolls or as necessary.

5A—3 INSTALLATION

Flashings to be installed at all points in the structure where projections or meetings of dissimilar materials require them. See drawings for details. Examples are projecting heads of windows and doors, capping for foundation insulation, crickets behind chimneys, etc. All flashings to be installed so that one edge is free to move. Only the concealed edge of flashings is to be nailed.

5A—4 PAINTING

All terne flashings to be painted before installation with Tin-O-Lin red iron oxide paint as distributed by Calbar Inc., 2626 N. Martha St., Philadelphia, PA 19125. Synthetic paints by other manufacturers are not acceptable. Paint must be applied by brush.

Division 5
Metals

SECTION 5B—TERNE ROOFS

5B—1 GENERAL REQUIREMENTS

Applicable provisions of the Agreement and of Division 1—General Requirements of the specifications govern the work of this section.

5B—2 QUALIFICATIONS

Lead-coated steel roofing material to be as manufactured by Follansbee Steel
Corp., Follansbee, WV 26037. Material to be IC (28-gauge) with 40-lb. lead
coating. Material to be supplied in 50' rolls, 24" or 28" wide.

5B—3 INSTALLATION

Standing-seam pans to be shop-formed on a standard metal brake in accordance with standard sheet metal practices. Edges to be formed over standard
galvanized roof edge. Use venting cap at ridge as shown on details. Pans to
be anchored with concealed clips spaced a maximum of 24" o.c.

Diamond-pattern metal roof pans may be hand-formed from square sheets.
Pans to be anchored with concealed clips in similar fashion to standing-seam.
Minimum roof slope 6/12.

5B—4 PAINTING

All terne to be painted before installation with Tin-O-Lin red iron oxide paint.
Synthetic paint by other manufacturers invalidates guarantee. Paint to be ordered from Calbar Inc., 2626 N. Martha St., Philadelphia, PA 19125. Order Tin-
O-Lin in red primer. Red primer may be used as finish coat or top-coated with
colored finish coat. Two brushed coats are required.

5B—5 GUARANTEE

All 40-lb. terne roofing to be guaranteed for twenty (20) years from date of
sale, provided material is painted as described above.

Division 6
Carpentry

SECTION 6A—WOOD SIDINGS

6A—1 GENERAL REQUIREMENTS

Applicable provisions of the Agreement and of Division 1—General Requirements of the specifications govern the work of this section.

6A—2 MATERIALS

Siding for board-on-board and board-and-batten patterns to be roughsawn No. 2 pine in widths as shown on drawings.

Siding for planed tongue-and-groove pattern to be 1X6 or 1X8 V-jointed cedar.

All nails to be noncorrosive; hot-dipped galvanized or aluminum. Do not use aluminum nails with cedar siding.

6A—3 INSTALLATION

Board-on-board pattern to have all windows, doors, and top and bottom perimeters cased before starting siding installation. All sidings to be double face-nailed. Board-on-board and board-and-batten patterns to be nailed so that sidings boards "float," i.e., each board is nailed separately to permit expansion and contraction and prevent splitting.

6A—4 WORK OF OTHER SECTIONS

Wherever possible, sidings shall be finished both sides before installation. See Section 7A.

Caulking to be applied between joints as installation progresses rather than surface-applied later. See Section 7C.

Division 6
Carpentry

SECTION 6B—WOOD SHINGLES

6B—1 GENERAL REQUIREMENTS

Applicable provisions of the Agreement and of Division 1—General Requirements of the specifications govern the work of this section.

6B—2 MATERIALS

Cedar shingles for sidewalls shall be No. 2 Red Label 18 Perfections, rebutted and rejointed for tight fit.

Nails shall be 4d hot-dipped galvanized or stainless steel.

6B—3 APPLICATION

Shingles to be applied over nailable sheathing (plywood or wood plank) and 15-lb. building felt. Shingles to be single-coursed with 8½″ to the weather. First course to be doubled.

Sidewall shingles shall be spaced apart not less than ⅛″ or more than ¼″. Vertical joints in any course shall be not less than 1½″ away from joints in adjacent courses.

Nails shall be driven just flush. Nailheads should not crush the wood. Nails to be not more than ¾″ away from edges of shingles and just above the butt line of the next course up the wall.

Division 6
Carpentry

SECTION 6C—FINISH CARPENTRY

6C—1 GENERAL REQUIREMENTS

Applicable provisions of the Agreement and of Division 1—General Requirements of the specifications govern the work of this section.

6C—2 QUALIFICATIONS

Finish wood shall conform to Voluntary Products Standard PS-20-76; Maximum moisture content 15%. All plywood materials shall meet the requirements of Product Standard PS I-66 for Softwood Plywood/Construction and Industrial.

6C—3 MATERIALS

Lumber for paneling, shelving, and cabinets to be of species as selected by owner. Material to be kiln- or air-dried to maximum 22% moisture content.

Plastic laminates shall be minimum .030″ thickness manufactured by Formica or equal.

6C—4 INSTALLATION

All material to be installed in a neat and workmanlike manner with tightly fitted joints. Wherever possible, simple butt joints are to be used. Dowels should be used to secure butt joints in load-bearing construction such as shelving. All material to be prime-coated on all faces immediately to prevent warpage.

Division 7
Moisture Control

SECTION 7A—WATERPROOFING

7A—1 GENERAL REQUIREMENTS

Applicable provisions of the Agreement and of Division 1—General Requirements of the specifications govern the work of this section.

7A—2 QUALIFICATIONS

All products shall bear one of the following trade names:

Woodlife
Cuprinol
Sealtreat

7A—3 MATERIALS

Apply water-repellant preservative conforming to Federal Specification SSA-
114b to all exterior wood materials exposed to weather.

7A—4 APPLICATION

Apply to above material in strict accordance with manufacturers' printed directions. The addition of pigmented stain to the above products is permitted.
Stir preservative frequently to insure adequate and even dispersion of stain.

7A/1

Division 7
Moisture Control

SECTION 7B—NEOPRENE ROOFING

7B—1 GENERAL REQUIREMENTS

Applicable provisions of the Agreement and of Division 1—General Requirements of the specifications govern the work of this section.

7B—2 QUALIFICATIONS

Neoprene/Hypalon waterproofing to be as manufactured by DuPont and distributed by Gates Engineering, 100 S. West St., Wilmington, DE 19801.

Medium density overlaid plywood to be United States Plywood Duraply.

Neoprene caulking and joint reinforcing tape to be supplied by Gates Engineering.

7B—3 APPLICATION

Material to be applied over sound substrate adequately sloped to drain. Surface must be pitched sufficiently to prevent standing water. Material can be applied to concrete or wood. All joints or cracks to be filled with neoprene caulking and covered with fiberglass tape before final installation of neoprene coating.

First coat of neoprene to be cut one half with xylene solvent. Plywood to be coated before installation on roof deck.

Neoprene to be applied with a heavy roller to a 20-mil dry-cure thickness. Application to be checked with wet film gauge. Apply two extra coats to areas with fiberglass tape.

Hypalon finish coat to be applied in two layers. White sand may be sprinkled over final coat to reduce slipperiness if desired.

Division 7
Moisture Control

SECTION 7C—SEALANTS

7C—1 GENERAL REQUIREMENTS

Applicable provisions of the Agreement and of Division 1—General Requirements of the specifications govern the work of this section.

7C—2 QUALIFICATIONS

All products shall be furnished by one of the following manufacturers:

Tremco Mfg. Co.: Mono caulking
Sonneborn-DeSoto: Sonac
W. R. Grace & Co.: Daraseal-A

7C—3 MATERIALS

Shall conform to Federal Specification TTS-230

7C—4 APPLICATION

Seal all joints between dissimilar materials and between all construction joints. Clean all joints before caulking. Sealant to be applied over round polyethylene foam rod compressed into joint.

Division 8
Doors, Windows, Skylights, and Greenhouses

SECTION 8A—WOOD DOORS

8A—1 GENERAL REQUIREMENTS

Applicable provisions of the Agreement and of Division 1—General Requirements of the specifications govern the work of this section.

8A—2 MATERIALS

Finish wood shall comply with applicable AWI standards. Wood to be of species as selected by owner.

Glue shall be a two-component epoxy of permanent weatherproof type, such
as Aerobond 2178, manufactured by Adhesive Engineering Co., 1411 Industrial Rd., San Carlos, CA 94070.

Dowels to be commercial-grade hardwood.

8A—3 DOOR TYPES

Doors to be constructed of three types as follows:

Wood-Framed Insulated Glass: Door frame to be 2″-thick wood frame designed to accommodate standard ⅝″-thick tempered insulating glass. Frame
to be constructed of one layer of 5/4 wood and one layer of 3/4 wood overlapped and doweled together at corners. All joints to be bonded with epoxy.

Wood-Framed Paneled Doors: Construction is similar to glass doors except
that glass area is filled in with one or more panels. Panels to be constructed of
¾″ tongue-and-groove finish lumber. Panel boards may be run either vertically or diagonally.

Solid-Wood Door with Crossbuck: Doors to be constructed of 2X6 tongue-
and-goove decking with a Z-shaped crossbuck recessed ¾″ into one face of
door. Crossbuck to be recessed into face opposite V-joints.

8A—4 FINISHES

All surfaces of doors including all edges to be finished immediately upon
completion to prevent warpage.

Division 8
Doors, Windows, Skylights, and Greenhouses

SECTION 8B—WINDOWS

8B—1 GENERAL REQUIREMENTS

Applicable provisions of the Agreement and of Division 1—General Requirements of the specifications govern the work of this section.

8B—2 MATERIALS

Window sash shall be standard utility sash treated with water-repellant wood preservative similar to Cuprinol. Framing members for window casing to be 2X6 framing-grade lumber selected for appearance and quality. Weatherstripping to be automotive-grade sponge neoprene bonded with contact cement. Hardware to be standard piano hinges, cam-action latches, and sash hooks.

8B—3 CONSTRUCTION

Window frame to be made of framing lumber with butt joints sealed with Mono caulking and anchored with wood screws. Window stops shall be nailed and bedded in Mono. Weatherstripping to be carefully applied to provide a weathertight seal at corners. Cam-action latches to be installed so that they fully compress sponge weatherstripping to provide a weathertight seal.

8B—4 GLAZING AND SCREENS

Sash are factory glazed with single glazing. Windows to be double-glazed with a layer of ⅛″ acrylic plastic, Plexiglas, or equal. Inside screen to be constructed of aluminum screen frame sections and installed on inside face of window stops. Optional storm sash to be installed in same position. Provide neoprene sponge weatherstripping for screen and storm sash. Screening to be fiberglass; aluminum screening is not permitted.

Division 8
Doors, Windows, Skylights, and Greenhouses

SECTION 8C—SKYLIGHTS AND GREENHOUSES

8C—1 GENERAL REQUIREMENTS

Applicable provisions of the Agreement and of Division 1—General Requirements of the specifications govern the work of this section.

8C—2 MATERIALS

Glazing materials for breakfront-type greenhouses and fixed skylights shall be ¼"-thick acrylic plastic similar to Plexiglas. Ventilating skylights to be Ventarama or approved equal. Glass for sloped-front greenhouses to be standard-size tempered glass units, 45X76 or other standard size as required. Units to be single or double layer as required. All glazing units to be bedded in Mono caulking with a weathertight trim board applied over glass edges. Sealant for glass-to-glass edges to be clear silicone by GE or Dow-Corning.

8C—3 INSTALLATION OF SKYLIGHTS

Ventarama skylights to be installed in strict accordance with manufacturers' printed directions. Acrylic plastic skylights to be installed in "shingle" fashion, with the top edge slipped underneath the roofing material and the sides and bottom overlapping by 4". Plexiglas to be anchored to roof deck with round-head wood screws with flat washers spaced exactly 8" o.c. Plexiglas to be bedded in Mono and the screw heads to be sealed with same.

8C—4 INSTALLATION OF GREENHOUSE GLAZING

Acrylic plastic (Plexiglas) greenhouse glazing to be installed with wood screws and Mono in similar fashion to skylights. Plexiglas to entirely cover exposed face of wood framing members to protect them from weather.

Insulating glass panels to be set on two 2"-long, ¼"-thick bearing blocks at one-quarter points (none required at center). Glass to be anchored in place with 1X2 batten strips set in Mono and fastened with wood screws at 12" o.c.

Division 9
Finishes

SECTION 9A—GYPSUM DRYWALL

9A—1 GENERAL REQUIREMENTS

Applicable provisions of the Agreement and of Division 1—General Requirements of the specifications govern the work of this section.

9A—2 QUALIFICATIONS

All products shall be furnished by the same manufacturer; one of the following:

United States Gypsum Co.
National Gypsum Co.
Celotex Corp.

9A—3 MATERIALS

All gypsum board shall be square-edged; furnish thicknesses as shown on finish schedule in sheets as large as practical. Furnish ⅝"-thick, fire-rated gypsum board where indicated.

9A—4 INSTALLATION

Gypsum board shall be installed in sheets as large as practical. Wherever possible, sheets to be installed with long dimension horizontal. Sheets to be anchored with Sheetrock screws spaced as recommended by manufacturer.

Double-layer systems shall have joints staggered. Second layer to be bonded with an approved adhesive.

First coat of spackling to be United States Gypsum Durobond 90 rapid-drying compound to prevent cracking and fill large voids. Other materials not permitted. Spackling to be three-coat system. Final finish to be completely free of visible defects.

Division 9
Finishes

SECTION 9B—PLASTERING

9B—1 GENERAL REQUIREMENTS

Applicable provisions of the Agreement and of Division 1—General Requirements of the specifications govern the work of this section.

9B—2 QUALIFICATIONS

All products shall have one of the following trade names:

Gypsolite
Structolite
Litemix

9B—3 MATERIALS

All materials to have same batch number. Each batch to be tested before application to insure freshness. Store materials in dry place.

9B—4 APPLICATION

Plaster to be installed over Styrofoam base. Diamond mesh wire to be installed over face of Styrofoam as reinforcement. Two coats of plaster to be used. Second coat to be smoothed to a rustic finish.

9B—5 PROTECTION

Plaster shall be protected from extreme heat or cold until it has cured. Maintain temperatures above 50°F. Keep wall surface damp in hot weather. Wall to be thoroughly wet down every three hours for first two days.

Division 9
Finishes

SECTION 9C—PAINTING AND FINISHING

9C—1 GENERAL REQUIREMENTS

Applicable provisions of the Agreement and of Division 1—General Requirements of the specifications govern the work of this section.

9C—2 QUALIFICATIONS

All products shall be furnished by one of the following manufacturers:

Martin-Seymour
Sherwin Williams
Glidden
Pittsburgh
Pratt and Lambert

9C—3 MATERIALS

All interior gypsum board (Sheetrock) and plaster (if desired) to receive two coats of latex base paint. Colors to be as selected by owner.

9C—4 PROTECTION

Adjacent materials to be masked to protect them from paint overrun. Wherever possible, trim members to be applied after painting is completed.

9C—5 APPLICATION

Application to be with 18″, commercial-type roller. Brush application is not permitted due to poor surface texture resulting from brushing.

9C—6 COLORS

Colors shall match Martin-Seymour Williamsburg collection, Turco Colour Cupboard, or other color chips submitted by owner.

Division 10
Masonry

SECTION 10A—BRICK FLOORS

10A—1   GENERAL REQUIREMENTS

Applicable provisions of the Agreement and of Division 1—General Requirements of the specifications govern the work of this section.

10A—2   MATERIALS

Brick for pavers shall be of uniform size and shape, with surface suitable for an exposed floor.

Mortar to be job-mixed from cement and sand. Premixed mortar is not permitted unless enriched with cement.

Setting bed to be a 6/1 sand-cement mixture to provide a stable bed for brick. Sand-cement mixture to be installed over a thoroughly compacted sand/gravel bed.

10A—3   INSTALLATION

Bricks to be dry-set over sand bed in desired pattern. Bricks may be set either with flush or open joints depending upon aesthetic preference and uniformity of brick. (Used or irregular brick must be set with open joints filled with mortar.)

Brick set with flush joints to have sand swept flush into the joints. Sand is sealed in place with polyurethane varnish.

Brick with open joints to be grouted by "dry-pack" method. Brick surface to be sealed first with one coat of final finish to prevent mortar staining. Mortar is mixed to damp consistency and swept into open joints. Mortar is then packed into joints with blunt instrument approximately the same width as the mortar joint. Brick must be thoroughly wet down before and after dry-pack installation.

10A—4   FINISHES

After mortar is thoroughly dry, scrub all excess mortar from surface of brick and apply desired finish. Finish may be paste wax, silicone masonry waterproofing compound, or polyurethane varnish. Use varnish for the most durable finish.

Division 10
Masonry

SECTION 10B— MASONRY WALLS AND
CHIMNEYS; RUMSFORD FIREPLACES

10B—1   GENERAL REQUIREMENTS

Applicable provisions of the Agreement and of Division 1—General Requirements of the specifications govern the work of this section.

10B—2   MATERIALS

Brick shall be as selected by owner. Flue liners to be of round cross section,
rather than square or rectangular. Steel damper and air intake slide to be
fabricated of plate as shown on drawings. All areas subject to high heat to
have flue liners with fire clay mortar. Fireplaces to be lined with firebrick.

10B—3   MASONRY WALLS

Masonry heat-storage walls to be laid up in conventional fashion in pattern
and color as selected by owner. Flues for heating appliances to be fully lined
with round clay tile flue liners. Flues for heat-storage system may be unlined.

10B—4   RUMSFORD FIREPLACES

Rumsford fireplaces to be laid with large, reflective backwall and widely angled sides to reflect the maximum amount of heat into the living area. Conventional stock steel dampers are not suitable and must not be used. Damper to
be continuous across the entire front face of the fireplace. Damper closure to
be constructed of a 2X2X¼" steel angle with a ¾" eye bolt welded to it for
operation with a poker.

10B—5   OUTSIDE AIR INTAKES

All combustion devices connected to the chimney or heat-storage wall, including Rumsford fireplaces, to have direct outside air intake. Air intakes to be
screened and to have positive damper closure.

Division 11
Mechanical

SECTION 11A—PLUMBING

11A—1   GENERAL REQUIREMENTS

Applicable provisions of the Agreement and of Division 1—General Requirements govern the work of this section.

11A—2   WORK INCLUDED

This division includes furnishing and installation of submersible deep well pump, supply piping from well to house, hot- and cold-water piping, hot-water heater, PVC drainage system, and connection and installation of sewage disposal system.

11A—3   PUMP (If required)

Pump and all controls and associated equipment shall be as manufactured by Goulds or Meyers. Install pump in well with pitless adaptor. Verify proper depth of pump with well-driller before installation of pump.

11A—4   WATER SERVICE AND SUPPLY PIPING

Install underground water service from well to utility room. Service to be 1" heavy-duty plastic. Furnish and install type "L" hard copper hot- and cold-water supply pipes to all fixtures indicated on plans. Pipe to have solder-type fittings. Provide control valves as necessary for proper control of piping and equipment.

Furnish and install hot-water heater of fuel type as selected by owner.

11A—5   SOIL, WASTE, AND VENTS

Soil, waste, and vent lines shall be run as required to connect fixtures as shown on drawings. All offsets shall be made at an angle of not more than 45°, and all horizontal runs shall have a pitch of not less than $\frac{1}{8}$" to the foot unless otherwise approved.

Install piping without undue strains or stresses. No structural member shall be weakened by cutting, notching, or otherwise unless provision is made for carrying the structural load and approved by the Architect.

Soil, waste, and vent lines aboveground, within the building, shall be Schedule 40 PVC. Connection from house to sewage disposal system shall be 4" cast iron.

11A—6   PLUMBING FIXTURES

Plumbing fixtures and fittings shall be Gerber, Sears, or equal. Flush-type toilets shall use a maximum of 3½ gallons of water per flush.

Faucets, traps, and wastes shall be Gerber or Sterling. Faucets and shower heads shall be equipped with water-conserving, flow restriction devices. Note: If a compact system with smaller size piping is used, flow restrictive devices may be eliminated.

11A—7   SEWAGE DISPOSAL SYSTEMS

Furnish and install sewage system as required by local health department. Note: Special permits and extra supervision may be required for alternative-type disposal systems.

Division 11
Mechanical

SECTION 11B—HEATING

11B—1 GENERAL REQUIREMENTS

Applicable provisions of the Agreement and of Division 1—General Requirements of the specifications govern the work of this section.

11B—2 WORK INCLUDED

Furnish and install electric radiant heat-panel backup system for all spaces shown on working drawings. Each heater to be individually controlled by thermostat as shown on drawings. Equipment to be of sufficient capacity to insure 65°F. inside temperature with 0°F. outside temperature. Provide mechanical exhaust of no more than 2 air changes per hour for toilets, showers, and range.

11B—3 MATERIALS

Heating elements shall be sealed with silicone compound and mounted in extruded aluminum frames. Units shall be as manufactured by Aztech International, Continental Radiant Glass Heat Co., or TVI Corp., Inc.

Division 11
Mechanical Work

SECTION 11C—AIR CONDITIONING AND
VENTILATION

11C—1 GENERAL REQUIREMENTS

Applicable provisions of the Agreement and of Division 1—General Requirements of the specifications govern the work of this section.

11C—2 MATERIALS

Furnish a single-unit heat pump similar to the single-unit, through-the-wall model marketed by Sears. Unit shall be reversible for either heating or cooling. Unit to be completely wired and plumbed at factory.

Ductwork to be galvanized sheet metal, sized and gauged according to ASHRAE standards. No paning of ducts will be allowed. All cutting and patching for ductwork to be done by general contractor.

All supply ducts to be covered with 1″, ¾-lb.-density fiberglass insulation with vinyl vapor barrier.

11C—3 INSTALLATION

Unit shall be installed through the wall of the utility core. Ductwork shall be run to major living spaces as indicated on drawings. Unit to be tested for operation in all modes. System to be complete with all controls, outside fan intake, ductwork, and supply and return grilles.

11C—4 VENTILATION

A system providing for fresh air to be fan-circulated directly from outside shall be interconnected to the heat-pump system and shall make use of the same duct system.

11C—5 PERFORMANCE, WARRANTIES

Equipment and ductwork system to be sufficient to insure 65°F. inside temperature with 0°F. outside temperature in wintertime, and 15°F. inside drop from outside temperature in summertime. 50% relative humidity to be maintained in summer.

Any defective equipment to be replaced at no expense to owner during first year of operation. Compressor to carry a five-year warranty for replacement.

11C/1

Division 12
Electrical

SECTION 12A—ELECTRIC WORK

12A—1   GENERAL REQUIREMENTS

Applicable provisions of the Agreement and of Division 1—General Requirements of the specifications govern the work of this section.

12A—2   WORK INCLUDED

Furnish and install a complete electrical system including all labor materials, equipment, lighting fixtures with lamps, switches, dimmers, receptacles, outlet boxes, motor wiring, wiring, and everything else necessary and/or required to produce a complete, safe, legal, and properly operating electrical system as herein specified.

12A—3   MATERIALS

Provide a 100A, 120/240V, single-phase, 3-wire service. Provide meter pan and meter wiring in accordance with utility company's requirements. Terminate electric service conduit as per utility company's requirements.

Panel board: Shall be of dead-front, snap-in circuit-breaker-type, breaker sizes as required.

Single pole, three-way switches; silent action type.

Receptacles: duplex 15A, 125V, grounded type. Provide GFI protection where required by code.

All devices and plates to be white. Approved manufacturers: AH&H, Hubbell, P&S or equal.

12A—4   WIRING

Branch circuit wiring shall be Romex 12/2 with ground. Lighting: A maximum of 1,600 watts per 20A circuit is permitted for lighting. Receptacles: Install on separate circuit (20A) with maximum of eight devices.

12A—5   LIGHTING FIXTURES

Install fixtures where indicated on drawings. Generally fixtures are either concealed 40W fluorescent strips or porcelain bases with exposed G-40-type bulbs. No recessed fixtures are permitted in insulated ceiling spaces.

Plans for Basic Saltbox House

All other books on building houses falter when it comes to plans for actually building the houses. High-speed, economical printing and binding techniques do not permit a set of plans to be included in most books. If a printer folds plans and inserts them into a pocket, it increases the price of the book by $5 to $10. Most authors either reproduce plans so small that they are useless or require you to order plans by mail at considerable expense. The very essence of this book is to provide an economical, easy means of building your own house. With this in mind, I have provided readers with the necessary plans—at a readable scale. I have also provided a quick, easy way to make modifications to the set of plans. There is one catch, however. *You* have to do some work to make all of this possible.

My standard plans are usually drawn at ¼-inch scale on 17X22-inch sheets of paper. I chose this size because it is a multiple of 8½X11 inches. When folded in quarters, the large sheet becomes a standard page size. Taking advantage of this size, I have reproduced each sheet in four sections; they are bound at the back of this book. The quarter-sheets can be easily reproduced on a standard Xerox machine. You can either cut them out of the book on the dotted line, or fold the book flat and xerox or photocopy the desired number of copies on a standard copier.

The four sections of each sheet of working drawings are bound in pairs facing in opposite directions so that they can be assembled into one large sheet. There are lines ⅛ inch from one long and one short edge with little hash marks. These are trim lines. Using a straightedge and a razor blade, remove ⅛ inch from two sides of all sheets as indicated. There is a numbered circle at the corner of each sheet. Take each set of four sheets and place the numbered corners together to form one large sheet. Now tape the sheets together with transparent tape and you have a complete set of plans. If you wish, you can type your name and address in the title block before assembling the plans to make them look more official.

The final touch to the plans is that there are built-in provisions for several versions. The plans have reference grid lines just like a road map. These serve two functions. First, they allow you to describe accurately the location of some detail or portion of a plan to someone over a phone or in a letter without actually pointing it out or going into a very lengthy and possibly misconstrued explanation. Second, the grid lines allow me to offer

several variations with the same set of plans. The last several pages of the plan set contain variations for the basic set. To make modifications, just cut out the desired revisions on the grid lines and glue them to the original plans before xeroxing those sections of the plans. In this fashion, you can have the basic house with just a carport or add the dormer and extra upstairs bedroom, enclosed garage and workshop, or extra loft space. You can even change the plans at a later date so that these additions can be made to your house. The drawings here show how your house might grow in stages.

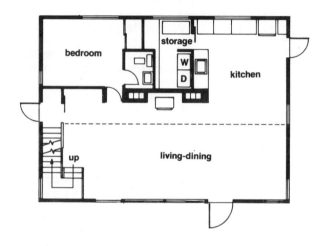

First-floor plan — basic house.

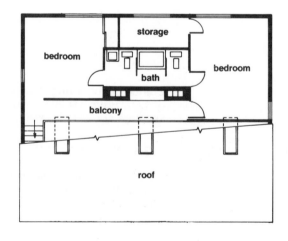

Second-floor plan — basic house.

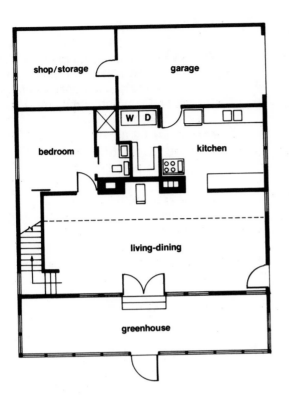

First-floor plan — basic house, expanded version.

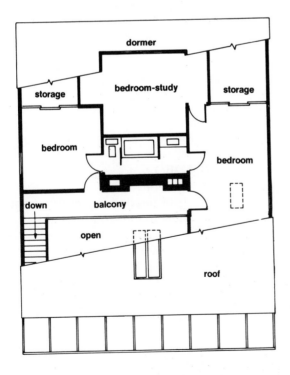

Second-floor plan — basic house, expanded version.

Materials List for Basic Saltbox House

This materials list should be used as a general guide for estimating purposes only. I strongly encourage you to make modifications to the basic house to adapt it to suit your individual needs and tastes.

The list is made up specifically for the basic saltbox house with a 12-foot-long, sloping-front greenhouse and a carport. For other variations, quantities will have to be modified accordingly.

Foundation types and required depths vary considerably for different parts of the country. The materials listed for the three types of foundation assume that you are building on a flat site with a uniform 4-foot-deep foundation. These figures must be modified to suit your local conditions.

Exterior sheathing is listed as the number of sheets of standard-size sheathing required. It should be reviewed in conjunction with the "Insulation Requirements" table in Chapter 10 to determine the type and thickness of material required for each face of your house.

Foundations: Materials for three different types of foundation are listed; a pressure-treated-post-type foundation, a grade beam foundation, and a standard concrete block foundation.

Pressure-treated post

5	6X6/10′ pressure-treated posts, cut in two
16	2X6/12′ pressure-treated sill plates
2	2X6/14′ pressure-treated sill plates
2	2X8/14′ pressure-treated sill plates
8	4X8X¼″ cement-asbestos board (Johns-Manville "Transite")
16	4X8 sheets rigid urethane insulation board (This is an integral part of the embedded system. See "Insulation Requirements" in Chapter 10 for recommended thicknesses.)
1	cu. yd. 3,000-psi concrete for fireplace footing

Concrete grade beam

12	cu. yd. 3,000-psi concrete
1	100'-roll 6X6X10/10 mesh reinforcing wire for concrete
24	⅝"X10" anchor bolts
16	2X6/12'
4	2X6/14'
	(Save this lumber for later reuse as girts.)

Concrete block

80	6X8X16 3-core lightweight block
316	8X8X16 3-core lightweight block
7	cu. yd. 3,000-psi concrete
16	20' lengths #4 steel reinforcing bars
24	¾"X12" anchor bolts
130	8" Dur-O-Wall wire reinforcement

Chimney: Materials are shown for basic concrete block chimney with two flues. Quantities for three flues are shown in parentheses.

800 (766)	8X8X16 3-core lightweight block
20 (30)	6"-diameter round clay flue tiles, 2' long
2 (3)	6" clay thimbles
35	80-lb. bags ready-mixed mortar
4	80-lb. bags cement, to be mixed with ready-mixed mortar for extra strength
	Note: A brick chimney requires about 10,000 brick and about ten times the mortar quantities. Premixed mortar is not economical for a brick chimney; buy cement and sand and mix your own.
1	can refractory cement or fire clay, required for joints in flue liners and connection between thimble and flue liner
2 (3)	slate, precast concrete, or steel plate flue caps

Framing: Framing can be done either with standard framing lumber laminated into larger members or with solid beams. Solid beams are listed first on framing list with laminated members following in parentheses. Exterior beams should be laminated in any case. Solid beams should be roughsawn pine, #1 or better. Roughsawn hardwoods can also be used. Any knots should be in the upper half of the beam.

Posts and beams

Exterior posts

30	2X6/8'
	(These are concealed in exterior walls and are easier to fabricate if laminated; may be solid if desired.)

Exposed posts b2 & c2

2	6X6/8' (4 2X6/8' & 2 2X4/8")

Main beams: column lines b2-3 & c2-3

2	6X12/16' (4 2X12/16' & 2 2X10/16')

Exterior beams: column lines a, d, 1, 3, & 4

	(16 2X12/12' & 4 2X12/14')

Intermediate beams: column lines ab, bc, & cd

13	4X10/12' (26 2X10/12' with 26 1X8/12" spacers)

Flooring: Use 2X6 tongue-and-groove decking for finish floor and finish ceiling. Spruce works well, #1 pine is second choice, fir is third choice. Select carefully, and be prepared to return bad material.

End bays

60	2X6/16'

Center bay

30	2X6/14'

Loft

30	2X6/12'

Wall framing: Douglas fir or spruce-pine-fir (SPF) are commonly stocked lumberyard framing members; #1 roughsawn pine is excellent if codes permit. Use only planed, pressure-treated members for sill plate.

Sill

8	2X6/12'
2	2X6/14'
	(Not needed if pressure-treated post foundation is used.)

Girts

60	2X6/8'
125	2X6/12'
12	2X6/14'

Plates and nailers

50	2X6/12'
50	2X6/16'
30	2X4/16'

Interior studs

125	2X4/8'

Roof framing: Conventional rafter system. Twenty-four-foot-long rafters may have to be special-ordered in your area. Check price and quality carefully before placing order.

Front rafters
19 2X12/24′
Front overhang
19 2X12/8′
Rear rafters
10 2X12/12′
Carport rafters
9 2X12/24′
(If carport is omitted, order 19 2X12/12′.)
Fascias
14 2X12/14′ (3 sides planed)
Sheathing
45 4X8X½″ 5-ply fir CDX plywood
125 ½″ plyclips

Alternate roof framing: Purlin system. Lateral girts as in pole barns. Roof sheathing may be omitted if ribbed metal roofing is used. Size of girts may be reduced for mild climates or seasonal-use buildings.

Main beams, front
8 2X12/24′
6 2X6/12′ for blocking
Main beams, rear
4 2X12/24′
4 2X6/12′ spacers
4 2X12/12′
(Make all beams at rear 12′ if carport is omitted.)
Purlins (secondary framing)
54 2X12/12′
Note: 2X10s or 2X8s may be substituted in mild climates.

Exterior Skins

Sheathing: Sheathing should be selected according to insulation values recommended in the "Insulation Requirements" table in Chapter 10. Total number of panels is shown. If plywood bracing is not used for corners, TECO or Stanley steel bracing must be added; 1,800 square feet are required.

55 4X8 sheets of desired material and thickness
or
110 2X8 sheets.

Siding: Area to be covered is 1,800 square feet for basic saltbox house. Add 10 percent for garage/workshop and dormer. Note that different patterns vary considerably in quantity.

Board on board
2,500 lineal ft. 1X6
2,500 lineal ft. 1X8
Board and batten
2,100 board ft. 1X8
3,000 lineal ft. 1X2
Tongue and groove
2,400 board feet

Roofing: Basic saltbox with carport is 18 square. If carport is omitted, deduct 3 square (a square equals 100 sq. ft. of roofing and is the professional ordering measure.)

Asphalt shingles
18 sq. 15-lb. felt roofing paper
18 sq. 235-lb. self-sealing shingles
50 lb. ½″ galvanized roof nails
16 10′ lengths galvanized drip edge
Terne roofing
16 rolls 28″X50′ IC 40-lb. terne
or
18 rolls 24″X50′ IC 40-lb. terne
18 sq. rosin-coated building paper
6 gal. Tin-O-Lin red iron oxide paint (6 additional gal. of finish if different color is desired.)
10 lb. 2″ galvanized roof nails
Ribbed galvanized roofing
43 34″X12′ sheets metal roofing
18 4′ closure strips
10 lb. neoprene washered nails
Neoprene/Hypalon roof
10 gal. H-10 neoprene
5 gal. Hypalon finish-coat in color desired
12 tubes neoprene caulking
2 rolls fiberglass
2 gal. xylene thinner

Insulation and Interior Finishes and Trims

Insulation: These are typical insulation thicknesses. See "Insulation Requirements" in Chapter 10 for recommended types and thicknesses for different climates.

Wall insulation
1,800 sq. ft., 6″ thick

Ceiling insulation
   1,400   sq. ft., 12" thick
Rigid perimeter insulation
     18   4X8X2"
Vapor barrier
      4   rolls 10'X100' 6 mil polyethylene

Wall Finishes: Materials are listed in total areas to be covered. Finishes will vary to suit owners' tastes.
Ceiling
   1,400   sq. ft. material (includes waste)
Walls
   3,500   sq. ft. material (includes waste)

Stairs: Stairs are simple, open-riser, modern design with plain handrail.
Stringers
     2   2X12/14' roughsawn or clear pine
Treads
     3   2X12/14' clear pine, spruce, or oak
Handrail
     1   2X6/14' oak
Newel post
     1   4X4/8' oak, cut in half

Brick floor: A brick or masonry floor set in sand is preferred for temperature stability. A monolithic concrete floor with resilient floor covering can also be used.
   5,100   4" by 8" brick pavers (new or used)
     14   cu. yd. concrete & 1,000 sq. ft. 6X6X10/10 mesh if alternate slab is used
   1,000   sq. ft. of tile or sheet goods are required as a finish material, or concrete can be waxed

Windows and doors: Door and window sizes are shown on the working drawings for various configurations. These can be either homemade or manufactured items. Window and door configurations should be varied to adapt house to specific site. For this reason, no specific quantities are listed. See working drawings for standard size table.

Window and door trim: Milcor L-channel metal trim, or ¾" wood corner moldings, quantities as required. Approximately 1,160 lineal feet for openings shown on basic plan.

Baseboard
    30   1X4/16' resawn pine

Closet rods
   ½" or ¾" galvanized pipe (salvage)

Kitchen, pantry, and closet shelves
    24   1X10/12' clear pine or leftover siding

Kitchen cabinets: These are steel-framed cabinets with Formica fronts and shelves. Fronts can readily be replaced with wood if desired.
     2   Sears 65 K 63442 LH
     2   Sears 65 K 63432 LH
     1   Sears 65 K 63412 LH
     1   Sears 65 K 6359 LH
   (End-panel set for use as sink front.)

Paint and finishes
     4   5-gal. cans flat latex paint
     2   cases polyurethane varnish for brick and tongue-and-groove flooring
     2   cases Minwax Colonial Pine stain for post and beam structure
     3   5-gal. cans clear or pigmented Cuprinol or Woodlife
     1   case Mono caulking compound

Nails and Hardware
     3   50' rolls ½" by 6" fiberglass sill sealer
    50   lb. 6d common nails
    50   lb. 8d common nails
   100   lb. 10d common nails
    25   lb. 16d common nails
    25   lb. 20d common nails
    20   lb. 4" barn spikes
    20   lb. 6" barn spikes
    40   4"X12" truss straps
    10   lb. 8d galvanized finish nails
    10   lb. 10d galvanized finish nails
    10   lb. 16d galvanized finish nails
    50   lb. 16d cement-coated "CC" sinkers for decking
    50   lb. Sheetrock screws (if Sheetrock is used)
    20   lb. 4d finish nails
    20   lb. 6d finish nails
    10   lb. 8d finish nails
    10   lb. 10d finish nails

Plumbing Supplies

Pressure tank fittings

1   42-gal. captive-air pressure tank with pump controls (if pump is used)
1   ¾″ sweat gate valve
1   ¼″ threaded pressure gauge
1   Harvard tank cross
1   ½″ boiler drain
1   1¼″ galvanized plug
2   ¼″ brass plugs
1   tapped check control valve
1   ¼″ brass nipple, 6″ long
1   pressure switch
1   1″ male adapter (nylon insert)
2   1″ 90° elbow nylon inserts
6   stainless steel screw-type band clamps
1   galvanized reducing coupling, 1¼″ to ¾″
1   copper sweat reducing coupling, ¾″ to ½″
    (Above fittings except gate valve are unnecessary if gravity-type water system is used.)

Hot-water heater fittings: Many different types of water heaters have been described, so none is included here. Select carefully from the recommendations under "Recommended Efficient Appliances and Equipment for Energy-Saving Houses."

2   ¾″ copper sweat male fitting adapters
2   ¾″ to ½″ copper sweat reducing couplings
2   ½″ sweat seat valves

Copper supply fittings

18   10′ lengths ½″ type "L" copper tubing
1   10′ length ¾″ type "L" copper tubing
    5-lb. roll 60-40 solid-core solder
1   roll plumbers emery cloth
1   6-oz. can soldering paste flux
1   ½″ plumbers wire brush
1   roll Teflon pipe tape
1   wax closet ring
6   ½″ copper sweat street elbows
32   ½″ copper 90° elbows
16   ½″ copper tees
6   ½″ copper caps
10   ½″ copper couplings

2   ½″ sweat boiler drain valves
5   ½″ sweat chrome supply angle valves (with ⅜″ compression fittings)
4   18″ chrome-plated supply pipe, ⅜″ diameter
1   18″ closet supply pipe, ⅜″ diameter
1   8″ outdoor freezeless faucet
1   ½″ threaded brass 90° coupling

Plastic drainage pipe

1   16-oz. can PVC or ABS cement
4   1½″ PVC slip joint connector to 1½″ chrome sink drain
1   1½″ PVC slip joint connector to 1¼″ bath sink drain
12   1½″ PVC 90° elbows
6   3″ PVC tees
6   3″ PVC 90° elbows
6   3″ PVC couplings
4   3″ to 1½″ PVC reducing couplings
1   3″ cleanout access plug insert
10   10′ lengths 3″ PVC pipe
3   10′ lengths 1½″ PVC pipe
1   3′ length oakum
1   tube butyl caulking

Electric supplies: These materials are for a minimum installation with no heavy loads. If resistance heating, electric range, central air conditioning, etc. are added, the main service, service panel, and breakers will have to be changed.

1   weather head
1   service cable, 30′, & 10 cable straps
3   service cable connectors
1   meter pan
1   4′ ground cable, #4 AWG
1   ground clamp
1   100A service panel 120/240V; flush-mounted, 12-circuit; Bryant, Murray, or Sears
1   20A GFI breaker
6   20A single pole breakers
1   30A 2-pole breaker for backup radiant panels (if used)
4   250′ rolls, 12/2 with ground, Romex cable
1   box cable staples (100)
2   boxes Ideal #22 two-piece wire connectors (wire nuts)

10 squeeze-type cable connectors for main panel

56 Slater S-18r plastic outlet boxes

5 floor outlets; cast housing, brass cover, complete unit with receptacle

32 receptacles, Slater 3232 WH

15 single-pole switches, Slater 660 WH

4 double-pole switches, Slater 663 WH

31 cover plates for receptacles, Slater S-94071

19 cover plates for switches, Slater S-94101

1 weatherproof receptacle cover plate

6 4″ octagonal plastic ceiling boxes

8 porcelain sockets; 2 with pull-chains

8 40W, single lamp, utility-type fluorescent strips with Class A ballasts and Duro-Test Vita Lite bulbs

8 G-40, 60W, globe-type bulbs, Duro-Test or Norelco

3 weatherproof outside sockets, complete with weatherproof housing and 100W floodlight, Swieviler S100

2 Bryant or Honeywell combination heat rise/smoke detector. Line voltage with battery backup.

Greenhouse

2 2X6/8′ (pressure-treated)

1 2X6/12′ (pressure-treated)

4 4X8/10′ framing members

3 45X92X⅝″ tempered glass

1 4X8X¼″ AC plywood (pressure-treated)

4 1X4/10′ cedar battens

1 4X8X¼″ Plexiglas for end panels

Bibliography

American Institute of Timber Construction. *Timber Construction Manual.* New York: John Wiley & Sons, 1974.

American Water Works Association. *Water Quality & Treatment: A Handbook for Public Water Supplies.* New York: McGraw-Hill, 1971.

Anderson, K. E. *Water Well Handbook.* Missouri Water Well Driller's Association, P.O. Box 250, Rolla, MO 65401.

Anderson, L. O. *How to Build a Wood Frame House.* New York: Dover Publications, 1973.

————. *Low-Cost Homes for Rural America.* USDA Handbook #36, Superintendent of Documents, U.S. Government Printing Office, Washington, DC 20402.

Eccli, Eugene. *Low-Cost Energy-Efficient Shelter.* Emmaus, Pa, Rodale Press, 1976.

Fowler, Orson S. *The Octagon House, a Home for All.* New York: Dover Publications, republished 1973.

Helion, Inc. *Simplified Windpower Systems for Experimenters.* Helion Inc., Box 445, Brownsville, CA 95919

Housesmiths. *The Timber Framing Book.* Housesmiths, P.O. Box 1496, Boulder, CO 80306.

Kern, Ken. *The Owner-Built Home.* New York; Charles Scribner's Sons, 1975.

Kidd, Donald M., and Siy, Louis J. *Hand Woodworking Tools.* New York: Van Nostrand Reinhold, 1962.

Larkin, David. *The Paintings of Carl Larsson.* Bearsville, New York: Peacock Press, 1976.

Mazria, Edward. *The Passive Solar Energy Book.* Emmaus, Pa.: Rodale Press, 1979.

Pacey, Arnold. *Sanitation in Developing Countries.* New York: John Wiley & Sons, 1978.

Park, Jack, and Schwind, Dick. *Wind Power for Farms, Homes, and Small Industry.* Washington, D.C.: The Energy Research and Development Administration.

Ramsey, Charles G., and Sleeper, Harold R. *Architectural Graphic Standards.* New York: John Wiley & Sons, 1970.

Rictor, H. P. *Wiring Simplified.* Saint Paul, Minn.: Park Publishing, 1978.

Rudstrom, Lennart, and Larsson, Carl. *A Home.* New York: G. P. Putnam's Sons, 1974.

Scharff, Robert. *The Complete Book of Home Workshop Tools.* New York: McGraw-Hill, 1979.

Sheldon, Jay. *Wood Heat Safety.* Charlotte, Vt.: Garden Way Publishing Co., 1979.

Stoner, Carol, ed. *Goodbye to the Flush Toilet.* Emmaus, Pa.: Rodale Press, 1977.

U.S. Department of Agriculture. *Living on a Few Acres.* 001-000-03809-5, Superintendent of Documents, U.S. Government Printing Office, Washington, DC 20402.

U.S. Environmental Protection Agency. *Manual of Individual Water Supply Systems.* 055-001-00626-8, Superintendent of Documents, U.S. Government Printing Office, Washington, DC 20402.

Wade, Alex, and Ewenstein, Neal. *30 Energy-Efficient Houses . . . You Can Build.* Emmaus, Pa.: Rodale Press, 1977.

Wagner, E. G., and Lanoix, J. N. *Water Supply for Rural Areas and Small Communities.* Geneva, Switzerland: World Health Organization, 1959.

Warshall, Peter. *Septic Tank Practices.* New York: Doubleday, 1979.

Wass, Alonzo. *Methods and Materials of Residential Construction.* Reston, Va.: Reston Publishing Co., 1977.

Wing, Charles and Cole, John N. *From the Ground Up.* Boston: Little, Brown & Co., 1977.

Index

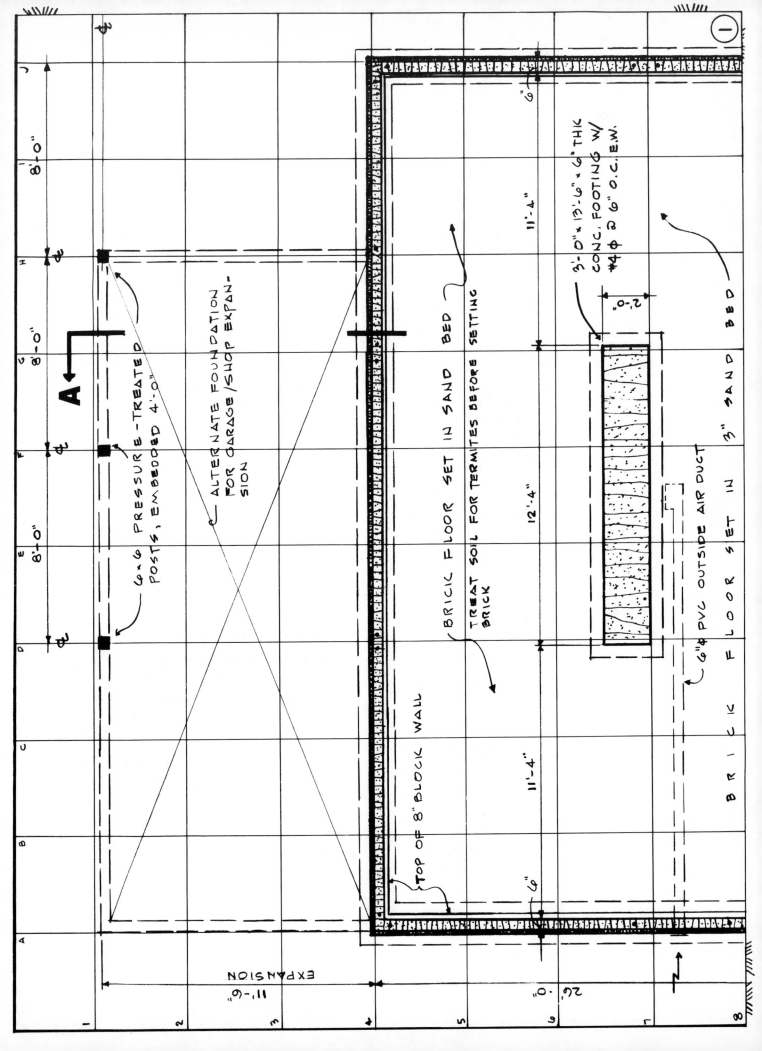

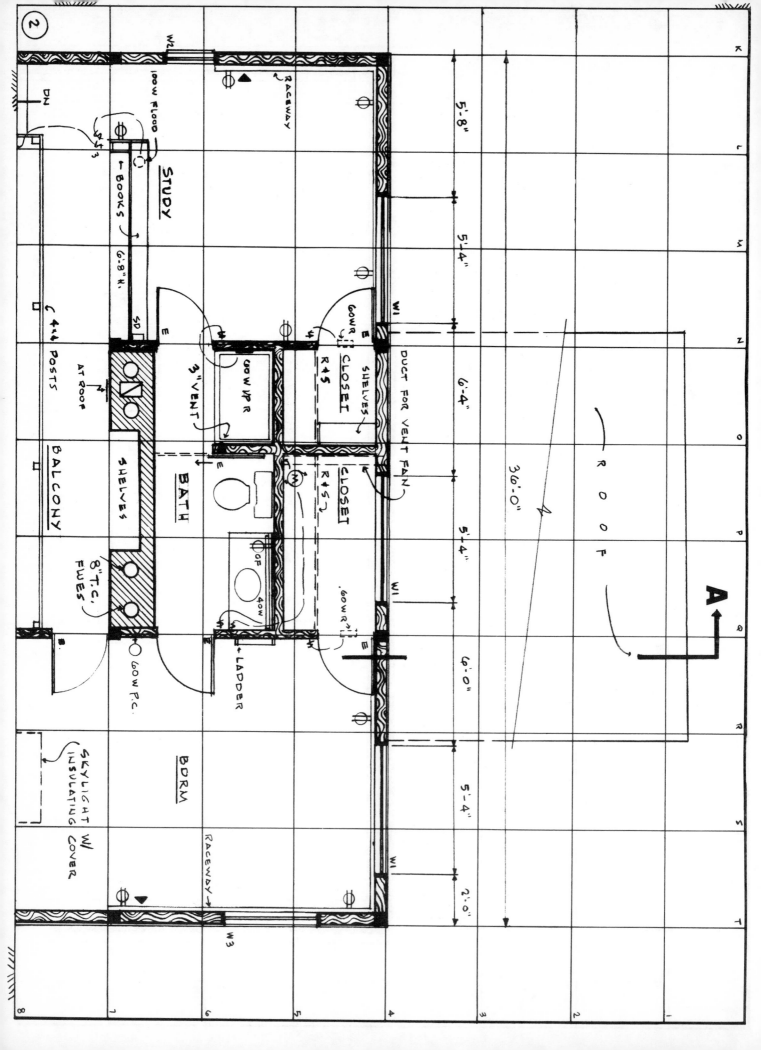

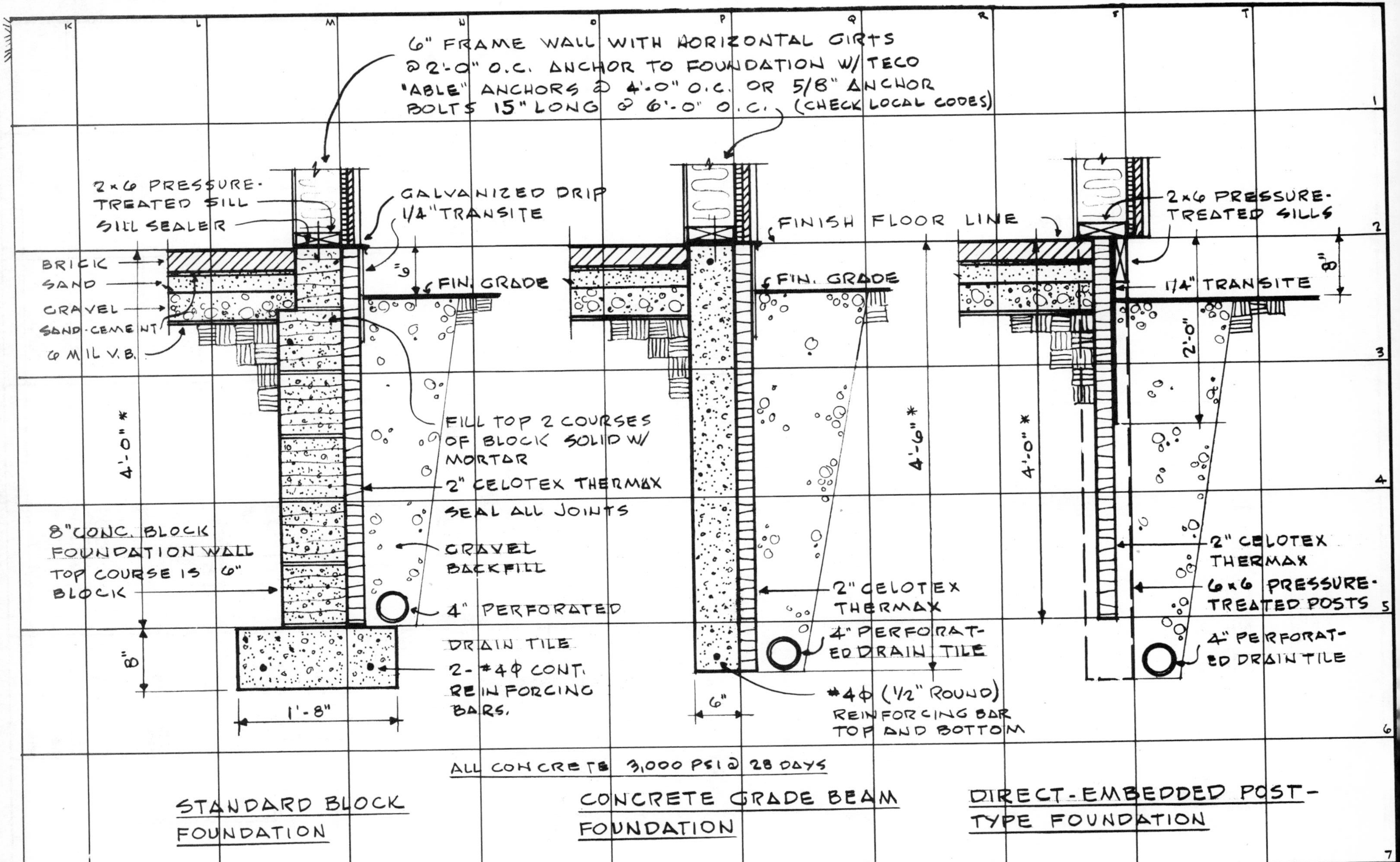

FOUNDATION DETAILS

SCALE 3/4" = 1'-0"

STANDARD BLOCK FOUNDATION

- 2×6 PRESSURE-TREATED SILL SEALER
- BRICK
- SAND
- GRAVEL
- SAND-CEMENT
- 6 MIL V.B.
- GALVANIZED DRIP 1/4" TRANSITE
- FIN. GRADE
- FILL TOP 2 COURSES OF BLOCK SOLID W/ MORTAR
- 2" CELOTEX THERMAX
- SEAL ALL JOINTS
- GRAVEL BACKFILL
- 4" PERFORATED
- DRAIN TILE
- 2-#4∅ CONT. REINFORCING BARS.
- 8" CONC. BLOCK FOUNDATION WALL TOP COURSE IS 6" BLOCK
- 6" FRAME WALL WITH HORIZONTAL GIRTS @ 2'-0" O.C. ANCHOR TO FOUNDATION W/ TECO "ABLE" ANCHORS @ 4'-0" O.C. OR 5/8" ANCHOR BOLTS 15" LONG @ 6'-0" O.C. (CHECK LOCAL CODES)
- 6"
- 1'-8"
- 8"
- * 4'-0"

CONCRETE GRADE BEAM FOUNDATION

- FINISH FLOOR LINE
- FIN. GRADE
- 2" CELOTEX THERMAX
- 4" PERFORATED DRAIN TILE
- #4∅ (1/2" ROUND) REINFORCING BAR TOP AND BOTTOM
- 6"
- * 4'-6"
- ALL CONCRETE 3,000 PSI @ 28 DAYS

DIRECT-EMBEDDED POST-TYPE FOUNDATION

- 2×6 PRESSURE-TREATED SILLS
- 8"
- 1/4" TRANSITE
- 2'-0"
- 2" CELOTEX THERMAX
- 6×6 PRESSURE-TREATED POSTS
- 4" PERFORATED DRAIN TILE
- * 4'-0"

* ADJUST DEPTH OF FOUNDATION TO SUIT LOCAL CLIMATIC CONDITIONS. FOUNDATION SHOULD EXTEND BELOW FROST LINE; MINIMUM DEPTH 2'-0". EMBEDDED POSTS SHOULD BE BURIED 4'-0" MINIMUM FOR STABILITY. ALL FOUNDATIONS SHOULD REST ON UNDISTURBED SOIL OF 3,000 PSI MINIMUM BEARING CAPACITY. FOR OTHER CONDITIONS, CONSULT LOCAL ENGINEER.

1

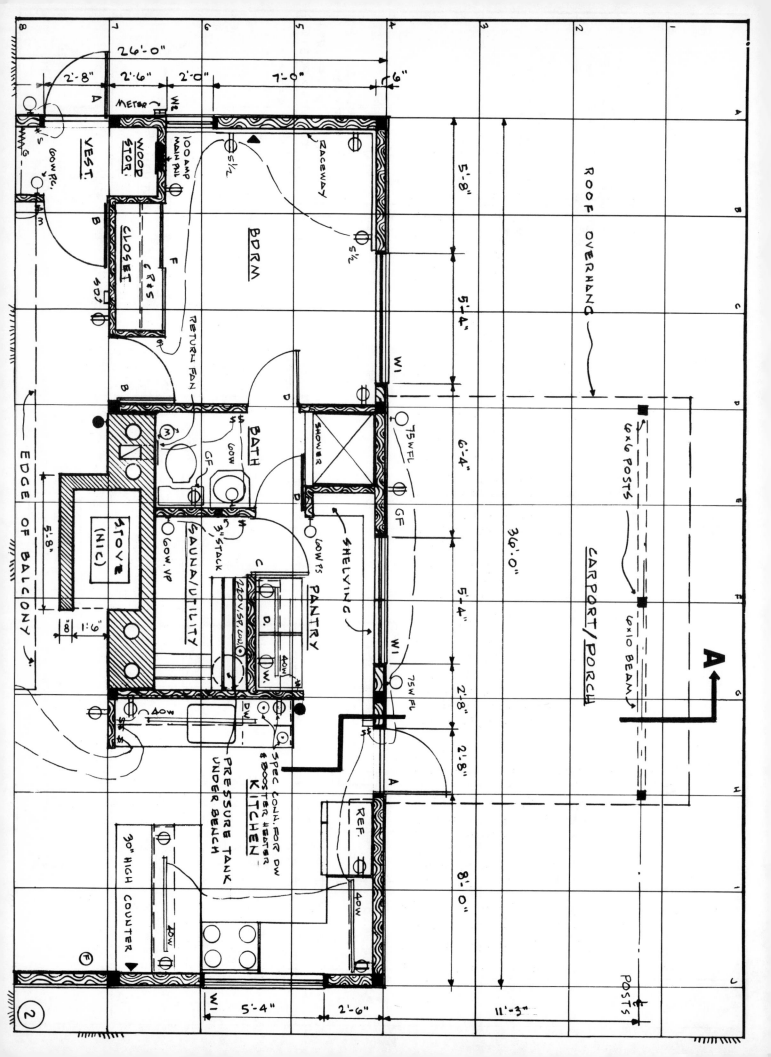

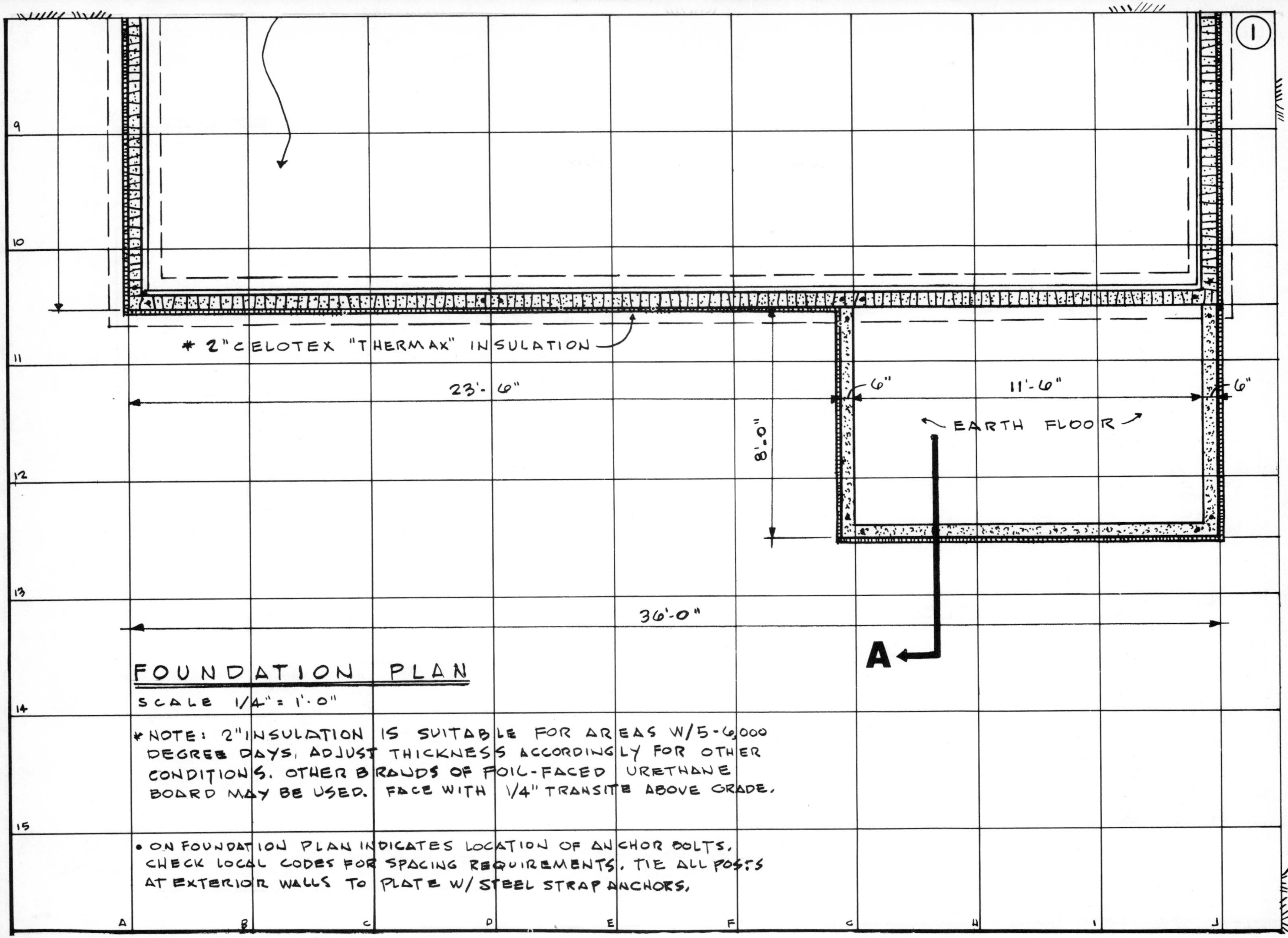

1
* 2" CELOTEX "THERMAX" INSULATION
23'-6"
6"
11'-6"
6"
8'-0"
EARTH FLOOR
36'-0"
A
9
10
11
12
13
A
B
C
D
E
F
G
H
I
J

FOUNDATION PLAN

SCALE 1/4" = 1'-0"

* NOTE: 2" INSULATION IS SUITABLE FOR AREAS W/5-6,000 DEGREE DAYS. ADJUST THICKNESS ACCORDINGLY FOR OTHER CONDITIONS. OTHER BRANDS OF FOIL-FACED URETHANE BOARD MAY BE USED. FACE WITH 1/4" TRANSITE ABOVE GRADE.

• ON FOUNDATION PLAN INDICATES LOCATION OF ANCHOR BOLTS. CHECK LOCAL CODES FOR SPACING REQUIREMENTS. TIE ALL POSTS AT EXTERIOR WALLS TO PLATE W/ STEEL STRAP ANCHORS.

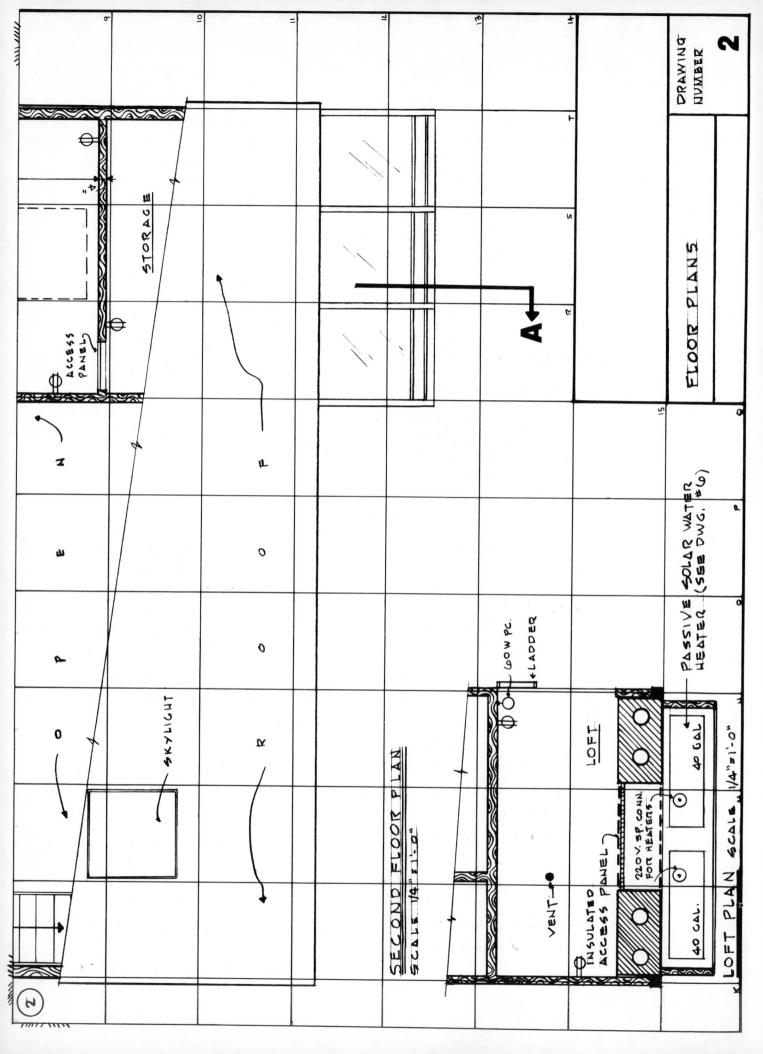

OPEN TO FLOOR

STORAGE

ACCESS PANEL

N

SKYLIGHT

SECOND FLOOR PLAN
SCALE 1/4"=1'-0"

A

LOFT

60W PC.

LADDER

VENT

INSULATED ACCESS PANEL

220V. SP. CONN. FOR HEATERS

40 GAL.

40 GAL.

PASSIVE SOLAR WATER HEATER (SEE DWG. #9)

LOFT PLAN SCALE 1/4"=1'-0"

FLOOR PLANS

DRAWING NUMBER

2

GENERAL NOTES:

THESE PLANS ARE EXEMPTED FROM THE COPYRIGHT OF THIS BOOK TO THE EXTENT THAT THEY MAY BE FREELY REPRODUCED. IN RETURN, THE AUTHOR AND PUBLISHER ARE ABSOLVED OF ANY LIABILITY IN CONJUNCTION WITH THEIR USE.

THEY ARE FLEXIBLE AND EASILY CHANGED AND EXPANDED. DWGS. #6 AND #7 PROVIDE OVERLAYS FOR AN OPTIONAL GARAGE/SHOP, EXTRA BEDROOM, COMPOSTING TOILET, AND VARIOUS MECHANICAL SYSTEMS. CUT OUT ANY FEATURES DESIRED FROM #6 AND USE AS OVERLAYS ON PLAN AND SECTION SHEET. NOTE THAT DWG. #6 BE-COMES LARGER AS A RESULT OF THE EXPANSION AND MUST BE FOLDED TO MATCH OTHER SHEETS IN THIS SET OF PLANS. CORRECTIONS MAY BE MADE WITH TYPEWRITER CORRECTION FLUID OR BY SIMPLY XING OUT UNWANTED FEATURES.

SOME AREAS OF THE COUNTRY WILL REQUIRE THAT A LOCAL ARCHI-TECT OR ENGINEER'S NAME APPEAR ON THE DRAWINGS. THE BOTTOM PORTION OF THE TITLE BLOCK IS LEFT BLANK FOR THIS PURPOSE. YOU CAN ALSO PUT YOUR NAME IN THIS SPACE IF DESIRED. A BLANK DRAWING SHEET IS PROVIDED AT THE END OF THIS SET OF DRAWINGS FOR MOD-IFICATIONS OR ADDITIONS BY YOU OR A LOCAL PROFESSIONAL. THE UPPER BLANK PORTION OF THE TITLE BLOCK SHOULD HAVE PROJECT NAME AND EXACT LOCATION. ALSO DATE THE FINAL DRAWINGS.

ABBREVIATIONS AND SYMBOLS

CONT.	CONTINUOUS
CONC.	CONCRETE
O.C.	ON CENTER
∅	DIAMETER (ROUND)
DWG.	DRAWING
MIL.	MILLIMETER
E.W.	EACH WAY
GAL.	GALLON
PSI	POUNDS PER SQUARE INCH
N.I.C.	NOT IN CONTRACT
T/	TOP OF
W/	WITH

R&S — POD & SHELF

———— LINE FOR JOINING SECTIONS OF DRAWINGS

⭢A — LOCATION OF BUILDING CROSS SECTION

③ — NUMBER FOR SMALL SHEETS. PLACE FOUR NUMBERED CORNERS TOGETHER TO FORM ONE DRAWING.

MATERIALS INDICATIONS

CONCRETE	
CONCRETE BLOCK	
BRICK	
SAND	
GRAVEL	
EARTH	
WOOD FRAMING (SMALL SCALE)	
RIGID INSULATION	
BATT OR FILL INSULATION	
STRUCTURAL POSTS	WOOD BEAMS IN CROSS SECTION
CENTER LINE	LOCATION OF OBJECT ABOVE PLANE SHOWN IN PLANS. ALSO CUTTING LINE FOR REMOVING PLAN SHEETS FROM BOOK.

FOUNDATION PLAN & DETAILS
GENERAL NOTES

DRAWING NUMBER: 1

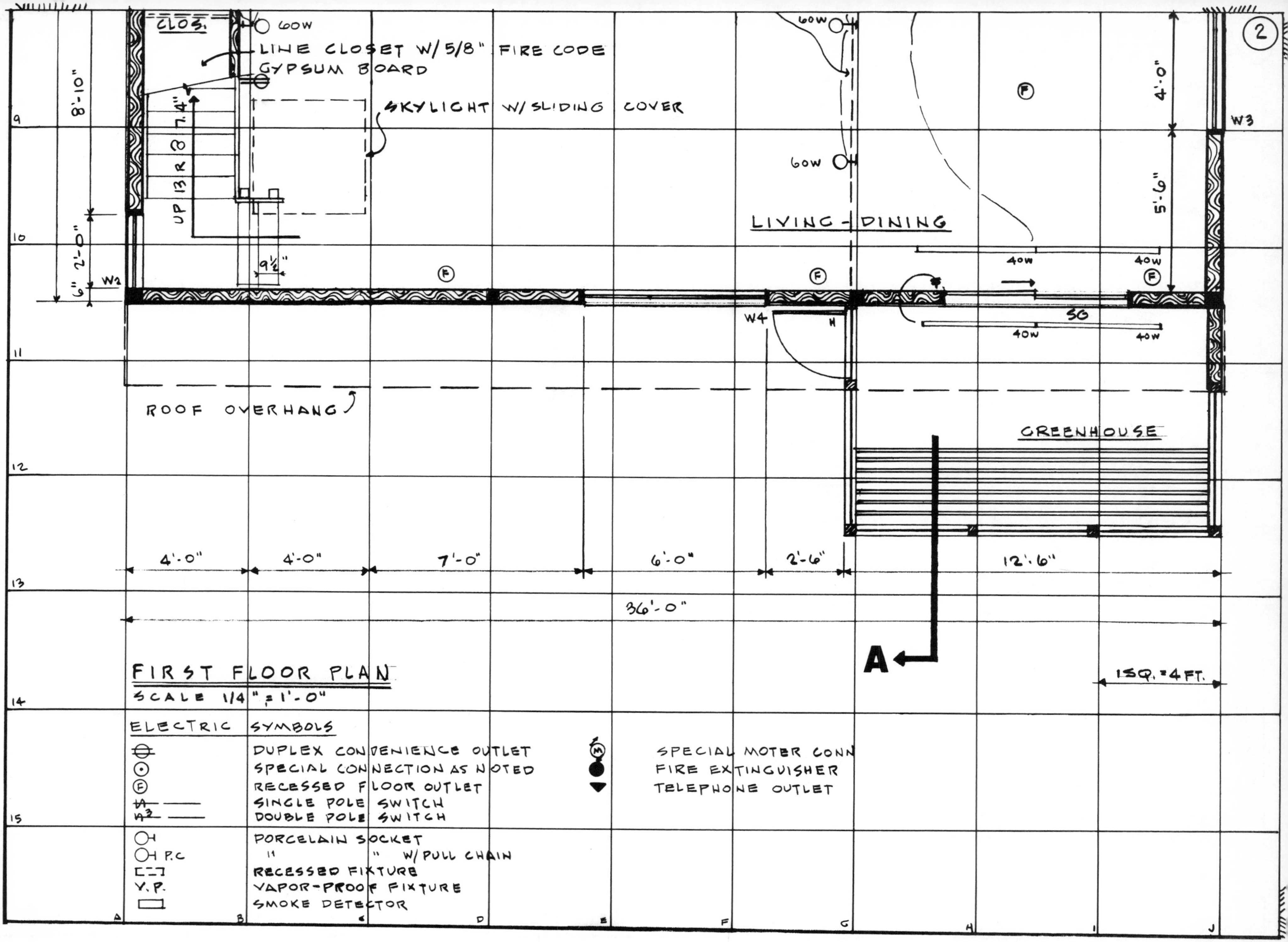

FIRST FLOOR PLAN
SCALE 1/4"=1'-0"

GREENHOUSE

LIVING-DINING

SKYLIGHT W/ SLIDING COVER

LINE CLOSET W/ 5/8" FIRE CODE GYPSUM BOARD

CLOS.

ROOF OVERHANG

UP 13R @ 7½"

W3 · W4 · W2

40W · 60W · SD

4'-0" · 5'-6" · 12'-6" · 2'-6" · 6'-0" · 36'-0" · 7'-0" · 4'-0" · 9½" · 8'-10" · 2'-0" · 6"

1 SQ.=4 FT.

A

ELECTRIC SYMBOLS

DUPLEX CONVENIENCE OUTLET
SPECIAL CONNECTION AS NOTED
RECESSED FLOOR OUTLET
SINGLE POLE SWITCH
DOUBLE POLE SWITCH

PORCELAIN SOCKET
"   W/PULL CHAIN
RECESSED FIXTURE
VAPOR-PROOF FIXTURE
SMOKE DETECTOR

SPECIAL MOTER CONN
FIRE EXTINGUISHER
TELEPHONE OUTLET

S_1
S_2
H.P.C
V.P.

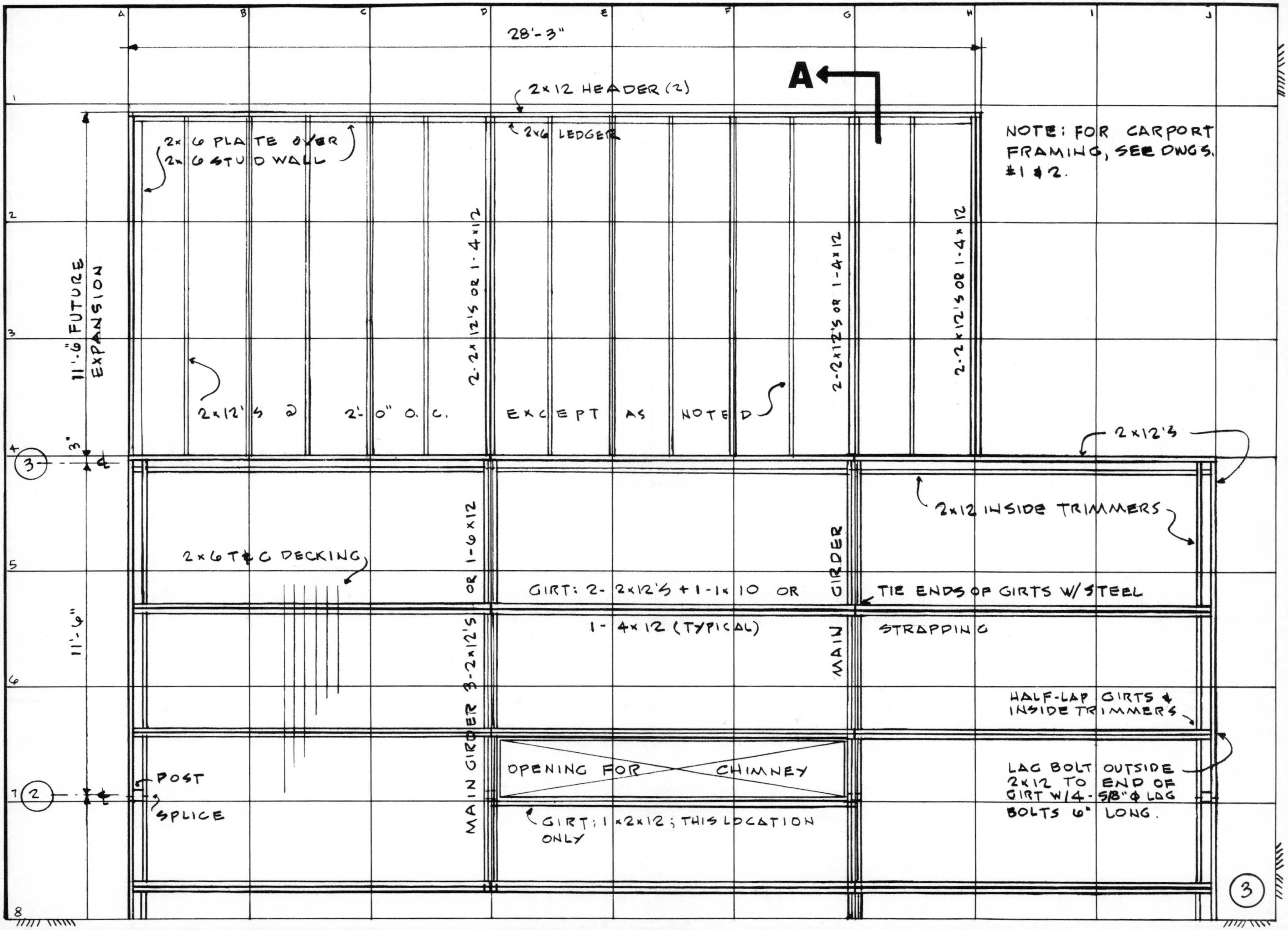
28'-3"
A
2x12 HEADER (2)
2x6 LEDGER
NOTE: FOR CARPORT FRAMING, SEE DWGS. #1 & 2.
2x6 PLATE OVER 2x6 STUD WALL
11'-6" FUTURE EXPANSION
2-2x12'S OR 1-4x12
2-2x12'S OR 1-4x12
2-2x12'S OR 1-4x12
2x12'S @ 2'-0" O.C. EXCEPT AS NOTED
3"
2x12'S
2x12 INSIDE TRIMMERS
2x6 T&G DECKING
MAIN GIRDER 3-2x12'S OR 1-6x12
GIRT: 2-2x12'S + 1-1x10 OR 1-4x12 (TYPICAL)
MAIN GIRDER
TIE ENDS OF GIRTS W/ STEEL STRAPPING
11'-6"
HALF-LAP GIRTS & INSIDE TRIMMERS
OPENING FOR CHIMNEY
LAG BOLT OUTSIDE 2x12 TO END OF GIRT W/ 4-5/8"Φ LAG BOLTS 6" LONG.
POST SPLICE
GIRT: 1x2x12; THIS LOCATION ONLY
3
2
3

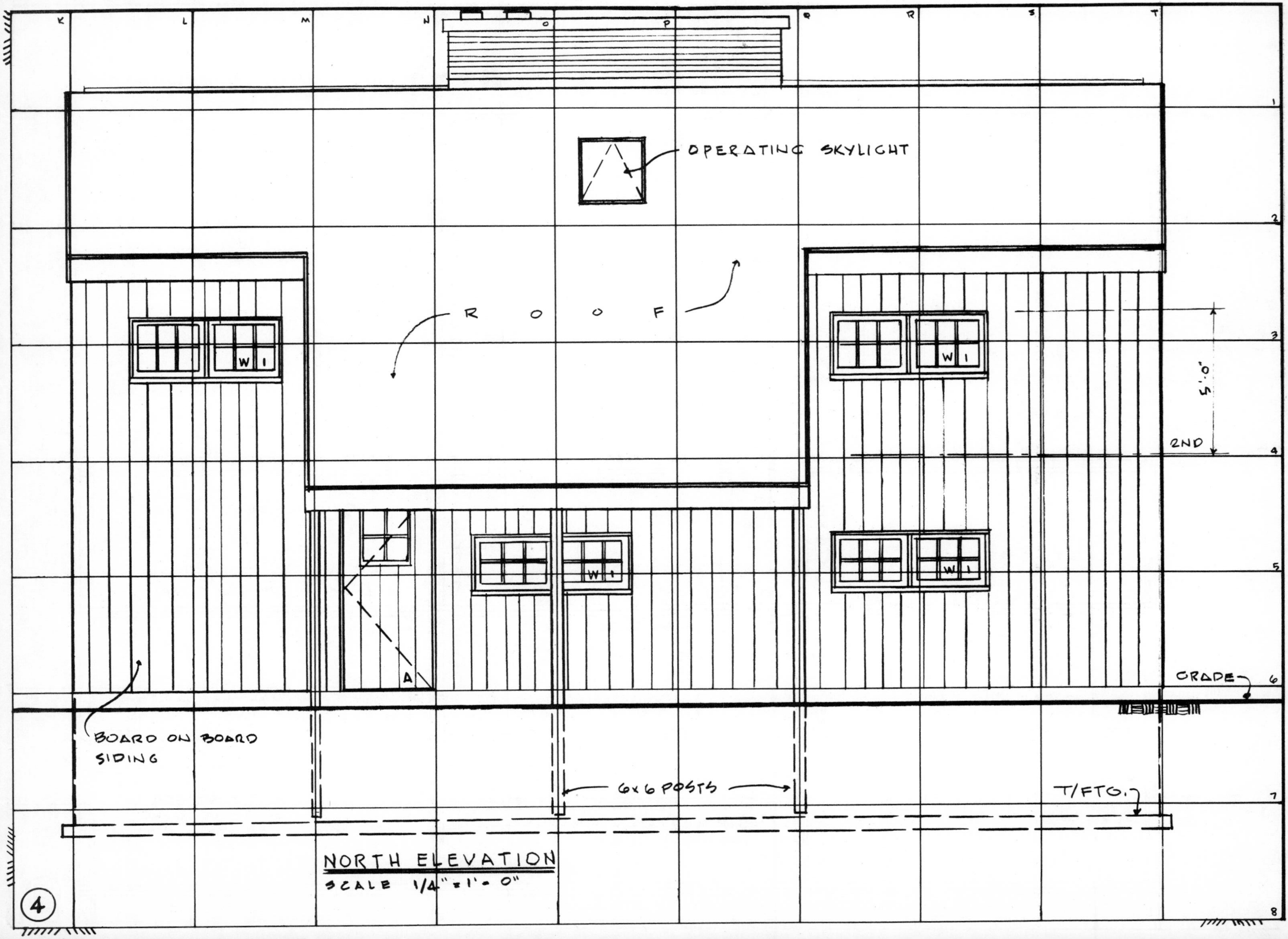

NORTH ELEVATION

SCALE 1/4" = 1'-0"

BOARD ON BOARD SIDING

6×6 POSTS

T/FTG.

ROOF

OPERATING SKYLIGHT

GRADE

2ND

5'-0"

W-1

W-1

W-1

W-1

A

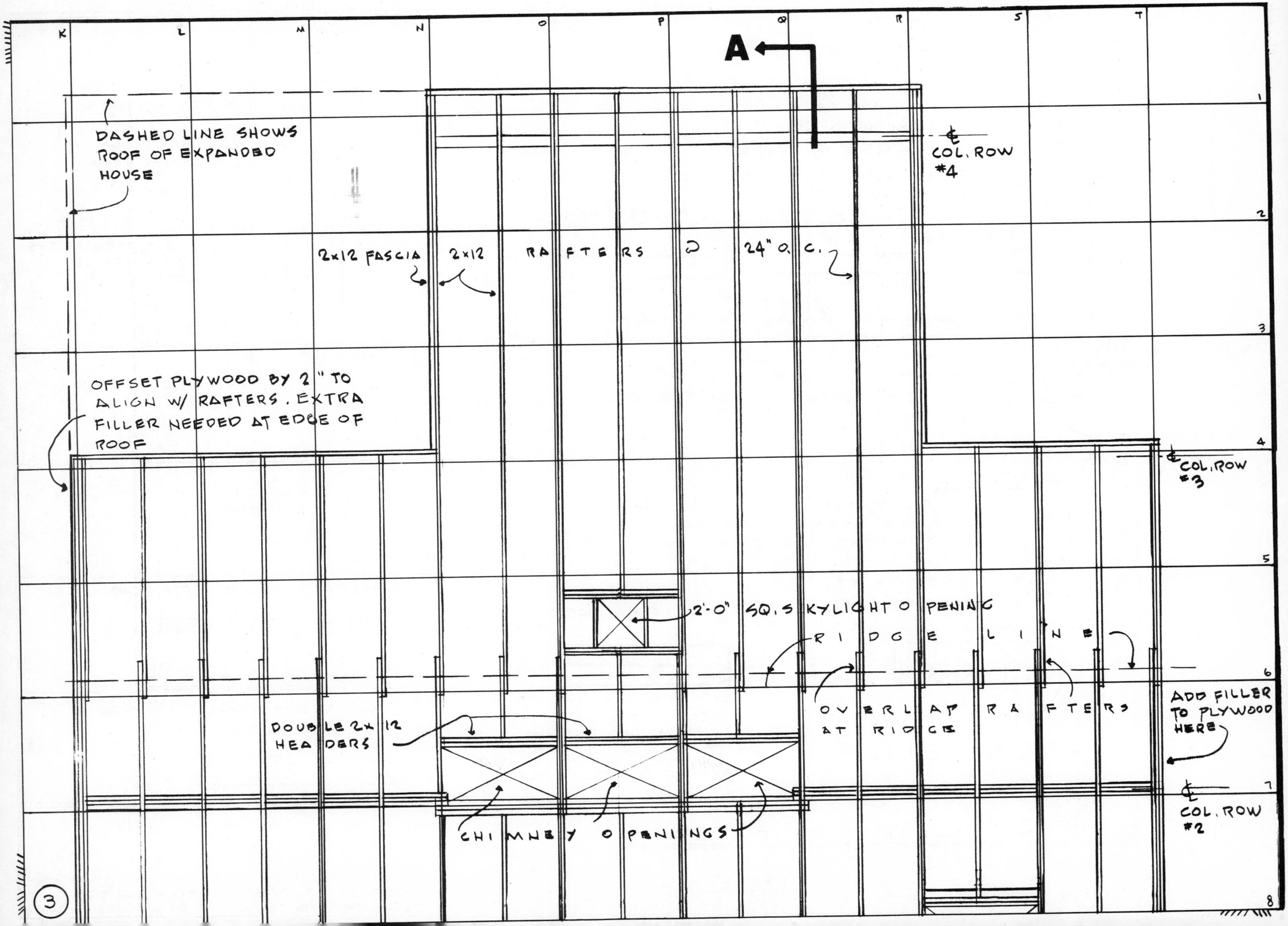
A
DASHED LINE SHOWS ROOF OF EXPANDED HOUSE
COL. ROW #4
2x12 FASCIA
2x12 RAFTERS @ 24" O.C.
OFFSET PLYWOOD BY 2" TO ALIGN W/ RAFTERS. EXTRA FILLER NEEDED AT EDGE OF ROOF
COL. ROW #3
2'-0" SQ. SKYLIGHT OPENING
RIDGE LINE
OVERLAP RAFTERS AT RIDGE
DOUBLE 2x12 HEADERS
ADD FILLER TO PLYWOOD HERE
COL. ROW #2
CHIMNEY OPENINGS
K
L
M
N
O
P
Q
R
S
T
1
2
3
4
5
6
7
8
3

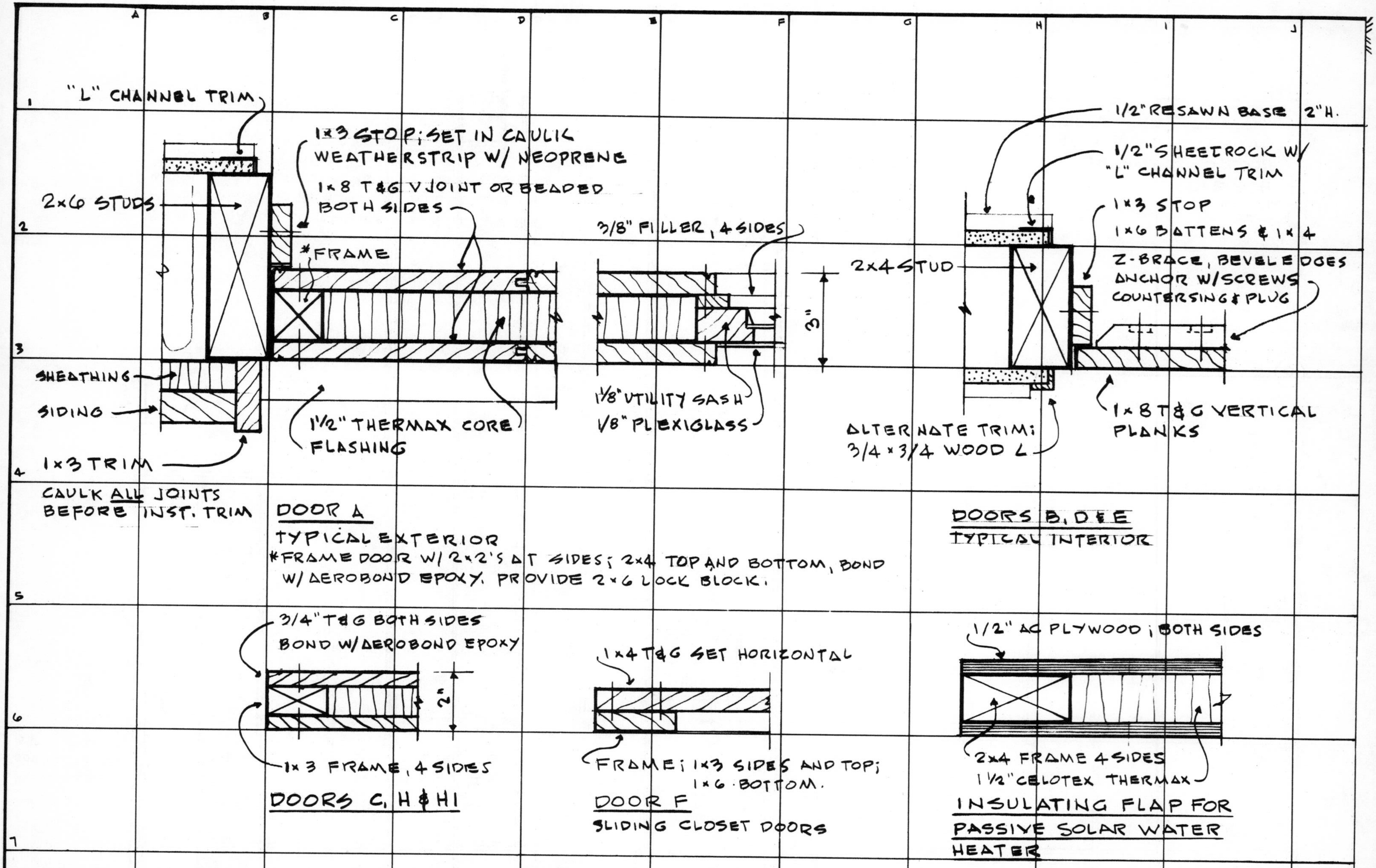

DOOR AND INSULATING PANEL DETAILS

"L" CHANNEL TRIM

2×6 STUDS

SHEATHING

SIDING

1×3 TRIM

CAULK ALL JOINTS BEFORE INST. TRIM

1×3 FRAME, 4 SIDES

3/4" T&G BOTH SIDES BOND W/AEROBOND EPOXY

2"

DOORS C, H & HI

1×3 STOP; SET IN CAULK WEATHERSTRIP W/ NEOPRENE

1×8 T&G V JOINT OR BEADED BOTH SIDES

#FRAME

DOOR A
TYPICAL EXTERIOR
*FRAME DOOR W/ 2×2'S AT SIDES; 2×4 TOP AND BOTTOM, BOND
W/ AEROBOND EPOXY. PROVIDE 2×6 LOCK BLOCK.

1½" THERMAX CORE

1½" THERMAX FLASHING

3/8" FILLER, 4 SIDES

1/8" UTILITY SASH
1/8" PLEXIGLASS

ALTERNATE TRIM:
3/4 × 3/4 WOOD L

3"

2×4 STUD

1×4 T&G SET HORIZONTAL

FRAME; 1×3 SIDES AND TOP;
1×6 BOTTOM.

DOOR F
SLIDING CLOSET DOORS

DOORS B, D & E
TYPICAL INTERIOR

1/2" AC PLYWOOD; BOTH SIDES

2×4 FRAME 4 SIDES
1½" CELOTEX THERMAX

INSULATING FLAP FOR
PASSIVE SOLAR WATER
HEATER

1/2" RESAWN BASE 2" H.

1/2" SHEETROCK W/
"L" CHANNEL TRIM

1×3 STOP
1×6 BATTENS & 1×4

Z-BRACE, BEVELED EDGES
ANCHOR W/ SCREWS
COUNTERSINK & PLUG

1×8 T&G VERTICAL
PLANKS

NOTE!

ALL WOOD USED FOR DOORS & MILLWORK
TO BE THOROUGHLY SEASONED, PAINT OR
SEAL BOTH SIDES & ALL EDGES AT ONCE.

SCALE 3" = 1'-0"

1 SQ = 4"

4

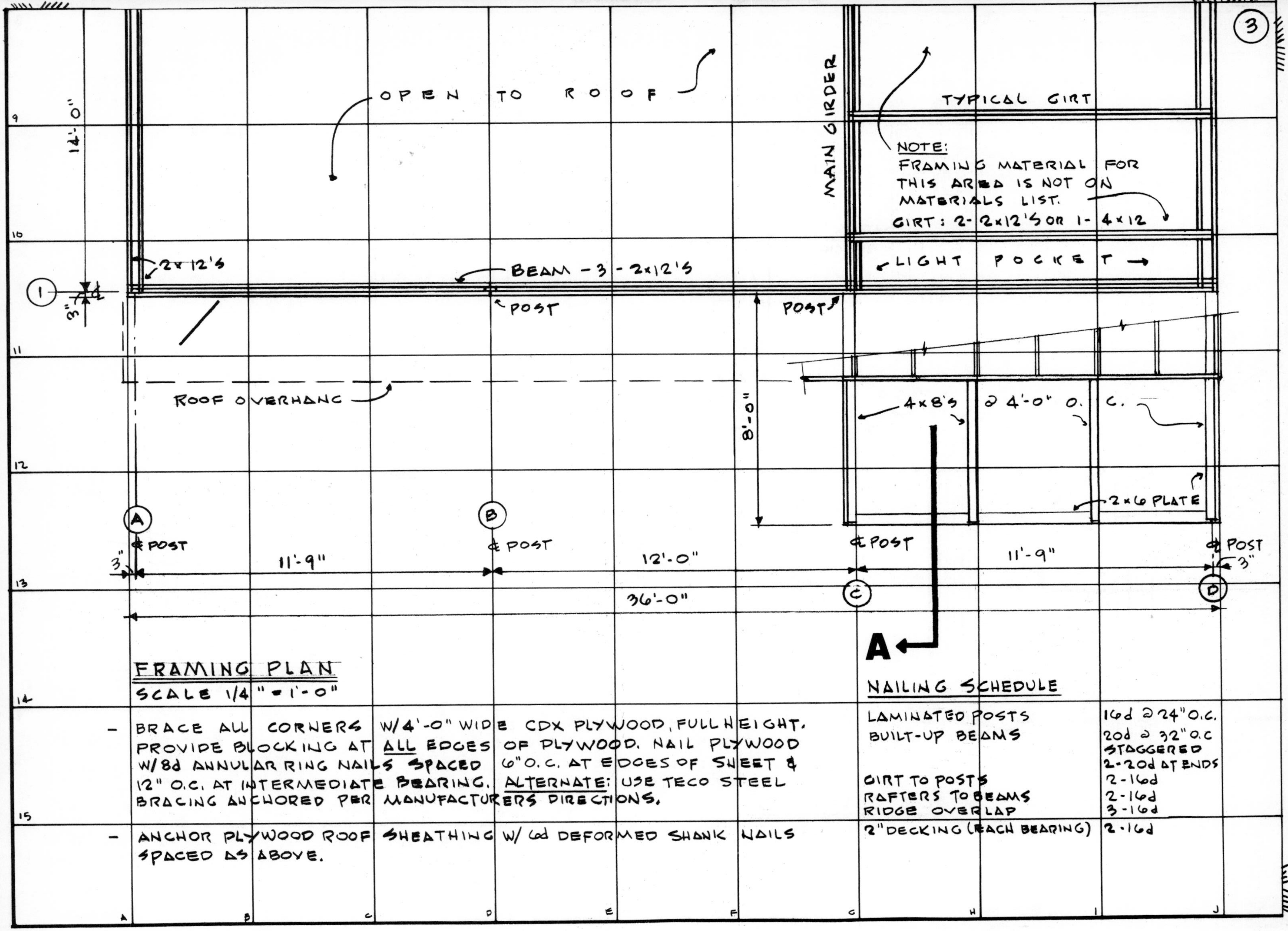

FRAMING PLAN

SCALE 1/4" = 1'-0"

NAILING SCHEDULE

LAMINATED POSTS	16d @ 24"O.C.
BUILT-UP BEAMS	20d @ 32"O.C. STAGGERED
	2-20d AT ENDS
GIRT TO POSTS	2-16d
RAFTERS TO BEAMS	2-16d
RIDGE OVERLAP	3-16d
2" DECKING (EACH BEARING)	2-16d

BRACE ALL CORNERS W/4'-0" WIDE CDX PLYWOOD, FULL HEIGHT. PROVIDE BLOCKING AT ALL EDGES OF PLYWOOD, NAIL PLYWOOD W/8d ANNULAR RING NAILS SPACED 6"O.C. AT EDGES OF SHEET & 12"O.C. AT INTERMEDIATE BEARING. ALTERNATE: USE TECO STEEL BRACING ANCHORED PER MANUFACTURERS DIRECTIONS.

ANCHOR PLYWOOD ROOF SHEATHING W/ 6d DEFORMED SHANK NAILS SPACED AS ABOVE.

NOTE:
FRAMING MATERIAL FOR THIS AREA IS NOT ON MATERIALS LIST.
GIRT: 2-2x12'S or 1-4x12

TYPICAL GIRT

MAIN GIRDER

LIGHT POCKET

OPEN TO ROOF

ROOF OVERHANG

BEAM - 3 - 2x12'S

2x12'S

POST

¢ POST

4x8'S @ 4'-0" O.C.

2x6 PLATE

14'-0"

3"
1/4"

11'-9"

12'-0"

36'-0"

8'-0"

A

3" ¢ POST

B ¢ POST

C ¢ POST

D ¢ POST 3"

1 9 10 11 12 13 14 15

3

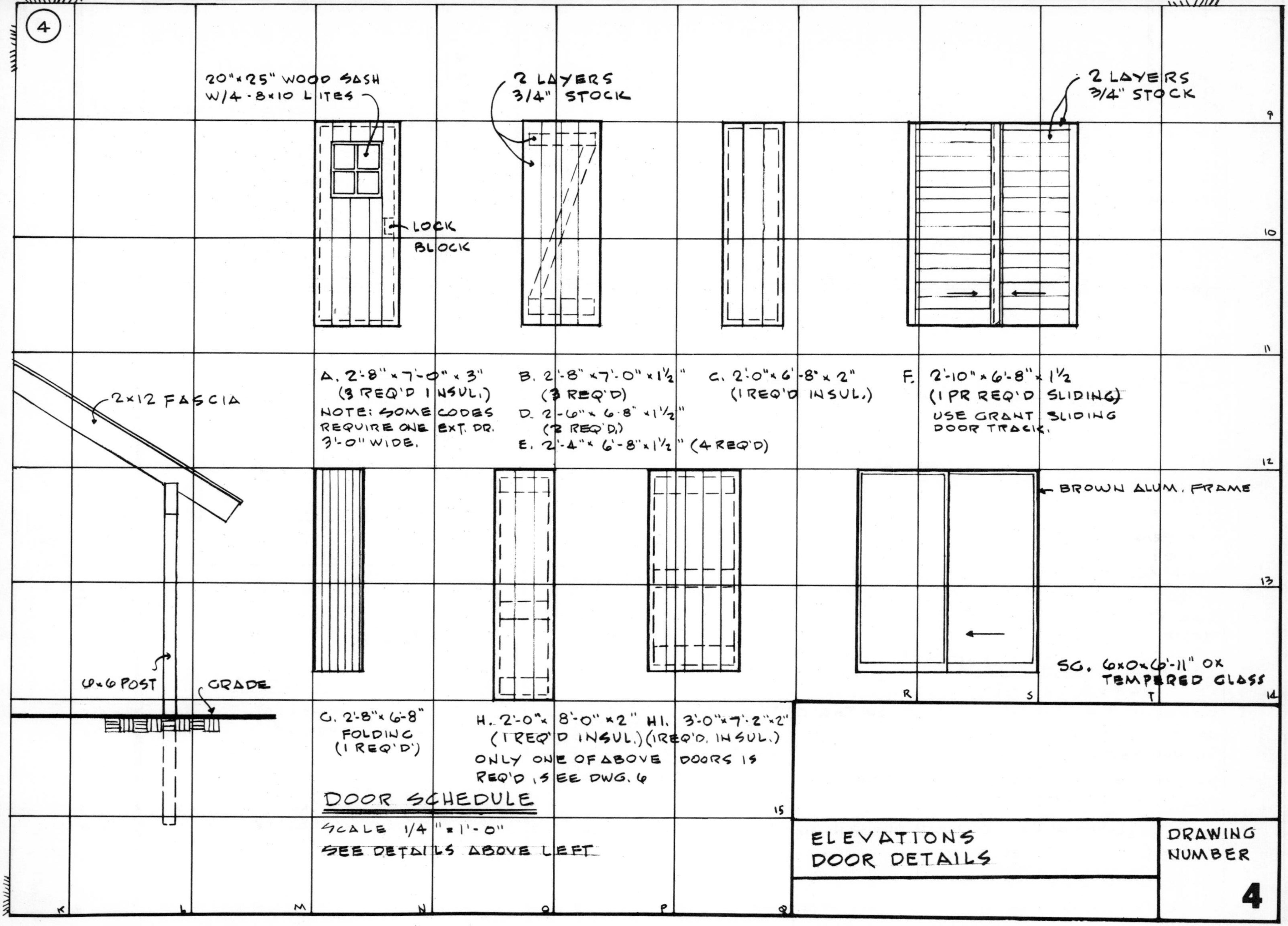

2 LAYERS 3/4" STOCK

2 LAYERS 3/4" STOCK

20"×25" WOOD SASH W/4 - 8×10 LITES

LOCK BLOCK

2×12 FASCIA

6×6 POST

GRADE

BROWN ALUM. FRAME

SG. 6'-0"×6'-11" OX TEMPERED GLASS

A. 2'-8"×7'-0"×3" (3 REQ'D INSUL.)

NOTE: SOME CODES REQUIRE ONE EXT. DR. 3'-0" WIDE.

B. 2'-8"×7'-0"×1½" (3 REQ'D)

C. 2'-0"×6'-8"×2" (1 REQ'D INSUL.)

D. 2'-0"×6'-8"×1½" (2 REQ'D)

E. 2'-4"×6'-8"×1½" (4 REQ'D)

F. 2'-10"×6'-8"×1½" (1 PR REQ'D SLIDING) USE GRANT SLIDING DOOR TRACK.

G. 2'-8"×6'-8" FOLDING (1 REQ'D)

H. 2'-0"×8'-0"×2" (1 REQ'D INSUL.)

HI. 3'-0"×7'-2"×2" (1 REQ'D. INSUL.) ONLY ONE OF ABOVE DOORS IS REQ'D (SEE DWG. 6)

DOOR SCHEDULE

SCALE 1/4"=1'-0"

SEE DETAILS ABOVE LEFT

ELEVATIONS DOOR DETAILS

DRAWING NUMBER

4

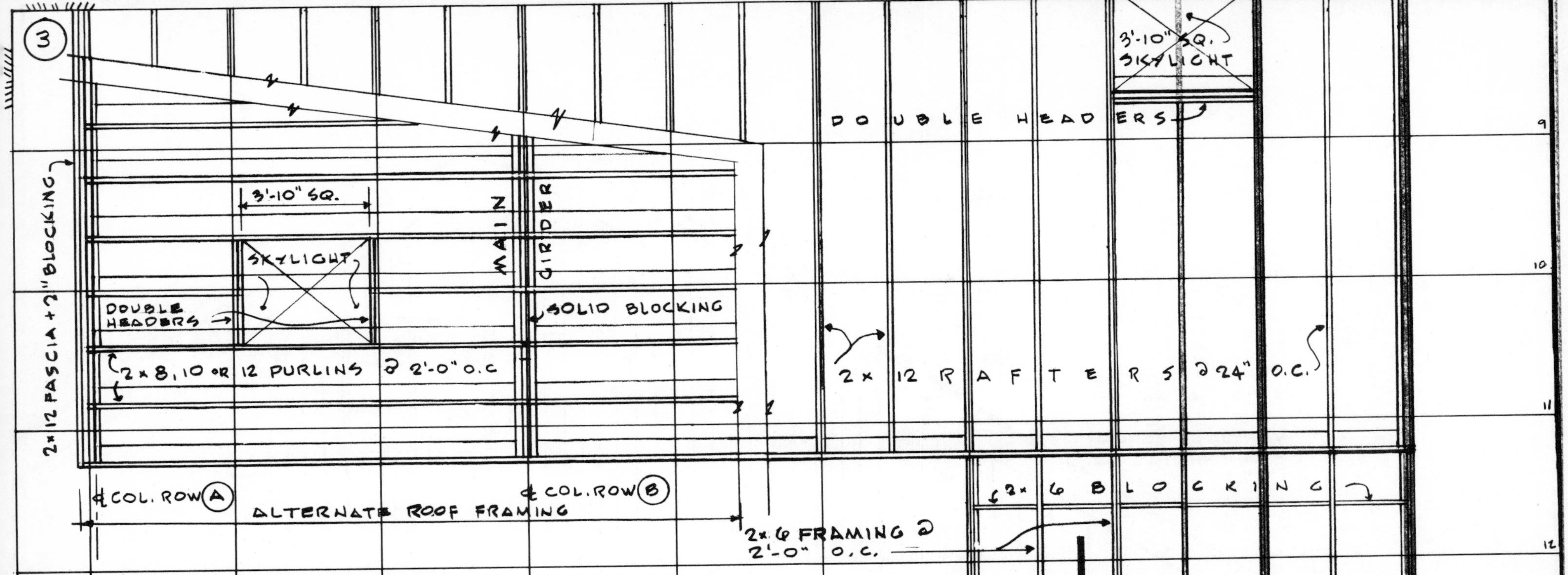

ROOF FRAMING PLAN

SCALE 1/4" = 1'-0"

- THE FRAMING SYSTEM IS OVERSIZED TO ACCOMMODATE HEAVY INSULATION. THE BEAM AT COL. LINE 1, FLOOR SUPPORT BEAMS AT LINES B & C, AND ROOF SUPPORT BEAMS AT LINE 2 & 3 ARE MODERATELY STRESSED. THESE SHOULD HAVE A MINIMUM FLEXURAL STRESS "f" OF 1,650 PSI, MEETING THE REQUIREMENTS OF A MAJOR GRADING AUTHORITY; NELMA, SPIB, WCLIB, WWPA OR NLGA (CANADIAN) STRENGTHS OF VARIOUS SPECIES AND GRADES OF LUMBER VARY GREATLY; CLEAR TIMBERS FREE OF KNOTS OR SHAKES IN MOST SPECIES OF PINE, SPRUCE, HEMLOCK OR FIR WILL MEET THESE MINIMUM REQUIREMENTS.

- FRAMING FOR MEMBERS OTHER THAN THE CRITICAL ONES NOTED ABOVE CAN BE ALMOST ANY SOUND, LOCALLY MILLED LUMBER. ROOF RAFTERS SHOULD BE SPACED @ 16" O.C. IN AREAS OF VERY HEAVY SNOW LOADS.

- DO NOT USE THE ALTERNATE ROOF FRAMING SYSTEM IN AREAS OF HEAVY SNOW LOADS.

- USE LOCALLY-MILLED AIR-DRIED LUMBER WHERE POSSIBLE, IT REQUIRES ABOUT 1/3 AS MUCH ENERGY AS COMMERCIAL LUMBER.

- REFERENCE FOR LUMBER GRADING: TIMBER CONSTRUCTION MANUAL, JOHN WILEY & SONS, INC., 1974

2×12 FASCIA + 2" BLOCKING

DOUBLE HEADERS

2×8, 10 OR 12 PURLINS @ 2'-0" O.C.

3'-10" SQ.

SKYLIGHT

MAIN GIRDER

SOLID BLOCKING

& COL. ROW A

ALTERNATE ROOF FRAMING

& COL. ROW B

2×6 FRAMING @ 2'-0" O.C.

2×12 RAFTERS @ 24" O.C.

DOUBLE HEADERS

3'-10" SQ. SKYLIGHT

& COL. ROW C

2×6 BLOCKING

2×6 BLOCKING

2×6 SILL

FRAMING PLAN FOR BREAKFRONT GREENHOUSE.

A

& COL. ROW D

FRAMING PLANS
STRUCTURAL NOTES

DRAWING NUMBER

3

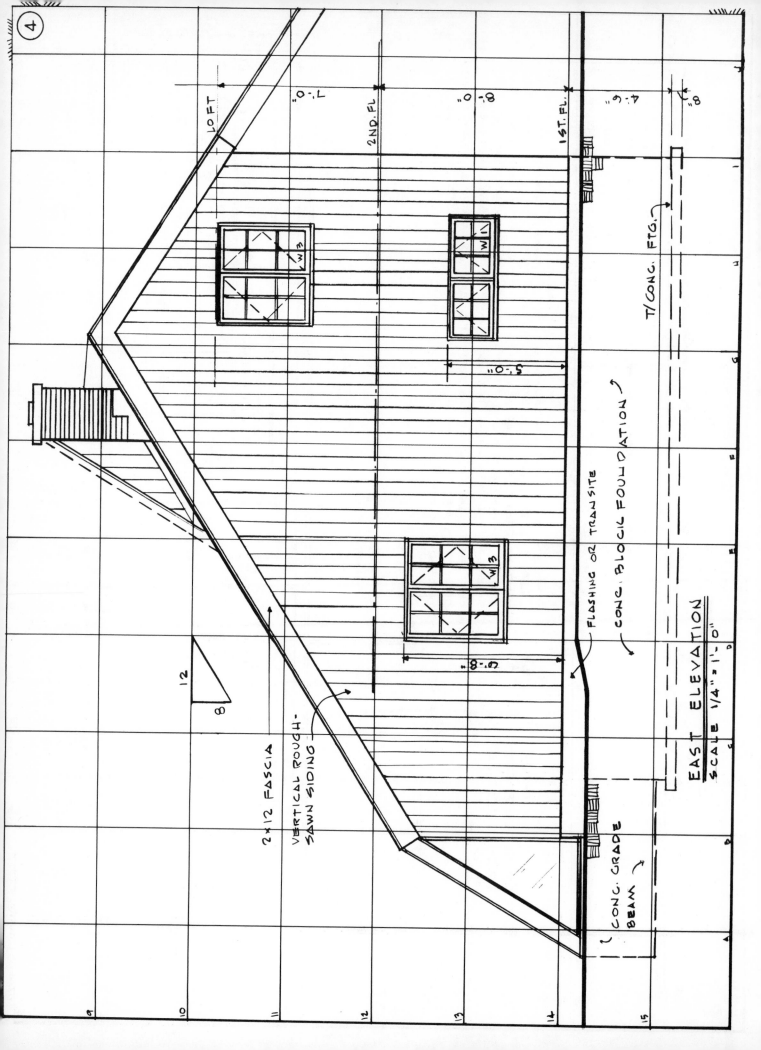

EAST ELEVATION
SCALE 1/4" = 1'-0"

LOFT

7'-0"
2ND. FL.

8'-0"
1ST. FL.

4'-6"

8"

T/CONC. FTG.

CONC. BLOCK FOUNDATION

FLASHING OR TRANSITE

CONC. GRADE BEAM

2×12 FASCIA

VERTICAL ROUGH-SAWN SIDING

12
8

W3

W1

W3

5'-0"

8'-0"

4

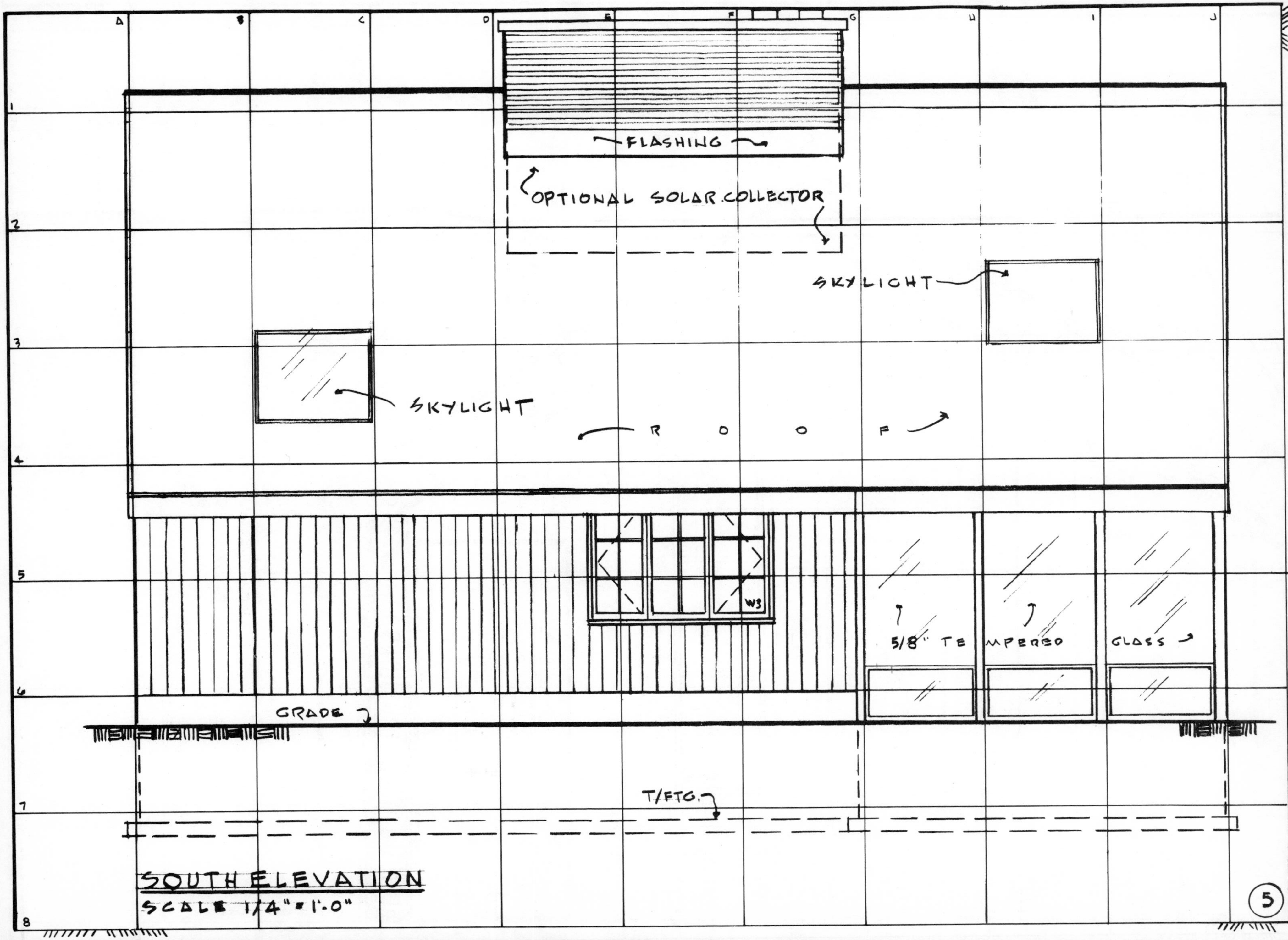

SOUTH ELEVATION
SCALE 1/4" = 1'-0"

OPTIONAL SOLAR COLLECTOR
FLASHING
SKYLIGHT
SKYLIGHT
ROOF
GLASS
5/8" TE MPERED
W3
GRADE
T/FTG.

⑤

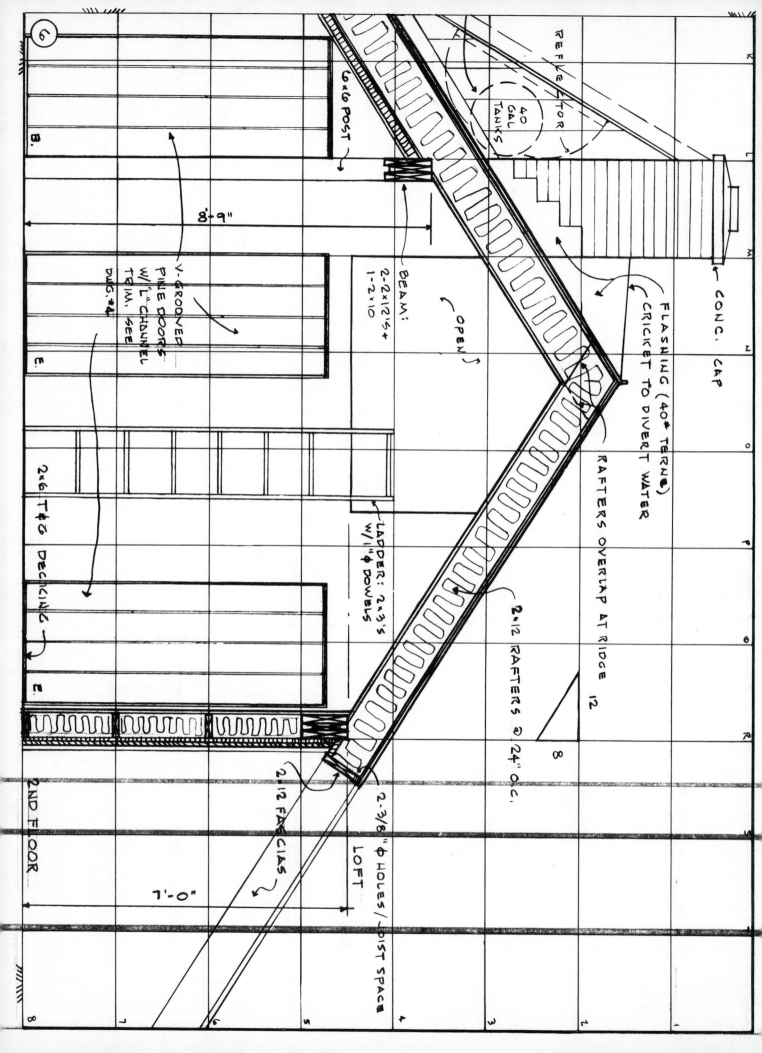

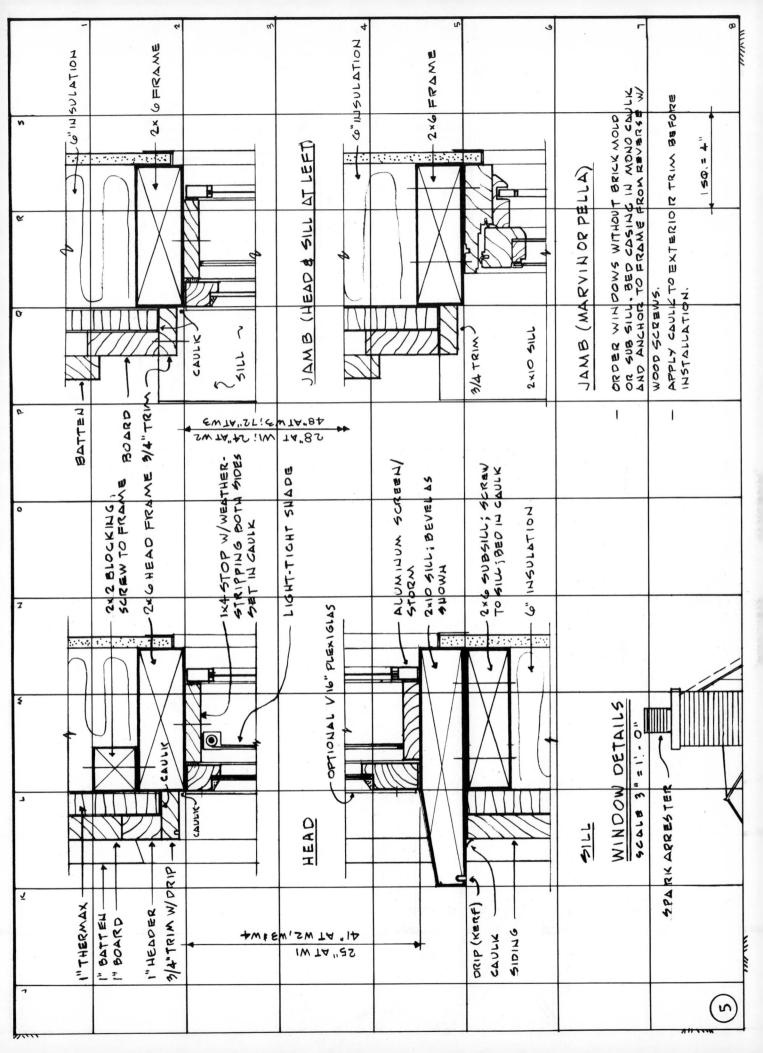

WINDOW DETAILS
SCALE 3"=1'-0"

HEAD

SILL

JAMB (HEAD & SILL AT LEFT)

JAMB (MARVIN OR PELLA)

ORDER WINDOWS WITHOUT BRICK MOLD OR SUB SILL. BED CASING IN MONO CAULK AND ANCHOR TO FRAME FROM REVERSE W/ WOOD SCREWS.
APPLY CAULK TO EXTERIOR TRIM BEFORE INSTALLATION.

SPARK ARRESTER

1 SQ. = 4"

1" THERMAX
1" BATTEN
1" BOARD
1" HEADER
3/4" TRIM W/ DRIP

25" AT W1
41" AT W2, W3, W4

DRIP (KERF)
CAULK
SIDING

2x2 BLOCKING; SCREW TO FRAME
2x6 HEAD FRAME 3/4" TRIM
1x4 STOP W/ WEATHER-STRIPPING BOTH SIDES SET IN CAULK
LIGHT-TIGHT SHADE
OPTIONAL 1/16" PLEXIGLAS

ALUMINUM SCREEN/STORM
2x10 SILL SHOWN
2x6 SUBSILL; SCREW TO SILL; BED IN CAULK
6" INSULATION

BATTEN
BOARD
CAULK

6" INSULATION
2x6 FRAME

28" AT W1; 24" AT W2
48" AT W3; 72" AT W3

CAULK
SILL

6" INSULATION
2x6 FRAME

3/4" TRIM
2x10 SILL

5

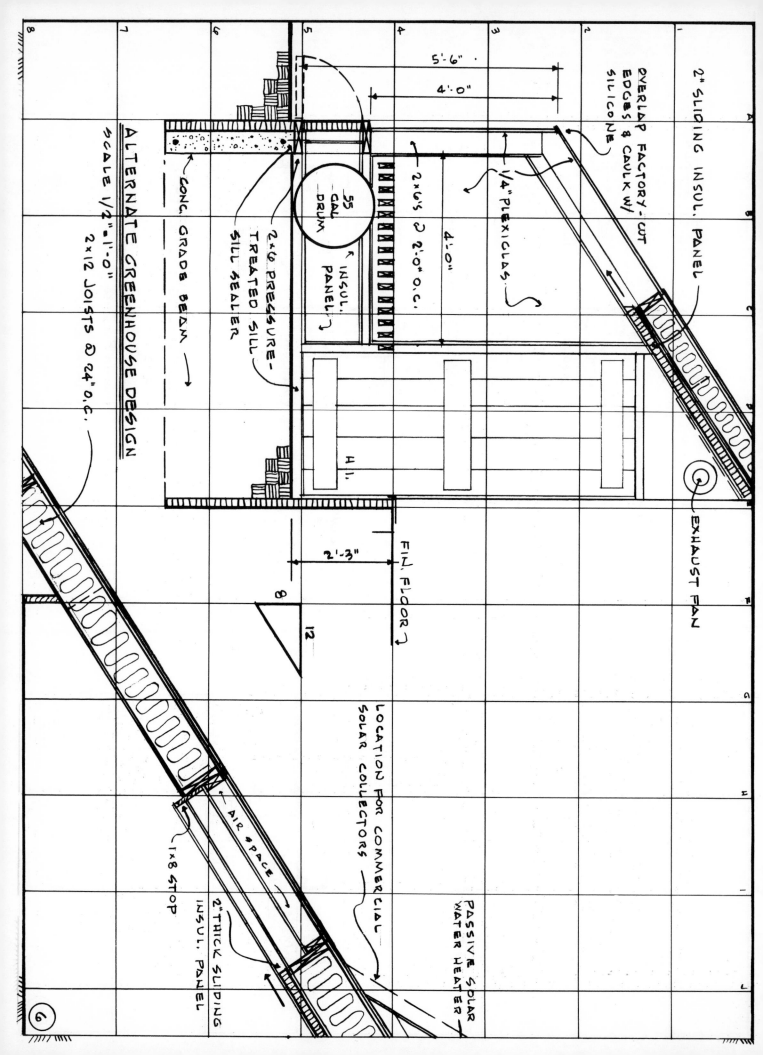

2" SLIDING INSUL. PANEL

OVERLAP FACTORY - CUT
EDGES & CAULK W/
SILICONE

1/4" PLEXIGLAS

2×6'S @ 2'-0" O.C.

55
GAL
DRUM

INSUL.
PANEL

2×6 PRESSURE-
TREATED SILL

SILL SEALER

CONC. GRADE BEAM

ALTERNATE GREENHOUSE DESIGN

SCALE 1/2"=1'-0"

2×12 JOISTS @ 24" O.C.

5'-6"

4'-0"

4'-0"

FILL

2'-3"

8

12

FIN. FLOOR

EXHAUST FAN

LOCATION FOR COMMERCIAL
SOLAR COLLECTORS

PASSIVE SOLAR
WATER HEATER

AIR SPACE

1×8 STOP

2" THICK SLIDING
INSUL. PANEL

⑥

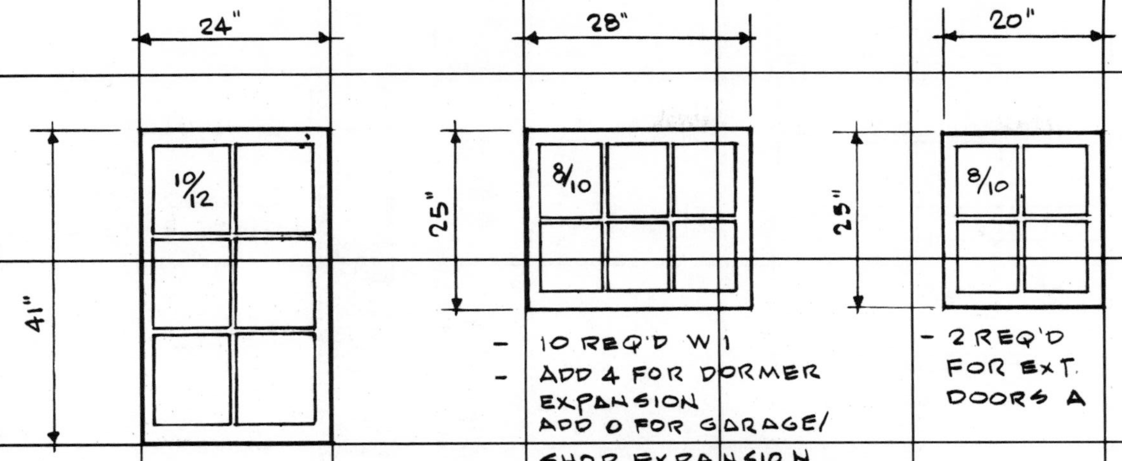

WINDOW SCHEDULE

SCALE 1/2" = 1'-0"

COMMERCIAL WINDOWS

THE FOLLOWING HIGH-QUALITY COMMERCIAL WINDOWS ARE OF A
SIMILAR SIZE TO THE WINDOWS SHOWN ABOVE AND ON THE ELEVATIONS.

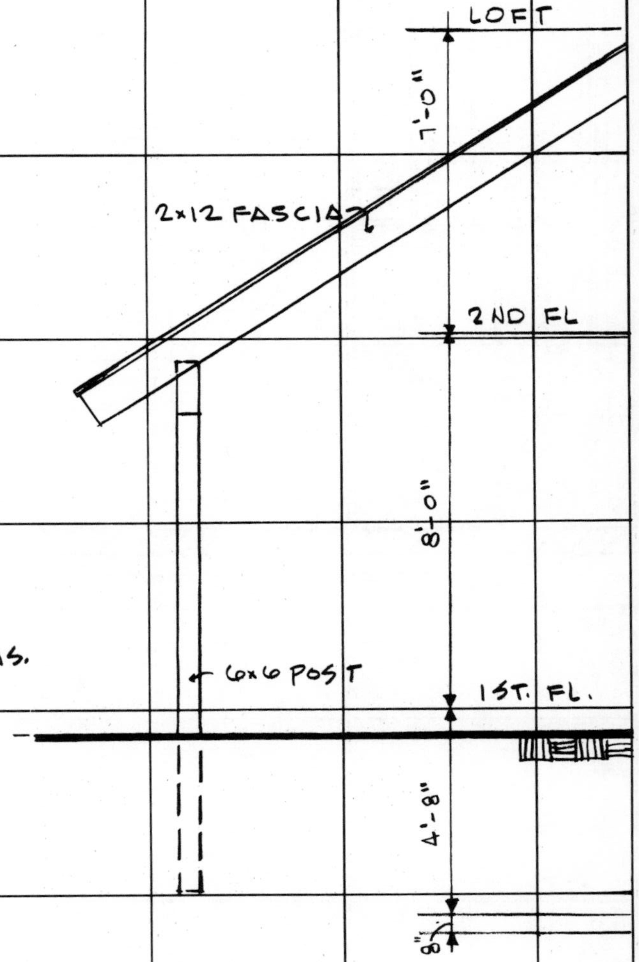

MARVIN WINDOWS WARROAD, MN 56763

CASEMENTS: 3-2040
  2-2040-2
  1-2040-3 OR 1 #4-24 LITE FIXED SASH

AWNING: 10-2822 OR 5-5-2816 SINGLE SLIDE.

PELLA ROLSCREEN CO., PELLA IA 50218

CASEMENTS: 3-2036-WC1
  2-2036-WC1
  1-2036-WC2
  1-2036-WC3 OR 1-6048 WC 20 LITE FIXED
  5-2820 WA21

AWNING: 5-2820 WA21

ORDER YOUR WINDOWS W/ SCREENS AND DOUBLE-GLAZING.
ORDER THEM WITHOUT BRICK MOLDS, EXTENSION JAMBS OR
SUB-SILL. MARVIN CAN FURNISH CLEAR, UNFINISHED WINDOWS.

41"   24"

10/12

10 REQ'D.
W2, W3, W4

1 — STANDARD 1 1/8" PONDEROSA PINE
UTILITY SASH. SEE DETAILS ABOVE

25"   28"

8/10

10 REQ'D W1
ADD 4 FOR DORMER
EXPANSION
ADD 0 FOR GARAGE/

1 — SHOP EXPANSION
ADD 2 IF BOTH EXPANSIONS
ARE DONE TOGETHER.

25"   20"

8/10

2 REQ'D
FOR EXT.
DOORS A

2×12 FASCIA

6×6 POST

7'-0"   LOFT

8'-0"   2ND FL.

4'-8"   8"   1 ST. FL.

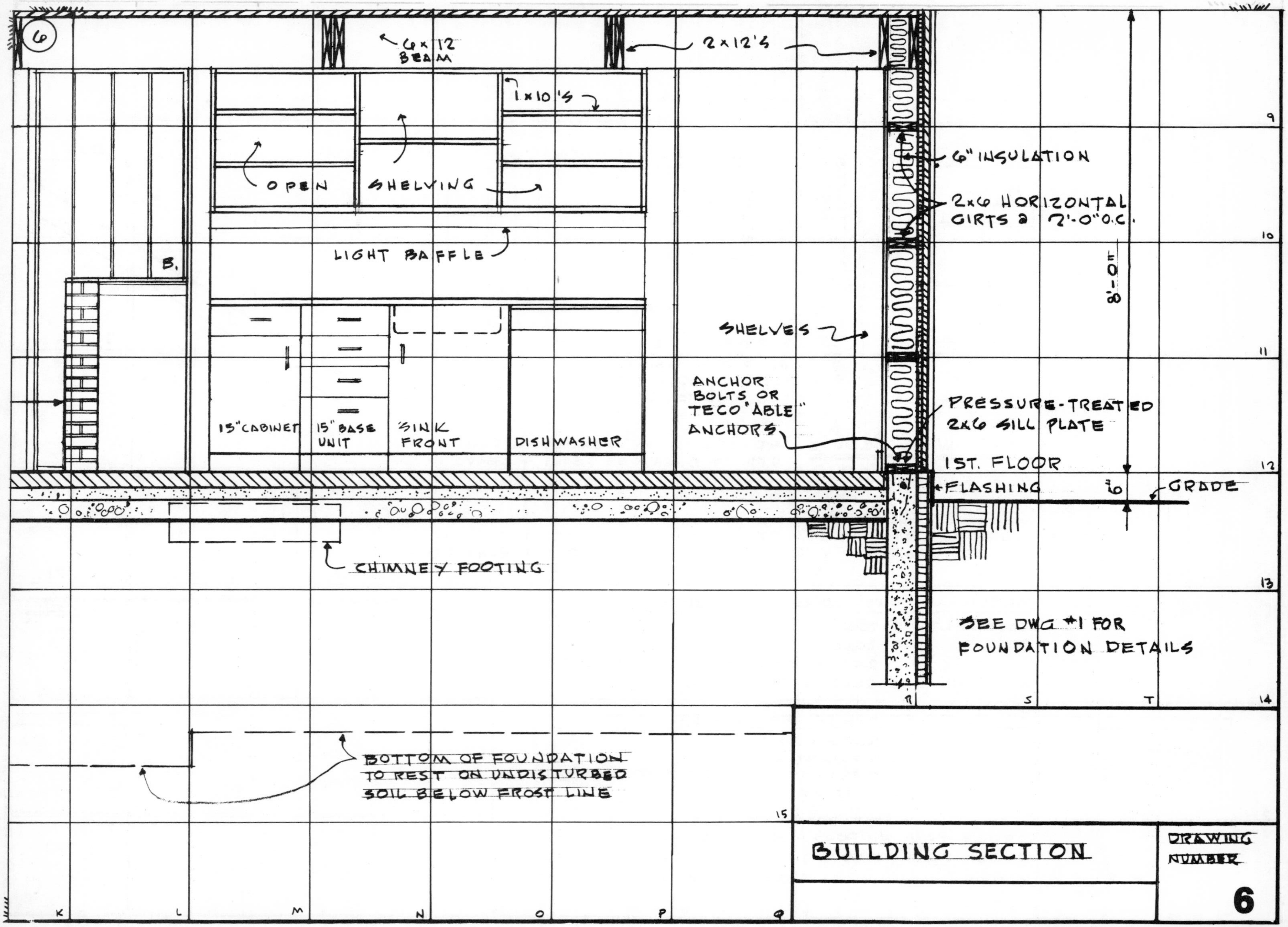

BUILDING SECTION

6" INSULATION

2x6 HORIZONTAL GIRTS @ 2'-0" O.C.

8'-0"

PRESSURE-TREATED 2x6 SILL PLATE

1ST FLOOR

GRADE

FLASHING

SEE DWG #1 FOR FOUNDATION DETAILS

2 x 12's

SHELVES

ANCHOR BOLTS OR "TECO'ABLE" ANCHORS

6 x 12 BEAM

1x10's

OPEN SHELVING

LIGHT BAFFLE

DISHWASHER

SINK FRONT

15" BASE UNIT

15" CABINET

CHIMNEY FOOTING

BOTTOM OF FOUNDATION TO REST ON UNDISTURBED SOIL BELOW FROST LINE

DRAWING NUMBER

6

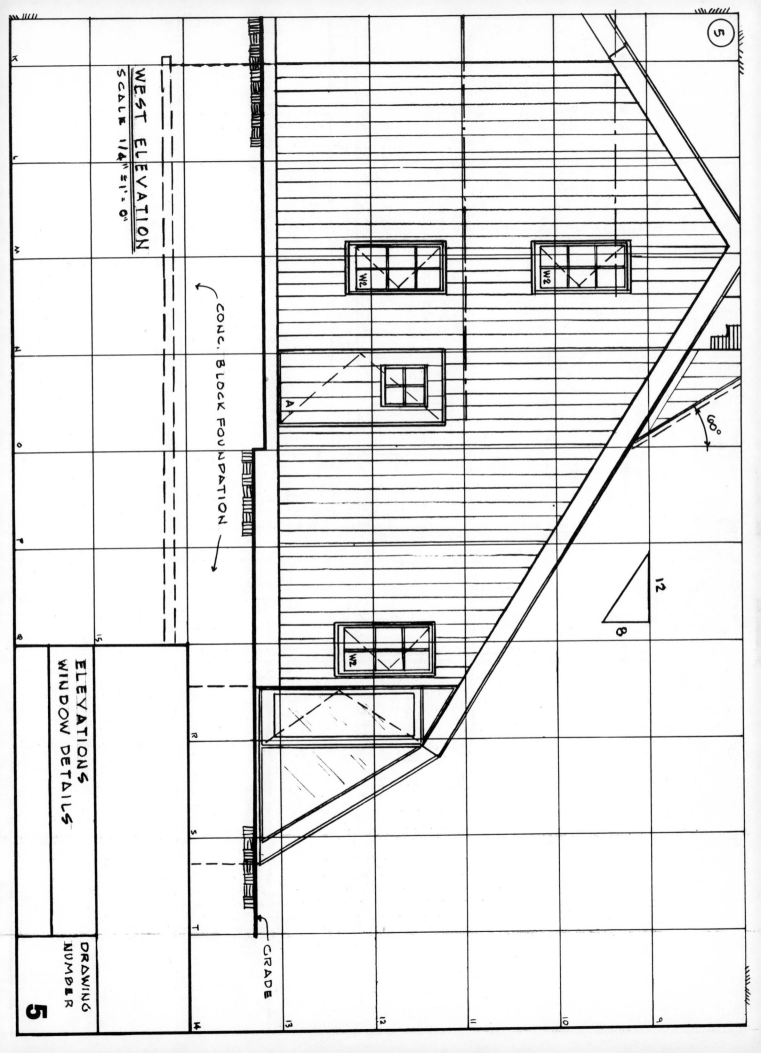

WEST ELEVATION
SCALE 1/4" = 1'-0"

CONC. BLOCK FOUNDATION

GRADE

12
8

60°

W2
W2
A
W2

ELEVATIONS
WINDOW DETAILS

DRAWING
NUMBER

5

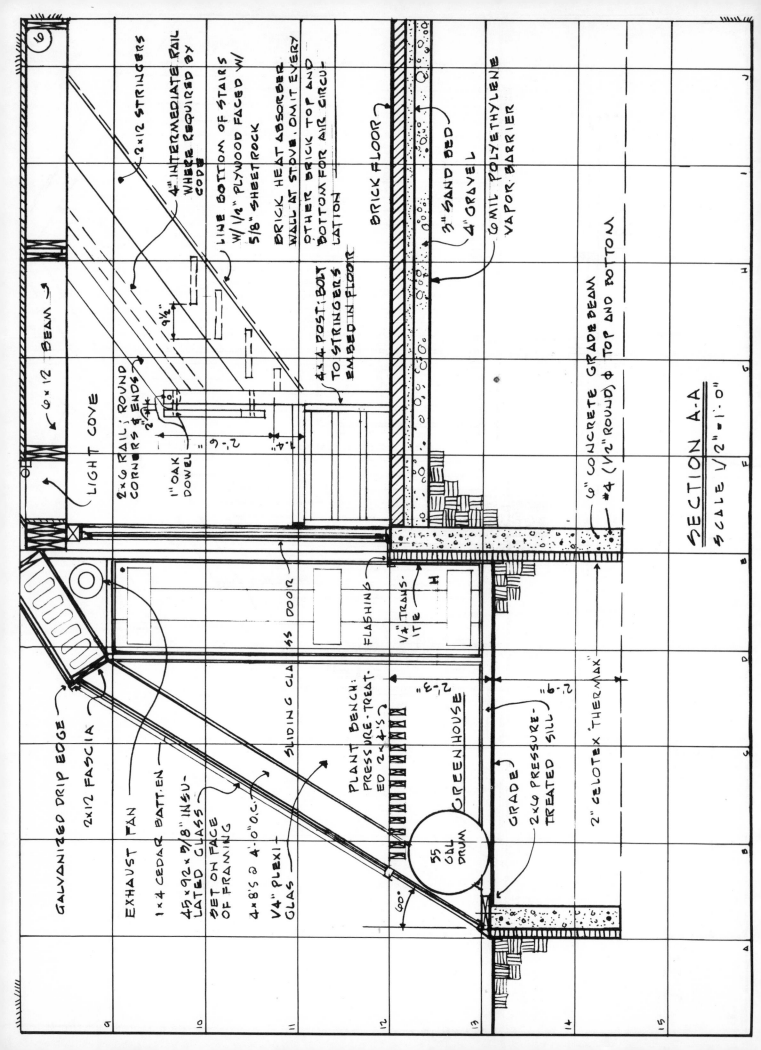

GALVANIZED DRIP EDGE

2x12 FASCIA

EXHAUST FAN

1x4 CEDAR BATTEN

45"x92"x 7/8" INSU-LATED GLASS

SET ON FACE OF FRAMING

4x8's @ 4'-0" O.C.

1/4" PLEXI-GLAS

LIGHT COVE

6 x 12 BEAM

2x6 RAIL; ROUND CORNERS & ENDS

2'-4"

1" OAK DOWEL

2'-6"

1'-4"

2x12 STRINGERS

4" INTERMEDIATE RAIL WHERE REQUIRED BY CODE

9 1/2"

LINE BOTTOM OF STAIRS W/ 1/4" PLYWOOD FACED W/ 5/8" SHEETROCK

BRICK HEAT ABSORBER WALL AT STOVE, OMIT EVERY OTHER BRICK TOP AND BOTTOM FOR AIR CIRCU-LATION

4x4 POST; BOLT TO STRINGERS EMBED IN FLOOR

SLIDING GLASS DOOR

FLASHING

1/4" TRANS-ITE

PLANT BENCH: PRESSURE-TREAT-ED 2x4's

2'-3"

55 GAL DRUM

GREENHOUSE

2'-6"

GRADE

2x6 PRESSURE-TREATED SILL

2" CELOTEX "THERMAX"

60°

BRICK FLOOR

3" SAND BED

4" GRAVEL

6 MIL POLYETHYLENE VAPOR BARRIER

6" CONCRETE GRADE BEAM

#4 (1/2" ROUND) ∅ TOP AND BOTTOM

SECTION A-A

SCALE 1/2" = 1'-0"

6

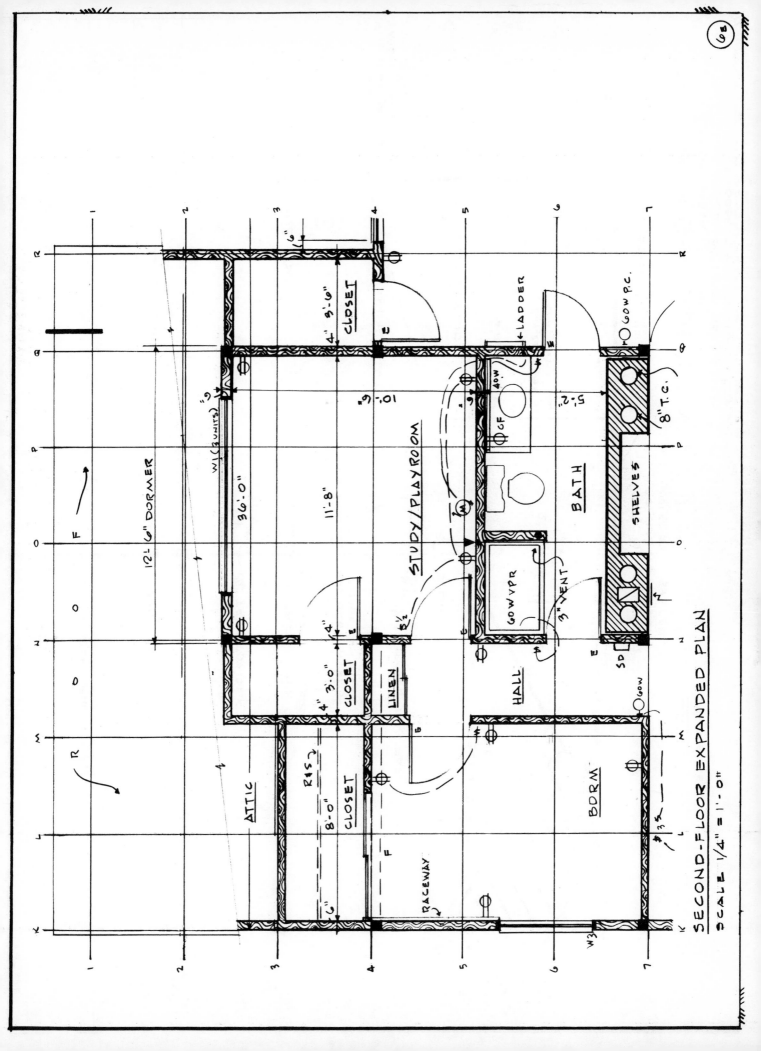

SECOND-FLOOR EXPANDED PLAN

SCALE 1/4" = 1'-0"

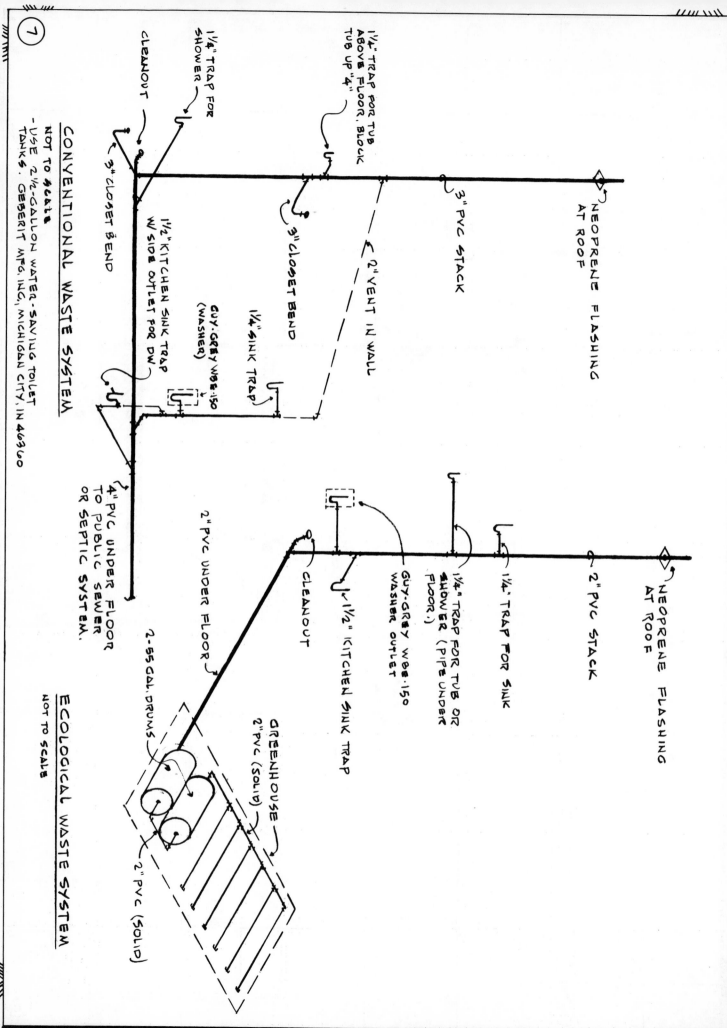

CONVENTIONAL WASTE SYSTEM

NOT TO SCALE

- USE 2½-GALLON WATER-SAVING TOILET TANKS. GEBERIT MFG. INC., MICHIGAN CITY, IN 46360

Labels (top diagram):

- NEOPRENE FLASHING AT ROOF
- 3" PVC STACK
- 2" VENT IN WALL
- 1½" TRAP FOR TUB ABOVE FLOOR, BLOCK TUB UP "4"
- 1½" TRAP FOR SHOWER
- CLEANOUT
- 3" CLOSET BEND
- 3" CLOSET BEND
- 1½" SINK TRAP
- 1½" KITCHEN SINK TRAP W/ SIDE OUTLET FOR DW
- GUY-GREY WBB-150 (WASHER)
- 4" PVC UNDER FLOOR TO PUBLIC SEWER OR SEPTIC SYSTEM.

ECOLOGICAL WASTE SYSTEM

NOT TO SCALE

Labels (bottom diagram):

- NEOPRENE FLASHING AT ROOF
- 2" PVC STACK
- 1½" TRAP FOR SINK
- 1½" TRAP FOR TUB OR SHOWER (PIPE UNDER FLOOR.)
- GUY-GREY WBB-150 WASHER OUTLET
- 1½" KITCHEN SINK TRAP
- CLEANOUT
- 2" PVC UNDER FLOOR
- 2-55 GAL. DRUMS
- GREENHOUSE 2" PVC (SOLID)
- 2" PVC (SOLID)

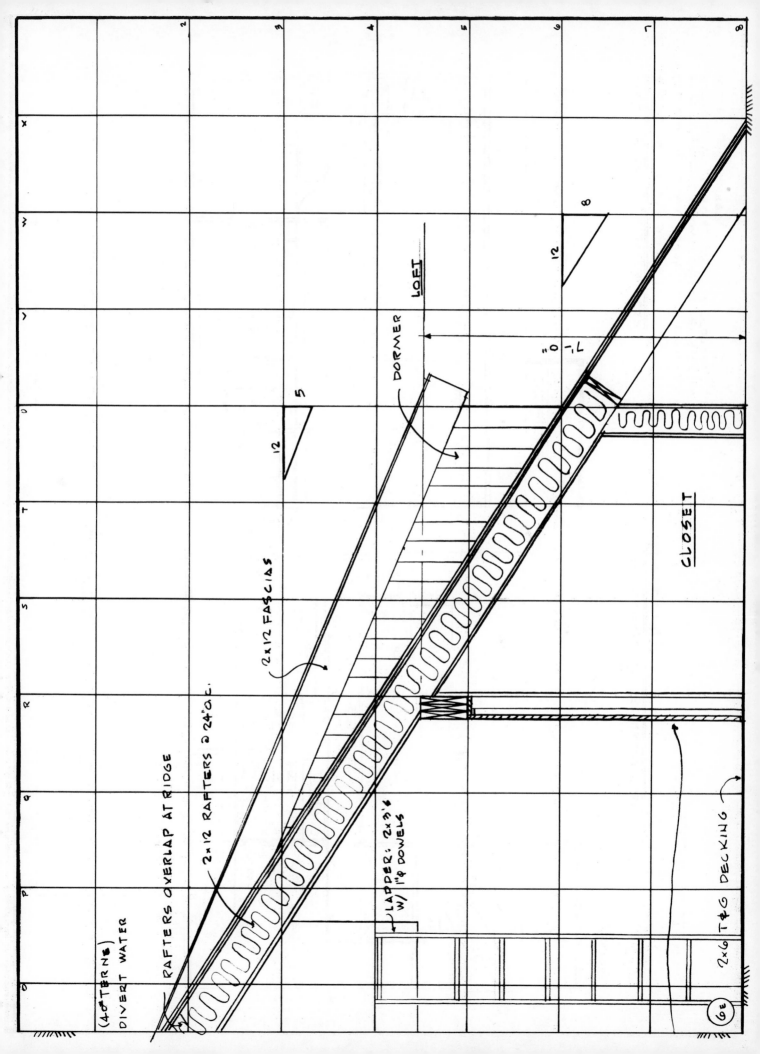

(40° TERNE)
DIVERT WATER

RAFTERS OVERLAP AT RIDGE

2×12 RAFTERS @ 24" O.C.

2×12 FASCIAS

LADDER: 2×3's
W/ 1"ø DOWELS

2×6 T&G DECKING

DORMER

LOFT

7'-0"

CLOSET

12 / 5

12 / 8

6E

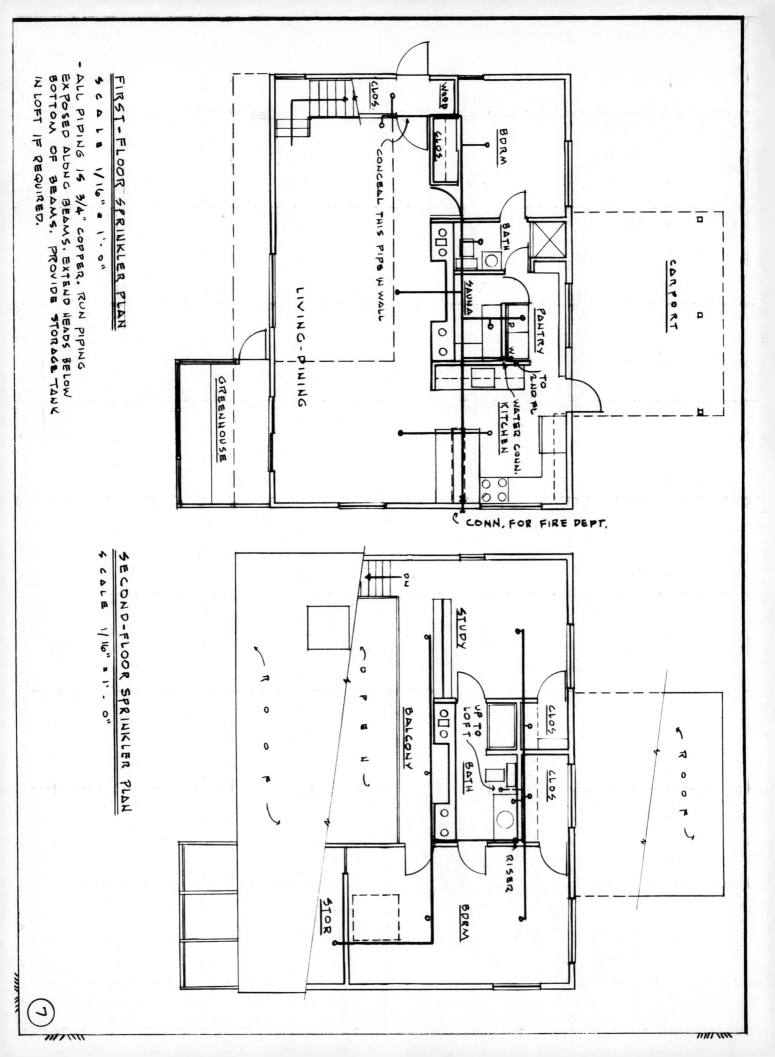

FIRST-FLOOR SPRINKLER PLAN

Scale 1/16" = 1'-0"

- ALL PIPING IS 3/4" COPPER. RUN PIPING EXPOSED ALONG BEAMS. EXTEND HEADS BELOW BOTTOM OF BEAMS. PROVIDE STORAGE TANK IN LOFT IF REQUIRED.

CONCEAL THIS PIPE IN WALL

CLOS.
WOOD
CLOS.
BDRM
BATH
SAUNA
PANTRY
D W
TO 2ND FL.
WATER CONN.
KITCHEN
LIVING-DINING
GREENHOUSE
CARPORT

CONN. FOR FIRE DEPT.

SECOND-FLOOR SPRINKLER PLAN

Scale 1/16" = 1'-0"

DN
STUDY
BALCONY
OPEN
ROOF
UP TO LOFT
CLOS
BATH
CLOS
RISER
BDRM
STOR
ROOF

⑦

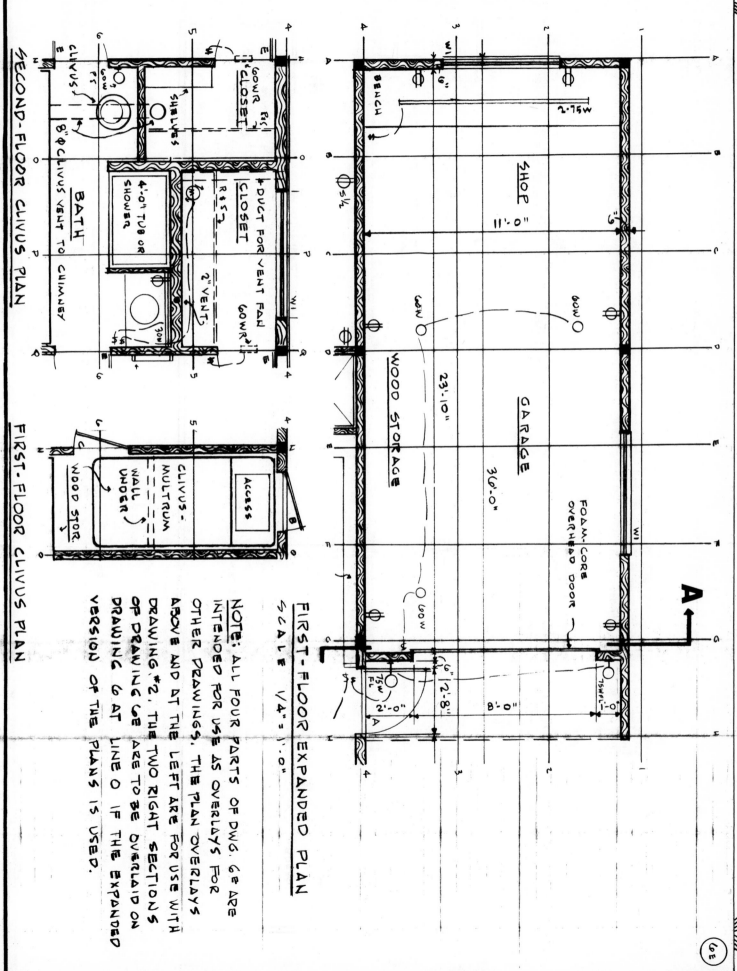

SECOND-FLOOR CLIVUS PLAN

FIRST-FLOOR CLIVUS PLAN

FIRST-FLOOR EXPANDED PLAN

SCALE 1/4" = 1'-0"

NOTE: ALL FOUR PARTS OF DWG. 6E ARE INTENDED FOR USE AS OVERLAYS FOR OTHER DRAWINGS. THE PLAN OVERLAYS ABOVE AND AT THE LEFT ARE FOR USE WITH DRAWING #2. THE TWO RIGHT SECTIONS OF DRAWING 6E ARE TO BE OVERLAID ON DRAWING 6 AT LINE O IF THE EXPANDED VERSION OF THE PLANS IS USED.

SHOP
11'-0"

GARAGE
36'-0"

WOOD STORAGE
23'-10"

FOAM-CORE
OVERHEAD DOOR

BENCH

2·75W

CLIVUS VENT TO CHIMNEY
8"⌀ CLIVUS

BATH
4'-0" TUB OR SHOWER

CLOSET

"CLOSET"

SHELVES

DUCT FOR VENT FAN

2" VENT

WOOD STOR.

CLIVUS - MULTRUM
WALL UNDER

ACCESS

8'-0"

2'-8"

2'-0"

A

6E

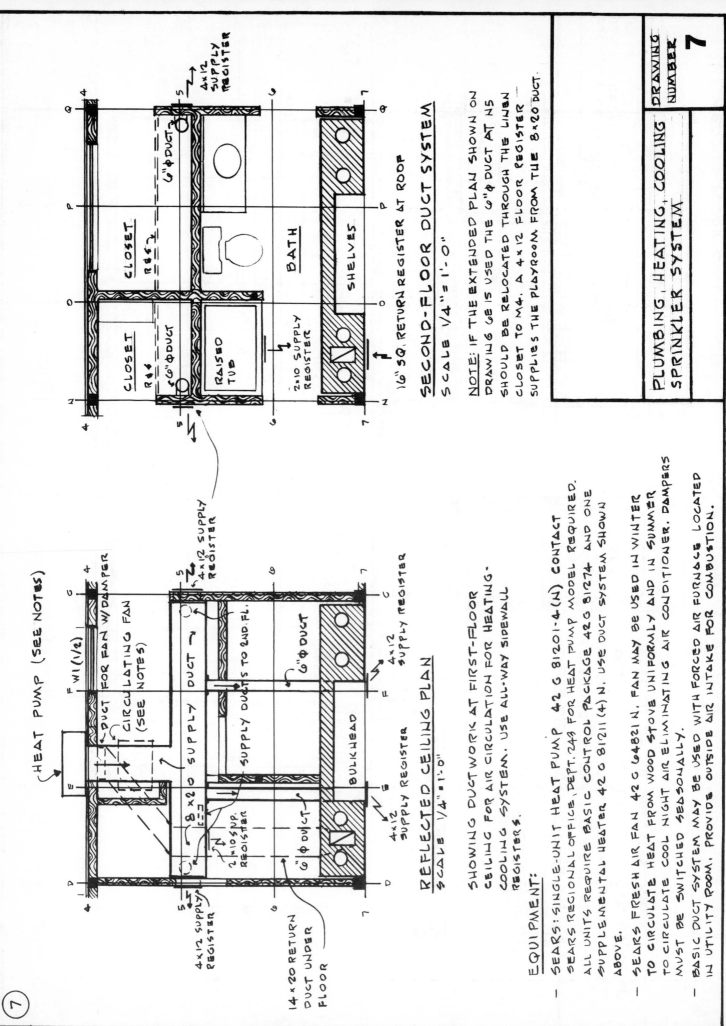

SECOND-FLOOR DUCT SYSTEM

SCALE 1/4" = 1'-0"

CLOSET R&6

CLOSET R&6

RAISED TUB

2x10 SUPPLY REGISTER

CLOSET R&6 2

BATH

SHELVES

4x12 SUPPLY REGISTER

6"ø DUCT

6"ø DUCT

6"ø DUCT

16" SQ. RETURN REGISTER AT ROOF

NOTE: IF THE EXTENDED PLAN SHOWN ON DRAWING G6 IS USED THE 6"ø DUCT AT N5 SHOULD BE RELOCATED THROUGH THE LINEN CLOSET TO M4. A 4x12 FLOOR REGISTER SUPPLIES THE PLAYROOM FROM THE 8x20 DUCT.

REFLECTED CEILING PLAN

SCALE 1/4" = 1'-0"

HEAT PUMP (SEE NOTES)

WI (1½)

DUCT FOR FAN W/DAMPER

CIRCULATING FAN (SEE NOTES)

8 x 20 SUPPLY DUCT

SUPPLY DUCTS TO 2ND. FL.

2x10 SUP. REGISTER

6"ø DUCT

BULKHEAD

4x12 SUPPLY REGISTER

4x12 SUPPLY REGISTER

6"ø DUCT

4x12 SUPPLY REGISTER

14 x 20 RETURN DUCT UNDER FLOOR

SHOWING DUCTWORK AT FIRST-FLOOR CEILING FOR AIR CIRCULATION FOR HEATING-COOLING SYSTEM. USE ALL-WAY SIDEWALL REGISTERS.

EQUIPMENT:

- SEARS: SINGLE-UNIT HEAT PUMP 42 G 81201-4 (N) CONTACT SEARS REGIONAL OFFICE, DEPT. 243 FOR HEAT PUMP MODEL REQUIRED. ALL UNITS REQUIRE BASIC CONTROL PACKAGE 42 G 81274 AND ONE SUPPLEMENTAL HEATER 42 G 81211 (4) N. USE DUCT SYSTEM SHOWN ABOVE.

- SEARS FRESH AIR FAN 42 G 64821 N. FAN MAY BE USED IN WINTER TO CIRCULATE HEAT FROM WOOD STOVE UNIFORMLY AND IN SUMMER TO CIRCULATE COOL NIGHT AIR ELIMINATING AIR CONDITIONER. DAMPERS MUST BE SWITCHED SEASONALLY.

- BASIC DUCT SYSTEM MAY BE USED WITH FORCED AIR FURNACE LOCATED IN UTILITY ROOM. PROVIDE OUTSIDE AIR INTAKE FOR COMBUSTION.

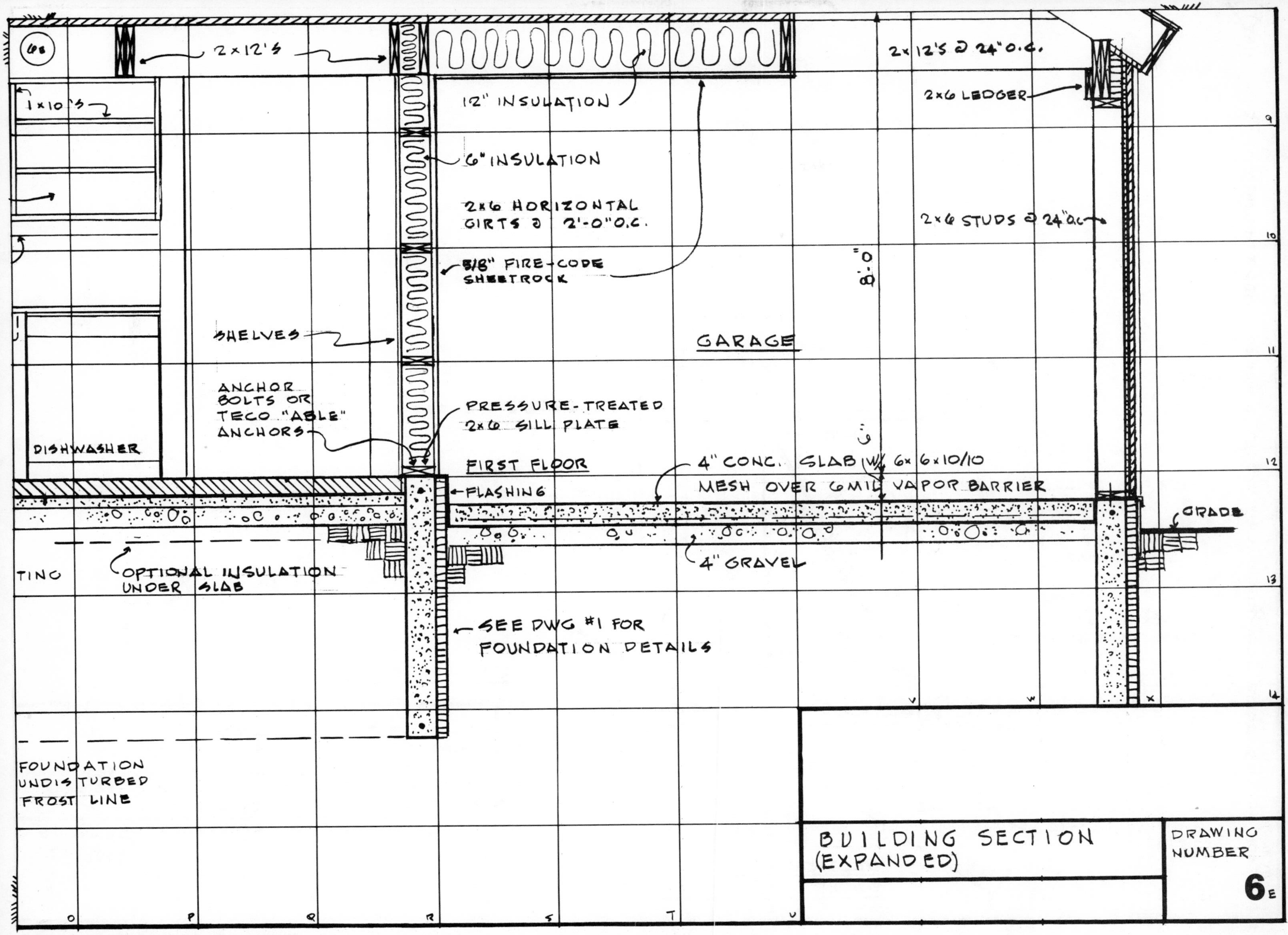
2x12's
1x10's
12" INSULATION
2x12's @ 24" O.C.
2x6 LEDGER
6" INSULATION
2x6 HORIZONTAL GIRTS @ 2'-0" O.C.
2x6 STUDS @ 24" O.C.
5/8" FIRE-CODE SHEETROCK
8'-0"
SHELVES
GARAGE
ANCHOR BOLTS OR TECO "ABLE" ANCHORS
PRESSURE-TREATED 2x6 SILL PLATE
DISHWASHER
FIRST FLOOR
4" CONC. SLAB W/ 6x6x10/10 MESH OVER 6 MIL VAPOR BARRIER
6"
FLASHING
GRADE
OPTIONAL INSULATION UNDER SLAB
TING
4" GRAVEL
SEE DWG #1 FOR FOUNDATION DETAILS
FOUNDATION UNDISTURBED FROST LINE

BUILDING SECTION (EXPANDED)

DRAWING NUMBER 6E

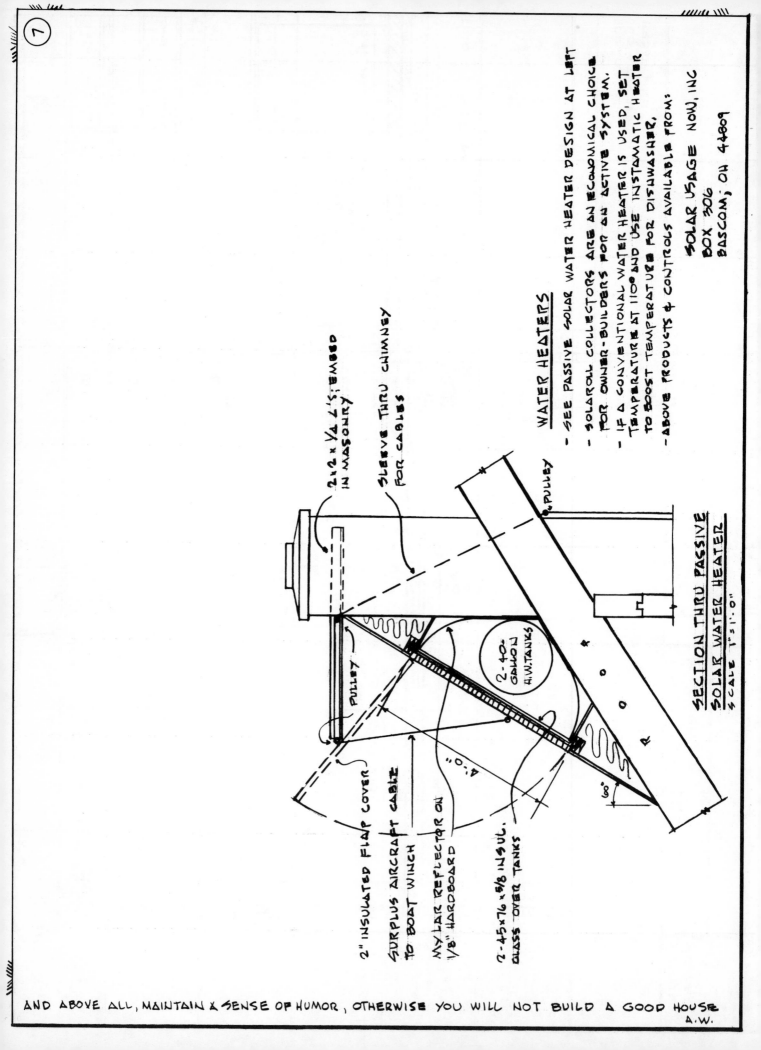

WATER HEATERS

- SEE PASSIVE SOLAR WATER HEATER DESIGN AT LEFT
- SOLAROLL COLLECTORS ARE AN ECONOMICAL CHOICE FOR OWNER-BUILDERS FOR AN ACTIVE SYSTEM.
- IF A CONVENTIONAL WATER HEATER IS USED, SET TEMPERATURE AT 110° AND USE INSTAMATIC HEATER TO BOOST TEMPERATURE FOR DISHWASHER,
- ABOVE PRODUCTS & CONTROLS AVAILABLE FROM:

SOLAR USAGE NOW, INC
BOX 306
BASCOM, OH 44809

2½ x ¼ L's; EMBED IN MASONRY

SLEEVE THRU CHIMNEY FOR CABLES

PULLEY

2 - 40 GALLON H.W.TANKS

PULLEY

SECTION THRU PASSIVE SOLAR WATER HEATER
SCALE 1"=1'-0"

8°

4'-0"

2" INSULATED FLAP COVER

SURPLUS AIRCRAFT CABLE TO BOAT WINCH

MYLAR REFLECTOR ON ⅛" HARDBOARD

2 - 45 x 76 x ⅝ INSUL. GLASS OVER TANKS

AND ABOVE ALL, MAINTAIN A SENSE OF HUMOR, OTHERWISE YOU WILL NOT BUILD A GOOD HOUSE
A.W.

DRAWING NUMBER